Industry and the European Union

Industry and the European Union

Analysing Policies for Business

Edited by

Michael Darmer
*Industry and Trade Counsellor at the Danish Permanent
Representation to the European Union*

and

Laurens Kuyper
*Industry and Trade Counsellor at the Netherlands Permanent
Representation to the European Union*

Edward Elgar
Cheltenham, UK • Northampton, MA, USA

Published by
Edward Elgar Publishing Limited
Glensanda House
Montpellier Parade
Cheltenham
Glos GL50 1UA
UK

Edward Elgar Publishing, Inc.
136 West Street
Suite 202
Northampton
Massachusetts 01060
USA

A catalogue record for this book
is available from the British Library

Library of Congress Cataloguing in Publication Data
Industry and the European union: analysing policies for business / edited by
Michael Darmer and Laurens Kuyper
    p. cm.
    Includes bibliographical references (p.).
    1. Industrial policy—European Union countries. 2. Labor
policy—European Union countries. 3. European Union
countries—Commercial policy. 4. European Union countries—Foreign
economic relations. I. Darmer, Michael, 1963– II. Kuypers, Laurens, 1945–

HD3616.E812 155 2000
338.94—dc21   00–34796

ISBN 1 84064 390 0
Printed and bound in Great Britain by MPG Books Ltd, Bodmin, Cornwall

Contents

Figures

Tables

Boxes

Preface

This book is a most valuable contribution to the understanding of the complexity of European policies and their impact on individual businesses and industry as a whole. That focus makes this book unique. All in all, there are only a few books about the industrial policy of the European Union and none with such a focus.

The book has chosen to analyse that focus from the policy point of view, rather than the traditional approach of industrial sectors. This is well justified taking into account the evolution of industrial policy in recent years, from sector-specific actions to a more horizontal approach. It demonstrates how modern industrial policy combines aims and effects from several other policies that, in different ways, all affect economic operators

When choosing a policy approach, there always is a dilemma concerning how much to explain about the policy in question. The book does not fall into the trap of trying to do justice to all policy areas covered. Instead it focuses, within each of those policy areas, on the issues which are of importance for business and industry. That is the common thread throughout the book.

The book is comprehensive in the sense that it covers all policy areas of relevance for business and industry, not only the more obvious ones, such as competition or research policy, but also environment and Trans-European Networks; maybe not industrial policy in the traditional sense, but with a growing impact on industry

This well-structured book has been written by experienced practitioners who are working in the relevant policy areas each day. It also is an advantage that all contributors have unique insights in the actual processes that create European policies.

Their backgrounds, from five different Member States – Denmark, the Netherlands, United Kingdom, Germany and Belgium – produce an international approach, which adds extra flavour to the book.

Because of its unique focus, this book will be of particular interest to all of those interested in and affected by industrial policy, for example, students, business people, interest groups and policymakers. It will fit well within courses of European studies, international business and international political economy. Better understanding the motivation and reasoning behind policies that affect industry is vital for anyone who is or will be involved in this area. Furthermore, the globalisation of the economy, the competitive environment and the policies that influence it, will also attract attention to the book from outside Europe.

Prof. Dr. Karel van Miert,
President of Universiteit Nyenrode,
Member of the European Commission (1989–1999)

Foreword

The idea for this book was born when Michael Darmer was teaching European studies at Copenhagen Business School. Michael was not able to find a good and recent book about the industrial policy of the European Union. In the end, he created his own teaching material based on a policy approach. During teaching, the focus changed from industrial policy in general into how EU industrial policy and other policies of importance to industry actually affect industry in its daily decision making. This concept was developed further interactively between the students and Michael. It became clear that there was a need as well as a market for a textbook along these ideas.

When Michael was posted as Industrial Counsellor at the Danish Permanent Representation to the European Union in Brussels he met Laurens Kuyper, already an experienced Industrial Counsellor at the Netherlands Permanent Representation to the European Union. Together they finalised the concept of the book and selected the contributors – all experienced professionals within their respective fields. They helped to produce this book in their personal capacities, expressing their personal views on the areas covered by their contributions.

We could not have written a book of such comprehensiveness and practical focus anywhere else than in Brussels with all its expertise and information at hand. We believe and hope that the reader recognises that this book is more than just a traditional desk-study. It is a unique book written in Brussels by practitioners working in Brussels.

Contributors

Svend Albæk, Principal Administrator, Merger Task Force, DG-Competition, European Commission.

Manfred Bergmann, Head of Unit, DG-Economic and Financial Affairs, European Commission.

Michael Darmer, Industry and Trade Counsellor at the Danish Permanent Representation to the European Union.

Adriaan Dierx, Principal Administrator, DG-Economic and Financial Affairs, European Commission.

Kevin Flowers, Coordinator 6th Environmental Action Plan, DG-Environment, European Commission.

Fabienne Ilzkovitz, Head of Unit, DG-Economic and Financial Affairs, European Commission, Professor, Université Libre de Bruxelles.

Laurens Kuyper, Industry and Trade Counsellor at the Dutch Permanent Representation to the European Union.

Robert Madelin, Director, DG-Trade, European Commission.

Oscar Schouw, Economic Expert, DG-Competition, European Commission.

Jan H. Schmidt, Director, DG-Economic and Financial Affairs, European Commission.

Robert-Jan H.M. Smits, Head of Unit, DG-Research, European Commission.

PART ONE

Introduction

1. A Definition of EU Industrial Policy

Michael Darmer

Issues and questions relating to the industrial policy of the European Union are from time to time being dealt with in newspapers, magazines, television and so on. Questions vary depending on who is dealing with them, be it the businessman, the politician, the student and so on. These questions can usually be summarised into the following three fundamental questions: Does the EU have an industrial policy? What does it look like? and How does it affect companies?

The businessmen know from everyday experience that the EU adopts legislation that has tremendous effects on its companies. But very often these legislative measures are labelled as something else such as environment policy, internal market regulation, or competition rules. So can it be called industrial policy?

Politicians certainly believe that the EU has an industrial policy, because they are aware that no less than two Directorate Generals in the Commission are responsible for what most people associate with industrial policy (Directorate General for Enterprises and Directorate General for Competition); and that there is an Industry and Energy Council[1] which meets regularly to discuss subjects of importance to business and industry. But it is more difficult to point to the concrete results of these meetings and how they affect business and industry.

Students usually know about Article 157 on industry in the Treaty and that a special treaty regulates the coal and steel industry until halfway through the year 2002. This is basic knowledge in many EU courses. But when it comes to naming specific initiatives, knowledge is often more sparse.

This widespread uncertainty about the contents of the industrial policy of the European Union is due to several reasons. One is that apart from specialised newspapers and magazines, European industrial policy is not very well covered. Many newspapers, measured in terms of circulation, have a limited coverage of industrial policy, and especially European industrial policy. Another reason is that industrial policy is a rather complex issue. Here again there is a difference between the national and the European level. At the national level industrial policy initiatives are part of the national

---

[1] The Industry Council was merged with the Energy Council in 2000.

political process, which is of general interest. This is usually not the case at the European level. Last but not least the industrial policy of the European Union is not well defined. It is difficult enough to define industrial policy in general economic terms and it becomes even more difficult to do so at Community level.

The overall aim of this book is to answer the three questions mentioned in the beginning of this section. In doing so, we first have to give our definition of what we consider as the industrial policy of the European Union. That is the main aim of this first Chapter.

In the next sections we analyse different definitions of industrial policy from an economic point of view and look at its different orientations. In Section 2 we use the economic concepts and findings from Section 1 and apply them to the Amsterdam Treaty. This leads us to our definition of the industrial policy of the European Union. In an ideal world one would then have a set of industrial policy instruments at disposal to form the best possible policy mix. But in reality, the different policy instruments have more than one purpose to fulfil which sometimes creates a conflict. Furthermore, the political process in the EU makes it very difficult to apply what, from a more theoretical point of view, looks like the best mix. In Section 3 we look at how the different policy instruments interact and sometimes conflict before we conclude in Section 4 and give an indication of the scope of the book.

1.1 INDUSTRIAL POLICY FROM AN ECONOMIC POINT OF VIEW

Over time, many different definitions of what is meant by industrial policy have been given, ranging from a very broad definition which includes everything that might affect a company, to a more narrow one including only specific measures oriented towards specific sectors. The problem was and still is that there is some sense in both approaches. In the following we will study these two approaches in further detail.

A Broad Definition of Industrial Policy

A broad approach might include health systems, social welfare systems and kindergartens. Health systems make it possible for employees to be treated so that they can return to work faster. Social welfare systems make it possible to lay off employees in times of recession, at the expense of the State instead of the company, and to have them available when the economic situation improves. Finally in more modern times kindergartens make it possible for many women to be available on the job market.

The unemployment benefit system, including the terms of dismissal, does affect companies,[2] and a precondition for fulfilling labour demand was the recruitment of women which again was possible only because the number of kindergartens was doubled many times in the 1960s and 1970s in most northern European countries.[3] But do these examples constitute industrial policy? Not in our opinion. There are many other reasons for basic welfare systems like unemployment benefit, health care and childcare, so this broad approach does not provide a very satisfactory definition of industrial policy.

An example of the broader approach and a frequently used definition of industrial policy is found in Johnson (1984) who defines it as: 'industrial policy means the initiation and co-ordination of governmental initiatives to leverage upward the productivity and competitiveness of the whole economy and of particular industries in it'.

This approach suggests that everything that has an influence on the productivity and competitiveness of the whole economy can be regarded as industrial policy, including social welfare systems if they add to the productivity and the competitiveness of the economy (which they often do since they are essential for the functioning of a modern industrialised nation). In this sense the industrial policy role of the government is to co-ordinate the different political initiatives in a way which increases the productivity and competitiveness of industry.

A somewhat similar approach can be found at Community level where the European Business Test Panel was set up as a pilot project as a response to the Action Plan for the Single Market. The test panel will calculate the cost of adjustments and give an estimate of the administrative burdens on companies of new legislative proposals from the Commission.

Another example at Community level of the same broad approach to industrial policy is found in the competitiveness debate that has taken place in the Industry Council from April 1997 onwards. In the medium-term working programme for the this ongoing debate, which was welcomed by the Industry Council in November 1998, the following was stated:

> The priority goal is to enhance the competitiveness of industry by creating a favourable economic and regulatory environment. Some horizontal aspects which have an impact on the way this environment is shaped, and thus on the competitiveness of industry, are parallel or exclusively dealt with by other councils – e.g. Environment and Consumer Protection, Research and Innovation.

---

[2] For instance in Denmark it is relatively easy to dismiss employees, who as a general rule have a maximum six months notice. This should be seen together with a relatively high unemployment benefit and an industrial structure with almost only small and medium-sized companies. The public sector has taken on the responsibility for fluctuations in labour demand. In other Member States like Spain and Portugal the responsibility for fluctuations in labour demand lies to a much higher degree with the companies. It is relatively more difficult to dismiss employees and the unemployment benefit is relatively low.

[3] Today the EU can support the building of kindergartens in order to improve equal opportunities for men and women in less developed regions.

The Council (Industry) should therefore devote itself, with the support of the Commission, to the questions 1) of how interdependencies in the fields falling within the scope of several Councils, while also having an impact on competitiveness, can be considered, and 2) how it can be ensured that the initiatives of other Councils in areas which are decisive for the creation of favourable conditions enhancing the competitiveness of industry and promoting economic growth are coherent; such areas include the completion of the internal market, consumer and environmental protection, the liberalisation of network services, especially in telecommunications, energy and transport (Council of the European Union, 1998).

For a more comprehensive discussion of the policies for the competitiveness of the European industry see Chapter 2.

In our view the broad approach does not give a satisfactory definition of industrial policy. Many or most of the policy areas covered in this approach have different main priorities, and wherever a possible effect on industry is taken into account it is balanced against the main aim of the policy and other indirect effects. Furthermore, the broad approach is difficult to handle since almost everything can affect the competitiveness of business and industry at a certain time.

A Narrow Definition of Industrial Policy

A very narrow approach would be to limit the definition of industrial policy to specific aid schemes targeted at specific sectors in order to improve future economic growth.

Like the broad approach, the narrow approach to industrial policy is not really satisfactory since it excludes more horizontal measures like aid schemes for research and development or small and medium sized enterprises or legislative measures which we consider as part of industrial policy.

An example of a more narrow definition is found in Tyson and Zysman (1983), who give the following definition of industrial policy: 'Industrial policy, ... means government policy aimed at or motivated by problems within specific sectors'.

This approach is also very easily identified at Community level for example, in the coal and steel sectors, textile and clothing, automotive industry and shipbuilding. One example of this sector-oriented industrial policy is found in the shipbuilding sector. In 1997 the Council allowed substantial aid to be given to shipyards in Germany (€371million; equal to DM 728 million), Greece (€175 million; equal to GRD 54,525 million) and Spain (€815 million; equal to Psa 135,028 million). The purpose of this aid was to facilitate an urgent and comprehensive restructuring in order to make these yards competitive and financially viable. Since the shipbuilding industry faced excess capacity worldwide it was part of the Council's decision that capacity should be reduced significantly in Germany and Spain. See also Chapter 13.

Besides the differences in scope there is another important difference between Johnson's definition and the definition of Tyson and Zysman. While Johnson seems to take the approach that everything that *affects* industry is industrial policy, Tyson and Zysman seem to take the approach that it should not only affect industry but it should also be motivated and *aimed* at industry.

Different Schools of Industrial Policy – Liberals vs. Interventionists

Despite the differences in definitions, Tyson, Zysman and Johnson are all in favour of government intervention in the area of industrial policy. Not all economists share the same positive attitude towards industrial policy. Krugman and Obstfeld (1988) are much more reluctant because of the risk that government interventions might distort the functioning of the market. They give the following definition of industrial policy: 'Industrial policy is an attempt by a government to encourage resources to move into particular sectors that the government views as important to future economic growth'.

According to Krugman and Obstfeld industrial policy means that resources are transferred to specific sectors as a result of government intervention. This means that industrial policy supports certain industrial sectors at the expense of other industrial sectors and the consumers. Somebody has to pay in the sense that they will be worse off, for instance in terms of higher taxes in order to subsidise certain sectors or companies. The justification is that the social benefits of subsidising are expected to be higher than the costs. Krugman and Obstfeld argue that this is only the case when and if the public sector is better than the private sector at 'picking the winners' in terms of future growth potential. If this is not the case, the private sector itself will allocate the necessary resources in order to get a higher return on investments. And this goes for both financial and human resources. If the returns of financial investments are expected to be higher in one sector than others, finance will flow into this sector in order to get higher profit. The same goes for human resources. If the job opportunities and/or the wages are expected to be higher in one sector, people tend to move into this sector. According to Krugman and Obstfeld this means that only in a situation where the private sector systematically underestimates the future growth potential in the economy can an intervention by the public sector be justified. Krugman and Obstfeld find it very difficult to justify why the private sector should make this kind of error systematically or be so shortsighted.

Other economists like Geroski (1989), Jacquemin (1987), Grossman (1990) disagree with Krugman and Obstfeldt. They point to three types of arguments that in their opinion justify government intervention. These are market failure, changes in comparative advantages and a wish to facilitate structural changes.

Market failures exist when the functioning of the free market leads to lower economic growth than would otherwise have been the case. Market failures can be caused by, for example, large fixed costs of entry into a market, externalities or asymmetry of information. The best known example is positive externalities stemming from research and development. Externalities arise when the actions of one party affect the wellbeing of another in a way which the market does not account for. In the case of research and development the use of knowledge by one party does not prevent its simultaneous use by another which makes it a positive externality. It may be difficult to prevent others from also making use of your research and development despite patent and copyright laws. Private agents will only bear the cost of research efforts to the extent that they can capture private rewards. The private rewards are smaller than total rewards since others also benefit from your research and development. This means that too little will be invested in research and development compared to what is optimal from a national point of view. Consequently, the government should promote research and development (see Grossman, 1990 and Tirole, 1988).

In most economic literature, the comparative advantages of a nation or a region are taken for granted, because it is more convenient and because they are not easily altered in the short run. The short-run perspective is the commonly used perspective in economic theory. But comparative advantages are not static. Parts of these changes are expected to be influenced by, for example, industrial policy. Some comparative advantages depend on natural resources – one would expect Spain to be better at growing oranges than Sweden – but others are man-made like the computer industry of the United States or the car industry in Japan. Many believe that government, through industrial policy and other policies affecting industrial performance, can create a competitive environment. A competitive environment fosters competitive industries, which may lead to competitive advantages. Factors which seem to be of importance in creating competitive advantages include, among other things, research connections between universities and industry, enforcement of strict product, safety and environmental standards, strong antitrust policies and easy access to capital for innovative purpose (see, for example, Porter, 1990).

Structural adjustment can be a very painful and harmful process for the industry, region or sometimes nation in question, especially if the adjustment process is carried out over a short time period by market forces through, for instance, closure of large enterprises. In a case of overcapacity in a sector, customers, investors and others may lose faith in the ability of the sector to produce rent, which may lead to a larger reduction in capacity than actually required. And because of general uncertainty about where the actual equilibrium is and what the future will bring, in a sector already hit by recession, it can be very difficult to attract new investment. To this must be added the unemployment and the social costs arising from a large reduction in capacity. These costs can be of vital importance for a region that is very dependent on a single sector, which at the same time experiences severe recession. In this case industrial policy is often called for, in order to reduce the total adjustment costs. The remedies used are State aid in order to facilitate closures and retrain the unemployed for jobs in other and more prosperous sectors, investment aid in order to make the remaining industry competitive and economically viable, and the attraction of new companies in other sectors in order to diversify the industrial structure of the region. Buigues and Sapir (1993) emphasise that industrial policy includes measures aimed at declining sectors as well as policies oriented towards the future.

Those who believe and support an active industrial policy are sometimes referred to as interventionists and those who are against are sometimes referred to as liberals because of their faith in the free market.

The liberals do not deny that market failures exist, but they do not believe that governments have sufficient information and the right instruments at their disposal to overcome these market failures. Furthermore, government intervention will lead to other market distortions, and the liberals do not believe that market distortions that result from government intervention will lead to a more optimal situation than a free market economy, with the market failures it contains.

With respect to using industrial policy to improve competitive advantages the liberals are sceptical as well. They recognise that the comparative advantages of nations are not static. They evolve over time and across nations. Nations lose their competitive advantages in certain activities and gain them elsewhere. The liberals believe that the only aim of the government should be to create a stable economic and legislative environment, so that the competitive advantages can emerge in those sectors, where the market conditions are favourable. The liberals do not believe that the government should intervene in favour of one or more specific sectors for the reasons mentioned above. Governments do not have the necessary information to 'pick the winners', and the liberals see no reason why the public sector should be better than the private sector at picking the sectors which may form the competitive advantages of tomorrow.

Finally, the liberals are not convinced that it is actually possible to lower the adjustment costs by using industrial policy, because adjustment costs are often influenced by a number of rigid factors such as the unwillingness to accept lower wages, the unwillingness to relocate interregionally or the unwillingness to accept retraining. When skills are less industry-specific, general wage rigidities caused by collective bargaining may prevent redundant labour from offering lower wages so as to obtain jobs.

As we have seen, it is possible to argue both for and against industrial policy – a concept that at the same time is not well defined. So is this the end of the story of industrial policy? Clearly not. Companies *are* heavily influenced by decisions made by the public sector, and almost *all* industrialised nations try, to various degrees, to create the best possible business environment in order to promote industrial performance, taking into account the specific structure of the industry and the specific problems and challenges it has to face.

Clear-cut liberal or interventionist implementation of industrial policy does not exist in reality. A modern industrialised country is simply too complex for such a simple approach. In an industrialised country, legislation affects industry, and there are economic and industrial challenges that must be met as well. Industrial policy will in reality always be a mix of the two. This does not prevent countries from having clear preferences or orientations for one of the two schools. This is also the case in the EU. Each Member State in the EU has a distinct national industrial policy even though there are also certain common characteristics.

One group of Member States like the UK, the Netherlands and Denmark has a clear preference for a market-oriented industrial policy, based on a liberal approach. In general these Member States do not reject public sector intervention, as long as the measures are horizontal, that is, not limited to specific sectors or individual companies. Examples are general research and development initiatives open to all sectors and companies, or SME initiatives. These countries will normally be against sector-oriented initiatives and operational, rescue or investment aid to individual companies.

Another group like France, Italy and Spain has a long tradition for a high degree of public sector intervention. In France for instance, the government has actively participated in developing national champions, has given massive support to individual companies and specific sectors and many companies are or have been owned or controlled by the public sector (see Box 1.1).

Box 1.1   Different schools of practical industrial policy in the EU

The UK and France represent the different approaches towards industrial policy within the European Union.

The UK is known for having a market-oriented attitude towards industrial policy, which is recognised in the UK's competitiveness programme, which among other things says that maintenance of a stable macroeconomic environment is seen as the most important contribution the government can make to improve competitiveness. Low inflation and sound public financing are considered to be essential. The government intends to influence competitiveness indirectly by means of partnership and sponsorship. Sponsorship is the means by which government works with individual sectors to address factors affecting their competitiveness. It is stressed that sponsorship implies neither picking winners nor subsidising non-competitive industries. Partnership involves government working with business wherever it can. It is stated that in a market economy the primary responsibility for improving competitiveness must lie with firms. However, it is also recognised that when market imperfections limit the scope for firms to improve competitiveness, the government may need to intervene. This would take the form of: providing a stable macroeconomic environment; maintaining and developing open and competitive world markets and reducing barriers to trade; removing unnecessary burdens on business by means of deregulation (with particular attention to SMEs); ensuring a favourable environment for inward investment; and improving value for money and standards in services that are best provided by the public sector (for example, education).

France has a long tradition for an active industrial policy. In the 1970s and in the first half of the 1980s France pursued a market-segment policy and a policy where specific branches of the industry were promoted. The idea was that the modernisation of the industrial system relied on the State. The instruments were State intervention, sector-based plans and nationalisation. In the second half of the 1980s French industrial policy changed. There is now a consensus that to reactivate growth, enterprises must have the means to make the most of the opportunities opened up to them by the globalisation of trade and to capitalise on their assets in the global market place. Seen in this light, the role of the State is to create a favourable and attractive environment for entrepreneurship and to provide enterprises with the stimulus they need to develop their competitiveness.

Even though there has been a change in French industrial policy, the State is more visible in France than in most of the other Member States in the European Union. With a particular focus on 'key technologies' which are related to the 'picking winners' theory, the French government still plays an active role in industrial research and development. For instance, since 1989 the government has introduced measures to encourage firms to invest in the development of innovative products or processes of strategic importance (Major Innovative Projects). In the same vein, a study entitled 'Key technologies for French industry in the year 2000' identified areas of technological expertise, which would have positive spin-offs for French industry in the future. A call for project proposals was issued to firms in industry to develop work on the technologies thus identified.

Source: OECD (1996) and OECD (1998)

There are other definitions of industrial policy – some of which have been brought forward in relation to the industrial policy of the European Union. Buigues and Sapir (1993) define industrial policy as 'the set of measures applied by governments to deal with the process of structural adjustment associated with changes in comparative advantage. It includes measures aimed at declining sectors as well as policies oriented towards the future'. Buigues and Sapir are in line with and Tyson and Zysman. They define an industrial policy measure according to the aim to be fulfilled by the measure. However, Buigues and Sapir have a more broad perspective which, in relation to the European Union, includes the Internal Market regulations and trade policy. Buigues and Sapir also distinguish between budgetary and regulatory instruments.

Gual (1995) defines industrial policy as 'the set of government interventions that by way of taxes (or subsidies) and regulations on domestic products or factors of production attempt to modify the allocation of domestic resources that results from the free operation of the market'. This definition is very broad and includes taxes and regulations on labour and capital, agricultural subsidies, accelerated depreciation allowances and financial market regulations. In order to limit the scope Gual focuses on three types of actions. These are strategic industrial policies, structural adjustment policies and horizontal policies. When transferring this definition to EU level: 'the EU industrial policy comprises some policies related to the completion of the Internal Market, Research and Development policies and sector specific policies'.

Pelkmans (1997) defines industrial policy as 'all government intervention aiming specifically at influencing industrial change by affecting the incentives to produce industrial goods or incentives to enter/exit specific industrial goods markets'. Pelkmans has a fairly broad definition of industrial policy. However, he also has a number of interesting observations. According to Pelkmans, there is an overall set of policies that somehow affect industry. He regards industrial policy as a narrow subset of this range of policies, but he also finds that there is a set of policies, which are wider than industrial policy but narrower than the overall set of policies affecting industry, and these he calls policies for industry.

None of the definitions in this section provide an adequate definition of the industrial policy of the European Union, but some of them contain interesting features, which we will take up in the next section. We will now turn to the Treaty itself in order to see if it can provide the clarity we are looking for.

1.2 INDUSTRIAL POLICY WITHIN THE EUROPEAN UNION

From the beginning, the European Communities possessed elements of industrial policy. The basis of the 1951 Treaty of Paris (European Community for Coal and Steel, ECSC) is indeed industrial policy and the Treaty of Rome (1957) included some clear elements of such a policy. But it was not until the Maastricht Treaty, agreed in December 1991, that an actual title concerning industrial policy appeared in the Treaty (for a historical background see Chapter 2). Title XVI of the present (Amsterdam) Treaty contains Article 157 about industry (see Box 1.2).

Box 1.2   Title XVI: Industry, Article 157 of the Treaty

The Community and the Member States shall ensure that the conditions necessary for the competitiveness of the Community's industry exist. For that purpose, in accordance with a system of open and competitive markets, their action shall be aimed at:
–   speeding up the adjustment of industry to structural changes;
–   encouraging an environment favourable to initiative and to the development of undertakings throughout the Community, particularly small and medium-sized undertakings;
–   encouraging an environment favourable to co-operation between undertakings;
–   fostering better exploitation of the industrial potential of policies of innovation, research and technological development.
1. The Member States shall consult each other in liaison with the Commission and, where necessary, shall co-ordinate their action. The Commission may take useful initiative to promote such co-ordination.
2. The Community shall contribute to the achievement of the objectives set   out   in paragraph 1 through the policies and activities it pursues under other provisions of this Treaty. The Council, acting unanimously on a proposal from the Commission, after consulting the European Parliament and the Economic and Social Committee, may decide on specific measures in support of action taken in the Member States to achieve the objectives set out in paragraph 1.

This Title shall not provide a basis for the introduction by the Community of any measures which lead to a distortion of competition.

When we wish to define the industrial policy of the European Union it is necessary to recall that the Treaty sets certain limitations, compared to what is possible at national level. For example, it is at present not possible to use tax incentives for industrial purposes at EU level. At the national level, this is a commonly used instrument. Therefore we will have to go through the Treaty and in particular examine Article 157 in order to see what the possibilities are for carrying out industrial policy at Community level.

When we examine Article 157 of the Treaty it becomes clear that the Community has an explicit industrial policy whose aim it is to 'ensure that the conditions necessary for the competitiveness of the Community's industry exist', and that any actions should be 'in accordance with a system of open and competitive markets'. The philosophy of Article 157 is clearly market-oriented. This is emphasised by the fact that the aim should be pursued through the policies and activities 'under other provisions of the Treaty', and by the sentence that the article does not provide a basis for introducing any measures 'which could lead to a distortion of competition'. Any new measures based on Article 157 require a unanimous decision by the Council.[4]

Even though the article itself sets the aim of the Community's industrial policy and at the same time clearly limits its use, it is by no means clear what is meant by stating that the aim should be pursued through the policies and activities under other provisions of the Treaty. As a guideline the article highlights four areas to which special attention should be paid. These are; adjustment of industry to industrial changes; small and medium-sized enterprises (SMEs); co-operation between companies and, finally, research and technological development. It is therefore necessary to go through the Treaty to identify those policies and activities that can be used for industrial purposes. In that respect we will use the findings in the previous section.

Recall that Johnson's definition seems too broad and not really manageable on an ex ante basis. All policy areas could be of importance to industry at some moment of time, even though at present it may not seem very likely. On the other hand, Tyson and Zysman's definition does not seem really useful either. Their definition is too narrow and excludes horizontal measures which have become increasingly important. But from our analysis above, we can develop some principles by which we will define the industrial policy of the European Union.

Tyson and Zysman, Buigues and Sapir and Pelkmans seem to have a point when they focus on initiatives *aimed* at or *motivated* by problems within specific sectors. The idea that one can characterise initiatives by their direction and motivation seems well founded. It is after all difficult to understand why an initiative aimed at industry, with the intention of improving the competitiveness of the industry, should not be labelled as industrial policy. So the direction seems to be a useful criterion to identify industrial policy. But it cannot stand alone, because this would, for example,

---

[4]   Some have argued that the Maastricht Treaty and Article 157 did not change anything since Article 157 requires unanimity which already was possible through Article 308 (former Article 235) and since the aim of Article 157 shall be pursued through other policies. But in our opinion it does make a difference. First, it makes it explicitly clear that the Community has an industrial policy including its aim. Secondly, it puts upon the Commission an obligation to pursue this aim through communications, proposals and so on. And finally, new policies have been introduced with a clear industrial scope, for example, the research and development policy. See also Chapter 11.

mean that an environmental regulation, which is directed at industry and imposes heavy burdens on it, should be labelled as industrial policy. This is clearly not the case. There is no doubt that in this example the regulation is aimed directly at industry, but it is also clear that the main objective is to improve the environment and not the competitiveness of the industry.

So in order to define a policy area as part of EU industrial policy, it both has to be *aimed* at industry and at the same time has as its *main priority* the promotion of industry's competitiveness. Such a definition is in full accordance with Article 157 of the Treaty. The policy areas that fulfil these criteria will comprise our first category of policy areas. But as the above example shows, there are many policy areas which may not be labelled initially as industrial policy because they have other main priorities, but which nevertheless have an important impact on industry and therefore should be taken into consideration. These areas form our second category. This is in line with Pelkmans who, as mentioned above, states that there are other policy areas of importance to industry than the ones labelled as industrial policy.

Finally there is also a third category of policy areas, which may or may not have an influence on industry. If it does affect industry, however, it is likely to be of less importance.

With these three categories in mind, we will go through Part Three of the Treaty – 'Community Policies' to identify the industrial policy of the European Union and other policies of importance to industry. The first category of policy areas is aimed at industry and has as its main priority to improve the competitiveness of industry. This is what we regard as the industrial policy of the European Union. It contains the following titles: title VI Common rules on competition, taxation and approximation of laws; title XI Social policy, education, vocational training and youth; title XVI Industry; title XVII Economic and social cohesion; title XVIII Research and technological development.

Title VI on common rules on competition, taxation and approximation of laws contains, in Chapter one, the rules of competition which are rules applicable to companies and rules for aid granted to companies by States. The rules applicable to companies cover agreements that prevent, restrict or distort competition within the common market, abuse of dominant positions in the common market and control of mergers. The State aid rules prevent, as a general rule, Member States from granting aid to companies, which may distort competition. There is no doubt that these rules must be considered as industrial policy in accordance with our definition. They are aimed at industry and have, as their main priority, the maintaining of a competitive environment that improves competitiveness. Title VI also contains a chapter on tax provisions, which will be dealt with in relation to the Economic and Monetary Union. The title also contains a chapter on approximation of laws which will be dealt with in relation to the Internal Market.

Title XVI on industry contains Article 157, which is the umbrella for the Union's industrial policy. As stated earlier it says that the objectives should be pursued mainly under policies and activities other than Article 157. Therefore only a few initiatives have had Article 157 as their legal basis.

One of the fundamental reasons for industrial policy is, as mentioned above, to facilitate structural adjustments. This purpose is also recognised in Article 157 where actions should be aimed at 'speeding up adjustment of industry to structural changes'. As well as in title XVII, concerning economic and social cohesion, where it is pointed out, that the European Regional Development Fund (ERDF) shall 'assist in the conversion of declining industrial regions' (Article 160); one of the ways to achieve this goal is to give investment aid directly to individual companies. The aim of the European Social Fund (ESF) is *inter alia* to facilitate workers' 'adaptation to industrial changes and to changes in production systems, in particular through vocational training'. While the ERDF operates regionally, the ESF is available throughout the Community. Both Funds assist companies directly. The other parts of title XI, social policy, education, vocational training and youth belong in category one.

Research and technological development policy has as one of its main objectives to improve the competitiveness of European industry. Article 163 of the Treaty states that 'the Community shall have the objective of strengthening the scientific and technological bases of Community industry and encouraging it to become more competitive at international level'. Research policy has other aims than just to improve the competitiveness of the European industry, but it still is one of the main objectives.

Category two, that is areas with other main priorities than industry, but which nevertheless have an important impact on industry, includes the following titles: title I Free movement of goods; title III Free movement of persons, services and capital; title V Transport; title VII Economic and monetary policy; title IX Common commercial policy; title X Customs cooperation; title XV Trans-European networks; title XIX Environment.

The free movement of goods and the free movement of persons, services and capital form, together with approximation of laws (Articles 94–97, chapter three of title VI), the Internal Market. There is no doubt that the Internal Market is of major importance to all business and industry and as such would qualify to be labelled as industrial policy. In fact many people like Buigues and Sapir (1993) see it this way. But the Internal Market contains many other aspects which only have a remote and indirect impact on business and industry, such as, for example, social security for migrant workers and financial regulation for insurance companies. With our definition of industrial policy, the Internal Market would have to be placed in category two.

Transport and Trans-European Networks are partly linked together since Trans-European Networks are a designation for transport networks, energy networks and telecommunication networks. The transport sector and the transport infrastructure as well as the energy infrastructure are of vital importance to business and industry. Without cheap and reliable transport and energy infrastructures the competitiveness of the Community's industry would be seriously affected in a negative way. But these networks are of importance not only to industry. They are fundamental to a modern industrial community including households and the public sector. So even though these networks are important to industry they are not *aimed* at industry. Telecommunication networks are somewhat different. The development of telecommunication networks is closely linked with the industrial policy ambition of developing a strong and competitive IT sector in Europe (see Chapter 13). In our opinion it is not possible to separate the two, and therefore we regard the development of telecommunication networks as part of industrial policy.

The Economic and Monetary Union and tax provisions (Articles 90-93, Chapter two of title VI) are somewhat similar to transport infrastructure. Stable economic conditions in terms of stable exchange rates within the Union, low inflation and relatively stable interest rates are important to the business environment and as such to the competitiveness of the European industry. However, stable economic conditions do not create competitive companies on their own. There are many examples of competitive companies located in regions with economic instability. On the other hand, there is no doubt that stable economic conditions are an important factor. Stable economic conditions mean that companies can concentrate on what they do best – produce whatever they produce.

According to basic economic theory, the optimal trade policy is to create and maintain free trade: that is, freedom to exchange commodities, manufactures and services across international frontiers without penalties or discriminatory hidden obstacles. Any limitation in free trade, the theory establishes, will leave the world worse off, in the sense that world income would be lower than it would otherwise have been. There are various reasons for this. One is that the global benefits of free trade would be unevenly distributed, with some sectors in a given country losing revenue (and perhaps closing down) while others gain profits and grow. Therefore, trade policy is sometimes used for industrial policy reasons – mainly to protect less competitive sectors internally – via, for example, import restrictions and export subsidies. 'Free trade' in practice being unobtainable, the international community has pursued since 1947 a regime (first under the GATT and now under the World Trade Organisation) geared toward 'open trade': that is the least restrictive possible trade regime, based on clearly defined and published rules. Progressively more ambitious trade liberalising commitments have reduced the extent to which trade policy can be used for industrial policy reasons to protect less competitive sectors. There remain, however, exceptions to open trade, notably where the trade policy instrument is used for foreign policy purposes (for example sanctions on South Africa, Libya or Cuba) or in order to ensure that exports are not diverted by unfriendly powers to advance their nuclear or military equipment strategies. To sum up, the main aim of trade policy as currently formulated is to maintain a progressively more liberal and in any case open and non-discriminatory regime for world trade. The increasingly ambitious multilateral rulebook of WTO limits the scope for using trade policy as an industrial policy tool very considerably. For these reasons, we include trade policy in category two.

Environmental policy clearly has another main priority than increasing the productivity of the European Union. However, environmental regulation increasingly interferes with the production of business and industry, as has been illustrated by the efforts to reduce CO_2 emissions, the polluter pays principle and the precautionary principle. Environmental initiatives are usually associated with increased burdens and cost of production. However, environmental initiatives can also lead to increased competitiveness through the principle of first movers' advantage, not to mention an environmental industrial sector of increasing importance like the recycling industry.

The areas which, in our opinion, fall into category three, that is, areas with none or only a limited effect on industry, include title II Agriculture; title IV Visas, asylum, immigration and other policies related to the free movement of persons; title VIII Employment; title XII Culture; title XIII Public health; title XIV Consumer protection; title XX Development co-operation.

The agricultural sector is heavily regulated by the EU, giving the Union an indirect influence on, for example, the food industry. But the agricultural sector and its very specific rules are outside the scope of this book. Visas, asylum, immigration and other policies related to the free movement of persons might have an influence on the labour supply, and as such on industry, but the effect is expected to be limited. The new title (included in the Amsterdam Treaty) about employment may also have an influence on the labour supply. The purpose though is to co-ordinate the employment policy of the Member States, in close co-operation with them, and to monitor the result. No new regulation or support schemes are introduced under this title.

Culture may have an influence on the entertainment industry which after all is a growing industry, but the importance of the Community initiatives in this area are still very limited compared to the wide range of initiatives at national level. Public health may have some influence on the pharmaceutical and biochemical sectors, which are sectors of major importance to the European Union, but as with culture, the importance of the Community for this sector is rather limited and only indirect compared to the importance of national policies. Consumer protection may impose burdens on industry in general and may lead to first movers advantages, but the importance to industry of this title is expected to be limit and only indirect. Development co-operation is of some importance to industry, because of the aid programmes involved, which may be of direct benefit to European companies. When we put this title in category three after all, it is because the main aim is different and only of limited importance to industry since most of the aid is going to aid organisations and so on.

We have now gone through the Community policies and grouped them into three categories; those whose main priority is to affect industry, those with a significant effect on the industry, but which have other main priorities and finally those with only a limited influence on industry. In conformity with Article 157 of the Treaty, we regard the first category as 'The Industrial Policy of the European Union'. It consists of both regulatory instruments and budgetary instruments. The second category we regard as 'Policies of Importance to Industry'. This group consists of both internal and external policies. A model of the EU's industrial policy and other important policies affecting industry is shown in Figure 1.1.

Figure 1.1   Industrial policy of the European Union and policies of importance to industry

Internal policies of importance to industry:			
Internal Market ↓	**EMU policy** ↓	**Transport policy** ↓	**Environment** ↓
Industrial policy			
Regulatory instruments:		**Budgetary instruments:**	
• Competition rules for companies - Agreements - Dominant position - Merger control • State aid rules - Block exemption - Procedural regulation • Sector-specific issues		• Research and development • SMEs • Structural Funds - Regional development Fund - Social Fund - Community initiatives - Cohesion Fund • Sector-specific issues	
External policies of importance to industry: ↑ **Trade policy**			

Each of the subjects in the figure will be dealt with in separate chapters: policies of importance to industry in Part Two and the industrial policy of the European Union in Part Three.

In this section we have seen that the aim of the industrial policy of the European Union is clearly formulated in the Treaty. However, when it comes to the instruments to implement it, the Treaty is rather unclear. By using the economic findings from Section 1 we managed to define the industrial policy of the European Union and its instruments.

The notion 'instrument' may give the impression that policymakers can at any time chose the instrument expected to be most effective to address the situation in mind. This is not the case. Different instruments may be in conflict with one another and the decision making process for the different instruments varies significantly as we will see in the next section. For these reasons, it is not always possible to choose what appears to be the best instrument.

1.3 POLICY CONFLICTS

Policy instruments may conflict. Not only may different policy instruments clash with different policy objectives, but different instruments with the same objective may also clash, as mentioned by Gual (1995). An example of a conflict between industrial policy instruments is the conflict between a strong competition policy on the one hand and the interventionist idea of doing something special for individual firms, a sector or even large segments such as SMEs on the other. An example of the conflict between industrial policy objectives and other policy objectives could be that burdens are imposed on industry for environmental reasons while the Community at the same time tries to improve competitiveness by limiting the administrative burden in other areas.

The conflict between a strong competition policy with the fundamental aim of securing an optimal and equal playing field on the one hand, and an interventionist industrial policy favouring individual companies or sectors on the other, is also a conflict between the different schools of industrial policy mentioned above. A strong competition policy is most in line with a liberal industrial policy. In case of an interventionist policy regime, pursuing a lax competition policy that allows for different kinds of exemptions can solve this conflict. This is to some extent the case in EU where block exemptions exist for, for example, pre-competitive agreements within research and development. However, the general attitude of Community policy in this area is, after all, liberal. The merger regulation is in itself a contradiction. On the one hand, economies of scale are generally accepted, that is, that efficiency increases with the size of the company, and to that extent, mergers should be seen as a way to increase efficiency. On the other hand, the merger regulation should prevent the creation of a dominant position that might lead to less efficiency.

As mentioned in the previous section, the main purpose of trade policy is to develop open world trade. When trade policy is used as an industrial policy instrument it is very often used to protect local industries *from* world trade. Trade policy may also conflict with the industrial policy objective of improving competitiveness since it removes the incentive for protected industries to carry out the necessary adjustments to changed market conditions.

Not all instruments are available at all times. The flexibility that is found at national level does not exist at EU level. Most, if not all, EU aid schemes have the form of multiannual programmes, which are adopted through a Council regulation, for example, the framework programmes for research and development, the multiannual programme for SMEs and the Structural Funds. It is very difficult to adjust these policies in the period the programmes are running.

The question of consistency may also arise due to the differences in implementation of the instruments. As we have seen, any measure under Article 157 requires unanimity. This can have practical consequences as was seen in the case of high-definition television (HDTV), where the UK, according to Bourgeois and Demaret (1995), used its 'veto right' to force through a sizeable reduction of the funding initially proposed. Unanimity is also required in relation to the general Structural Funds regulation while the European Regional Development Fund and the European Social Fund are adopted by qualified majority and in co-decision with the European Parliament. Qualified majority and co-decision are also necessary in relation to framework programmes in the field of Research and Development. As mentioned above, trade policy is sometimes used as an industrial policy instrument, and in this field decisions are taken by the Council acting by qualified majority or, with respect to dumping, by a simple majority. In the field of competition and State aid, the Commission has exclusive power to take final decisions, as it has been especially entrusted with the task of implementing Articles 81 and 82, as well as the merger regulation and the State aid rules.

Both in regional and research policy, the objectives are pursued through multiannual programmes, which are not easily altered within the programming period. This makes it difficult to use this kind of instrument when unexpected events occur. In that case, it will be necessary to use instruments which are more suitable for addressing ad hoc problems. In many cases, the proper instrument, from an economic point of view, would be to address the problems directly by using the provisions of, for example, Article 157. But since Article 157 requires unanimity, which can be difficult to obtain, trade policy is sometimes used as the second best option, because qualified or simple majority voting is politically easier to apply. The preference for trade policy should also be seen in the light of the fact that trade policy may create revenue, while industrial policy may lead to increased spending.

Differences may also occur for political reasons. Politics is a matter of compromise especially in the European Union, where the Commission has to make compromises through consultation procedures internally in the Commission before it adopts a proposal. The Council amends the proposal of the Commission in order to get a compromise text which can secure the necessary votes to be adopted. Finally, in more and more cases, it is also necessary to make compromises with the European Parliament in view of increased use of the co-decision procedure. Thus the political process may substantially have altered what was originally intended.

All of these aspects mentioned above have to be taken into account when studying the industrial policy of the European Union and the other policies affecting industry and their interaction.

1.4 CONCLUSIONS AND HOW THIS BOOK IS ORGANISED

In this chapter we have seen that there is no such thing as a single definition of industrial policy, neither in general economic terms, nor at the EU level. The economic arguments range from very broad ones including everything which could possibly affect industry to very narrow approaches looking only at specific sector initiatives. None of these approaches was applicable for our purpose of defining the industrial policy of the European Union.

Not only is it difficult to define industrial policy, but it could also be questioned whether industrial policy objectives should be pursued at all. Some argue that industrial policy can be justified due to market failures and changes in comparative advantages, while others do not believe that a situation with public interventions will lead to a more optimal situation than the free market situation, since the public does not have the necessary information and instruments at its disposal to overcome these failures and because public interventions in themselves distort the market. The difference in attitude has led to different schools of industrial policy, which are sometimes referred to as interventionists and liberals. Although, in reality, industrial policy is pursued through a mix, these different schools are easily recognised in the different Member States' attitude towards industrial policy.

The basis of the industrial policy of the European Union is Article 157, which may be clear concerning the objective of the Unions industrial policy, but which is rather unclear towards its instruments. The objective is to ensure that the conditions necessary for the competitiveness of the Community's industry exist. However, the instruments to achieve this objective have to be found under other provisions of the Treaty. We used economic findings to go through the Treaty identifying three categories of policy areas.

The first one consists of policy areas whose main aim and priority is to affect industry. The second one consists of policy areas with a significant affect on industry, but which have other main priorities. The third one consists of policy areas with a limited influence on industry. The first category we regard as the industrial policy of the European Union. The second category we regard as important policies affecting industry. This categorisation gives the scope of the book. The first category will be subject to closer examination in Part Three. The second category will be dealt with in Part Two. The last category will not be dealt with in any further detail.

The application of industrial policy and the co-ordination with other policies affecting industry can be difficult because the different instruments may conflict with one another. These aspects will be taken into account in the different Chapters where relevant.

BIBLIOGRAPHY

Bourgeois, H. J. and Demaret, Paul (1995), The Working of EC Policies on Competition, Industry and Trade: a legal analysis, in Pierre Buigues, Alexis Jacquemin and André Sapir, (eds.), *European policies on competition, trade and industry: Conflict and complementarities*. Edward Elgar Publishing Company, Vermont.

Buigues, Pierre and Sapir, André (1993), Community Industrial Policy, in P. Nicolaides (ed.), *Industrial Policy in the European Community: A Necessary Response to Economic Integration?* European Institute of Public Administration, Maastricht.

Council of the European Union (1998), Presidency Note to Industry Council, *Ongoing debate on industrial competitiveness. Medium-Term Working Programme,* Doc. 12233/98, 20 October 1998.

Council regulation No 1013/97 of 2 June 1997 on Aid to certain shipyards under restructuring, OJ No. L 148/1, 06.06.1997.

Darmer, Michael (1992), EF's nye industripolitik, *Samfundsøkonomen, 1992:7.*

Darmer, Michael (1995), EU's industripolitik, *Samfundsøkonomen, 1995:1.*

Darmer, Michael and Pettersson, Preben S. (1991), Dansk elektronikindustri i den internationale konkurrence, *Økonomi og politik 1991:3.*

Davis, Evan (1993), Industrial Policy in an Integrated European Economy, in P. Nicolaides (ed.), *Industrial Policy in the European Community: A Necessary Response to Economic Integration?* European Institute of Public Administration, Maastricht.

European Commission (1990), *Industrial Policy in an Open and Competition Based Environment. Guidelines for a Community Policy*, COM(90) 556, Brussels 16 November 1990.

European Commission (1991), *European Industrial Policy for the 1990s*, Bulletin of the European Communities, Suppl. 3/91.

European Commission (1997), *Action Plan for the Single Market,* CSE(97)1, 4 June 1997.

European Commission (1998), *Virksomhedspanelet, et Pilotprojekt,* COM(98) 197, 30 March 1998.

Geroski, P.A. (1989), European Industrial Policy and Industrial Policy in Europe, *Oxford Review of Economic Policy,* Vol 5, No. 2.

Grossman, Gene M. (1990), Promoting new industrial activity: A survey of recent arguments and evidence, *OECD Economic Studies,* No. 14, 1990.

Gual, Jordi (1995): The three common policies: An economic analysis, in Pierre Buigues, Alexis Jacquemin and André Sapir, (eds.), *European Policies on Competition, Trade and Industry: Conflict and complementarities*, Edward Elgar Publishing Company, Vermont.

Jacquemin, Alexis (1987), *The New Industrial Organisation: Market Forces and Strategic Behaviour*, Clarendon Press, Oxford..

Johnson, Chalmers (1984), The Idea of Industrial Policy, in Chalmers Johnson (ed.) *The Industrial Policy Debate.*

Krugman, Paul R. and Obstfeld, Maurice (1988), *International Economics. Theory and Policy*, Glenview, IL.

Ministeriet for Erhvervspolitisk Samordning (1993), *Erhvervsredegørelse 1993.*

Nicolaides, Phedon (1993), Industrial Policy: The Problem of Reconciling Definitions, Intentions and Effects, in P. Nicolaides (ed.), *Industrial Policy in the European Community: A Necessary Response to Economic Integration?* European Institute of Public Administration, Maastricht.

OECD (1996), *Industrial Competitiveness,* OECD, Paris.

OECD (1998), *Policies for Industrial Development and Competitiveness.* DSTI/IND(97)28/FINAL, OLIS 12-May-1998.

Pelkmans, Jacques (1997), *European Integration: Methods and Economic Analysis,* Addison Wesley Longman, Essex.

Porter, Michael E. (1990), The competitive advantage of nations, *Harvard Business Review*, March–April 1990.

Tirole (1988), *The Theory of Industrial Organization,* The MIT Press, Massachusetts Institute of Technology, Cambridge, Massachusetts.

Tyson, Laura and Zysman, John (1983), American Industry in International Competition, in J. Zysman and L. Tyson (eds.), *American Industry in International Competition: Government Policies and Corporate Strategies,* Cornell University Press, London.

2. A Policy for the Competitiveness of European Industry

Laurens Kuyper

Industrial policy, under whatever name, is not a new phenomenon. Every government takes account of the wellbeing of its manufacturing industry and services. For the European Union, however, industrial policy only has a short history.

Industrial policy as such was not included in the Treaty of Rome (1957), but it has found a specific place in the present Treaty of Amsterdam (1998). In that period its character and content changed drastically, and also evolved from typically government activity towards closer co-operation with industry itself.

The first section of this chapter takes a look at the beginning, when it was the Commission, and only the Commission, that tried to create a policy competence on Community level. From the first Council of Industry Ministers (1980) onwards, the Community struggled to find an industrial policy philosophy that would be acceptable to all Member States. The section ends with the first show of consensus (1990).

The second section builds on that consensus and the progressive implementation of a real European industrial policy. The end of sector-specific industrial policy, which was common in the earlier period, was put into effect; the Community did choose for a horizontal policy in this area. Successive activities, like the Information Society, managed to set this horizontal approach into building blocks around the central theme of competitiveness and a favourable business environment. In this period a closer involvement of industry became a normal part of policymaking, through advisory groups and intensified dialogue.

The third section looks at Europe's competitiveness, as follows from the improved data and information on the performance of European industry in comparison with its main trading partners.

2.1 THE DEVELOPMENT OF INDUSTRIAL POLICY

The first years of the European Community were devoted to the objective of creating the Customs Union. With its completion on 1 July 1968, goods could move freely within the Community area (of six Member States) without running up against tariff obstacles. But, in the view of the Commission, this broadening of the market 'has not so far been paralleled by a similar process of broadening the structures of production' (Bulletin 2–1969). Therefore, closing this gap between the market and the structure of production had to be the first task of a Community industrial policy.

Such a policy should be based on general conditions to help and encourage the structural adaptation of firms and on specific measures: 'some industries need the intervention and support of the public authorities' (ibid.).

First Steps

In a memorandum on an industrial policy (18 March 1970), the Commission presented its first ideas for an industrial strategy at Community level. A structural policy directed essentially to an integrated industrial network was needed because of the 'inadequate degree of efficiency and, by the same token, competitiveness of Community industry, when measured by the standards of its main rivals'. And also because the production structures had remained national, which meant that restructuring (adaptation to change) mainly takes place on exclusively national lines. The memorandum concludes that competitiveness is a necessity and that 'the process of permanent change which is a feature of modern economies cannot be left to market forces alone' (Bulletin 5–1970).

The Council (July 1970) resolved to assign the investigation of priorities in this area to a group of senior civil servants. The report of this group indicated a broad measure of agreement and also proposed to set up a Standing Committee on Industrial Policy (which never was established).

The Paris Summit Conference of October 1972 recognised the need 'to try and provide a uniform basis for industry throughout the Community'. This motivated the Commission to propose the industrial and technological policy programme (Communication of 7 May 1973, Bulletin 5–1973) it intended to follow up. Its priorities were: removal of barriers to trade, progressive and effective opening-up of public and semi-public contracts, promoting inter-company competition at European level, and sectors facing special problems; the Commission concluded that 'some industrial sectors deserve special attention either because they are under a crisis or because restructuration at European level is high priority for them'. In view of this, it announced proposals for the sectors aeronautics, data processing, heavy mechanical and electrical plant, uranium-enrichment, shipbuilding, textiles and paper.

The ensuing Council debate on industrial policy set out the guidelines for a European industrial policy; the issues (Box 2.1) in the Council Resolution would remain on the agenda for the coming years. It marked the starting point of industrial policy discussions between the Member States at Community level.

Box 2.1   Industrial policy issues

Abolition of technical barriers to trade in foodstuffs and industrial products
Gradual and effective liberalisation of public contracts
Abolition of fiscal barriers to closer relations between undertakings
Abolition of legal barriers to closer relations between undertakings
European-scale promotion of competitive advanced technology undertakings
Conversion and modernisation of certain sectors of industry
Preparation of measures to guarantee that concentrations affecting undertakings established in the Community are in keeping with Community economic and social objectives, and the maintenance of fair competition both in the Common Market and on outside markets in accordance with the provisions of the treaties
Measures concerning exports and, in particular, credit insurance
Supplies of raw materials, in particular of non-ferrous metals
The Commission shall draw up an annual report on the implementation of the programme.

Source: Council of the European Community (1973)

The oil crises and the following global recession diminished those ambitions. Instead, the Community's main subject for discussion turned to possible ways to alleviate the problems of industry, trying to create a specific policy with a view to alleviating the most immediate employment problems or in response to 'strategic' considerations. These actions were often designed or applied in such a way as to produce the wrong kind of adjustment, and they were not always co-ordinated with each other. In practice, European industrial policy in this period was predominantly sectoral in nature, because the many national worries in declining sectors like steel, shipbuilding and textiles were put on the desk of the Commission to solve the mainly external problems through the Community's trade policy competence.

Concepts like 'strategic industries' were often used in the debate, in order to protect large well-established and domestically controlled firms. Policy instruments such as subsidies and soft loans became very popular, as they were regarded, at the time, as substituting the perceived failures of the market mechanism.

Industry Ministers in Council

In 1980 European Industry Ministers did meet for the first time in the Community context, informally. Although they had formal meetings when discussing the problems in the steel industry (Steel Council), they continued these informal meetings until May 1984; in October of that year they started to have formal meetings as Industry Council.

Industry Commissioner Davignon inspired the first meeting in Venice, Italy (11 June 1980), referring to the serious crisis in the steel industry in 1977, which endangered the Community's internal solidarity, and to the problematic situation of the Community's economy. Positive adjustment, free trade, fair competition and completion of the internal market must be the guiding principles of European industrial policy, supported by the attention given to new areas such as telecommunications and biotechnology.

Referring to the difficult period through which the European economy was passing in 1980/81, the European Parliament expressed its disappointment about the lack of co-operation on industrial policy between the Member States, as well as about lack of agreement within the Council and about the absence of initiatives on the part of the Commission (Report Delorozoy of 27 April 1981). According to the Parliament, the Commission's Memorandum of 1973 was still relevant for promoting a true industrial policy in the Community.

In a Resolution (1981) it stressed the need for a 'policy of industrial co-operation', asked for more money in the Community budget,[1] and suggested the setting-up of an Industrial Policy Committee under the Council, as well as the creation of sectoral co-operation committees ('for determining the policies to be applied in certain major industrial sectors'). The Parliament even discussed the use of the budget to force the Council and the Commission to get a true industrial policy off the ground.

In its Communication to the Council on 'A Community Strategy to Develop Europe's Industry' (European Commission, 1981a), the Commission suggested to turn the internal market into 'a genuine European industrial continuum, but with an element of Community preference in cases where industrial development involves the participation of the public authorities'. In the same document the Commission concluded that research and development in the Community was unsatisfactory, both in the scale of research requirements and the resources available. A new industrial R&D programme for the long term was proposed: to develop European capacities for the production of microprocessors and opto-electronic equipment and for

---

[1]   Of the 1980 budget only 0.04 per cent was targeted for the industrial sector.

the transmission, management and processing of information. In close co-operation with twelve large companies this later developed into the ESPRIT program.

The Communication was welcomed as the first attempt to compare the Community's overall industrial performance with its main trading partners. But its approach did not meet with general approval in the Council (13 January 1982); the Directors-General for Industry of the Member States[2] were asked to prepare a new Council debate on the implementation of a Community industrial strategy. The DG's also expressed their opinion about the Commission's idea that companies which are producing within the Community should benefit from Community 'preference': in view of difficulties encountered in exporting to certain third countries, industries from those countries should be treated less favourably than European companies in the areas of common commercial policy, technical standards and public procurement. The opposing opinion was that such an instrument to discriminate against third countries is not acceptable, especially in view of the Community's international obligations.

Such a 'Community preference' disappeared in the Council, but continued to come up in the following years, often under the guise of attempts to 'define' European enterprises.

Another steel crisis in the mid1980s, together with problems in the European shipbuilding industry, dominated in this period the discussions in the Industry Council. Therefore the Commission's first analysis of the competitiveness of European industry (1986) was only discussed in general terms and did not get a great deal of attention.

Towards a New Policy

Throughout the Community's first two decades the concept of (European) industrial policy divided the Member States. Most of them regarded this area as belonging exclusively to the national domain – claiming that their national policies did not distort competition at home, did not raise prices to consumers and were based on rational economic criteria.

This attitude of Member States left little or no space for a common European policy. Whenever there was a problematic situation for a specific industry or sector, as has been the case in areas troubled by strong international competition, like steel and textiles, the European Commission was called upon to soften the blow. 'Defensive' industrial policy was the apt description.

From the mid 1980s onwards the political environment began to change, enabling a general acceptance of the guiding principles for an industrial policy at Community level. The old controversies between Member States, referred to in Chapter 1, started to disappear. The experiences with the

---

[2]   Established in 1975 to assist the Commission.

troubled sectors were, to put it mildly, no success, and everyone began to accept that governments are not in a good position to manage microeconomic processes, but do have an important influence on the business environment. From that starting point, a new approach to European industrial policy was developing.

It was industry itself, pressing governments to put a greater effort in the completion of the internal market in order to eliminate the still existing barriers between Member States' markets. The Commission's White Paper 'Completing the Internal Market' (COM(85) 310, 14 June, 1985), unanimously endorsed by the Heads of Governments in June of that year, aimed at just doing that, by the end of 1992. It created a period of great optimism and determination in Europe, although the major trading partners and competitors of the Community feared it would make Europe a fortress, closed to the outside world. This situation is analysed in Chapter 7.

The change in attitude became manifest in the preparation of a new Commission document on industrial policy: during the year 1990 the Directors-General of Industry from the Member States discussed the possible content of this document, in close co-operation with the Commission's officials. Agreement was reached about the need to found European policy on the development of competitiveness of European industry and on continued structural adjustment. In October 1990 the Industry Ministers discussed the ideas of the Commission for a comprehensive industrial policy. A few days later the final European Commission Communication (1990) was published. [3]

In the document the Commission built upon the emerging consensus, with the main focus on the creation of the right business environment, while at the same time broadening the industry policy domain to include all those policies which influence the structural adjustment of industry. Its key question is: 'which conditions need to be present in order to strengthen the optimal allocation of resources by market forces, towards accelerating structural adjustment and towards improving industrial competitiveness and the industrial and particularly technological long term framework'. Guiding principles are openness, horizontal and subsidiarity.

Maintaining an open approach to markets also included an effective implementation of rules, which guarantee the proper functioning of trade, both inside and outside the Community. Emphasising a horizontal approach was at the expense of sectoral policies, recognising the failures of the past.

The principle of subsidiarity meant that the Community only tackles those tasks that cannot be done better at the national level. This implied the necessity to define the economically relevant markets so that industrial policy

---

[3]   Regarded by the OECD, 1991, as the politically most important policy initiative during 1990, 'not only because of its novelty (it is the first EC document outlining a Community industrial policy approach, but also because it reflects a convergence of views and an implicit agreement on common principles between Member States that have until now often followed rather different industrial policy approaches'.

can identify the correct mix of Community, national and local responsibilities.

At the same time the Commission settled the main conceptual question, that had been at the heart of the debate on industrial policy, that is, what is the role of government: 'The main responsibility for industrial competitiveness must lie with firms themselves, but they should be able to expect from public authorities clear and predictable conditions for their activities.'

In an annex to the document, the Commission analysed the relative position of the Community's industry on global markets. It shows a relatively stable Community share in world exports since the 1970s, but in relation to its main competitors its position is not so strong, in particular in expanding markets such as Japan. The 1989 position in exports of the EU, Japan and the US is shown in Figure 2.1. Improvements in investment and cost of capital for equipment are necessary in view of the growing importance of innovation and technology as source of competitiveness. Figure 2.2 illustrates the importance of the Union's investment in the US, as well as the relative minor flow of Japanese investments into the EU and the US.

Figure 2.1   Exports EU–US–Japan (1989) in billion €

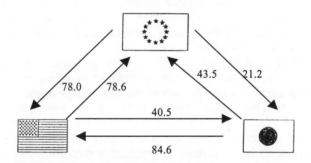

Source: European Commission (1990)

An analysis of revealed comparative advantage (for the first time in a document to the Industry Council) showed a favourable position of European industry in almost half of the examined 100 product categories. This analysis, showing European strengths in specific segments of industry and not in industrial sectors or industry as a whole, underlined the need for leaving behind the traditional policy approach.

Figure 2.2   Foreign direct investment EU–US–Japan (1989) in billion €

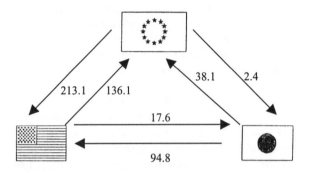

Source: European Commission (1990)

The Change is Settled

The Industry Council of 26 November 1990 unanimously agreed to achieve the goal of an industrial policy of the Community that would take into account 'the complexities of the situation both internal and external to the Community as well as allow a more balanced development and greater economic and social cohesion within the Community'. The Council also endorsed the conclusions of the Commission's document and encouraged it to continue its work and its studies.

This Council marked the end of sector-specific industrial policy, in the sense of the recent past. It did not put an end to differences between Member States about the practical consequences of the new European policy. But it did create a suitable basis for European consensus. The Intergovernmental Conference (1991) that was set up to modernise the Treaty, introduced 'the strengthening of the competitiveness of Community industry' as a general obligation (Article 3) in the revised Treaty. It also succeeded, not without much difficulty because not all Member States were convinced that it was necessary, to introduce a separate Title XIII on Industry (Article 130) in the revised Treaty of the European Union (Maastricht, 1991).

The change in policy character agreed upon did not significantly change the content of the Industry Council meetings: problems in the steel, textiles and shipbuilding industry retained an important place on the agenda.

To overcome difficulties in the steel industry – prices collapsed 30 per cent on the Community market, as mentioned in Chapter 13 – some Member States did feel they needed to grant large amounts of state aid to steel companies, while at the same time attempts were made to restructure the sector in the Community. The failure of these attempts did, undoubtedly, influence the mood in which it would become easier to change the character of European industrial policy.

The new, not sector-specific, approach became gradually visible in the Union's activities in relation to subjects such as: electronics and information technology (a Council Resolution was adopted on 18 November 1991), biotechnology, maritime industry, small and medium-sized enterprises (a Council Resolution on the action programme for SMEs was adopted on 27 May 1991), environment, industrial co-operation, and an annual debate on the Community's competition policy.

2.2   AN INDUSTRAL COMPETITIVENESS POLICY FOR THE EUROPEAN UNION

As the revised Treaty obliged the Community *and* the Member States to ensure that the conditions necessary for the competitiveness of the Community's industry exist, it also puts an obligation on the Member States to consult each other (in liaison with the Commission) and co-ordinate, where necessary, their actions. This confirms that industrial policy remains a national competence, only limited in the sense that information and co-ordination take place in order to fulfil the objective of competitiveness. Therein lies the role of the Community: helping to achieve that objective by taking horizontal measures. The Council may also decide to take specific measures to support Member States' actions in this area, but the agreement of all Member States is necessary.

The requirement of unanimity showed that, in spite of the general acceptance of the concept of industrial policy on Community level, there remained worries about the danger of returning to the sector-specific measures of the past. It was a reflection of the recurrent discussion between Industry Ministers about the horizontal character of European industrial policy, whenever the Commission proposed a document on the situation in a given sector of industry.

New challenges were facing industry, such as the intensifying international competition and the economic recession in 1992/93, emphasising the need to improve the employment situation in the Community. Industry added its advice: 'bring the costs down, cut the regulations, and raise the quality' (European Round Table of Industrialists, 1993; UNICE, 1994).

Competitiveness of European industry became the most important priority, not only because it had been written into the Treaty, but also because it is economically necessary for the welfare of the European Union. The Industry Council of April 1994 invited the Commission to report annually on the state of Europe's competitiveness, so as to facilitate the debate about possible measures on Community level.

Information Society

At the same time Industry Commissioner Bangemann's High Level Group, published its report ('Europe and the global information society') to the European Council of Corfu (1994), calling for a market-driven approach, which seemed to be necessary in view of Europe's position in the information and communication technologies sector (ICT). As Figure 2.3 shows, the US continued to stay ahead of both the EU and Japan. The Union is even farther behind when comparing ICT expenditure per capita.

The High Level group recommended accelerated liberalisation of telecommunication, with the clear intention to contribute to the competitiveness of Europe's industry.

Figure 2.3   ICT as a percentage of GDP

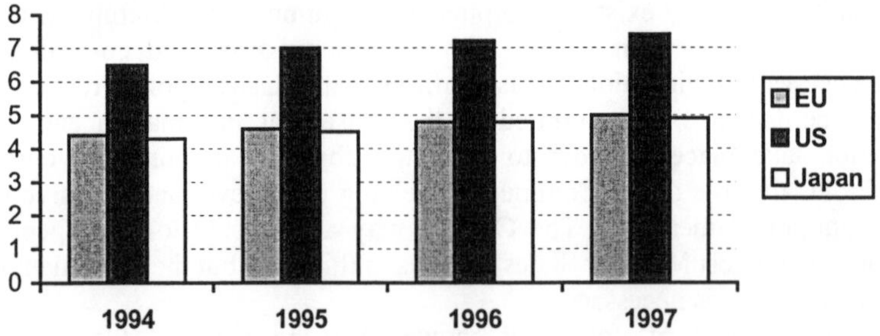

Source: EITO, European Commission (1998a)

The European Council invited the Commission to set up an Action Plan covering the measures needed at Community level. This Action Plan, 'Europe's Way to the Information Society' (COM(94) 347, 19 July 1994), was published one month later and welcomed by a combined Council of Industry and Telecommunications Ministers in September 1994. In that meeting the divergences of opinion between Member States could not be bridged concerning decisions that should be taken on the principles (and a timetable) for the liberalisation of the telecommunications infrastructure.

Information society technologies continue to grow in importance; they are becoming essential for the competitive performance of industry. The EU part is increasing slowly as a percentage of GDP (see Figure 2.3); compared to the US, Europe and Japan are still lagging behind. The Union is even farther behind when comparing ICT expenditure per capita.

Within the larger goal of realising the Information Society, the information and communication technology industry occupies the heart of the Commission's work. Its Communication on electronic commerce[4]

---

[4]   A European Initiative in Electronic Commerce, COM(1997) 157 of 16 April 1997; Council conclusions of 13 November 1997.

received full support from the Industry Ministers. The Commission foresees electronic commerce as the driver for change in traditional sectors, because it goes beyond information technology in the sense that it would need re-rethinking of business organisation; 'for a company going online is not a technology decision but a strategic decision'.[5]

In conformity with the present approach to industrial policy, the Council re-stated that the primary responsibility lies with businesses themselves. The role for government, again, should focus on creating a favourable business environment, a clear and predictable legal and regulatory framework, and – especially with a view to electronic commerce development – liberalising telecommunication markets. European industry is perceived to be strong in certain key areas (mobile communication, digital television, and financial services) but is not taking up the challenges offered by the information society.

Competitiveness

In that setting the Commission also published its Communication on 'An industrial competitiveness policy for the European Union' (1994), pointing out for the Member States where improvements for the sake of competitiveness could be made. It focused on four areas: intangible investment, industrial co-operation, fair competition, and the role of public authorities. The document also attempted to mitigate industry's alarming sounds about the Europe's competitiveness:

> assessments of the state of EU industry are being made in a context of economic crisis when it is difficult to determine to what extent the unfavourable comparison of certain quantitative factors is not a reflection of the poor economic environment.

According to the Commission the Union's industrial competitiveness had improved: increasing export of goods, decreasing trade deficits with the USA and Japan, growth in research and development effort by big enterprises, downward unit labour-cost trends. On the other hand, the Union's weaknesses were still there: declining share of worldwide exports of manufactured goods (as shown in Figure 2.4), low presence and trade deficit in high-technology products, slower improvement of productivity, weaker public research and development effort.

---

[5] European Commission Staff Working Paper: A catalyst for European competitiveness, SEC(99)1291.

*Figure 2.4   Market shares as a percentage of world exports of manufactured
goods*

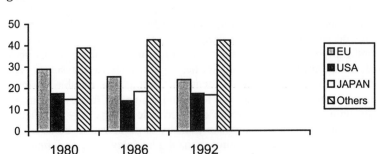

Source: OECD; European Commission (1994)

The Industry Ministers reiterated, in a Council Resolution (OJ C 343, 6
December 1994), their approval of the guiding principles for European
industrial policy, and welcomed the Commission's Communication in which
the possibilities for action are outlined. This reception showed that not all
Member States supported the ideas for European action; some countries saw
in the approach of the Commission a danger of deviating from the consensus
that European industrial policy should maintain its horizontal character in all
circumstances.

In following-up this Resolution, the Commission presented an Action
Programme (COM(95)87, 22 March 1995) for strengthening the
competitiveness of European industry: reinforce the Internal Market and
improve its functioning; co-ordinate R&D policy with the needs of industry;
information society; and promote industrial co-operation. Consequently, the
Council adopted a decision on the implementation of this Programme,
including the publication of an annual report on competitiveness.

The New Policy is Taking Shape

Looking back at the period 1990–94, quite a number of actions of the
Commission did reach the Industry Council, while in the same period major
developments took place elsewhere, like the reunification of Germany, the
conclusion of the Urugay Round and the establishment of the World Trade
Organisation, or the changes in central and eastern Europe. At the start of
1995 Sweden, Finland and Austria joined the European Union.

Renewed efforts on the completion and functioning of the internal market,
the proposals on energy and transport networks and on financing the trans-
European networks, as well as the process of liberalisation of
telecommunication and the strengthening of research and development, were
all aimed to contribute to improving Europe's competitiveness. Political
attention towards information and communication technologies increased

significantly, as the Industry Ministers stressed the importance of the Information Society for the competitiveness of European industry[6] and its priorities.[7]

To this was added the growing awareness that policies concerning environmental protection not only had an increasing impact on industry, but also could be influenced by industry itself. The Industry Council of May 1995 recognised this.

The Intergovernmental Conference that started in 1996 to adapt the Treaty concluded in the end (Amsterdam, 1997) that the legal basis for industrial policy should remain as it was decided in Maastricht (1991). There was some discussion about the voting majority needed for taking specific measures in this area, but the text stayed as it was – unanimity for changing it could not be found. The former Article 130 now became Article 157. The European Council, however, again stressed its importance: 'competitiveness of European industry provides the foundation for growth, creating jobs and raising living standards'.

Industry as Adviser

In order to assist the Commission in its task to enhance competitiveness, the European Council of Essen (1994) recommended setting up a Competitiveness Advisory Group, consisting of high level experts. The group stressed the need to finalise the still not completed internal market so as to enable European enterprises to face stronger competition abroad, and to enhance human resources so as to promote flexibility in economic adjustment. In its reports[8] the group advised giving priority to: the reform of infrastructure services and the utilities sector, support of innovative SMEs, the company and environmental policy, the redesigning and reinforcing of education and training beyond basic levels, as well as flexibility in labour markets.

The strong influence of industry, manifested by advisory groups such as this, and the increased dialogue between the Commission and the organisations of industry and trade unions, pointed at the way industry itself uses tools to determine its position in the market. Companies compare their own performance with the best in the world and then try to find a way to do as well or better. The High Level Group on Benchmarking,[9] composed of representatives from industry, trade unions and the civil society, was given the task of assisting the Commission in this area.

---

[6]   Resolution on the industrial aspects of the information society, of 27 November 1995.
[7]   Resolution of 21 November 1996, OJ C 372 of 12 December 1996.
[8]   Presented to the European Councils of Cannes (June 1995), Madrid (December 1995) and Florence (June 1996)
[9]   Established (1998) by Commissioner Bangemann to advise him on how to use benchmarking as a tool to improve European industrial competitiveness.

Benchmarking

For companies the use of benchmarking has been an efficient way of improving productivity and competitiveness. The European Commission's (1996b) Communication demonstrated its belief in benchmarking as a tool for comparing performance in the different key areas of the economy and society that determine economic success. It was further developed in a Communication (1997) on 'Benchmarking, implementation of an instrument available to economic actors and public authorities'.

According to the High Level Group, Europe in general lags behind the USA in terms of awareness and use of benchmarking in various sectors. 'For the competitiveness of Europe, benchmarking must be applied not only by private enterprises but also by the public sector'. Industry strongly advised the Commission to benchmark the quality and performance of the public services of governments that make up an important part of the business climate, in order to identify the limiting factors that hinder the competitiveness of industry in Europe. According to industry, 'Europe's problems have been analysed quite thoroughly. We therefore need to move from analysis to action'.

Not all Member States were immediately convinced that it would be possible, or useful, to benchmark government policies as they worked out as framework conditions in the business environment. In spite of the strong support (by UNICE) for the Commission's initiative, it took several steps to move forward in that direction: first, the Commission had to analyse already existing benchmark practices; then there had to be some pilot projects; this had to be concluded by an evaluation. This process took three years (1997–99) to complete; the Industry Council of April 1999 agreed to the ongoing development of benchmarking as an instrument for improving competitiveness, and called on the Commission to identify practical steps to develop benchmarking of framework conditions. In the meantime the Commission continued its activities in this area: a website[10] was set up (1998) on the Internet providing information about these activities as well as links to other relevant benchmarking sites elsewhere. In 1997 the European Benchmarking Network was established, including representatives of over 400 organisations interested in benchmarking.

Role of Industry Council

In the Union's division of labour between the institutions it is the task of the Commission to present proposals, and it is up to the Council – in many cases together with the European Parliament – to decide upon them. For Industry Ministers, since they met in the Industry Council, most of these decisions have been on measures in specific sectors like steel and shipbuilding.

---

[10]   http://www.benchmarking-in-europe.com

The change in European policy, moving from sector-specific to horizontal approaches, reduced the need for taking decisions considerably. Since then, Industry Ministers mostly discussed communications of the Commission or they were able to debate the Commission's activities, such as the annual Competition report. The Industry Council needed to find a new area of competence, which it found in the central issue of competitiveness of European industry; closer co-operation with other components of the Council, such as Internal Market, Energy, and Environment had to be organised.[11] In the move to modernise the role of the Industry Council, the Ministers also aimed to involve European industry closer with the Council's activities. As this could not be done within the formal context of the Council, industry was (beginning in 1997) invited to discuss with Ministers in an informal session on the night before the Industry Council meeting.

2.3   THE STATE OF EUROPE'S COMPETITIVENESS

As had been requested by the Industry Council Resolution in 1994,[12] the Commission published its first Report on this issue in 1996. It examines the competitive performance of the European economy in general, and of European industry in particular. Part of the report concerns intangible investment, research and development, human resources, innovation and protection of the environment. The report, however, does not draw any conclusions from the stated decline in Europe's competitiveness (in rate of growth of GDP, in share of world exports, in share of inward foreign direct investment, in employment and job creation). The Union could not match the performance of its main competitors (Table 2.1), but showed clear improvements.

Table 2.1   Trade in total manufacturing

	Market shares*		Trade balance 1000 million €		Annual growth in % Exports	Imports
	1989	1996	1989	1996	1989	1996
EU	27.0	26.9	28.1	130.2	7.9	5.3
Japan	19.2	14.5	121.7	107.4	3.7	7.8
USA	20.2	18.8	-125.1	-146.4	6.8	5.5
Other	35.4	42.0	-1.9	-123.3	9.2	11.3

Note:* Market shares: exports as a percentage of world imports

Source: COMPET, WIFO calculations, European Commission (1998a)

---

[11]   This process is still going on (2000).
[12]   Resolution of 21 November 1994 on strengthening the competitiveness of European industry.

The 1998 Report has a different set-up: the first part presents a general assessment of Europe's competitive performance and the problems encountered, while the second part focuses on the strengths and weaknesses of the European manufacturing sector and compares its sectoral specialisation with that of the USA and of Japan. It is the Commission's intention to link the report with the agreed use of benchmarking; thus it would contribute to identifying key trends and weaknesses. This in turn can provide the basis for informed debate on key competitiveness factors in the Industry Council. The objective is to establish a continuous cycle of issue identification, weakness diagnosis, results reporting and ongoing review of progress.

The Report derives four policy issues arising from the data: maintaining the horizontal character of industrial policy is essential; industry must continue to upgrade (industrial policy therefore must promote innovation, adaptability and upgrading human capital); elimination of institutional barriers to the creative and flexible management of change; and policies directed at the diffusion of best practices within the European Union (leading to upward convergence and disappearing of disparities).

The main conclusion of the Competitiveness Reports is that European industry is, in general, competitive. The good performance of industry on export markets emphasises the strengths of European industry. Employment growth is better than it has been in the past decade, as shown in Figure 2.5.

The Union's trade balance for manufactured goods is positive and increased in the 1990's, while the market shares of Japan and the US decreased. This is an indication of the health of manufacturing industry in Europe.

Figure 2.5   Employment growth in percentage per annum

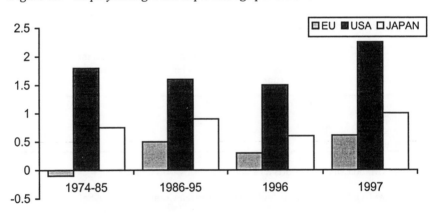

Source: OECD; IFO calculations, European Commission (1998a)

Europe has got a quality mark-up: the EU's trade surplus is generated by a quality premium in the sense that exports are more highly valued than imports. Figure 2.6 illustrates the Union's position.

Figure 2.6   Exports EU–US–Japan (1998) in billion €

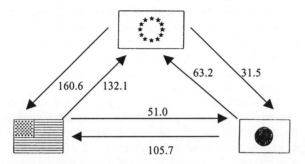

Source: European Commission (1999)

Europe is more specialised in relatively high added-value products, especially traditional products. It is strongly positioned in mainstream manufacturing and the research-intensive industries outside the information technologies; the EU is competitive in machinery, vehicles and chemical sectors, which contribute considerably to the trade surplus. However, compared to the USA, European performance is not too good in ICT-related research-intensive industries and in the fast moving markets, where competitive advantage is based on intangible investment in research and marketing.

According to the Competitiveness Reports and the annual publications of the Panorama, the picture for the Union is generally positive, but some weaknesses in Europe's performance, as compared with the US and Japan, continue to exist (Box 2.2).

Box 2.2   Weaknesses of European industry

• The level of R&D spending
• European enterprises form relatively few alliances in advanced technologies
• Undeveloped specialisation in sectors with high growth, highly differentiated products and requiring a strong market strategy
• No strong presence in the business service sector
• Risk-capital funds invest insufficiently in new and high technology industries

Source: Panorama, 1997; Competitiveness report 1998

One of these weaknesses is the performance in the field of innovation: all studies and reports show that Europe has insufficient innovative capacity. Of the present 25 biggest American firms, 19 did not exist or were very small before 1960 (at that date, neither Microsoft nor Intel existed). A look at the 25 biggest European firms show that none of them is new and they have all existed for more than 30 years.

Europe's industry performance is lagging behind the US and Japan when looking at expenditure by business on R&D (Table 2.2), as well as international patenting. R&D per unit GDP was around 1.2 per cent during the period 1985–97. In the same period this percentage varied between 1.8 and 2.1 for Japan and the USA. In absolute terms the US allocated €170 billion in 1997, compared to €127 billion in the EU.

Existing data also show that the take-up of research results in the EU is less efficient: the number of patent applications is a rough indication of the economic relevant R&D output. Measured by the number of first applications per million inhabitants on an annual basis, Japan shows the best performance with around 150 inventions in 1994. The inventions per capita were around 100 in the US that year. The European Union, however, had the lowest performance: around 50 inventions per capita. These figures show a gap vis-à-vis Japan and the US.

The business–R&D ratio and the number of patents applied indicate that the innovation speed in the EU is relatively lower compared to Japan and the USA. As R&D is crucial for the future competitiveness of industry, the European R&D performance is too weak to enhance the Union's competitiveness. The European innovation system is, in fact, fragmented – not in line with the integration effects of the internal market – and a disadvantage in this respect. The many national innovation systems involve the risk, according to the Commission (1999a) 'of aiming limited resources at too many national institutions with similar functions and objectives across the countries'. In this context, the real European weakness therefore has to be the absence of converting Europe's technological and scientific knowledge to effective business opportunities.

Table 2.2   Business R&D

	EU	USA	Japan
Business expenditure per capita in €	175	456	369
Share of total R&D (1994–96)	60.6	71.8	71.1
Number of patents per 10 000 inhabitants in 1996	2.62	4.03	–

Source: OECD (1998), European Commission (1998, 2000)

Another weak point concerns the relatively few alliances of European enterprises in advanced technology fields. Such alliances may help companies to keep up with technological developments, by sharing high technological risks and increasing costs of advanced R&D, as well as by gaining access to know-how of other firms.

Non-equity R&D agreements have become the most prevalent mode of global industrial R&D co-operation. Research partnerships grew at an average of almost 11 per cent per year worldwide between 1980 and 1994, particularly in information technologies, biotechnology and new materials. However, more than five times as many technological alliances are formed between US firms than between European companies.[13]

Underdeveloped specialisation in sectors with high growth such as the information technology industry is another concern of the Union. High technology enterprises are important for future growth: the ICT industry generates many new jobs (see Chapter 13). On average, European firms invest less in ICT and have a lower ICT expenditure per capita than firms in Japan or the US. These figures show a relatively limited use of information technology in Europe.

European industry has no strong presence in the business service sector. In fields like logistics, business and legal consultancy and auditing, Europe lags behind. In financial services, for instance, the capital productivity in the US is about 30 per cent higher.

The fact that the sums invested by venture capital funds in high technology in Europe are minimal is a weak point as well: companies in the early stages of development received 7.4 per cent of the total investments from European venture capital funds against 34 per cent in the US.

Other weak points are the prices of basic services like energy, transportation and communication, which are higher in the EU than in the US, or the lower labour productivity compared to Japan or the US.

But nevertheless, in general, European industry is in good shape, as the general indicators show – with the exception of employment (Table 2.3). In a way, it is a paradox. European industry showed excellent performances in such sectors as chemicals, pharmaceuticals, foodstuffs and oil refining. American and Japanese groups dominated in electronics and computing. A situation of co-leadership existed in the car industry. The 200 biggest industrial groups in the world in the early nineties demonstrate this: 69 of them were European, 64 from the US, and 53 Japanese (Panorama, 1997).

---

[13] The competitiveness of European enterprises in the face of globalisation: how it can be encouraged, COM(98) 718 Final.

Table 2.3   Average annual rate of change

	GDP			Investment			Employment		
	1970–1980	1980–1990	1990–1998	1970–1980	1980–1990	1990–1998	1970–1980	1980–1990	1990–1998
EU	2.9	2.4	1.8	1.5	2.5	0.8	0.3	0.6	0.0
Eurozone	3.2	2.4	1.8	1.7	2.2	0.6	0.3	0.6	0.0
USA	3.2	2.9	2.7	3.6	2.4	5.4	2.4	1.8	1.3
Japan	4.5	4.0	1.1	3.5	5.2	–0.4	0.8	1.2	0.5
Austria	3.6	2.3	2.1	3.7	2.5	3.1	0.3	1.1	1.1
Belgium	3.4	1.9	1.7	2.3	2.3	0.9	0.2	0.2	0.2
Denmark	2.2	2.0	2.7	–0.8	1.6	4.4	0.7	0.7	0.3
Finland	3.4	3.1	1.5	2.1	3.4	–2.5	0.9	0.6	–1.3
France	3.3	2.4	1.6	2.5	2.3	–0.3	0.5	0.3	0.2
Germany	2.7	2.2	2.0	1.2	1.6	0.9	0.1	0.6	–0.5
Greece	4.6	0.7	1.9	2.8	–0.4	3.3	0.7	1.0	0.5
Ireland	4.7	3.6	7.7	5.7	0.5	5.6	0.9	–0.2	2.9
Italy	3.6	2.2	1.2	1.7	1.6	–0.4	0.6	0.4	–0.6
Luxembourg	2.6	4.5	5.0	2.6	3.7	5.9	1.2	1.7	3.0
Netherlands	3.0	2.2	2.6	0.2	1.9	2.6	0.7	1.1	1.7
Portugal	4.7	3.2	2.4	4.1	3.0	4.4	0.4	1.2	0.4
Spain	3.5	3.0	2.1	1.6	5.2	1.4	–0.6	0.9	0.6
Sweden	2.0	2.0	1.0	0.6	3.3	–2.2	0.9	0.5	–1.4
UK	1.9	2.7	2.0	0.5	4.3	2.0	0.3	0.8	0.0

Source: European Commission (1999c; 1999d)

Globalisation

In 1999 the Commission published a reflection document which describes the principal challenges that the European Union must face up to in order to benefit from globalisation (European Commission, 1999a). It signals the need for Europe to adapt its industrial policy, 'notably to spread the enterprise culture and encourage risk-taking and to promote the emergence of innovative companies able and willing to conquer the world market'. It also calls upon all economic, social and political players in the European Union to co-operate in what should be Europe's ambition, that is, to be present in the leading industrial and service sectors.

The report seeks to add to the existing concept of industrial policy a sense of urgency, inspired by the globalisation of the economy. The challenges for the Union's industry stem from the economic evolution worldwide. Competitiveness factors are evolving: quality, speed, customisation, a product's image and after-sales service are overtaking traditional cost factors. These new factors require intangible investments such as organisational skills, training and research. Knowledge-based industries are outstripping traditional sectors in growth, capitalisation and exportability. Electronic commerce is becoming a determining catalyst in terms of greater market transparency, immediate global competition and changing business potentials. Research and development requires a compressed timeframe. SMEs are able to rapidly leap from a simple idea to world leader in their field.

Global companies try to optimise the value chain. Activities with a relatively low return may be outsourced or re-localised (to the most favourable business climate) to improve the performance of the company as a whole. Companies may specialise on their core competencies to increase their performance and to exploit what they are good at. Such strategies as 'back to the core business', 'specialisation', 'optimising scale of certain activities' all redefine the value chain. It is no longer considered necessary that a company controls all activities that are in the interest of the final product. This affects the concept of competitiveness. Traditionally, competitiveness is a term to measure the relative strength of a company, and thus it does not seem very useful to apply this concept to European industry or sectors, because the sector may no longer cover all activities necessary for a complete value chain. Developments such as cross-border equity, rapid rotation of ownership, the geographical identity of companies becoming more diffuse, make it even more difficult to measure competitiveness.

In a globalised economy only certain activities of the value chain may be viable in a certain region. In this perspective, the 'framework conditions' determining the business climate for certain activities are gaining more importance, leading to the policy question: are the framework conditions competitive? This replaces, in a way, the traditional question about the competitiveness of industry. Factors such as the level of corporate income tax, the wage level, the availability of a skilled labour force, the quality of government, all determine which activities of the value chain should be located in a certain region. Global companies continuously optimising the value chain by relocating activities will seek for the optimal framework conditions to increase the return on equity and its shareholder value. In its document the Commission recognised this effect of globalisation:

> As companies slice up the value chain of their products and services across separate markets, traditional criteria focussing on individual sectors are becoming less appropriate. The true yardstick for competitiveness should not be sectors, but, rather activities and markets.

The Industry Council of April 1999 discussed the Commission's document, but did not draw any conclusions from it. The Ministers agreed with the areas of particular relevance to the competitiveness of European industry, as described in the document, but they intended to take positions about them when proposals for action would be presented to them.

2.4 CONCLUSION

European industrial policy, in the sense of guidance on Community level policy, has developed from one side of the spectrum to the other; from the Commission's belief in a central role for itself, to the market-orientation of today. The state of the European Union's competitiveness at the beginning of a new century gives ample reason for that change of focus.

European industry has no strong presence in the business services sector; insufficient externalisation; underdeveloped specialisation; relatively few alliances in advanced technology areas; difficult access to financial markets; a low level of R&D spending; not enough exploitation of research results; high costs for achieving intellectual property protection; not enough co-operation in research projects. In this situation the Commission proposes to counteract these weaknesses by actions in the area of intangible investments, such as improving the level of and return on research resources. Education and training, in particular connected with the 'spirit of enterprise', need to be addressed, as well as improving access to the world market, promoting fair rules of the game at a world level, and making full use of the information society and electronic commerce.

By emphasising these elements, the Commission moves further away from the traditional approaches for industrial policy, in particular from sectorally oriented policies (see Chapter 13). Improving framework conditions or improving the business environment are becoming the new focal points for policy development; this can be characterised as a market-oriented approach. Ultimately market forces determine the industrial structure – Darwin has come to our economic society: survival of the fittest companies.

BIBLIOGRAPHY

Bangemann, Martin (1992), *Meeting the Global Challenge: Establishing a Successful European Industrial Policy*, Kogan Page, London.

Beije, Paul (ed.) (1987), *Towards a New European Industrial Policy*, Croom Helm, London.

Brittan, Sir Leon (1991), Does Europe have an industrial policy? Speech for the Chamber of Commerce, Aachen.

Colonna di Paliano, Guido (1969), *Industrial Policy. Problems and Outlook*, Bulletin EC, 2–1969, Office for Official Publications, Luxembourg.

Colonna di Paliano, Guido (1970), *The Case for a Common Industrial Policy*, Bulletin EC, 5–1970, Office for Official Publications, Luxembourg.

Competitiveness Advisory Group, *Enhancing European Competitiveness,* reports to the European Council, 1995–1997, Brussels.

Council of the European Community (1973), *Resolution* 17 December 1973, OJ 1973, C.117.

Council of the European Community (1979), *Resolution* 11 September 1979, OJ 1979, C.231/1.

Curzon Price, Victoria (1981), *Industrial Policies in the European Community*, London.

European Commission (1970), *The Industrial Policy of the Community*, Office for Official Publications, Luxembourg.

European Commission (1972), *Industrial Policy. Status report of the Community's work,* Bulletin EC, 6–1972.

European Commission (1975), Working paper: Elements of a common policy on industrial changes, Spinelli paper).

European Commission (1981a), *The European Community's Industrial Strategy*, COM (81) 639 of 3 November 1981.

European Commission (1981b), *Industrial policies in the Community. State intervention and structural adjustment*, Study Group Report.

European Commission (1988), *The Competitiveness of European Industry*, Office for Official Publications, Luxembourg.

European Commission (1990), *Industrial policy in an open and competitive environment. Guidelines for a Community Approach,* COM (90) 556 of 16 November 1990, Office for Official Publications, Luxembourg.

European Commission (1994a), *An Industrial Competitiveness Policy for the European Union*, COM(94) 319 of 14 September 1994, Office for Official Publications, Luxembourg.

European Commission (1994b), *Europe's Way to the Information Society,* COM(94) 347, Office for Official Publications, Luxembourg.

European Commission (1995), *Action programme to Strengthen the Competitiveness of European Industry*, COM(95) 87, Office for Official Publications, Luxembourg.

European Commission (1996a), *The Competitiveness Report*, Office for Official Publications, Luxembourg.

European Commission (1996b), *Benchmarking the Competitiveness of European Industry*, COM(96) 463 of 9 October 1996, Office for Official Publications, Luxembourg.

European Commission (1997), *Benchmarking: Implementation of an Instrument Available to Economic Actors and Public Authorities*, COM(97) 153 of 16 April 1997, Office for Official Publications, Luxembourg.

European Commission (1998a), *The Competitiveness Report*, Office for Official Publications, Luxembourg.

European Commission (1998b), *Managing Change,* Final report of the High Level group on economic and social implications of industrial change, Office for Official Publications, Luxembourg.

European Commission (1999a), *The Competitiveness of European Enterprises in the Face of Globalisation*, COM(1998) 718 of 20 January 1999, Office for Official Publications, Luxembourg.

European Commission (1999b), *First Report by the High Level group on Benchmarking,* Brussels, Office for Official Publications, Luxembourg.

European Commission (1999c), *Structural Change and Adjustment in European Manufacturing,* COM(1999) 465, Office for Official Publications, Luxembourg.

European Commission (1999d), *The Competitiveness of European Industry, 1999 Report,* Staff Working Paper, SEC(1999) 1555, Brussels.

European Commission (1999c), *Report on the Functioning of Community Product and Capital Markets,* COM(99) 10, Office for Official Publications, Luxembourg.

European Parliament (1981), *Report on Industrial Co-operation between Member States,* 27 April 1981.

European Round Table of Industrialists (1993), *Beating the Crisis,* Brussels.

European Round Table of Industrialists (1996), *Benchmarking for Policymakers. The Way to Competitiveness, Growth and Job Creation.* Brussels.

European Round Table of Industrialists (1998), *Job Creation and Competitiveness through Innovation,* Brussels.

Kuyper, Laurens (1984), *Ontwikkelingen in het Europese industriebeleid,* Ministerie van Economische Zaken, Den Haag.

Pierce, Joan, Sutton, John and Batchelor, Roy (1985), *Protection and Industrial Policy in Europe,* Royal Institute of International Affairs, London.

Romano Prodi (1998), *European Industry and Finance in International Competition,* Jean Monnet lecture, 20 March 1998.

UNICE (1994), *Making Europe more Competitive. Towards world-class performance,* Brussels.

UNICE (1998), *European Competitiveness,* Brussels.

UNICE (1999), *Fostering Entrepreneurship in Europe. The UNICE Benchmarking Report,* Brussels.

VNO (1993), *Industrial Policy. A Comparative Analysis,* The Hague.

PART TWO

Policies of Importance to Industry

3. The Internal Market – Economic Heart of the Union

Laurens Kuyper

The internal, or common, market is described in the Treaty of Rome as: 'an area without internal frontiers in which the free movement of goods, persons, services and capital is ensured in accordance with the Treaty'. It was one of the main objectives for the founding Member States to link their economies in order to create a market in which every participant is free to invest, produce, work, buy and sell, to apply or obtain services under conditions of competition which have not been artificially distorted wherever economic conditions are most favourable.

This meant that all barriers to trade between Member States had to be eliminated. In the first decades of the Community tariffs and quota restrictions between Member States were eliminated rather quickly.[1] Opening up national markets and abolishing national restrictions to trade, the so-called non-tariff barriers proved to be more difficult. This was partly due to the negotiating process that needed the consent of all Member States for the adoption of harmonised rules.

The difficulties of that approach caused a severe slowdown in the intended integration of the European economies. In the early 1980s, European business revived interest in integration, as it experienced a reduction of its competitiveness in relation to its US and Japanese competitors.

The Commission's report on the 'costs of non-Europe' (1988b) demonstrated that there was much to gain from completing the internal market of the Community. Together with mounting pressure from industry to complete the original single market intention, it became the starting point for the first of the Commission's internal market action plans: the White Paper 'Completing the Internal Market (1985)' listed almost 300 measures needed to achieve the single market as meant in the Treaty. The strong support from succeeding European Summits, as well as enlarging the possibilities for qualified majority voting in the Single European Act, which came into force on 1 July 1987, created a new wave of enthusiasm for European integration.

---

[1] For industrial products, the last quantitative restrictions within the Community were abolished on 31 December 1961.

At the end of the 1990s, almost all of the necessary measures had been adopted and were in force. The process of harmonising national rules continued, although in a manner different from the past. The focus of the ongoing work changed to the functioning of the internal market, set out in the Commission's 'Strategic programme for the internal market' (COM(93) 256) and explicitly supported by the Union's Heads of Government for making the internal market work.

The Treaty gives several explanations concerning the character of the internal market, such as 'in accordance with the principle of an open market economy with free competition' (Article 3a), 'a system ensuring that competition in the internal market is not distorted' (Article 3g), or 'a properly functioning common market' (Article 3h). In that sense, all policies treated in this book play a role in the European internal market.

This chapter takes a look at the Community's activities to complete the internal market in regard to industry's needs: the first section considers the harmonisation of national laws and standardisation, the second section deals with public procurement, while the third section addresses the present situation. The fourth section looks at several other areas within the internal market that are of interest to business.

3.1 HARMONISATION AND STANDARDS

Creating a common market implies that national rules do not act as barriers to trade between Member States that frustrate the free movement of goods, services, persons and capital. The development of economic integration demands a flexible procedure for harmonising such national rules, including the availability of adequate standards, as well as respecting the concerns of consumers and companies.

Free Movement

Free movement (Article 28 of the Treaty) of goods, in particular, is essential for companies to be able to reap the benefits of a large home market.

Technical barriers, such as different national product standards, impede the free movement of goods. Until the mid-1980s, the harmonisation of the relevant national laws, that is, the adoption of European regulations that would ensure the free circulation of goods, was a long and cumbersome process. The decision to replace national standards with new European ones needed the unanimous consent of the Member States. It often took ten years or more to achieve total harmonisation, that is, Community measures which deny Member States the power to maintain deviating rules. Other possibilities for harmonisation are: minimum harmonisation, when Member States are free to apply stricter or more far-reaching requirements; or optional harmonisation, whereby Community measures have to be complied with in the Community, but Member States are free to maintain their own rules as well. There also could be partial harmonisation, such as the type approval systems concerning cars, which has been replaced by total harmonisation since 1996 (Directive 92/53/EEC, OJ 1992 L-225).

The possibilities for derogation from the principle of free movement are restrictive and only justified (Article 30) on grounds of:

> public morality, public policy or public security; the protection of health and life of humans, animals or plants; the protection of national treasures possessing artistic, historic or archaeological value; or the protection of industrial and commercial property. Such prohibitions or restrictions shall not, however, constitute a means of arbitrary discrimination or a disguised restriction on trade between Member States.

Such exceptions are no longer justified if Community legislation has come into force in the same area.

In order to manage such exemptions, a procedure for the exchange of information has been established,[2] which requires the Member State to notify the Commission of measures preventing the free movement of a model or a type of a product which has been made or sold legally in another Member State.

Mutual Recognition

One of the greatest contributions to the internal market came from a German company called Rewe Zentral AG, that wanted to import the liqueur Cassis de Dijon into West Germany (1978), but was denied because it did not contain enough alcohol by German standards. The Court of Justice (Case 120/78 of 20 February 1970, OJ 1980 C-256) did not accept the German government's claim that its standards did not discriminate between German and foreign drinks. Germany had no right to block the import of a product that was lawfully on sale in France, unless it could show that there is an overriding health, safety or environmental reason to prevent such trade circulation, and no alternative exists that would create less barriers to trade.

This case became the start of a new approach to industrial standards in the Community. It made 'mutual recognition' the cornerstone of the internal market and was taken up in the Single European Act: 'The Council may decide that provisions in force in a Member State must be recognised as being equivalent to those applied by another member State'. The matter is now governed by Community legislation.[3]

The principle of mutual recognition allows free movement of goods and services without the need for harmonisation of national legislation at

---

[2]   Decision 3052/95, OJ 1995 L-321; it came into effect as of 1 January 1997.
[3]   Council Regulation 1576/89/EEC, OJ 1989 L-160; and Council Regulation 3378/94, OJ 1994 L-366; Commission Communication COM(93) 669 OJ 1993 C-353.

Community level. A Member State may not forbid the sale on its territory of a product lawfully produced and marketed in another Member State, even if that product is produced according to specifications that are different from those applied to its own products. The same principle applies to services.

There is, however, no Community provision that prevents a Member State from putting its own industry in a less favourable position than its competitors in other Member States.

Most Member States have their own standards and laws which are important in setting quality and safety requirements for goods sold in their national home market. National standards bodies, such as DIN (Germany) and AFNOR (France) draw up the standards. When different standards apply in other Member States these can be barriers to trade and thus fragment the internal market.

National technical barriers[4] that are barriers to trade are disappearing, by either harmonising them on the European level, or by mutual recognition of each other's regulations. To avoid the erection of new barriers, the Member States are required to notify the Commission and other Member States in advance of proposals for new technical regulations (Directive 83/189[5]).

The Commission is very active in pursuing complaints about the failure of Member States to respect their obligations under mutual recognition. It forces the Member States to include in their national regulations a statement saying that 'requirements in force in another Member State of the European Union, which provide an equivalent level of security, will also be accepted'. One example out of many was the Spanish legislation that limited the description 'beer' to beer with an alcohol content of more than 3 per cent; low-alcohol and alcohol-free beer was thus excluded from the Spanish market, although these were legally produced and marketed as such in the other Member States. The mutual recognition clause provided the necessary free circulation of those beers.

New Approach

The Commission's White Paper (1985) opened up a new avenue to avoid the long, painstaking process of harmonising national technical measures into a European Directive. Under the 'New Approach', Directives are confined to setting the essential requirements for health, safety, consumer protection and the environment; the relevant technical details (European standards) are worked out subsequently by the European standards bodies CEN, CENELEC and ETSI.[6]

---

4   In the mid-1980s there were some 100 00 technical regulations.
5   OJ 1983 L-109, now replaced by Directive 98/34, in order to include rules relating to information society services.
6   CEN: Comité Européen de Normalisation, established in 1961; CENELEC: Comité Européen de Normalisation Electro-technique, established in 1962; ETSI: European Telecommunications Standard Institute.

All products covered by these Directives must meet the essential requirements; when they do, they will carry an Conformité Européenne (CE) mark that allows them to be circulated freely in the Community. No Member State will then be able to refuse them entry on technical grounds.

As these standards are not compulsory, a manufacturer is free to opt for other specifications; if he does, he has to demonstrate conformity with the essential requirements of the relevant Directive, and has to have his product tested by a certification authority. Before the CE mark can be affixed to the product, the manufacturer must follow certain procedures; these may differ for each directive and each product. Applicable procedures are: declaration of conformity (manufacturer's declaration); compiling a technical construction file; applying for and filing an EC–type examination certificate; compiling a user manual; and affixing the CE mark.

The CE mark does not more than indicate that the manufacturer has undergone all assessment procedures required for the product; it is not a quality mark.

The change from unanimous voting to qualitative majority voting that the Single Act in 1987 introduced for New Approach Directives accelerated the harmonisation process considerably. CEN and CENELEC were relatively inactive until the introduction of the New Approach and experienced difficulties in keeping up with the development of the European standards needed. By 1996, both organisations had produced some 5000 standards; in view of the Directives adopted[7] these correspond to 25 per cent of the standards needed.

The testing and certification institutes are themselves required to satisfy criteria. These relate to independence, expertise and administrative precision. They are part of a set of European standards (EN 45000 series) and based on internationally accepted guidelines (ISO).

In 1990 the Commission established the European Organisation for Testing and Certification (EOTC), under a memorandum of understanding with CEN, CENELEC and the EFTA countries, in order to provide 'the appropriate framework with regard to conformity assessment issues'.

Under the New Approach, the Commission mandates the European standards organisations to draft European technical standards. These bodies use, wherever possible, the international standards of the ISO (International Organisation for Standardisation) and IEC (International Electrotechnical Commission); they only adopt European standards when international standards do not exist.   When an EU Directive is developed and the European standards organisations have started their standard-making activities, Member States have to refrain from setting their own national standards. Standards for products not regulated in a Directive may still be

---

[7]   Such as: simple pressure vessels, toys, machinery, electromagnetic compatibility, gas appliances, personal protective equipment, lifts, active implantable medical devices.

developed at the national level; in that case, the principle of mutual recognition of national standards applies (Table 3.1).

Table 3.1   Production of mandated standards under the New Approach

	Mandated	Ratified	Pending approval	In preparation
CEN	2182	633	847	702
CENELEC	231	103	33	95
ETSI	143	86	29	28
Public Procurement	349	92	172	85
Total	2905	914	1081	910

Source: European Commission (1999e)

Consumers

The Treaty of Rome did not contain a basis for a specific consumer policy in the internal market; Community legislation was primarily targeted at protecting the buyers of goods and thus, indirectly, catering to consumers' interests. The Commission's first action programme for a consumer policy (OJ 1975 C-92) provided a framework for fundamental rights for consumers: protection of health and safety; economic interests; right to damages; right to information and education; and the right to be represented. All Member States give consumers a general right in law to seek redress; some have national legislation, for instance, to prevent practices that are unfair to consumers, while others leave room for self-regulation by the market.

In the beginning, Community legislation was limited to safety and health aspects of cosmetics, food labelling and misleading advertising. With the 1987 Single Act [8] consumers entered into all Community activities for the achievement of the internal market: product safety, unfair contract terms, cross-border payments, distance selling, and so on.

The Maastricht Treaty gave consumer policy a place of its own in Article 129a (now Article 153). A number of legislative actions followed: financial services, consumer access to justice, food law, sale of consumer goods and associated guarantees, injunctions, contracts negotiated at a distance, comparative advertising, and cross-border transfers. The British BSE[9] crisis and Belgian problems with dioxin found in chicken meat put the emphasis on consumer health and food safety.[10]

The Treaty of Amsterdam introduced a new Article 153, the general aim being the protection of the health, safety and economic interests of consumers, and the promotion of their right both to information and

---

[8] 'Measures designed to protect consumers, ensuring a high level of protection'.
[9] Mad-cow disease in the UK that led to an export ban for British meat.
[10] Conclusions of the Luxembourg European Council of December 1997.

education, and to organise themselves in order to safeguard their interests. Consumer protection must now be taken into account in other Community policies and activities.

Individual rights

The European rules that are applicable to all persons and companies in the Union give them a right to claim damages from Member States that do not take up these rules in their national legislation.

Directives are addressed to the Member States, who are obliged to transpose them into national law. If they are not doing that, they may become liable to pay damages, as judgements of the Court of Justice have demonstrated.

In the ruling on the Francovich Case (Case 9/90), the Court established that Member States have to make good loss and damage caused to individuals and companies by breaches of Community Directives which have not been transposed into national law. In the 'Brasserie du Pecheur' case (Cases 46 and 48/93), a French brewery was seeking damages from Germany, which according to an earlier judgement of the Court (in Case 178/84), had infringed Article 28 by insisting that imported beers respect its purity laws for beer, irrespective of whether they were legally manufactured in other Member States. In the 'Factortame' case, a series of Spanish companies operating fishing vessels were seeking damages after the Court had ruled in 1991 (Case C-221/89) that the United Kingdom had violated Article 43 by refusing these companies the right to establish themselves in the United Kingdom.

The rulings in these cases make clear that Member States can also be liable to make good damages arising from breaches of the directly applicable (without the need for implementing them into national legislation) rules of the Treaty. Member States have also to ensure that in their legal system means of redress exists for breaches of Community law under conditions no less favourable than for breaches of national law.

Liability of the Member State must meet the following conditions: the rule of Community law which has been infringed contains rights to individuals; the infringement is sufficiently serious; and there is a direct causal link between the breach of the Member State's obligation under Community law and the loss and damage suffered by the injured parties.

The Court has taken the protection of individual rights even further in a case concerning the failure of Belgium to notify to the Commission technical rules for alarm systems to be sold in Belgium. The ruling in this 'Securitel' Case (Case 194/94 of 30 April 1996) clarifies the right that individuals may invoke when Member States have not notified new draft technical rules.

Under Directive 83/189,[11] Member States are required to notify to the Commission new draft technical regulations and to postpone their adoption for three months, in order for the Commission and other Member States to examine them. The Court found the obligations of that Directive sufficiently precise to be invoked by individuals directly before national courts. If these obligations were invoked against a national regulation that had been adopted without prior notification or without respect of the duty to postpone its adoption, the regulation would be unenforceable against the individuals.

Impact

In the 'Costs of non-Europe' (the Cecchini Report), the Commission (1988b) attempted to estimate the reduction in costs that would follow from the completion of the internal market in 1992. Elimination of trade barriers and customs formalities, non-tariff barriers such as technical standards, and public procurement preferences, followed by increased competition and scale economies, would increase total national income by 2.5 per cent and the Community's GDP by between 3.2 and 6 per cent.

The Cecchini Report estimated the cost reduction due to the dismantling of customs procedures to be around 2 per cent of the value of goods traded (€13 to 24 billion). Opening up national procurement markets would result in cost reduction of around €17 billion. Employment would increase with 2 to 5 million new jobs.

One of the first steps to reap that benefit was the introduction of the Single Administrative Document on 1 January 1988 meant to facilitate the transition to the real internal market without frontiers. Each Member State had its own national forms for despatch and entry declarations, which were often complex and needed to be supported by an extensive range of other official documents. The Single Administrative Document, which contains only essential information, replaced a total of around 100 forms in trade between Member States.

Since 1 January 1993 all routine frontier controls at the internal borders of the Union have disappeared. The Single Administrative Document was abolished at the same time: from then on no document has to be shown at the internal frontiers of the Union. The Commission estimates this to have saved 60 million customs forms per year. A new system was introduced for taxes and to provide trade statistics (those are now reported by companies to Intrastat). The Commission estimates that the abolition of customs frontier controls alone reduced costs for traders, amounting to some €5 billion per year.

There are still checks, such as veterinary checks, but not any more at the Union's borders. The necessary checks are now carried out inside Member

---

[11]   OJ 1983 L-109, now replaced by Directive 98/34 OJ 1998 L-204 and Directive 98/48 OJ 1998 L-217.

States' territory, in the same way as such checks are made on domestic products moving within Member States, that is, without discrimination based on the origin of the goods or the mode of transport.

Figure 3.1   Share of trade within the EU in total trade, average

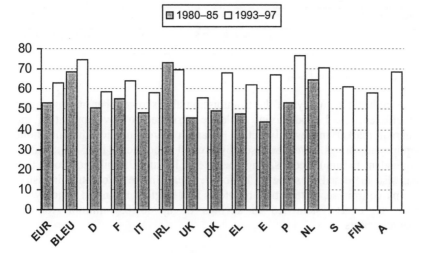

Source: Eurostat (1986); Commission (1998)

The Commission's Communication on the Impact and Effectiveness of the Single Market (1996) concluded that the internal market had a positive impact[12] on the competitiveness of European industry, although the benefits were not as high as the Cecchini Report estimated:

- in 1994, the GDP of the European Union was 1.1 to 1.5 per cent higher (€60–80 billion) than it would have been without the internal market, and up to 900 000 jobs were created;
- it is estimated that the 1994 average rate of inflation in the Union was 1.0 to 1.5 per cent lower than it would have been without the internal market;
- intra-Community trade increased from 61.2 per cent of total trade in manufactured goods between Member States in 1985 to 67.9 per cent in 1994 (see Figure 3.1);
- the flow of intra-Community investment increased fivefold between 1985 and 1993. In the first half of the 1990s, 44.4 per cent of world

---

[12] The same document, however, also stated that cross-border trade is still being hampered by delays in applying and enforcing the Single market rules at national level.

investments went to the European Union (compared with 28.2 per cent in the period 1982–87).

Table 3.2   Average intra-EU foreign direct investment inflows as a percentage of GDP, 1992–96

IRL	BLEU	NL	S	P	E	DK	UK	A	FIN	F	D	EL	I
3.9	2.9	2.9	1.4	1.1	0.9	0.8	0.8	0.7	0.6	0.5	0.4	0.4	0.4

Source: Commission (1998)

The studies and surveys of the Commission also showed that improvements in efficiency and productivity could be attributed to development of the internal market in several sectors. Examples are: in telecommunications equipment, prices have decreased by around 7 per cent (1985–95); this is equivalent to annual cost savings between €1.5 and 2.0 billion; production has also increased by some €1 billion per year. In the automotive industry, the move from separate national systems to a single harmonised Union-wide type approval system led to savings of up to €30 million for car manufacturers.

3.2 PUBLIC PROCUREMENT

As had been shown in the studies and reports that made estimates of the potential benefits of the internal market, the area of public procurement offers the best opportunities. Procurement accounts for more than 10 per cent of the Community's GDP (around €700 billion).

Progress in opening up this market has been slow: only 2 per cent of public contracts in the Community were awarded to companies from another Member State. All too often suppliers from other Member States come up against barriers which discourage them, such as the tendency to 'buy national'; the lack of information about contracts; discriminatory specifications; and complex tendering procedures.

The Treaty contains the fundamental principles contracting authorities have to observe when awarding contracts: the right of establishment (Article 43), the freedom to provide services (Article 49) and the prohibition of discrimination on grounds of nationality (Article 12).

Member States must allow individuals and companies from other Member States to establish and carry on a business in their territory, under the same conditions as laid down for their own nationals. The same principle of 'national treatment' applies to the freedom to provide (industrial and commercial) services. Exceptions are only allowed on grounds of public policy, public security or public health.

These principles, however, were not, as such, sufficient to bring about an internal market in the area of public procurement. There was no obligation to open up contracts to Community-wide competition.

The Community's objective is to co-ordinate national procedures for the award of public contracts in order to open up these contracts to effective Community-wide competition. To that end, Member States had to include competition, also from suppliers in other Member States, in their national tendering procedures when contracts have an estimated value above the relevant thresholds.

Legislation

The first Directives,[13] adopted in the 1970s, which co-ordinated public procurement procedures for works and supplies did not open markets to the extent hoped for. New Directives[14] to amend the existing ones intended to improve this situation. In the beginning of the 1990s the legislation was codified and thus formed the basic structure of the present Community's public procurement policy.

Four Directives[15] were adopted, covering works contracts, supply contracts service contracts and 'utilities' (in the sectors of water, energy, transport and telecommunications). Two Directives,[16] concerned with compliance followed these up to ensure that there is a proper remedy for any infringement committed during contract-award procedures.

With its 1996 Green Paper on public procurement, the Commission launched a discussion about the way this part of the Internal Market should develop, and incorporated the results in its Communication 'Public Procurement in the European Union' (European Commission, 1998). It concluded that public procurement in practice still seemed to be closed to offers from firms in other Member States, although the basic legal structure was in place. Therefore, the Commission stressed the need for maintaining this structure, but adapting it to the need for simplification and modernisation, with the clarification and consolidation of the existing rules, and ensuring that the rules are properly applied and enforced.

The existing legal framework does not apply to certain products in the field of defence, which are listed exhaustively; or to supplies which are declared secret or where the protection of the Member State's basic national security interests so requires. Also, certain types of contract governed by an

---

[13] 71/305/EEC OJ L-185 of 16 August 1971; 77/62/EEC OJ L-13 of 15 January 1977; 80/767/EEC OJ L-215 of 18 August 1980 (implementing the Community's obligations under the 1979 GATT Agreement on public procurement).

[14] 88/295/EEC OJ L-127 of 20 May 1988; 89/440/EEC OJ L-210 of 21 July 1989.

[15] 93/37/EEC OJ L-199 of 9 August 1993; 93/36/EEC OJ L-199 of 9 August 1993; 92/50/EEC OJ L-209 of 24 July 1992; 93/38/EEC OJ L-199 of 9 August 1993;.

[16] 89/665/EEC OJ L-209 of 24 July 1992; 92/13/EEC OJ L-76 of 23 March 1992.

international agreement or the particular procedure of an international organisation are excluded.

Contracting Authorities

Contracting authorities may choose between different award procedures: the *open* procedure (all interested suppliers may submit tenders); or the *restricted* procedure (only those suppliers so invited by the contracting authority may submit tenders).

In the cases listed exhaustively in the Directives (products manufactured purely for the purpose of research or experiment; and extreme urgency brought about by unforeseen events), contracting authorities may use the *negotiated* procedure (involving direct discussions between the purchaser and one or more suppliers of the purchaser's choice).

Selection criteria for suppliers have to do with their good reputation and technical capability. The criteria for awarding contracts must either be the lowest price or a combination of factors which persuade the purchaser that a tender is the most economically advantageous of those received.

The technical specifications relating to each contract must refer to national standards transposing European standards, to European technical approvals or to common technical specifications.

The Directives qualify as contracting authorities: the State; regional and local authorities; bodies governed by public law; and associations formed by one or more local or regional authorities or bodies governed by public law. There are more than 110,000 contracting authorities in the EU.

Contracts

Public works contracts are defined as

> contracts for pecuniary interest concluded in writing between a contractor and a contracting authority, which have as their object: either the execution, or both the execution and design, of works related to building and civil engineering, installation and building completion work; or the execution, by whatever means, of a work corresponding to the requirements specified by the contracting authority.

A work is defined by the Directive as 'the outcome of building or civil engineering works taken as a whole, that is sufficient of itself to fulfil an economic and technical function'.

Public supply contracts are 'contracts for pecuniary interest concluded in writing between a supplier and a contracting authority and involving the purchase, lease, rental or hire purchase, with or without option to buy, of products'. The delivery of such products may, in addition, include siting and installation operations.

Public service contracts are 'contracts in writing whereby a service provider provides services to a contracting authority in return for pecuniary consideration'. The Public Services Directive includes every activity not covered by the other public procurement Directives; certain services are excluded, because of their nature (such as contracts for broadcasting, research and development services contracts, or employment contracts). Public service concessions are also excluded.

Agreement on Government Procurement (GPA)

The Community is a party to the GATT Agreement on Government Procurement (GPA), which now belongs to the Union's legal system; this Agreement entered into force in the Union on 1 January 1996.[17]

Within the Community, the GPA creates rights for suppliers, contractors and service providers established in third countries which have signed the Agreement.[18] The European Directives deal exclusively with the relations between the contracting entities of the EU and companies established there (Box 3.1). The GPA does not change these relationships.

Box 3.1 Thresholds to which the Directives apply

Public works –	
Contracts with an estimated value excluding VAT of at least	€5 million
For central entities, in accordance with GPA	€5 150 548
Public supply and public services –	
Contracts with an estimated value excluding VAT of at least	€200 000
For central entities, in accordance with GPA	€133 914
The value of the thresholds in national currencies and the threshold in the GPA expressed in € are normally revised every two years (OJ 1988 C-22).	

In respect of contracts being awarded within one of the sectors covered by the GPA (water, electricity, urban transport, ports and airports sectors) a new obligation has been introduced to give information to candidates and tenderers, whose requests to participate or bids have not been retained. It is, however, specified that, exceptionally, some of the required information may be omitted, that is, where the legitimate commercial interests of public or private companies, including those of the winning firm, would otherwise be prejudiced.

---

[17] Council Decision 94/800/EEC of 22 December 1994, OJ 1994 L-336, which approves the agreements reached in the Uruguay Round of multilateral trade negotiations.

[18] Canada, South Korea, USA, Israel, Japan, Norway, Switzerland, Hong Kong.

Publication

Companies that want to compete for public contracts have different options to find the necessary information. Contracting entities are obliged to publish a notice announcing the intention to award a contract. Potential suppliers from all Member States are thus informed about public contracts in the European Union. Such notices must comply with prescribed models and are published in the Official Journal of the European Communities and in the TED[19] database in all official languages of the Communities. The TED database is more often used than the Official Journal, because it is faster and, by that, more up-to-date.

Recently, the Commission began to encourage contracting entities to publish comprehensive information about their tenders on the Internet, as part of the information system for public procurement (SIMAP).[20] As the use of information and communication technology increases, this will be the fastest source of information for companies.

There are also Guides to the Community rules available (on public supply contracts, public works contracts, and public procurement of services), as well as a specific Common Procurement Vocabulary[21] to assist contracting entities with their drawing up of their notices.

The legislative situation of public procurement in the internal market seems to be rather complete, notwithstanding the Member States' arrears in implementation. The business sector, however, is less positive: Almost 50 per cent of larger companies reporting obstacles to accessing procurement markets believe that purchasers are awarding contracts on the basis of criteria other than price and quality. Similarly, some 40 per cent of small firms indicate that their access to procurement markets is hindered by the lack of publication of calls for tenders. Obstacles in this sense do not always result from non-application of Community legislation, but are often barriers included in the use of national language and cultural traditions.

Contract Award Notices, which constitute a particularly important incentive for potential suppliers (by providing market information on the state of competition, price structure and so on), are published for approximately half of all tenders announced through an invitation to tender. Many of these Notices do not give any information on price/value of the contract (Table 3.3).

---

[19] Tenders Electronic Daily (TED) is available free of charge to Internet users.

[20] Système d'Information pour les Marches Publics. The SIMAP website (http://simap.eu.int) is the official procurement site of the EU; it provides information on the procurement market, on rules and procedures, and an on-line notification service.

[21] Commission Recommendation 96/527/EC OJ L-222 of 3 September 1996.

Table 3.3   Procurement Notices, 1993–97

	Total procurement (ECU billion)	All notices	Tender notices	Award notices
1993	688	67 192	39 397	21 118
1994	722	96 370	56 180	31 046
1995	750	127 770	77 310	38 855
1996	789	140 576	81 216	46 598
1997	831	155 185	87 757	53 377

Source: European Commission (1999b)

3.3   PRESENT SITUATION

A new Action Plan, published as 'Making the Single Market work' (European Commission, 1997a), and endorsed by the European Council in Amsterdam, defines four strategic targets:

- *Making the rules more effective.* The Single Market is based on confidence. Proper enforcement of the agreed common rules is the only way to achieve this goal. Simplification of rules at Community and national level is also essential to reduce the burden on business and create more jobs;
- *Dealing with key market distortions.* There is general agreement that tax barriers and anti-competitive behaviour constitute distortions that need to be tackled;
- *Removing sectoral obstacles to market integration.* The Single Market will only deliver its full potential if barriers that remain – and, of course, any new ones that emerge – are removed. This may require legislative action to fill gaps in the Single Market framework, but it also call for a significant change in national administrations' attitudes towards the Single Market;
- *Delivering a Single Market for the benefit of all citizens.* The Single Market generates employment, increases personal freedom and benefits consumers, while ensuring high levels of both health and safety and environmental protection. But further steps are needed, including steps to enhance the social dimension of the Single Market. And to enjoy their Single Market rights to the full, citizens must be aware of them and be able to obtain speedy redress.

A great deal of attention has focused on the implementation deficit, that is, the failure by Member States to implement on time Directives agreed by the Council and the Parliament. There is improvement: the percentage of Directives not yet implemented in all Member States has fallen from 35 per cent in June 1997 to 12.6 per cent in November 1999 (Single Market Scoreboard, No.1). But the internal market still is not yet fully realised in practice.

Embarrassment Effect

The Commission monitors the commitments of the Member States by means of a Single Market Scoreboard, published regularly since 1977. This will identify clearly which Member States have the best, and the worst, record on respecting Internal Market rules; it will take into account not only a Member State's record on implementing internal market Directives, but also indicators of its compliance with Community law. It is expected to have a positive effect ('peer pressure') because no Member State likes to be exposed as lawbreaker.

Simplifying the Rules

Launched in 1996, under pressure from industry calling for legislation that did not impose unnecessary constraints, SLIM[22] brings together small groups of experts and users, to identify existing problems and make recommendations to the Commission on how to improve the legislation. A new project, BEST,[23] suggested measures to reduce unnecessary administrative and regulatory burden on business; Chapter 12 gives a description of this project.

SLIM teams consist of five experts from national government services plus five experts from the users of the specific regulation; Member States which are not part of one of the teams, can contribute in writing. Until this moment, SLIM has addressed regulations in four phases: first, statistical obligations (Intrastat), construction products, recognition of diplomas and ornamental plants; second, VAT, nomenclature, fertilisers and banking; third, insurance, electro-magnetic compatibility, social security co-ordination; and fourth, company law, dangerous substances and pre-packaging.

Pre-packaging (products packed in given quantities not in the presence of the purchaser) has been governed by several Directives since 1975. Their complexity and the fact that they affect over 40 different categories of consumption products make them appropriate subjects for SLIM.

Dangerous substances: focus on Directive 67/548/EEC and in particular the issues of classification, packaging and labelling of dangerous chemicals and the placing on the market of chemicals in general. The Directive has been amended 8 times. Its annexes have been adapted to technical progress 23 times in order to take into account the continuous increase of scientific and technical knowledge in the field of dangerous chemical substances.

---

[22] Simpler Legislation for the Internal Market; COM(96) 559.
[23] Business Environment Simplification Task Force.

Dialogue with Business

In some Member States, the government explicitly consults business before enacting new legislation, or has at its disposal procedures for assessing the impact on business. Under the Single Market Action Plan a pilot project was set up to assess the potential costs and administrative consequences for business: the Business Test Panel. The Test Panel was consulted by the Commission in 1998 on a proposal to amend the VAT Directive on fiscal representation, as well as on a proposal to amend the Fourth Company Law Directive on companies' annual accounts. The reactions from businesses in this Panel were such that there was no need for the Commission to change the content of its proposals. The pilot project was concluded in the summer of 1999, and is being evaluated in order to decide whether such an approach to new legislation should be put on a permanent basis.

The Commission launched a One Stop Internet Shop,[24] as part of its permanent Dialogue with Business. It is intended for businesses (receiving 10 000 request per day) and can be used, free of charge, as a gateway to data, information and advice from many existing sources in the 11 languages of the EU.

Box 3.2　Example of information exchange

A Dutch company shipping timber to the UK was subjected to customs checks in a British harbour, involving the unpacking of its container. UK Customs charged the costs arising from that inspection to the Dutch company, which requested via the One Stop Internet Shop, the advice of its national contactpoint and enquired whether the customs authorities were entitled to make such charges. The Business contactpoint in The Hague identified this as a breach of the Treaty and forwarded the case to the respective Dutch authorities, which discussed the problem with its counterparts in the UK. The UK customs authorities have withdrawn the measure and refunded the fees paid by the company.

Source: Single Market News, European Commission, March 1999.

It also offers immediate access to a number of free advice services at European, national, regional and local level. In particular, the site offers direct access to over 230 Euro Info Centres, the Commission's largest business advice network – see Chapter 12. It contains the possibilities for companies to give feedback on the difficulties encountered. Business Contact points have been established in Member States to assist firms that encounter problems in the internal market, such as the example in Box 3.2. Such contacts offer the possibility to solve administrative blockages directly, with minimal involvement of governmental or legal procedures.

---

[24]　25 January 1999; http://europa.eu.int/business.

Compliance

Uniform enforcement of internal market rules is crucial to generating business confidence. Where Member States fail to comply with their obligations, the Commission increasingly turns to using the infringement proceedings.

These start with the Commission sending a letter of formal notice to the Member State, inviting its comments on the alleged breach of Community law. If the Member State's reaction is not satisfactory, the Commission then delivers a reasoned opinion, inviting the Member State to comply. The answer of the latter is decisive for the possible next stage, that is, the Commission referring the case to the Court of Justice.

These procedures take up a lot of time: reactions from Member States take between 80 to 90 days. When the Court is involved it can take 5–8 years before the dispute between Member State and Commission is resolved.

In recent years, the Commission deals annually with about 5000 infringement cases (all stages), half of which concern internal market rules; not every stage in these cases leads to the next one: in each stage the Member States' answers or reactions could resolve the dispute with the Commission. Nevertheless, the number of cases referred to the Court continues to be high; it shows that the state of completeness of the internal market still does not conform to the political commitments made in the Council.

Cardiff Process

The European Council in Cardiff (1998) again stressed the fundamental role the internal market must play to promote competitiveness, growth and employment in the Union, and also mentioned the positive effect of the Scoreboard.

The need for markets that perform flexibly and efficiently called for better co-ordination of the Member States' policies; it would be necessary to have a better insight in the integration process – of the integration of national economies into the European one, as well as of the integration of national industries into Europe-wide sectors. Monitoring this process requires a macroeconomic and a microeconomic co-ordination. This has become known as the Cardiff process, in which different formations of the Council have to deliver their input, contributing to the broad Economic Policy Guidelines for the Community, as explained in Chapter 4.

The Commission's first contribution to this process is the Report 'Economic Reform: Report on the functioning of Community product and capital markets' (1999a), considering the extent to which each particular market (goods, services, capital market) in the European Union really is integrated. The tools for the Union to use in this field are:

Monitoring market developments to identify areas in which adjustment may be required; enforcing the rules effectively; developing new policies to meet fresh challenges where necessary; and taking decisive action to deal with barriers within the Single Market and unnecessary constraints on economic activity.

The Commission warns that any remaining weakness in the internal market will result in efficiency losses for industry and reduce the capacity of markets to absorb shocks; managing what has been achieved and further developing the integration that strengthens the European internal market.

3.4   AREAS OF SPECIFIC ATTENTION

The internal market is not yet completed; special attention is needed for areas such as financial services (banking, insurance) and taxation.

Financial Services

The financial services sector accounts for some 6 per cent of the Union's GDP, and offers essential financial products to both industry and individual consumers. In practice, the markets for this sector have been mostly national; even today, there is no internal market to speak of in this area. The Cardiff European Council invited the Commission to table a 'framework for action' to improve the Single Market in financial services, in particular concerning the effectiveness of implementation of current legislation, as well as identifying weaknesses which may require amending legislation. The introduction of the Euro provides a strong incentive to realise the market's full potential.

In its Communication: 'Financial services – implementing the framework for financial market; Action Plan' (COM(1999) 232), the Commission reiterates the need for removal the remaining barriers to cross-border provision of financial services. Emphasis is put on effective enforcement of existing legislation and on flexible methods to adapt the rules to evolving market conditions, such as the growing importance of electronic commerce.

Taxation

The Union's legislative framework requires Member States' unanimous consent when addressing taxation issues. In a market where physical and technical barriers to trade have been progressively disappearing and where exchange rate fluctuations will no longer be possible, tax barriers have become visible as a source of distortion of competition within the internal market.

A Single Market in taxation, ideally, implies a uniformly applied system for companies' domestic and intra-Community transactions, especially in the area of indirect taxation. At the moment, firms that are active in Member States have to deal with over 200 different special arrangements and options concerning VAT alone.

The system of VAT that was introduced (Directives 91/680 and 92/111) when the frontier controls were abolished did not make companies happy, because it required complex arrangements so that goods can be exported zero-rated on VAT without fraud. The system, known as the system of the country of destination, was meant to be transitional, and in 1996 the Commission came forward with proposals for the definitive system, based on the country of origin. Companies prefer a system in which VAT would be paid in the country where the goods in question were bought, just as in domestic trade.

Most Member States opposed the proposed system because it would create a distortion of competition due to the divergence of rates in the Member States. For example in Sweden the VAT rate is 25 per cent, and in Luxembourg 15 per cent. At that moment, Member States were not prepared to accept further harmonisation of rates and structures, which would be necessary for the introduction of a new system. The plan for changing the system into a definitive system, based on the country of origin of the goods and services, failed. The Commission, reluctantly, had to accept that it, for the moment, would have to settle for improving the existing system. [25]

The area of direct taxation is still a matter for the Member States themselves. Some of them are of the opinion that a certain co-ordination in this area has to take place on a Community level; a first step is the so-called taxation package, adopted by the Council (Ecofin) on 1 December 1997.

This package deals with a code of conduct (combating harmful tax competition), taxation of interest on savings and the abolition of withholding taxes on interest and royalty payments in certain inter-company relations. The discussions on the package are difficult, and the deadline set for a final report has not been met. The main problems are still the code of conduct and the interest on savings.[26] The United Kingdom has insurmountable problems in taking Eurobonds into the scope of the interest on savings Directive. In view of this situation, it is not likely that the Union will arrive at a harmonised rule in this area.

That does not imply that nothing happened in this area in the past or that the Commission[27] is giving up trying to complete the internal market by

---

[25]   COM(96) 328 and a technical note (XXI/1156/96).

[26]   During 1998–99, the Commission tried, unsuccessfully for the time being, to find a compromise in suggesting that each Member State could have the choice between levying a withholding tax on the relevant income or providing information on that income to the competent tax authority. To avoid double taxation, the State in which the individual is resident would be obliged to credit withholding tax paid in another Member State.

[27]   'Taxation in the European Union' SEC(96) 487; and the informal ECOFIN Council in Verona, 13 April 1996.

adding to the already existing legislative framework, such as the parent–subsidiary Directive, the merger Directive, and the Directive on mutual assistance

Fiscal sovereignty, in conclusion, may have distorting effects on competition if the implementation of national tax rules favours domestic companies. Unfair tax competition is subjected to the rules of state aid and treated by the Commission accordingly.

Intervention Mechanism

The Amsterdam European Council was asked to react on angry complaints from companies transporting goods through France, where trucks from other Member States were blocked by French truckers on strike. The European Council mandated the Council (Internal Market) to find the means of effectively guaranteeing the free movement of goods in the internal market.

A Regulation was proposed and adopted[28] that, at least on paper, gives an answer to such problems. While recognising the right or freedom to strike, Member States have the duty to inform the Commission when such actions hinder the free movement of goods and they are obliged to take measures to remedy the situation. As with most cases of this nature, the embarrassment effect is expected to act as preventing trade barriers; the Commission cannot do more than request the Member State concerned to take all necessary measures to remove the obstacle.

European Company

Differences in taxation regimes, for instance, and workers representation in trans-European companies, force those companies to set up subsidiaries in other Member States. These differences complicate pan-European business and add to the cost of their operation. A European system would alleviate those costs.

The proposal for a European Company Statute has been on the Community's negotiating table for more than 30 years.[29] Its adoption has always been frustrated, in particular because of problems associated with choosing a suitable mechanism for the determination of the worker participation rules in the European Company.

To try and resolve this problem, a High-Level Group of Experts (Davignon Group, May 1997) suggested establishing the principle of free negotiations between the employers and employee representation. Member States, however, have not been able to overcome their differences on the issue.

---

[28] Regulation (EC) 2679/98 of 7 December 1998.
[29] The first concept was produced by Prof. Pieter Sanders in 1967.

In the Council (Social Affairs), discussions are concerned with the rules which should apply if an agreement cannot be agreed between the management and the worker's representatives. The intention is to preserve existing employee participation rights unless the employees themselves agree to the diminution or removal of these rights. The participating companies must also agree to the employee participation arrangements.

Company law aspects and taxation are dealt with in the Council (Internal Market). These matters will not be dealt with in the EU-Regulation concerned, but in separate measures in the future if deemed necessary.

BIBLIOGRAPHY

Agnelli, G. (1992), The Europe of 1992, *Foreign Affairs* 68.

Bakhoven, A.E. (1989), *The Completion of the Common Market in 1992*, Martinus Nijhoff, The Hague.

Buchan, David (1996), *The Single Market and Tomorrow's Europe, A Progress Report from the European Commission,* Kogan Page, London.

Burrows, F. (1987), *Free Movement in European Community Law*, Clarendon Press, Oxford.

Cecchini, P. (1988), *The European Challenge 1992 – the Benefits of a Single Market*, Vildwood House, Aldershot.

Dekker, Wisse (1984), *Europe-1990: an Agenda for Action*, Philips, Eindhoven.

Eurochambres (1994), *Non Tariff Barriers in the European Union,* Brussels.

European Commission (1985), *Completing the Internal Market, White Paper from the Commission*, COM(85) 310, June 1985, Brussels.

European Commission (1987), *Making a Success of the Single Act: a New Frontier for Europe,* COM(87) 100, Brussels.

European Commission (1988a), The economics of 1992: an assessment of the potential economic effects of completing the internal market on the European Economy, *European Economy, (March)* No. 35.

European Commission (1988b), *Research on the Costs of Non-Europe – Basic Findings*, 16 vols, COM(88) 650, Office for Official Publications, Luxembourg.

European Commission (1989), *Europe without Frontiers: Completing the Internal Market,* Office for Official Publications, Luxembourg.

European Commission (1993), *Strategic Programme for the Internal Market,* COM(93) 256, Office for Official Publications, Luxembourg.

European Commission (1994a), *Guide to the Implementation of Community Harmonisation Directives Based on the New Approach and the Global Approach*, Office for Official Publications, Luxembourg.

European Commission (1994b), *Abolition of Border Controls,* July 1994, Office for Official Publications, Luxembourg.

European Commission (1995), *National Regulations Affecting Products in the Internal Market, A Cause for Concern*, September 1995, Brussels.

European Commission (1996), *The Impact and Effectiveness of the Single Market*, COM(96) 520, October 1996, Brussels.

European Commission (1997a), *Action Programme for the Internal Market*, CSE(97) 1, June 1997, Brussels.

European Commission (1997b), *Public Procurement, Special Sectoral Report No.1*, November 1997, Brussels.

European Commission (1997c), *Guide to the Community Rules on Public Procurement of Services*, Office for Official Publications, Luxembourg.

European Commission (1997d), *Guide to the Community Rules on Public Works Contracts*, Office for Official Publications, Luxembourg.

European Commission (1997e), *Guide to the Community Rules on Public Supply Contracts*, Office for Official Publications, Luxembourg.

European Commission, *Single Market Scoreboard*, No. 1, November 1997; No. 2, May 1998; No. 3, November 1998; No. 4, June 1999; No. 5, December 1999, Office for Official Publications, Luxembourg.

European Commission (1998), *Public Procurement in the European Union*, COM(98) 143, March 1998, Brussels.

European Commission (1999a), *The Strategy for Europe's Internal Market*, COM(1999) 464, October 1999 and COM(1999) 624, November 1999, Brussels.

European Commission (1999b), *Report on the Functioning of Community Product and Capital Markets*, COM(99) 10, Brussels.

European Commission (1999c), *Assessment of the Single Market Action Plan*, COM(99) 74, February 1999, Brussels.

European Commission (1999d), *Mutual Recognition*, COM(99) 299, June 1999, Brussels.

European Commission (1999e), *Financial Services, Implementing the Framework for Financial Markets, Action Plan*, COM(1999) 232, Office for Official Publications, Luxembourg.

GAO (1990), *European Single Market, Issues of Concern to U.S. Exporters*, US General Accounting Office, February 1990.

Henderson, David (1989), *1992: The External Dimension*, Occasional Papers No. 25, Group of Thirty, New York/London.

Hoeller, Peter, and Louppe, Marie-Odile (1994), *The EC's Internal Market: Implementation and Economic Effects*, OECD Economics Studies No. 23.

Micossi, Stefano (1995), *Regulation and Deregulation of Industrial Products in the Internal Markets of the European Union*, speech, London.

Ministerie van Economische Zaken (1991), *Tien vragen en antwoorden over het CE-merk*, The Hague.

Ministerie van Economische Zaken (1988), *Zaken doen op de Europese interne markt*, The Hague.

Ministerie van Economische Zaken(1992), *Normalisatie en certificatie – sleutels voor kwaliteit*, The Hague.

Monti, Mario(1997), *Making the Single Market Work – The Next Steps*, speech, Brussels.

Moret Ernst & Young (1989), *...in een verenigd Europa,* Rotterdam.

Philip Morris Institute (1996), *Is the Single Market working?*

Rensberger, Roger A., van de Zande, Rene and Delaney, Helen (1997), *Standards Setting in the European Union*, US Dept of Commerce, Washington.

Sutherland, Peter et al.(1992), *Meeting the Challenge, The Internal Market after 1992,* Brussels.

VNO (1985), *Opheffing van technische handelsbelemmeringen in de EG,* The Hague.

4. Economic and Monetary Union – Reinforcing the Single Market

Adriaan Dierx, Fabienne Ilzkovitz and Jan H. Schmidt

The euro was launched on the 1ˢᵗ January 1999, with 11 EU Member States initially participating. This created the world's second largest single currency area in terms of GDP. Only the United States is larger. The euro was launched on the 1ˢᵗ January 1999, with 11 EU Member States initially participating. This created the world's second largest single currency area in terms of GDP. Only the United States is larger. With the possible entry of the remaining EU Member States as well as the EU enlargement candidates, the euro zone has the potential to become the largest integrated market for business in the world. Institutionally, the euro area consists of a single currency, a single monetary policy conducted by the European Central Bank (ECB), and a framework for the co-ordination of economic policy. The institutional set-up thus includes a centralised independent monetary policy authority and a decentralised although co-ordinated economic policy with neither a central fiscal policy nor a central political authority.

The euro will not just provide institutional changes and a single monetary policy, it is also expected to lead to more profound changes to economic policy conditions and the way to do business in the Single Market. The euro is seen to provide not only a single but also a stable currency, bringing both more stability and efficiency.

The EMU has created a framework for macroeconomic stability through the establishment of a single monetary policy directed towards price stability and the rules for sound public finances. The framework can bring increased economic activity due to lower and stable interest rates as well as more employment-friendly wage behaviour. Section 1 of this chapter describes the stability framework and discusses its consequences for growth and employment in EMU.

The EMU will also improve economic efficiency. The single currency will contribute to economic integration by reinforcing the EU Single Market. Greater price transparency and reduced costs for doing business across the borders will raise the level of competition and are expected to improve the competitiveness of the euro area. Wider and deeper capital markets will contribute to reducing the cost of capital on top of the fall in interest rates provided by the stability-oriented macroeconomic policy. These different effects of the euro on the functioning of product and capital markets are discussed in Section 2.

However, the potential benefits of greater stability and efficiency can only be realised through specific action to be undertaken by policymakers and business. EMU provides opportunities to improve the euro area economic situation, but it also carries challenges in terms of ensuring an adequate policy mix consisting of continued macroeconomic stability and further structural reforms. EMU is also a stimulus for industrial change and new ways of doing business. These changes will add to the ongoing restructuring process which has been put in motion by forces of globalisation, technological development and the establishment of the Single Market.

Amongst other things, competition will be fiercer. Certain sectors like, for example, the car industry, financial services and retail, will be more affected than others. In general, business will have to adapt to these changes and to seize the opportunities they will bring. Economic reforms would have to accompany and facilitate such an adjustment. The role of the Community would primarily be to establish a level playing field for business throughout the EU via the Single Market and Competition Policy and to push Member States to facilitate the necessary structural changes. Some structural reforms in the area of product and capital markets to make EMU a success are discussed in Section 3. Section 4 presents the main conclusions of our analysis.

4.1   EMU: A FRAMEWORK FOR MACROECONOMIC STABILITY

The Starting Point

Since the oil crisis of 1973, European economic performance has been hampered by a lack of macroeconomic stability and a reluctance to introduce the structural reforms necessary to make the EU economies more adaptive to the forces of globalisation and technological change.

High and increasing public deficits and debt fuelled inflationary expectations and crowded out private investments. High and unstable inflation rates contributed to inflated wage claims, leading to an uncertain business climate. Investment activity, economic growth and employment were thus dampened.

The instability and the subsequent need to tighten macroeconomic policy added to adverse demand shocks which, combined with institutional rigidities in both product and labour markets, caused lacklustre economic growth and persistently high unemployment in the 1980s and 1990s (European Commission, 1998a, 1999a; IMF, 1999; OECD, 1999a).

The Stability Framework

The introduction of the euro has, by definition, eliminated exchange rate instability between the participating Member States. Exchange rate variability is often considered to reduce trade and confidence on the part of business and consumers, thereby lowering economic growth. The empirical evidence of the impact of exchange variability on trade appears to indicate little effect of short-term exchange rate volatility, but more important effects of longer lasting exchange rate misalignments.

However, business surveys point to the danger of a loss of business confidence which may negatively affect both trade and investment (European Commission, 1990, p.73, 1995, p.2). Thus, in case of high volatility in exchange rates, firms might postpone decisions on investment, waiting for a clearer indication on future exchange rates.

Price stability and sound public finances are conditions for entry of an EU Member State into the euro zone. They became permanent features of the EMU system via the Maastricht Treaty and the Stability and Growth Pact.

The Treaty's chapter VII outlines the framework both in terms of institutional set-up and in terms of main elements of substance for a stability-oriented macroeconomic policy (see Box 4.1).

It was, however, felt that the Treaty articles on surveillance of budgetary deficits and sanctions needed more clarity. Some Member States feared that once countries had become members of the euro area, they might relax fiscal policies and jeopardise monetary policy and economic growth. It was also felt that in times of normal economic growth (around 2.5 per cent) Member States should create room for manoeuvre so that in times of more sluggish economic growth, budget deficits could be increased to stabilise the economies. The European Council therefore agreed to a Stability and Growth Pact in June 1997, which was outlined in legal form (see Box 4.2 for the main elements).

Economic theory points to welfare losses due to high inflation. Higher rates of inflation are usually associated with greater variability in inflation rates and, therefore, greater uncertainties, which may have a damaging effect on confidence and investment (Buti and Sapir, 1993, p.3). In such cases, both firms and consumers postpone decisions to invest or purchase important goods until prices are more stable.

Box 4.1　Treaty Articles on EMU

Chapter VII of the Treaty is entitled EMU and includes Articles 98 to 124.
The main elements of the Articles are highlighted below with reference to the relevant Articles in brackets:

- Member States should co-ordinate their economic policies to obtain economic growth and high employment respecting principles of stable prices and sound public finances (Article 98 with references to Articles 2 and 4)
- The main instrument for monitoring and co-ordinating economic policy is the Broad Economic Policy Recommendations on the basis of which specific recommendations can be given to individual Member States (Article 95)
- Overdraft facilities for public authorities with central banks and privileged access for public authorities to financial institutions are prohibited (Articles 101 and 102)
- Financial bailing-out of any public authority (Community, central, regional or local government) by the Community or other Member States is prohibited (Article 103)
- Member States are obliged to avoid excessive public deficits, the process leading to a decision on excessive deficits and the possibility of issuing sanctions in case of non-compliance with a Community decision to get rid of an excessive deficit (Article 104 with further specifics in the protocol on excessive deficits and in regulations on The Stability and Growth Pact – see Box 4.2)
- Price stability is the main objective of monetary policy conducted by the European Central Bank System (Article 105)
- The European Central Bank has the exclusive right to issue notes and to decide on the amount of coins to be circulated (Article 106)
- The European Central Bank System consists of the European Central Bank and the National Central Banks. Decisions on monetary policy are taken by the European Central Bank's Governing Council and its Executive Board (Article 107)
- The European Central Bank, the National Central Banks and the members of these central banks' decision making bodies are independent (Article 108).

Sounder public finances are expected to provide support for the price stability by fostering low and stable inflationary expectations. This would thus support low and stable interest rates. A sound fiscal policy will also allow a crowding-in of private investment, leading to lower interest rates. Lower interest rates reduce the cost of capital for both business and consumer borrowing. Investment and consumption will increase and will thus contribute to more growth and employment. Finally, lower deficits and public debt and higher public saving are necessary to create room in the budgets to deal with the budgetary impact of the ageing of the population. It is also necessary to create room in the budgets to cope with adverse economic shocks without putting pressure on interest rates (ibid., p.10).

Box 4.2   The Stability and Growth Pact

The core elements of the Stability and Growth Pact include:

- Pursuing country-specific 'medium-term objectives of budgetary positions close to balance or in surplus', so as to allow Member States to respect the 3 per cent budget deficit ceiling even during economic downturns. The Treaty only allows Member States to exceed the 3 per cent deficit ceiling in exceptional downturns.
- A recession is considered 'exceptional' if there is an annual fall of real GDP of at least 2 per cent. An annual fall of GDP of less than 2 per cent could nevertheless be considered exceptional in the light of further supporting evidence, such as the abruptness of the downturn or the accumulated loss of output relative to past trends. In any event, in evaluating whether the economic downturn is severe, the Member States will, as a rule, take an annual fall in real GDP of at least 0.75 per cent as a reference point.
- The excess of the deficit over 3 per cent of GDP will be considered temporary and thus allowed by the Pact only insofar as the 'exceptional' conditions mentioned above persist. Therefore, the deficit has to move back below the 3 per cent threshold in the year following that during which these 'exceptional' circumstances occurred.
- Putting in place an early-warning mechanism, under which Member States participating in the euro zone will have to submit stability programmes, while those not adopting the single currency will have to present convergence programmes. The Council will regularly examine both sets of programmes. The Council can issue a recommendation urging the Member State concerned to take adjustment measures, should significant slippage from the targets set in the programmes be identified.
- Speeding up the excessive deficit procedure. In order to avoid sanctions, the Member State concerned should bring back its deficit below the reference value two years after the occurrence of an excessive deficit and one year after its identification, unless special circumstances are given.

Specifying the scale of sanctions in the event of persistent excessive deficits. Sanctions are applied only on EMU members. The amount of the non-interest bearing deposit in the first year of application of the sanctions is composed of a fixed component equal to 0.2 per cent of GDP and a variable component equal to one tenth of the difference between the deficit and the 3 per cent reference value. A ceiling of 0.5 per cent of GDP is set. In each subsequent year, until the excessive deficit decision is abrogated, only the variable component will be applied. As a rule, a deposit is to be converted into a fine after two years if the excessive deficit persists. If no action is taken to correct the excessive deficit, sanctions can be imposed within the calendar year in which the decision on the existence of the excessive deficit is taken.

The Convergence Process

The Maastricht convergence criteria, which were the conditions for entry into EMU, have led to a rather spectacular downward convergence in inflation levels and equally spectacular improvements in public finances. From 1993 to 1999 inflation has come down from almost 4 to 1.25 per cent and the public deficits have been reduced from 6.25 to 1.5 per cent of GDP. Furthermore, this consolidation came about primarily through a better control of public spending. The ratio of public expenditures to GDP was reduced from 49.75 per cent in 1997 to 48.5 per cent in 1999 (see Figure 4.1).

Figure 4.1   Evolution of selected variables in the euro area, 1993–99

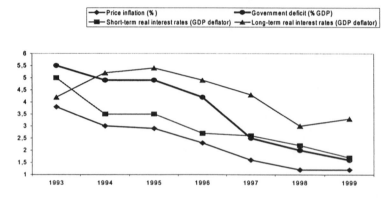

Recently improved economic prospects should help ensure that the EU Member States' deficits remain on track to meet the objective of the Stability and Growth Pact to achieve a budgetary balance or surplus by 2001/2002. Reaching this target would put public finances in a good position to meet future risks associated with the ageing of the European population.

The principal objective of the newly created European Central Bank is to maintain price stability within the euro area. The ECB, which has full control over monetary policy, has indicated that it considers price stability to be an inflation rate below 2 per cent. However, ECB will take into account other general economic objectives like growth and employment in situations where the primary task of maintaining price stability is not endangered. For example, in the beginning of 1999 the ECB lowered short-term interest rates by 0.5 per cent in the light of the international financial crisis and the sluggish economic activity in the euro area. However, in the Autumn of 1999, the ECB considered it necessary to counter accelerating private credit and money supply growth, rising industrial producer prices and the possibility of high wage settlements in up-coming pay negotiations. The bank raised short-term interest rates by 0.5 per cent, making it clear that it was determined to avoid any risk of inflation rising above 2 per cent. This was followed up by a rate hike of 0.25 per cent in February due to inflationary risks stemming mainly from an undervalued Euro.

A key factor explaining the subdued inflation levels has been wage moderation. Between 1993 and 1999 the annual rate of increase in nominal wage levels was reduced from 4.25 to 2.5 per cent. Supported by low inflation rates, real wage levels continued to rise by around 1 per cent annually, giving support to private consumption. At the same time, productivity was increasing sufficiently to obtain a continued reduction of real unit labour costs and support the profitability of private investments. Overall labour productivity increased by a little more than 1.5 per cent annually exceeding the increase in real wages and leading to an improvement in profitability.

It is too early to say whether real wages are responding more rapidly to changes in unemployment levels as a result of the convergence process and the introduction of the euro. However, the non-accommodative macroeconomic policy framework in EMU will have to be taken into account during the wage negotiations between the social partners. As a result, wage developments might be less likely to come into conflict with the stability objective. Such changes in wage behaviour would help avoid an unnecessary tightening of monetary or fiscal policies and would contribute to job creation.

Some economists suggest that the increased comparability of wage and price levels in EMU may lead to an upward convergence of wage levels to the levels found in the richer Member States. Alternatively, the increased wage and price transparency could lead to a common rate of wage increases across the euro area. Given the unavoidable differences in developments and levels of productivity between the countries, regions and sectors, such uniform wage developments would have negative consequences for employment (Buti and Sapir, 1998, p.19). In recent years, overall labour productivity increases have varied between 0.5 and 1 per cent in the Netherlands compared to 3.5 to 5 per cent in Ireland. Real wage developments have correspondingly been very different, ranging from slightly negative in the Netherlands to increases in Ireland, around 1.5–2 per cent. Had they been uniform, profits would have been squeezed in the Netherlands.

Growth and Employment in EMU

In the run-up to the adoption of the euro, two possible problems were raised. First, the macroeconomic policy mix in the euro area might be too much biased in favour of maintaining price stability, thus holding back business investment and consumer demand and leaving insufficient room for growth and employment. Second, the one-size-fits-all monetary policy would not permit one to overcome adverse economic conditions affecting only a part of the euro area (OECD, 1999). This is the problem related to what in economic literature is called shocks, that is, events like an oil price increase or a financial crisis which brings changes in economic activity. In the case of shocks common to the whole EU area, like an oil price increase, the common monetary policy can provide an adequate response via changes in interest rates and/or exchange rates. If the shock is asymmetric, and concerns only a limited number of countries, like the collapse of the Soviet Union, which triggered a crisis for the Finnish economy, the common monetary policy would not be the appropriate instrument to use. The right response to shocks depends on their character.[1]

The fear that the EMU policy framework would produce a too restrictive monetary and fiscal policy can be overcome by considering the already significant benefits of the convergence process described in the previous section. For example, the lower levels of inflation resulting from this process permitted the ECB to counter sluggish economic growth in the first half of 1999 by lowering interest rates. These cuts in interest rates came on top of the rate cuts that had taken place at the end of 1998. The ECB appears to be sensitive to general economic objectives other than price stability, provided of course that its principal objective of price stability is not at risk.

Furthermore, the central cause of slow growth and insufficient employment creation in the EU is not a bias in the present macroeconomic policy mix, but rather the structural rigidities in the product, labour and capital markets (compare Section 4). Such rigidities are delayed and limited deregulation of the telecommunications, energy and transport sectors, excessive red tape related to the creation of new businesses, high labour taxes and different regulations and taxation concerning financial markets. For an in-depth discussion on the effect of deregulation in telecom, energy and transport, see Chapter 5. The main benefit of a more accommodating macroeconomic policy would be to facilitate the structural reforms deemed necessary to encourage long-term growth and employment creation.

Reflecting on the second problem raised, it is evident that the different countries or regions within the euro area could be hit by different economic disturbances. The ability of the euro area to deal with such disturbances is limited by the relative immobility of the European labour force, at least in comparison with the United States. In addition, real wages are more rigid in the euro zone than in the US. As a result, economic shocks affecting certain regions or countries only could lead to substantial differences in unemployment rates. The single monetary policy would not be the suitable instrument to resolve such basically national or local economic problems, while equilibrating fiscal policies covering the whole territory of the euro area are much less developed than in the US federal system. In the US, as in national Member States, the federal budget – in the case of economic downturns in a single or a few states – distributes more public funds to and receives less taxes from these states. This compensates to a certain degree for

---

[1]   See for a discussion Buti and Sapir, pp. 24ff.

the lack of economic activity. The EU budget, amounting to 1.2 per cent of GDP and being a balanced budget cannot play such a stabilising role. On the other hand, national fiscal policies can be relaxed or tightened in order to deal with country-specific economic shocks. In this context, fiscal policy can play an important role due to the size of public finances in the EU economies, the condition being that a room for manoeuvre has been created in the budgets (Buti and Sapir, 1998; European Commission, 1996; OECD, 1999).

Furthermore, the ongoing process of economic integration of the euro area might make the so-called asymmetric shocks less likely, as it leads to an increased interdependence of the different economies. The introduction of the euro will further accelerate this process. So far, economic integration has not led to a significant increase in the sectoral specialisation of Member States but rather to an increased exchange of similar products between them. The integration process would thus seem to reduce the risk of a specific country being hit by a sectoral shock, while the other Member States would remain unaffected.

Another problem of the past is that Member States used to react in different ways to common shocks. In response to the oil crisis of 1973, for example, some countries resorted to currency depreciation, while others did not. The common stability-oriented economic policy framework of EMU will reduce the likelihood of a recurrence of this type of problem.

Finally, the appropriate response to an asymmetric shock (and in particular, a sector-specific shock) will often be a structural adjustment rather than a macroeconomic accommodation. In the case of a crisis due, for example, to low demand and relatively higher costs in the textile sector mostly hitting France, Italy and Portugal, the adequate response would rather seem to be out-sourcing of production, as it has taken place in other EU Member States and retraining of the laid-off work force. Therefore, the response should be neither a currency depreciation nor a loosening of fiscal policy.

In the present situation, the main economic problems of Europe relate not to macroeconomic policy but to the need to pursue and strengthen structural reforms to respond to globalisation and technological developments. Given the stability framework of EMU and the commitment to pursue this stability-oriented policy, it is, to a large extent, the structural rigidities which are responsible for Europe lagging behind the US in terms of competitiveness, economic growth and employment as shown in Figure 4.2 (European Commission , 1999b).

Figure 4.2   Relative standards of living in the EU and the US (1997, EU=100)

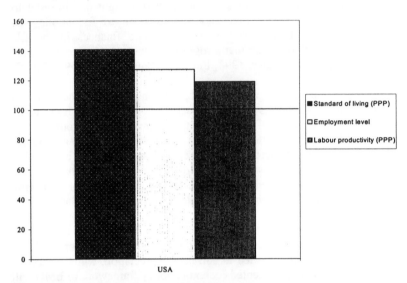

The differences amongst the euro zone members with respect to their structural problems and with respect to their pursuance of reform is, however, in itself a potential for differences in the impact of economic disturbances and can thus lead to problems for the stability-oriented macroeconomic policy, thus the need to pursue these structural reforms; compare the sections below.

4.2   THE EURO AND THE FUNCTIONING OF EUROPEAN PRODUCT AND CAPITAL MARKETS

Evidence on the Functioning of European Product Markets

As described in the previous section, Europe has been unable to match the US performance in terms of growth and job creation.[2] One explanation for this discrepancy is the high level of competition on the relatively integrated US product markets. European product markets, on the other hand, continue to be fragmented and relatively inefficient in spite of the significant progress made towards EU market integration. Even with a successful legal implementation of the Single Market Programme, a number of specific problem areas have been identified (European Commission, 1999b).

---

[2]   See European Commission (1998b) for further evidence.

First of all, the new legislation needs to be correctly enforced. Thus far, the degree of market opening varies greatly between countries and sectors. Beyond legislation, other problems continue to fragment Member State markets. The lack of opening up of public procurement and technical trade barriers, but also national policies unfriendly to competition, such as state aids and differences in taxation systems, are making cross-border market access more difficult.

Finally, continued differences in price levels between EU Member States suggest that producers and distributors continue to be able to segment markets and engage in price discrimination. The data presented in Table 4.1 suggest that on average the variation of prices between EU Member States is around 2 per cent higher than that between US metropolitan areas. However, differences in price variation between product categories are much more important.[3]

Insufficient competition also helps explain the relatively high price levels and low productivity in the EU in comparison with the United States. According to OECD data, 1996 EU price levels exceeded those in the US by 24 per cent, which should be attributed in part to the higher consumer tax burden in the EU (14.4 per cent compared with 5.5 per cent in the US). However, EU market inefficiencies are likely to have played an important role. In this respect, it is interesting to observe that the EU compares particularly badly to the US in some sectors (such as pharmaceuticals, chemicals, motor vehicles, beverages and so on) where EU markets are highly segmented, due to regulation, taxation or business strategies.

Table 4.1   A comparison of price dispersion in the EU and the US (%)

	EU (1997)	EU* (1997)	USA* (1998Q1)
Goods and services (aggregate)	15	13	11
Housing	30	29	26
Health care	19	21	16
Utilities	17	16	20
Transportation	15	12	10
Grocery items	17	14	8

Note: * Price data exclude taxes.
Source: Eurostat, Commission services, ACCRA.

Up to now, the main Union's response to these challenges has been to accelerate the move towards European market integration through the introduction of the euro. The single currency can be expected to improve the efficiency of product and capital markets, by reinforcing some of the benefits

---

[3]   See European Commission (1999c) for more details.

associated with the Single Market Programme which aimed to remove all non-tariff trade barriers between EU Member States by the end of 1992. First the elimination of exchange rate costs and risks in EMU should further stimulate intra-EU trade and investment flows.

Second, the increased price transparency should modify the degree and the nature of competition within the euro area and could lead to a further convergence of price levels between the Member States. Box 4.3 illustrates the sometimes important differences in pricing policies between multinationals.

Box 4.3   Strategic reaction to the euro by selected multinationals

Multinational companies tend to have fairly well developed European market strategies already. However, even within these companies the increased price transparency associated with the euro is sometimes viewed as a threat to profits obtained through price discrimination.

Emerson (1999) distinguishes between two types of multinationals. For suppliers of bulk commodities and semi-processed goods (Du Pont, for example) markets are already relatively transparent and the impact of the euro is expected to be minor. Nevertheless, Du Pont's policy is to work pro-actively towards price convergence in Europe, the Middle East and Africa with the aim of avoiding price harmonisation at the lowest currently available level. Du Pont sees supply and distribution strategies shifting from a national to a pan European focus, as distributors will form alliances in different countries and will operate bigger regional operations.

A second group of multinationals are the suppliers of branded consumer goods (Nestlé, for example). For these multinationals the price transparency effect of the euro could be more important. Nestlé makes a distinction between differentiated products for which there is no need to harmonise prices internationally, and internationally comparable products for which there is 'enormous' pressure from trade partners to harmonise prices at the lowest level. In response, Nestlé has decided to create price corridors for wholesale prices, leaving the decision on consumer prices to the retailer.

The elimination of non-tariff barriers foreseen in the Single Market Programme was an important step in the process of European market integration. In the run-up to the completion of the Single Market in 1992 price dispersion between EU Member States declined significantly. The coefficient of price variation fell from above 20 per cent in 1985 to 16 per cent in 1993.[4]

In the period 1993–97, however, EU market integration has failed to deliver a further convergence of prices and the level of price dispersion has remained stable at around 16 per cent (European Commission, 1999c). This halt in EU price convergence is all the more surprising, since trade figures show a continued rise in the level of intra-EU trade as a percentage of GDP

---

[4]   See DRI (1996) for a more detailed description.

(from 26.5 per cent in 1993 to 31.5 per cent in 1997). The strong currency movements of 1995 offer the best explanation for the unexpected halt in price convergence.

The Euro and the Level of Competition within the Single Market

The introduction of the euro should make the differences in price levels between countries in the euro area more transparent, especially after the euro coins and bills have been introduced in 2002. This greater price transparency will make it harder for producers to price discriminate, as consumers become more aware of any price differences existing and may decide to go for a cheaper purchase price abroad. As a result, the price levels in the euro area will face pressure to converge downward. Distributors have an even more crucial role. They are better placed and have a greater incentive to compare prices across countries than consumers.

Two alternative strategies to profit from the increasingly evident differences in price levels can be distinguished. The first strategy involves price arbitrage, that is, buying the product in the low-price country and selling it where it is more expensive. This would normally lead to a downward convergence of price levels. However, the greater clarity of price signals could also facilitate collusive behaviour amongst distributors. It would be much easier to maintain price levels that are similar to those of the competition. This second strategy would imply price convergence as well, but not necessarily to a lower level. However, as the EU competition law forbids collusion, the first strategy should be more common and a downward price convergence more likely. Similarly, the strict anti-inflationary discipline carried out by the ECB should lead to lower prices.[5]

Another channel through which the introduction of the single currency affects the conditions of competition in the euro area is by making it easier for firms to penetrate markets in other Member States. The elimination of currency transaction costs and the uncertainty of exchange rate fluctuations should reduce the costs and risks associated with doing business in the whole euro area. In practice, most firms appear to have adopted a rather defensive strategy in dealing with the arrival of the euro (see Box 4.4). Nevertheless, increased competition should force firms to become more efficient and productive.

---

[5]   See European Commission (1999c) for further details.

Box 4.4   Strategies of US and European firms in relation to EMU

According to a research report by KPMG and Harris (1998) 'EMU offers unparalleled opportunities for US businesses to expand their European sales and marketing programmes, but also offers new threats from European rivals within the new economic zone'. A survey of US and European business executives showed that most companies had a rather defensive strategy in relation to the coming arrival of the euro. The following strategic objectives were given the highest priority:

- ensure that one can operate in a single currency environment;
- minimise the commercial risks of EMU;
- minimise the costs of change; and
- minimise the costs of implementation

The first more offensive objective to 'Identify/exploit new European market opportunities' was ranked only in fifth place.

Thus, by deepening integration and raising the level of competition within European markets, the single currency could improve the conditions for an increase in the productive efficiency and international competitiveness of the European economy. However, further structural reforms aimed at improving the functioning of product and capital markets are an essential complement to market integration. This issue is developed in more detail below.

Finally, it is interesting to observe that the increased popularity of electronic commerce will have many of the same effects as the arrival of the euro. E-commerce helps reduce search and transaction costs, especially for cross-border purchases. With the increased ability of consumers to compare prices through a search of the Internet, producers may be forced to lower price levels. However, the Internet also permits producers to rapidly obtain information about the sales conditions offered by their competitors, allowing them to engage in collusion and driving up price levels (Shapiro and Varian, 1999). Both the euro and electronic commerce are therefore expected to reinforce competition and to lead to an increased convergence of price levels.

The Euro and the Integration of European Capital Markets

European companies have already been able to benefit from the reduction in interest rates associated with EMU convergence process (see above). The ongoing integration of EU capital markets opens up the potential for further reductions in the cost of capital. An integrated European capital market would be similar in size to the US market. As a result, it would be more liquid and efficient than the current national markets, offering firms the possibility to obtain investment capital at lower cost. In addition, the increased diversity of the European capital markets will make it easier for firms to find more suitable alternative sources of finance. This would be beneficial especially for firms with capital- or technology-intensive activities as well as for small and medium-sized enterprises which in Europe have tended to be highly dependent on bank financing. The example of the US capital market shows that there is still ample room for making the European market more responsive to the needs of business.

The arrival of the euro has given a stimulus to the integration of European capital markets. However, some obstacles to the full integration of European capital markets remain, including differences in the interpretation and implementation of (EU) financial market legislation; regulatory differences in areas such as pension funds; differences in national fiscal regimes; and technical barriers, for example in the field of payment systems. This indicates that further reforms are necessary in that area.

The International Role of the Euro

The euro has the potential to develop into a truly international currency used for invoicing and payment, even beyond the borders of the euro area. The economic weight of the area, a macroeconomic policy framework conducive to low levels of inflation and interest rates and the development of an integrated financial market are all factors that make the euro a more attractive currency. The share of EU trade[6] in world trade is around 20 per cent, a share similar to that of the United States. Nevertheless in 1995, only 13 per cent of world trade was denominated in German marks (the major European currency at the time), while more than 50 per cent was denominated in US dollars. This indicates that there is a good likelihood that the euro will be used more than the German mark in the past in international commercial transactions.

The cost of using the euro for invoicing or payment by companies located outside the euro area should be relatively low, especially if their trading partners are located within the euro area. The large size of the euro area should contribute to relatively low transaction and information costs associated with euro usage. One would therefore expect that the euro would be used intensively in transactions involving euro area companies. As Box 4.5 shows, some companies based within the euro area are taking pro-active measures to ensure that they are being billed in Eurasia. These companies would benefit by not having to carry the exchange rate risk normally associated with international trade. However, in situations where the transactions remain denominated in a currency other than the euro, exchange rate fluctuations continue to play a role. But it has to be highlighted that the sensitivity of the EU economy to international currency fluctuations has been significantly reduced. Whereas in the past EU trade involving currency

---

6   Excluding trade between EU Member States.

exchange amounted to around a quarter of GDP, with the arrival of the euro such trade is equivalent to around one tenth of GDP.

Box 4.5   Invoicing in Eurasia: a case study of a Dutch wholesaler in the printing industry

Many suppliers were based outside the European Union and operating in different currencies. To seize the opportunities and meet the challenge associated with the introduction of the euro, the company undertook the following actions:
- Contact suppliers based outside EMU countries to discuss the possibility of invoicing in euros as of 1 January 1999.
- Assess the financial and commercial impact of reduced exchange rate risks if non EMU suppliers were willing to invoice in euros.

Source: European Commission, Enterprise Policy (1999).

The Sectoral Impact of the Euro

The change in the business environment caused by the introduction of the euro will affect the various sectors of the economy in a positive way. But the intensity and the nature of its impact might differ according to some sectoral characteristics, such as the costs of the changeover, characteristics of the markets (degree of internationalisation, concentration of supply), importance of exchange rate transaction costs, sensitivity to exchange rate fluctuations, degree of price discrimination and corresponding dispersion of prices.

Recent studies by Ilzkovitz and Dierx (1999a, 1999b) make the argument that two sectoral characteristics, the trade orientation (intra- versus extra-EU trade) and the degree of price dispersion, are key to analysing the impact of the euro in the different industrial sectors. On the one hand, sectors with major markets inside the euro area will particularly benefit from the reduction in exchange rate transaction costs and the elimination of exchange risks while sectors more exposed to extra-EU competition will continue to be affected by the euro exchange rate. For these sectors, other characteristics, such as the degree of product differentiation, consumer loyalty, sunk costs, will also influence their sensitivity to exchange rate changes as the impact of exchange rate changes is more limited in sectors with imperfect competition and segmented markets. On the other hand, the greater transparency of prices should have principally an impact on sectors where the price dispersion between Member States is still high.

This simple framework can be used to investigate the impact of the euro in the various industrial sectors of the economy. For example, a sector such as the aerospace industry is already strongly internationalised at world level and, as a result, price dispersion is weak. Therefore, in the short term, the impact of the euro should be relatively limited in this industry. However, this impact could be greater in the longer term if the euro develops as an international currency and prices for aeroplanes are no longer denominated in dollars only. By contrast, in a sector such as the car industry, the impact of the euro would be stronger and more immediate for the following reasons. First, the car industry should benefit from the reduction in the exchange rate transaction costs and the elimination of exchange risks, because intra-EU trade is so significant. Secondly, one can also expect a major impact of the greater transparency of prices because the dispersion of car prices between EU Member States is still very high. With the arrival of the euro, car companies' strategies of market segmentation (for example, exclusive distribution agreements) will be less easy to implement. Finally, the arrival of the euro could speed up the ongoing restructuring process of the car industry, by facilitating cross-border alliances.

4.3   THE NEED FOR FURTHER STRUCTURAL REFORMS: SOME POLICY ISSUES

The Cardiff Process and the New Strategy for the Internal Market

Measures to improve the functioning of product and capital markets should help raise the level of competition, lower prices and the cost of capital, thereby enhancing the EU's competitiveness with ultimately positive effects on growth and employment creation. Member states' efforts to improve the business environment have been given a new stimulus by the 'Cardiff' process of economic and structural reform which was launched in June 1998. This process, which includes elements of peer review, benchmarking and identification of good and bad practices, aims at improving the functioning of European product and capital markets. Within the framework of the Cardiff process, a first annual review of national economic reform policies was conducted at the beginning of 1999 (European Commission, 1999b).

The new 'Strategy for Europe's Internal Market', launched in the fall of 1999, should also contribute to this reform process by furthering market integration and improving the regulatory environment for business. The new Internal Market strategy should be seen as a deepening of the Single Market Programme, which aimed at the elimination of all barriers to the free circulation of goods, services, capital and persons by the end of 1992. An evaluation of the Single Market Programme carried out in 1996 showed significant economic benefits, but identified areas for further improvements, which were addressed in part by the 1997 Action Plan for the Single Market. By 1999, however, the legal framework for the Single Market was largely established and the focus has shifted from primarily legal questions to the more economic aspects of the Internal Market, which were the focus on the Cardiff process as well. Here, we are referring to efforts to enhance the efficiency of products and capital markets and to improve the business environment. Measures to simplify the administrative burden on start-ups and to promote access to finance for innovative SMEs, a modernisation of competition rules and the continuation of the liberalisation of network industries are examples of actions envisaged in this Plan.

Within the framework of the Cardiff process the national governments and the Commission prepare year-end reports on the functioning of product and capital markets in the Member States and the European Union as a whole. On the basis of these reports, specific target actions under the Internal Market Strategy are identified by the Internal Market Council and country-specific recommendations in the area of product and capital markets are made to the Member States in the Broad Economic Policy Guidelines issued annually by the ECOFIN Council.

The Broad Economic Policy Guidelines play a central role in economic policy co-ordination as it covers a broad range of issues, including the necessary reforms of product, capital and labour markets as well as taxation issues. This central role is essential to guarantee the articulation between the different areas of reforms and between structural reforms and macro-economic policy, in particular given the proliferation of policy initiatives which take place at the moment in the area of economic reform.[7] Below we only deal with structural measures concerning product and capital markets. The need for reforms in labour markets is indicated in the beginning of this chapter.

A Strict Competition Policy

The benefits of better functioning product and capital markets in EMU can only be realised if the level of competition is allowed to increase. This is by no means evident as, for example, the increased price transparency associated with both the introduction of the euro and electronic commerce may facilitate collusive behaviour. In addition, the increased importance of economies of scale, particularly on the demand side (the so-called 'network externalities'), may reinforce monopolistic tendencies especially in the Information and Communication Technology (ICT) sectors. Therefore competition policy has an important role to play in safeguarding or enhancing the flexibility of product and service markets.

Nevertheless, any challenges to competition policy need to be seen in the context of an overall pro-competitive impact of EMU. As some companies will inevitably experience difficulties as a result of more intense competition,

---

[7]   Among these initiatives, one can mention the Cardiff, Luxembourg and Cologne processes as well as various action plans pertaining to specific domains. The Luxembourg process centres on an annual procedure dealing specifically with labour market issues. The Cologne process establishes a macroeconomic dialogue at Community level between all relevant policy actors, including the social partners. To that one should add the policy initiatives undertaken at the national level.

Member States are likely to experience strong pressure to protect these companies by means of state aids, notably rescue and restructuring aids. Such aids can lead to distortions of competition at the expense of more efficient companies.

Merger and acquisition activity is likely to increase as the increased facility of entering other markets within the euro area and elsewhere offers new opportunities to exploit economies of scale. This will especially be true for sectors such as financial services or business services where sales networks have previously been largely confined to national boundaries and where companies see prospects for obtaining important cost savings by enlarging these to a European scale. Some companies have already anticipated the arrival of the euro and over the period 1996–98 one has observed a strong increase in merger activities in sectors such as business services, hotels and catering, recreational and cultural services, and the chemical industry. On the other hand, competition will expose the weaknesses of less efficient companies, which will become prone to take-over bids.

Provided that market entry is easy, no major competition problems should result from the reduction in the total number of firms as inefficient firms exit and more efficient firms expand. Although the number of domestic suppliers in any local market will likely fall, the total number of actual or potential competitors in that market will increase after it has been incorporated into a wider geographic market.

The Need for Further Regulatory Reforms

Efforts by firms to reduce the level of competition can only be successful if made possible by a slack regulatory environment. Improving the regulatory environment is expected to increase the static and dynamic efficiency of the economy. By reinforcing competition, regulatory reform may help reduce costs, prices and mark-ups leading to a better allocation of resources, increased demand and growth. It can also stimulate managerial effort and force restructuring as the least efficient producers are eliminated from the market. Finally, it can create a more innovative business climate. All these effects improve the functioning of markets and thereby the capacity of the economy to respond to shocks (European Commission, 1999b). However, they may also imply adjustment costs in the short term because in most cases deregulation is accompanied by employment losses. This is the case, for example, when deregulation leads to a profound restructuring and employment lay-off in the incumbent and the employment creation in the new companies entering the market is insufficient to outweigh these employment losses or when technology development makes it possible to significantly improve productivity, which also results in employment reductions in the short term.

An improvement in the regulatory environment does not necessarily mean deregulation and it may also entail re-regulation provided that the new rules are better adapted to the new economic environment. In a changing business environment, regulations that were appropriate in the past may no longer be in the future. Governments are therefore a responsibility to continuous review regulations and assess their appropriateness in the current business environment. It is more common, however, that government regulations create an environment in which anti-competitive practices can prosper. Many European markets remain highly segmented due to differences national rules, regulations and practices.

In recent years, governments have become increasingly aware of the need to avoid unnecessary regulatory and administrative burdens on business. Efforts to lighten such burdens are being pursued both at the Community and the national levels. The Internal Market Strategy, for example, makes specific proposals to reduce the regulatory burden imposed on business in general, and small- and medium-sized enterprises in particular. However, significant progress remains to be made.

Three recent studies have attempted to analyse the link between performance and regulation. Although it is extremely difficult, work in this area is important to improve the public acceptance of the regulatory reforms by making it possible to identify their positive effects.

The first of these studies (Koedijk and Kremers, 1996) concludes that there is a link between regulation and two indices of economic performance: overall economic growth and productivity growth. Among the 11 countries under review, those with the lightest overall regulation (Ireland, the UK and Denmark) exhibit a trend growth rate in the market sector twice as large as that of the countries with the most rigid regulatory framework (Italy and Greece). In the other countries, either the relatively low degree of product market regulation more than compensates for their tight labour market regulation (Spain and Portugal) or the opposite holds (Belgium, France, Germany and the Netherlands). Another striking conclusion from this study is that it is product market regulation that has the larger influence on economic growth (twice that of labour market regulation).

The second study (OECD, 1999b; Nicoletti et al., 1999) compares the levels of product market regulation between the OECD Member States using various indicators (see Box 4.6). It shows a great variance in the level of regulation between EU Member States, with the regulatory burden being particularly heavy in Italy and much lighter in countries like the UK and Ireland. The OECD has also attempted to relate high regulation levels with poor economic performance. The outcome of such attempts at the aggregate national level has not been very convincing. Results at the sectoral level look more promising. One should add that the issue of regulation is particularly important for certain sectors including the network industries (telecommunications, transport, energy and the like) as well as retail distribution. It is on these sectors that the OECD has initially focused.

These studies are interesting because they have allowed the collection of, by means of a questionnaire, a lot of detailed information on regulatory frameworks in several countries.

Box 4.6 OECD indicators of product market regulation

The OECD has developed a set of indicators of product market regulation, making a distinction between four main categories:

- State control of the national economy (measured by public ownership and involvement of government in business operations);
- Barriers to entrepreneurship (including regulatory and administrative opacity; administrative burdens on start-ups; and barriers to competition);
- Explicit barriers to international trade and investment (such as tariffs, ownership barriers and discriminatory provisions); and
- Other regulatory barriers.

An initial investigation of these indicators appears to show that in all EU countries except the UK product markets are more regulated than in the United States, although for most of them regulation is no more stringent than in Japan. The difference between the US and the EU Member States is most striking in the area of state control.

Source: OECD, 1999b

Finally, a recent study made by the European Commission (1999d) shows that some interesting observations can be made on the impact of liberalisation in the telecommunications industry. It confirms the observation of the OECD study that liberalisation goes hand in hand with low prices. Regarding employment, there are short-term employment losses as the employment created by the new operators is insufficient to offset the lay-off by incumbents. However, the long-term prospects are better as the reduction in prices will increase demand and spread into other sectors, leading to competitiveness gains for the whole economy.

4.4 CONCLUSION

This chapter has analysed the different channels through which the EMU will change the business environment in the euro area. Section 1 has described the framework of stability which has been created and its impact on the macroeconomic performance of the euro area. Section 2 has considered the generally positive efficiency effects associated with the introduction of the euro by analysing its impact on product and capital markets. However, further structural reforms are needed to amplify the positive effects of EMU on the functioning of European markets. Section 3 has raised some industrial policy issues related to the functioning of product and capital markets.

By eliminating exchange rate variability and imposing price stability and sound public finances as conditions for entry, the EMU has created a framework of stability more favourable to growth and employment. In particular, inflation rates and public deficits have been significantly reduced from 1993 to 1999. It also appears that Member States have not relaxed their budgetary discipline and that wage moderation has also had a positive impact. The risk, sometimes mentioned, that the policy framework in EMU would be biased towards a restrictive policy, does not appear to be founded. The ECB has shown that it is ready to lower interest rates in a situation of sluggish growth provided that such a move does not endanger its primary objective of price stability.

Despite its improved macroeconomic results over the recent period, the EU continues to grow more slowly than the US and to suffer from low rates of employment. Despite progress in EU integration, the European markets continue to be fragmented and relatively inefficient. For example, the relatively high price levels and the higher price dispersion in the EU suggest that markets remain segmented, due to differences in regulation, taxation and business strategies.

Up to now, the main response to this problem has been to accelerate the move towards European integration through the introduction of the euro. The single currency can be expected to improve economic efficiency in several ways. Greater price transparency and reduced costs for doing business across borders will increase competition and are expected to improve the competitiveness of the euro area. Wider and deeper capital markets will contribute to reducing the cost of capital on top of the fall in interest rates provided by the stability-oriented macroeconomic policy. But further economic reforms are also necessary to improve the functioning of markets in EMU and to foster growth and employment.

This is the reason why, at the Community level, diverse initiatives have been taken to better co-ordinate and monitor structural reforms in the Member States. The main objectives of these initiatives are to improve the coherence and comprehensiveness of reforms, to increase their effectiveness, to better integrate structural reforms and macroeconomic policy and to maintain momentum in this process. Labour market reforms are particularly important and are dealt with in the Broad Economic Policy Guidelines and in the Employment Guidelines, which include recommendations on active labour market policies, reform of tax and benefit systems and of working time. In the area of product and capital markets, the Cardiff process and the new Single Market strategy, strict competition and further regulatory reforms play a central role. The Cardiff process aims at identifying good practices and problem areas in the functioning of product and capital markets. The competition policy guarantees that the pro-competitive effects of EMU are not jeopardised by an increase in state aids or other anti-competitive practices. Finally, further regulatory reforms are necessary to reduce the regulatory burden imposed on business and to create an economic climate more favourable to growth and innovation.

BIBILIOGRAPHY

Buti and Sapir (eds) (1998), *Economic Policy in EMU*, Clarendon Press, Oxford.

DRI (1996), Price competition and price convergence, *The Single Market Review*, Vol. 1, Sub-series V.

Emerson, Michael (1999), Euro strategies for business: Going for AAA, Report of a CEPS working party, Brussels.

European Commission (1990), One market, one money, *European Economy*, No. 44.

European Commission (1993), Stable money, sound finances: Community public finance in the perspective of EMU, *European Economy*, No. 53.

European Commission (1995), The impact of exchange-rate movements on trade within the Single Market, *European Economy, Reports and Studies*, No. 4.

European Commission (1996), Economic evaluation of the internal market, *European Economy, Reports and Studies*, No. 4.

European Commission (1998a), Growth and Employment in the Stability-oriented framework of EMU, *European Economy*, No. 65.

European Commission (1998b), European competitiveness in the Triad: Macroeconomic and structural aspects, *European Economy*, Supplement A, No. 7.

European Commission (1999a), EU economy: 1999 review, *Annual Economic Report, European Economy*, No. 69.

European Commission (1999b), Report on economic and structural reform in the EU, *European Economy*, Supplement A, No. 1.

European Commission (1999c), Market integration and differences in price levels between EU Member States, Study 4 in EU economy: 1999 review, *European Economy*, No. 69.

European Commission (1999d), Liberalisation of network industries: Economic impact and main policy issues, *European Economy*, forthcoming.

European Commission, Enterprise Policy (1999), *Your Business and the Euro: A Strategic Guide*, Office for Official Publications of the European Communities, Luxembourg.

Ilzkovitz, F. and Dierx, A. (1999a), From the Single Market to the Single Currency: New Challenges for European Companies in J.-V. Louis and H. Bronkhorst (eds), *The Euro and European Integration*, pp. 109–37.

Ilzkovitz, F. and Dierx, A. (1999b), Du marché unique à la monnaie unique: L'impact sectoriel de l'euro, *Economie Internationale*, Vol. 80.

IMF (1999), *1999 World Economic Outlook*, Washington.

Koedijk, K and Kremers, J. (1996), Market opening, regulation and growth in Europe, *Economic Policy*, No. 23, October.

KPMG and Harris (1998), US companies: Preparedness for the Economic and Monetary Union in Europe, research report.

Nicoletti, G., Scarpetta, S. and Boylaud, O. (1999), Summary indicators of product market regulation and employment protection legislation for the purpose of international comparisons, OECD Economics Department Working Paper, No. 226, December.

OECD (1999a), *EMU. Facts, Challenges and Policies*, OECD, Paris

OECD (1999b), Cross-country patterns of product market regulation, Chapter 7 in *OECD Economic Outlook*, December, OECD, Paris.

Shapiro, C. and Varian, H. (1999), *Information Rules: A strategic Guide to the Network Economy*, McGraw-Hill.

5. Efficient Trans-European Networks – the Backbone for a Competitive European Industry*

Manfred Bergmann

Comprehensive transport, communication and energy networks are a main source and a main means of industrial and economic development. Modern mass production would not have become the dominant feature of industrialised countries if it had not been for the development of more or less efficient infrastructure networks. With some notable exceptions, most goods transportation has been within national or local frontiers: even today most production in large countries is still for consumption within that country. Thus, the national orientation of networks to a large extent reflects their usage. It also reflects in part the role of physical boundaries in creating national political frontiers. Indeed, the consolidation of European nation states and the exploitation of all their economic and social potentials has been facilitated greatly by the development of national networks.[1]

This national orientation was characterised by neglecting cross-border links and, perhaps more importantly, by the parallel development of mutually incompatible national technologies and standards. However, the Single Market and globalisation now call the validity of this national orientation of the networks into question. Moreover, despite the dominance of domestic production for domestic markets, nowadays hardly any product, be it the breakfast egg or yoghurt or be it a computer or an aircraft, is produced or distributed without some stages of the production or distribution process having to rely on international links. Therefore, it is often said that the predominantly national orientation of networks has proven to be a real burden for European industry. This holds in particular for the design of transport networks with their incompatible technologies and standards and lack of sufficient cross-border links as it is making transport services more

* The author is grateful to Mark Hayden and Heinz Jansen for useful input and comments on earlier drafts.
[1] History even shows that this is true independent of time (e.g. the network of roman streets in the Roman Empire) and space (see for example, the role of creating the railway network in the United States of America for the shaping and consolidation of this country).

time consuming and more expensive for downstream industries. But this also held for the discriminatory rules governing access to the other networks until recently. Both the inadequate design and the discriminatory access rules are assumed also to have reduced demand for these services themselves and, by this, for their upstream industries. Substantial positive growth and employment potentials are still buried under these nationally oriented structures.

Therefore, European policies have gradually been put into place to overcome these shortcomings. The main aims of the European policies in supporting the better development and use of trans-European networks (TENs) and a European infrastructure are to reduce inefficiencies coming from this national orientation, and to promote competition. It is only recently that the aim to make the services provided through these networks environmentally and socially sustainable has been added to this political agenda.

This chapter deals with the policies undertaken and designed in this context, their implications for both the networks and their use as well as the implications for the European industry. The next section gives an overview of the development of the different networks. In Section 2 the reader will find an analysis of the shaping of the different Community policies, including their aims and their effects on the design and performance of the different networks. The focus, however, will be on transport policy given its importance for all industrial branches in Europe. Section 3 contains an analysis of the effects of these policies on the European industry, while Section 4 will provide a brief outlook.

5.1 THE DEVELOPMENT OF NETWORKS IN EUROPE

In the past, the transport networks were at the core of other such networks, such as, for example, postal services because information had to be delivered physically. Energy networks themselves did not exist until early this century. Rather economic activity was concentrated where energy (water or coal) was naturally abundant. It was not until transport networks (shipping, railways and roads) were sufficiently available and powerful that energy could be transported over longer distances.

However, technical inventions (electricity, telegraph) and the availability of liquid fossil fuels which could be transported with the help of pipelines allowed for the independent development of transport, energy and communication networks from the end of the nineteenth century. In the meantime, technical progress enables the distinction to be made between traditional networks, which depend on concrete physical infrastructure for transporting energy, information, goods or people, on the one hand, and modern networks such as, for example, air transport or satellite-based telecommunications which only need this physical infrastructure at the sending and at the receiving end of a transaction.

At the beginning of the twenty-first century transport, energy and communications networks are the backbones of efficient modern economies, and they have become important and dynamic sectors. Taken together these network industries account for some 11 per cent of gross value added and some 7 per cent of total employment in Europe. This compares to some 10 per cent of gross value added in the US and in Japan, and about 6 per cent of total employment in these countries.

For some time, the initially privately developed network industries have been exposed to heavy state intervention, often resulting in the public provision of these networks and related services. From an economic point of view public intervention could be justified mainly for two reasons. First, often these networks constituted 'natural monopolies', that is, due to technical constraints and falling average costs over the whole market range it was not efficient to establish competing parallel networks as such a solution would have been more expensive than to let the market be served by a single network. The resulting monopoly power, however, had to be contained by public regulators. Alternatively the government itself exploited it. Secondly, the vital importance of access to services provided with the help of these networks for virtually all economic transactions asked for a kind of 'public service obligation' imposed on network and service providers: everybody should have access to the network or the service at reasonable prices independent of the costs this access might entail for the network or service provider. This often resulted in a cross subsidisation of services in favour of those living in remote areas. However, in the end the lack of competition within networks and modes was substituted for by competition across modes.

Transport Networks

In the transport domain rail services dominating mass transport of goods were hard pressed by road services. Initially highly competitive because of their speed, reliability and capability to transport goods and services over long distances, railways lost out against road transport because they were unable to deliver what road transport could, and what was the final aim of all transport services: a complete door-to-door service. This competitive disadvantage was aggravated by the fact that most railway companies had been turned into public companies, almost 'by definition' not characterised by a vigorous strive for innovation, competitiveness or improved customer satisfaction.

The reaction of railway operators to this new challenge was quite defensive, that is, they tried to get protection against this new competition, and subsidies to compensate for their losses. Normally both were granted generously. Nevertheless, the railway sector could not offset its technical competitive disadvantage and, as can be seen from Table 5.1, by the end of the 1970s rail transport in all industrial countries had lost out against road transport for passenger transport. Governments investing heavily in a massive extension of the road network while at the same time neglecting investment to expand or modernise the railway infrastructure facilitated this tidal shift.[2] It was not until recently that policies were launched to revitalise railways.

Table 5.1   Basic transport indicators (000 million tkm)

	EU				US			
	1970	1980	1990	1997	1970	1980	1990	1996
Goods transport								
Total [a]	865	1113	1369	1644	2691	3433	3951	4842
Modal split into (in %)								
Road	47.6	56.2	67.9	73.1	22.4	23.6	27.2	29.7
Rail	32.7	25.8	18.6	14.4	41.5	39.1	38.2	40.9
Inland waterways	11.9	9.6	7.9	7.2	12.7	12.3	13.1	10.7
Pipelines	7.6	8.4	5.6	5.2	23.4	25.0	21.6	18.7
Passenger transport								
Total	2151	3069	4197	4825	3563	4424	5681	6818
Modal split into (in %)								
Car	73.6	76.0	78.7	78.5	91.4	88.7	85.7	85.7
Railway	10.1	8.2	6.5	5.8	0.5	0.4	0.4	0.3
Bus [b]	14.3	12.6	9.9	9.0	2.8	2.9	3.8	3.5
Air	2.0	3.1	4.9	6.7	5.3	8.0	10.2	10.5

Notes:
[a] Excluding intra EU short-sea shipping of 472 (1970), 778 (1980), 919 (1990) and 1124 bn tkm in 1997.
[b] Buses, coaches, trams and metro.

Source: European Commission (1999a)

---

[2]   In Europe, the length of the motorway system almost tripled between 1970 and 1996. Over the same period the length of the overall railway network declined by about 10 per cent (European Commission , 1999a).

However, in comparing the EU with the US one can see some striking differences:

- For passenger transport, rail and local public transport never played an important role in the US, while in Europe these modes were quite important in the past, but lost out against private road transport.
- For goods transport, contrary to Europe, railways in the US were and still are the most important transport mode. A reason for this might be the absence of short-sea shipping in the US. In Europe, this mode experienced almost as dynamic a growth performance as road transport. If one took railways and short-sea shipping together, these modes would still be more important than road transport in Europe, although with a declining market share.

Communication Networks

Also communication networks have undergone tremendous change, once again initiated by technical progress. Initially relying on private or public postal services the electronic form of communication and transmitting messages (telephone, telefax, Internet, videoconferences, and so on) has put the traditional postal service under much pressure. Besides enabling new forms of communication these services also have crowded out traditional ones as they could deliver the services in question at a fraction of the time and costs.[3] Once again, the lack of competition within a mode was substituted for by competition across modes, leaving traditional and sheltered services to loose out.

In principle, postal service operators were in public ownership, and there was often no separation between the regulating and supervising authority on the one side and the operator on the other side. Until recently, the national operator has had a quasi-monopoly on all postal services. It was not until the mid–1990s that some competition through private operators was introduced in parcel and express delivery.

As can be seen from Table 5.2, postal services are an economically important sector, but much less dynamically developing than the partially competing telecommunications sector. Today about 1.7 million people are employed in the European postal sector (of which about 1.4 million are employed by public service providers). Cross-border transactions contribute only about 4 per cent to the turnover of this sector.

---

[3]   The traditional postal services fulfilled two functions: the transport/ transmission of information (letters, newspapers and so on) and the transport of goods (parcels). It is mainly the first which is in danger of being crowded out by telecommunications services.

Table 5.2   Basic indicators on postal services, 1995

	EU	US	Japan
Employment (% of total)	0.8	0.6	0.7
Value added (% of GDP)	0.9	0.7	0.8
Letters/parcels (per inhabitant)	300	650	160
International deliveries (% of total)	4.0	0.5	1.1

Source: European Commission (1997c)

The telecommunications sector has developed very dynamically over the recent past. With an annual growth rate of about 8 per cent per year over the last decades has it been the fastest growing sector of the economy. Starting with a production structure which had all elements for constituting a 'natural monopoly' situation,[4] that is, copper-cable based telephone networks, traditional telecommunications providers also came under pressure from providers who based their services on less capital-intensive networks technologies, namely radio waves.

So far, incumbent providers were able to more or less cope with this emerging competition, *inter alia* by also exploiting the chances coming with this technical progress. This was facilitated by a new paradigm in regulatory policy: with only a slight delay the emergence of these new technologies was followed by deregulation and liberalisation of the services, which in turn made it possible to massively privatise formerly publicly owned network providers and operators. This might have freed entrepreneurial incentives, still remaining buried under cumbersome structures in the railway sector until recently.

As can be seen from Table 5.3 dynamic growth came mainly from the mobile phone sector and from the mushrooming of Internet use, both technologies taking off as late as in the late 1980s. Although Europe is still lagging behind the US in some parts of the telecommunications sector, it seems to be catching up, to innovate fast and to continue to have buoyant growth prospects.[5]

As a result of technical progress and deregulation the market for telecommunications services has been overhauled completely over the last decade.[6] One outcome of this was that the fifteen national monopolies were challenged by hundreds of new service providers, public monopolies have been privatised on a large scale, and the penetration of mobile phones and

---

[4]   With the given production technology it was more efficient and less costly to establish only one single and by this a monopolistic network instead of several competing ones.

[5]   For more details see OECD (1999a).

[6]   For more details see European Commission (1999b).

Internet access has dramatically increased, if compared to the penetration pattern of voice telephone over earlier decades.

Table 5.3   Basic indicators on telecommunications

	EU		US	Japan
	1997	1999	1997	1997
Penetration rates (in %)				
- Fixed telephone lines	52	55	66	48
- Mobile telephone lines	14	36	20	30
- Internet hosts	10	31	4	1
Market value (in $bn)	186.5	173.9	271.5	110.0
Spending/capita (in $)	499	578	946	875
Investment/capita (in $)	123		200	261
Employment share (in %)	0.6	0.6	0.7	0.4

Source: OECD (1999a); Telecommunications database, European Commission, (1999b)

Energy Networks

The establishment of the energy networks, that is, the electricity grid and gas and oil pipelines was characterised by a market constellation (capital-intensive production and distribution structures resulting in falling average costs) favourable for the establishment of 'natural monopolies'. As with the rail and communications networks, providers and users of the networks were in general identical, a distinction between the supply of energy and its distribution did not take place.

The changing market shares of the different fuel shares were driven by different factors: solid fuels have been on a declining trend since the 1950s, as cheap oil became available. As from the mid–1970s oil was partially substituted for by the more convenient gas. This was to a large extent also due to a diversification of fuel sources in the aftermath of the first oil price shock. This shock was also a driving force behind the growing market share of electricity, once the heavily subsidised nuclear power plants became commercially available.

In looking at Table 5.4 one can see that the gap between domestic production and domestic consumption widened in all industrialised regions of the world: the growth in primary production was more than offset by the dynamic growth in gross inland consumption.[7] The fuel mix in the US has

---

[7]   However, thanks to the exploration of oil and gas fields in the North Sea the import ratio for Europe has declined somewhat since the early 1980s.

been quite stable over the last four decades. However, the tide against the consumption of solid fuels has been dramatic in the EU and in Japan, while in the US solid fuels never played the same role. In Europe it has been mainly oil and natural gas, which benefited from this trend, while in Japan it was oil.

Table 5.4   Basic energy indicators (million tons of oil equivalent)

	EU			US			Japan		
	1960	1980	1997	1960	1980	1997	1960	1980	1997
Domestic production	355	584	767	965	1553	1684	47	43	107
Net imports	206	688	700	66	307	510	35	319	416
Total primary energy supply	546	1218	1421	1021	1812	2162	81	346	515
Total final consumption	399	885	1006	810	1320	1445	57	233	340
- solids (%)	48	10	4	11	4	2	46	10	7
- oil (%)	37	56	52	54	53	54	37	67	62
- natural gas (%)	5	17	22	24	26	23	3	4	6
- electricity (%)	9	14	18	7	13	19	14	19	23
- others (%)	2	3	5	4	4	3	0	0	1
Final consumptn/ capita (toe)	1.27	2.49	2.69	4.48	5.80	5.42	0.6	2.0	2.69
Import ratio[a] (in %)	52	78	70	8	23	35	61	137	122
Transformation ratio[b] (in %)	73	73	71	79	73	67	70	67	66

Notes:
[a] Net imports as a percentage of final consumption;
[b] Final consumption as a percentage of total energy supplies.

Source: OECD (1999b)

Also striking is the declining transformation ratio, that is, the ratio between total final consumption for energy purposes and total primary energy supply despite annual energy efficiency improvements of about 1 per cent. This is to a large extent explained by the trend towards 'high quality' energy. Indeed, electricity has more than doubled its share in total final energy consumption in the industrialised world from the 1960s to the end of the 1990s; it now accounts for one fifth of total energy consumption.

While the electricity grid in most industrialised countries was in public hands the pipeline networks were often built and financed by private companies, namely the big global players. However, from quite early on the different network providers for the same energy (electricity, oil, and gas) closely collaborated to meet erratic shifts in demand and to safeguard the security of supply. As a result, network structures were not only regional and national in their design, but also had the necessary international links.

Economic Issues in Network Analysis

From an economic point of view,[8] the historic development of transport, energy and telecommunication networks within Europe was of concern for several reasons:

- Features of 'natural monopoly' asked for state regulations to avoid monopolistic behaviour. However, often public ownership dominated these regulated sectors so that there was the imminent risk of collusion between the regulators and the regulated at the expense of the end users.
- Public ownership and monopolistic structures risked slowing down technical progress and adequate reactions to consumer needs.
- Lack of market competition, high market entry barriers and presence of collusion or regional monopolies led to an inadequate use and design of existing capacities, and price levels and price discrimination which were not satisfying from the viewpoint of consumers.
- The national orientation led to technical standards and design incompatible across borders, by this hindering the exploitation of the international network benefits.
- The non-inclusion of environmental externalities in supply and demand decisions risked to make certain developments environmentally unsustainable, for example, the modal shift in transport in favour of road transport.

Therefore policies had to be put in place to remedy and cope with these shortcomings and inefficiencies. Such policies were also required at the European level. The following section gives a brief overview on the European policy reaction and its impacts.

---

[8] For a more detailed reasoning see Bergman *et al.* (1998), Ilzkovitz *et al.* (1999) or Institut d'Economie Industrielle (1999).

5.2   THE MAKING OF EUROPEAN NETWORKS POLICIES

Given the above analysis it is quite natural that the European Union also tries to support Member States in their effort to get their network policies right. Inappropriately designed networks, incompatible national technologies and standards, and rigid and patchy rules of operating and using such networks are major stumbling blocks for further economic development and unleashing wealth-increasing entrepreneurial activity and creativity in Europe.

European Transport Policies

Already in the Treaty of 1957 founding the European Economic Community it was enshrined that Member States should pursue the objectives of European integration within the framework of a common transport policy. To this end

- common rules applicable to international transport should be laid down,
- the conditions under which non-resident carriers may operate transport services within a Member State should be defined (so-called *cabotage*), and
- further appropriate provisions were foreseen.

However, it was understood that the support of building trans-European infrastructures was not empowered by the Treaty. The late 1980s saw this seen as a major drawback. Therefore, the Maastricht Treaty of 1992 added to the above obligations of a Common Transport Policy that

- measures to improve transport safety should be envisaged, and that
- the Community should contribute to the establishment and development of trans-European networks to support the Internal Market and to enable citizens of the Union, economic operators and regional and local communities to derive full benefit from the setting-up of an area without internal frontiers.

Until 1985 the Common Transport Policy was practically non-existing as a consequence of continuing differences in approach between Member States.[9] Indeed, some Member States were characterised by stronger 'de-regulatory' or 'hands-off' traditions, with others preferring more interventionist or 'regulatory' approaches in the transport sector. These different approaches were, however, incompatible with each other. In consequence only tiny

---

[9]   For more details on the following see The EU Committee (1999).

measures on which a consensus could be reached were undertaken at the European level.

The lack of co-ordinated efforts at the European level and the high regulation density affecting the national transport sectors had led to considerable negative side-effects by the mid-1980s: border checks were numerous, and a complex patchwork of bilateral agreements impeded the development of significant international road and rail transport. The quantitative restrictions (quotas and contingents) regulating the road transport of goods between Member States increased transport prices and reduced supply possibilities. Over 50 per cent of all transported goods were regulated through contingents. Due to *cabotage* prohibitions in Member States it was estimated that until the late 1980s about one third of cross-border transport within the European Community were empty return journeys. In consequence, it was often more profitable for economic agents to invest in rent-seeking activities rather than to discover new markets.

However, in June 1985 the European Council approved the Commission White Paper (COM(85) 310) on the completion of the Single Market, which sketched out the details of a policy aiming at completing this tremendous task by 1992.[10] This White Paper stipulated amongst others that it was essential for the completion of the Single Market to abolish the existing restrictions on the provision of transport services. More specifically, it asked

- to lay down rules governing conditions of non-resident goods transport services not only for road carriers, but also for inland waterways, sea transport and air transport – all within a fixed time frame,
- to dismantle non-tariff barriers including border controls, to abolish transport quotas and the prohibition of *cabotage*.

Moreover, the White Paper also asked for common guidelines for policy fields outside a narrowly defined transport policy, but with significant implications for transport services, such as state aids, railway financing and infrastructure planning.

Important steps in liberalising transport services and creating the Single Market in transport were made eventually; 1986 saw progress for maritime transport (Regulations 4055/86 to 4058/86) and 1987 for air transport (Directive 87/601). In 1988 and in 1992 the Council liberalised the road carriage market (regulation 1841/88 and regulation 881/92).

However, adopting legislation at the European level and transposing and implementing it at the national level are sometimes two different matters. Indeed, the regularly published scoreboard of the Commission on the implementation of Single Market legislation shows that until 1998 only one out of two European Directives aiming at creating a single transport market

---

[10] For more details on this see the chapter on the Internal Market in this volume.

were transposed into national legislation in all Member States.[11] Only the telecommunications sector and public procurement had a worse record. This poor record might also serve as another example of the high levels of sensitivity towards European interference into the transport sector.

Despite its relatively slow transposition into national legislation the drive towards creating an integrated market for transport services has already had beneficial impacts. Transaction costs for cross-border transport services have come down substantially, and international competition has had its beneficial effects for downstream industries and end users. However, unsustainably fast growing road transport services have put environmental sustainability, safety and the balance between different modes of transport, including the issue of charging for infrastructure use, high on the Commission's future work programme (European Commission, 1996a, 1998b).

Until the adoption of the Maastricht Treaty the funding of infrastructure investment was exclusively part of a policy to give the peripheral countries and regions the potential to economically catch up with the rest of Europe. It was the Maastricht Treaty of 1992, which firstly created a legal basis for a trans-European infrastructure policy. In 1994 the so-called Christophersen group, created by the Council established a list of 14 priority TEN-transport projects (European Commission, 1995b), their location is shown in Figure 5.1. Important selection criteria were the supposed benefits for a trans-European transport network and the fact that their planning phase was already close to be completed. Moreover, they should be a manifestation of the new drive of the European policy of 'transforming a patchwork into a network' (European Commission, 1995c). For some projects even the construction phase was already quite advanced. All these projects are supposed to bring with them a huge traffic reorientation and re-location potential.

Three of these projects are already completed (the Oresund rail and road link between Denmark and Sweden and the new Malpensa airport close to Milano) or well advanced (namely the high speed rail link between Paris–Brussels, Cologne, Amsterdam and London), while some others are still in the planning phase. These priority projects are complemented by nine so-called pan-European transports 'corridors' linking central and Eastern Europe with its western counterpart (European Commission, 1997a).

---

[11]   See, on this, Chapter 3 in this volume.

Figure 5.1 The 14 priority TEN-transport projects

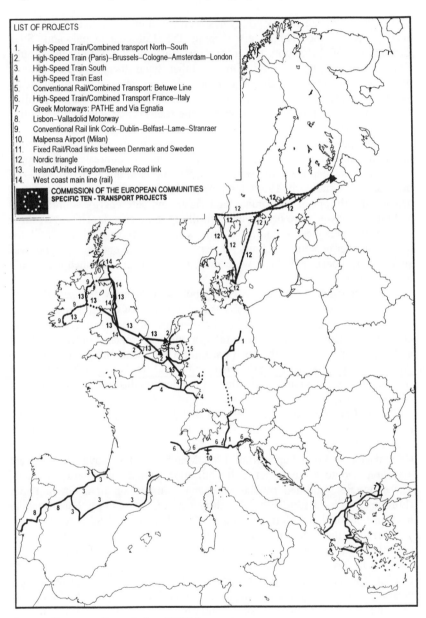

LIST OF PROJECTS

1. High-Speed Train/Combined transport North–South
2. High-Speed Train (Paris)–Brussels–Cologne–Amsterdam–London
3. High-Speed Train South
4. High-Speed Train East
5. Conventional Rail/Combined Transport: Betuwe Line
6. High-Speed Train/Combined Transport France–Italy
7. Greek Motorways: PATHE and Via Egnatia
8. Lisbon–Valladolid Motorway
9. Conventional Rail link Cork–Dublin–Belfast–Lame–Stranraer
10. Malpensa Airport (Milan)
11. Fixed Rail/Road links between Denmark and Sweden
12. Nordic triangle
13. Ireland/United Kingdom/Benelux Road link
14. West coast main line (rail)

COMMISSION OF THE EUROPEAN COMMUNITIES
SPECIFIC TEN - TRANSPORT PROJECTS

Source: European Commission (1996b).

European Energy Policy

So far, the European energy policy has been based on two pillars. On the one hand there is the Treaty establishing the European Coal and Steel Community of 1952 and the Treaty establishing the European Atomic Energy Community of 1957. On the other hand there are the general provisions for creating a Single European Market laid down in the Treaty establishing the European Economic Union. A legal basis for an explicit Common Energy Policy, comparable to the transport or agricultural policy does not (yet) exist.

Not surprisingly the European energy policy consists of two quite different elements. First, one can find policy initiatives addressing the supply of coal and nuclear as energy sources. Agreed upon in the post-war world of the late 1940s and early 1950s the purpose of these sectoral policies was to provide the European economies with cheap and safe energy sources. Coal and nuclear power were perceived as fulfilling these criteria. However, these legal provisions were set up at a time when European coal was still the dominant energy source (about 90 per cent of total energy demand was supplied by coal), and there were unfounded illusions of cheap and safe nuclear energy.

In consequence, the European energy policy of the early post-war decades was characterised by policies to foster the provision of cheap domestic coal, and to support research for making the civil use of nuclear energy possible and reliable. However, these sectorally oriented approaches entered a dead-end road in the 1980s as the legal basis for a European energy industry had not been adapted to the radically changing world (rocketing market share of first oil and then gas) and scientific and political doubts in the superiority of nuclear energy.

This did not hold for the other part of European energy policy that was embedded into the general rules shaping the creation of a European Single Market. On the contrary, with the new momentum generated by the Commission's White Paper from 1985 Member States' governments were also prepared to set on track a liberalisation of national energy markets. These policies, outlined by the European Commission in a Green Paper (European Commission, 1995a) culminated in Community Directives to liberalise national electricity markets in 1996 (Directive 96/92), and, in 1998, to liberalise the gas markets as well (Directive 98/30). Although only recently in place, the first effects for downstream industries and end users seem to be favourable. Falling prices and more flexible services seem to confirm the philosophy underlying the policy approach of progressively creating a single market and freeing market forces while simultaneously securing a certain regulatory supervision to avoid the abuse of a dominant position and to safeguard the public service obligation.

The upgrading and integration of the national energy networks has got little attention from the European policymakers, as the construction and financing of the energy networks had mainly been left to the publicly owned network operators. However, when reconsidering its network policies in the mid-1990s the Christophersen group also identified ten priority projects in the energy field that would be beneficial for an integrated European energy network (European Commission, 1995b). Key features of these projects are outlined in Box 5.1.

Box 5.1   Key features of the ten priority TEN-energy projects

---

Projects in the field of electricity distribution:

- Connecting the isolated Greek electricity grid with the Italian one through an under-sea cable, estimated investment costs: €300 million, financing through network operators, financing supported by grants from European Structural Funds and a loan from the EIB (European Investment Bank)
- Upgrading of interconnections between France and Italy estimated investment costs: €170 million, financing through network operators
- Upgrading of interconnections between France and Spain, estimated investment costs: €115 million, financing through network operators
- Upgrading of interconnections between Spain and Portugal, including an improvement of electricity networks within Portugal, estimated investment costs: €110 million, financing through network operators, supported by a EIB loan
- Improvement of electricity networks within Denmark (East–West link), estimated investment costs: €135 to 200 million

Projects in the field of gas networks:

- Introduction of natural gas in Greece, estimated investment costs: €1.3 to 1.5 billion, financing supported by grants from European Structural Funds and European loans
- Introduction of natural gas in Portugal, estimated investment costs €440 million, financing supported by grants from European Structural Funds and European loans
- Construction of a new gas supply pipeline Algeria–Morocco–Spain–France, estimated investment costs for first two phases Tanger–Tarifa and Tarifa–Cordoba €440 million, financing supported by a loan from the EIB
- Upgrading of an existing gas pipeline system between Ukraine and the EU

Source: European Commission (1995b)

European (Tele)communications Policy

The European policy in the field of communication networks is exclusively based on the legal provisions to create an integrated European market in which the freedom to provide services is guaranteed and the discrimination of non-resident service providers is not accepted. In this respect two different 'targets' for liberalisation can be identified: traditional postal services and more modern services and networks based on telecommunications networks.

While progress for the former could be characterised as rather 'modest', much progress was made in the field of liberalising telecommunications networks. The latter was helped by technical progress occurring at a time when the policy gear had shifted from 'over-cautious regulation and protection' to 'liberalisation and privatisation'.[12] This shift in gear might have been helped by the public perception that incumbent national telecommunication providers were exploiting their monopoly power at the expense of end-users. Since striving for a single European telecommunications market and liberalisation and privatisation started in the early 1990s the most important markets have undergone a dramatic change, resulting in a sharp decline of end-user prices without a corresponding deterioration in the quality of the services provided. Also the public service obligation does not seem to be endangered.

This large-scale structural change and privatisation did not lead to a massive shedding of labour, as feared by incumbent employees. On the contrary, falling prices and the rapid availability of new services let demand soar (this might serve as an indication of a highly priced elastic demand), new network providers entered the scene and overall job creation was positive. Moreover, the unleashing of entrepreneurial initiatives as a consequence of liberalisation and privatisation led to the development of numerous new markets and technologies.[13]

5.3 IMPACT ON EUROPEAN INDUSTRY

The European shortcomings in the field of transport, energy and communications networks did not trigger large spending out of the EU budget, except the above-mentioned financing of infrastructure projects in so-called peripheral regions in the context of the Structural and Cohesion Funds.[14] The focus was rather on changing the regulatory framework and stimulating investment at the national, regional and local level both by public and private legal entities.

The economic effects of these regulatory reforms are supposed to be tremendous, although hardly quantifiable. And given that large-scale liberalisation has taken effect only since the 1990s, we have not yet seen much of this. Nevertheless, it is possible to outline the mechanisms triggering these economic changes. To do so, it seems appropriate to distinguish the following different sectors of industry:

---

[12] For more details see European Commission (1994a); Bergman et al. (1998) and Ilzkovitz et al. (1999).

[13] More details on this in European Commission (1999b) and OECD (1999a). This trend confirms earlier studies on this issue, for example, the study by BIPE conducted for the European Commission. See BIPE (1997).

[14] For more details on the possibility of financing infrastructure projects under the Structural Funds and the Cohesion Fund see Chapter 10 in this volume.

- first, there are those industries that are benefiting from creating the physical infrastructure. These numerous industries, let us call them 'upstream industries', comprise a set of branches ranging from stone quarrying and road construction companies to the aerospace industry for launching telecommunications or telematics satellites.
- Secondly, there are those sectors that are providing the specialised services. Also these industries comprise totally different sectors, ranging from small road haulage enterprises to national railway companies or vertically integrated energy providers and global telecommunications companies.
- Finally, there are those sectors relying on the services that can only be provided with the help of these networks. These sectors, let us call them 'downstream sectors', effectively comprise the whole economy, including the 'upstream industries'.

Upstream Industries

Upstream industries clearly benefit from the growing use of existing infrastructures, an extension of physical infrastructures, or their modernisation. To this end, a policy aiming at the establishment, completion or modernisation of trans-European networks is warmly welcomed by these industries. This also holds for a policy aiming at the establishment of pan-European corridors through extending the western networks to the east.

Figures are easily available on how many jobs in these industries are created or secured by well-specified infrastructure projects. As an illustration, the above-mentioned 14 priority projects in the context of trans-European networks are estimated to temporarily create or secure roughly 250 000 jobs during the construction phase of these projects. However, as a stand alone analysis these figures cannot be taken as serious, as they neglect that the money could have been spent otherwise, and could also have created or secured jobs in other sectors. A more serious analysis would also have to take into account knock-on effects on other industries, on public and private spending and so on.

Such a general equilibrium analysis as opposed to a partial equilibrium analysis should normally precede the adoption of specific policy initiatives, and it is, indeed, normally undertaken for EU policies which are assumed to have a significant impact on certain industries or on the economy as a whole. Only policies with a positive benefit–cost ratio for society as a whole should be implemented. What such an analysis could look like is illustrated in Box 5.2. This analysis shows that the benefit–cost ratio of the above mentioned 14 projects is, indeed, substantially positive, including an estimated net creation of 130 000 to 230 000 permanent jobs.

Box 5.2   Economic implications of investments in trans-European transport networks

---

If one wants to analyse the economic implications of investments in infrastructure projects one has to distinguish between the construction and the operation phase of a project, and analyse the short-term demand-side effects and the long-term supply-side consequences.

The demand side effects of the construction will, in general, be transitional. They predominantly occur on the construction site itself, but also upstream industries benefit from such investment. Permanent effects will come about only during the operation phase, when the new infrastructure leads to cost savings in terms of faster or cheaper transport. Moreover, more efficient transport is not only a benefit in itself, it also increases the productivity of the economy. This supply-side effect can be used differently: increased labour productivity can be used for increased production or reduced labour demand and increased leisure time.

On the other hand, a euro spent on an infrastructure project cannot be used for other purposes, there must be a reduction either in consumption or in other types of investment, or both. Depending on capacity constraints in the economy and in directly affected sectors as well as the type of financing these projects alternative investment might be crowded out. Financing through borrowing might lead to an increase in interest rates, increased demand might set on higher inflation, so might higher labour productivity with respect to wages.

Simulations undertaken by Commission services (European Commission 1997) to estimate the economic effects of investing roughly €90 bn in the 14 projects show that short-term demand effects dominate the picture in the first decade. They lead to an increase in GDP, investment and employment. Then, and in parallel with the increasing use of the new infrastructure, the supply-side effects gradually gain momentum and dominate the picture in the long run. All in all, GDP might increase by up to 0.2 per cent, and employment might permanently rise by up to 230 000.

However, this analysis should also be seen in a broader context, as it, for example, assumes competition among upstream industries. Given that investment in transport infrastructure is predominantly financed out of public or quasi-public funds (the potential investor is a public company) intense competition must not be hampered by too rigid and too protective a public procurement policy. The European policy on public procurement is assumed to have a major positive impact on international competition by this economising on investment expenditure for trans-European networks.

The Commission's White Paper on Growth, Competitiveness and Employment (1994b) estimated that for the five-year period until 1999 the overall volume of direct investment to be mobilised for the different networks could amount to €400 billion. [15] In the meantime, much of these

---

[15]   €220 billion were assumed to go to transport, €150 billion to telecommunication and €13 billion to energy transport.

funds have been mobilised. This occurred mainly in a traditional fashion, that is, public funds for financing transport infrastructure investment, and private funds for the investment in telecommunication and energy transport networks.

However, more and more the distinction between public and private funds becomes blurred. On the one hand, formerly publicly-owned network and service providers and network investors are getting privatised. On the other hand, budget constraints have become biting and governments are looking for public private partnerships, that is, private money to match public money for certain, well-specified investment projects. So far, however, this latter initiative has had only a lukewarm response from private agents for two reasons: risks inherent in such long-term projects and uncertainty about the rate of return on the investment. The problems with the financing of the Channel tunnel might serve as examples in the first context. The problems of charging for individual chunks of a national and 'free of charge' motorway system may illustrate some facets of the latter.

Prospects for the upstream industries are all but bleak given the huge amounts of money at stake. An accelerated modernisation and extension of TENs which is at the heart of the European TENs policy contrasts with a gloomy outlook a decade ago, when highly regulated networks and public finances under severe tension did not allow the prediction of substantial investment activities in these fields. Moreover, the opening of Eastern Europe and a policy to promote pan-European corridors adds another positive note to this outlook.

Table 5.5   Pan-European infrastructure density, 1996 (m/1000km$^{2(a)}$)

	EU	CEEC[b]
Motorways	14.3	2.3
High speed railways	0.8	—

Notes:
(a)   length of infrastructure in meter per 1000 km^2 of area;
(b)   Bulgaria, Czech Republic, Estonia, Hungary, Latvia, Lithuania, Poland, Romania, Slovak Republic, Slovenia

Source: European Commission (1999a)

Table 5.5 gives an illustration of the potential for upstream industries for the transport sector, if eastern European infrastructure density with a pan-European component (that is, motorways and high-speed rail links) would have to be upgraded to western standards.

This, however, does not necessarily translate into a rosy outlook for the incumbents of these industries. On the contrary, the creation of the integrated

European market, the opening up of discriminatory and protective public procurement procedures and the profit orientation of the newly emerging network owners and providers will let only the fittest survive. Also new network technologies, especially in the sphere of communications might be different from existing ones. Thus, market entries in upstream industries are stimulated and substantial adjustment capabilities are required from the incumbents.

Network Service Providers

The successful creation of European regulatory frameworks for the different networks, successive national deregulation and liberalisation together with the connection of isolated networks and the gradual improvement of interconnections between Member States have resulted in a substantial facilitation of cross-boarder transactions for several services.[16] These changes have also intensified competition among network providers, as nationally sheltered networks had to be opened to non-resident operators.

These developments[17] have, on the one hand, put profit margins of formerly monopolistic and sheltered incumbents under pressure, especially as the rules for bailing them out with the help of State aid had become stricter. Consequently, incumbent network operators had to aim at more efficient production processes that also resulted in labour shedding. They also had to become more responsive to their clients' needs as new domestic and foreign competitors emerged through market entries and new access rules.

On the other hand, these new developments created new opportunities for innovative economic agents. Falling prices led to rising demand. The more liberal regulatory framework and technological developments allowed for new markets to emerge and new network providers to push innovation and new products. In the end, the 'Europeanisation' of networks, rules governing their use and economic transactions as a whole, have led to a complete overhaul of the structures characterising the provision of network services. Providers became vertically more disintegrated and more specialised, the cross-subsidisation of different services became more difficult, national providers entered European or even global alliances and powerful actors initially coming from other markets entered the scene.

This was most dramatic and visible for the telecommunications services, as can be seen from Table 5.6. Within some years 15 national operators have been replaced by hundreds of international, regional or even local operators, resulting in a sharp slump of prices for traditional producers without jeopardising the quality of the services.

---

[16] Rail services might still be an exception to this rule. Recent efforts to revitalise railway services and to create improved cross border transportation met substantial national resistance, and an end to this is not yet in sight.

[17] For more details of the following see Bergman et al. (1999).

Table 5.6 Impact of deregulation on prices and market structures in the telecommunications sector

	Number of operators 1999			Total % price variation 1997–99	
	(a)	(b)	(c)	(a)	(b)
Belgium	10	9	4	-23	-21
Denmark	11	11	3	-36	-30
Germany	47	47	4	-36	-67
Spain	10	10	4	-18	-27
Greece	1 (d)	1 (d)	3	-25	-16
France	31	31	3	-29	-55
Ireland	6	8	3	-54	-37
Italy	12	12	4	-28	-50
Luxembourg	6	7	4	-	-63
Netherlands	24	24	2	-33	-89
Austria	20	20	2	-41	-34
Portugal	1 (e)	1 (e)	5	-34	-49
Finland	19	14	3	3	-32
Sweden	22	22	4	-39	0
United Kingdom(f)	26	66	4	-10	0
EU-15	16	19	3	-27	-38

Notes:
(a) Long distance calls.
(b) International calls.
(c) Digital mobile market.
(d) Greece has been granted a derogation until 2001 for the introduction of competition in the national market.
(e) In Portugal four licences for the public network have been issued to date, but operators could not start commercial activity until 1 January 2000, owing to Portugal's derogation for the introduction of competition in the national market.
(f) Unweighted average.

What has been very visible for the telecommunications services seems now to be happening for the distribution of electricity, as is illustrated by Box 5.3. Enabled by the creation of a trans-European network for the distribution of electricity and the liberalisation of the European electricity market adopted by the Council in 1996, first signs of increased competition among service providers are emerging. This holds both domestically and internationally.

Box 5.3   Effects of the liberalisation of electricity markets

Liberalisation of the Community's electricity market under the terms of Directive 96/92 got underway in February 1999. Greece has a two-year derogation; two Member States – Belgium and Ireland – received a one-year derogation, so that they have now started opening their markets. As a consequence of delays in transposing the Directive into national law, both France and Luxembourg enjoyed a *de facto* derogation.

The Directive requires that an increasing share of domestic electricity consumption be gradually opened up to competition. This share was to increase from approximately 26 per cent in 1999 to 28 per cent in 2000 to some 33 per cent by 2003. The Commission will review the situation in the coming years, and may propose further liberalisation to take effect from 2006. In practice many Member States are already going beyond the minimum provisions of the Directive: in Germany, Finland, Sweden and the United Kingdom all customers are free to choose their electricity supplier. In the latter three countries, liberalisation preceded Community legislation.

Liberalisation of the Community's electricity market has taken place against a background of several years of falling prices, linked to declining energy costs and technological improvements in generation. The downward trend in electricity prices continued during the first half of 1999, notwithstanding a recovery in oil prices. Although it is too early to make a definitive judgement on the impact of liberalisation on prices to consumers, some indication of what may be expected may be gleaned from experience in the United Kingdom. When full market liberalisation took effect in 1999, all distributors cut their prices in an effort to attract new customers.

Further progress on the setting of transmission tariffs, in particular for cross-border electricity flows, remains to be made before a truly pan-European electricity market can emerge. The Commission continues to work with national electricity regulators and operators within the framework of the Florence European Regulatory Forum to reach a satisfactory agreement on this issue.

However, capacity constraints with respect to cross-border links and the existence of some still isolated electricity networks will require additional investment in trans-European infrastructures to reach all the economic benefits of integration and liberalisation.

With respect to transport networks, most of these changes have already been implemented for road transport, while rail transport is just undergoing substantial change. It is in the latter where the lack of compatibility between national infrastructure systems does not allow the efficient use of existing infrastructure. Five different electric powering systems, four different railway gauges, 16 different signalling systems and hundreds of incompatible national regulations are amongst the major stumbling blocks for using the railway network as a real trans-European one. On the one hand, these features shelter national rail companies against international competition. On the other hand, however, they render rail transport highly incompetitive *vis-à-vis* other modes of transport, finally resulting in the ever-lasting decline in market shares of this transport mode. The creation of a trans-European network for high speed passenger trains and conventional freight trains will therefore only be beneficial for rail operators if they are prepared to allow for a real trans-European use of these infrastructures and if they are in support of more compatible trans-European standards and regulations. So far, affected service providers seem to remain reluctant and lukewarm on these necessary structural adjustments. Goods transported internationally on trains still travel at an average speed of 20 kilometres an hour (European Commission, 1996d). However, deregulation and privatisation might gradually shift the balance of incentives of service providers and network owners in favour of a more efficient design and use of these networks.

Downstream Industries

The quality, density and comprehensiveness of trans-European networks and the rules governing their use affect downstream industries mainly with respect to localisation decisions and competitiveness.

Localisation decisions to a large extent depend on the availability and easy access to resources and their cost on the one side, and access to customers and markets on the other side.[18] This makes the quality of transport infrastructure an essential determinant of localisation decisions, namely of industry. A well-functioning, reliable and fast transport infrastructure is of special importance for those branches that rely on huge quantities of transported goods, or a speedy delivery of their inputs or products. While localisation decisions of companies developing computer software might predominantly be determined by the availability of a well-qualified labour force and high quality telecommunication networks, the decisions of traditional industries to a large extent depend also on the availability of an adequate transport infrastructure.

Of course, localisation decisions of industry will in the end be determined by the expected rate of return of the investment. However, this might result in a regional concentration of activities in central locations, while at the same time neglecting peripheral areas. This contrasts with European governments' preference for letting capital come to where the workers live rather than for workers to migrate there where capital materialises in factories. To this end, governments prefer a more even localisation of industry within their jurisdictions than would simply occur on the basis of market decisions. Consequently, governments try to influence the relative attractiveness of different regions for investors in favour of regionally more balanced economic activity and job creation.[19]

---

[18] Resources comprise work force and raw materials, (intermediate) goods and services.

[19] Of course, the smaller the jurisdiction the more accepted is a concentration of industrial sites as long as commuting is possible at reasonable costs for employees, and large-scale migration out of the jurisdiction for getting a job can be avoided.

This preference for capital over labour 'mobility' is also a core aim of the European Union's Regional Policy and the different funds in favour of so-called peripheral regions or regions with declining industrial activity. European policy tries to make these remote areas more interesting for potential investors by supporting Member States in coping with such problem regions, for example, by linking them to European networks or upgrading and modernising their infrastructure.

However, it should not be overlooked that trans-European transport networks mainly link central locations, be it in central regions or be it in peripheral regions. This holds especially for airports, seaports, high-speed passenger transport and so-called rail freight freeways. In the end, such networks could be harmful for non-central locations within central regions, if they were not supplemented by a dense network of high quality 'spokes' in such a 'hub and spoke' system.

Indeed, if the creation and modernisation of trans-European transport networks did not also result in improved links for non-central locations in both central and peripheral regions the negative side effects of such a policy might outpace its positive main effects. In such a case the money would have been better spent in upgrading these spokes rather than the trans-European hubs, because what counts in the end is the quality and speed of 'door-to-door' services. A high-speed train will not necessarily shorten the travel time to a remote location if it does not (contrary to the conventional train it replaces) serve all the locations any more.

Such concerns are of much less relevance for the other networks, be it road transport, telecommunications or energy networks. Road transport services are normally direct door-to-door services, while the availability of telecommunications services and energy networks means that the localisation decisions of industries are no longer of predominant importance. In Western Europe this holds even for the most peripheral regions.

The competitiveness of industrial locations is not only dependent on the quality but also on the price of the network services available. Indeed, the quality of the service and prices charged for it must be attractive for investors as well as for existing industries. Otherwise the long-term viability and international competitiveness of service-dependent enterprises and branches is at stake. Also knock-on effects of 'excessive' prices of transport, telecommunications and energy services on producer and consumer prices and on wages could have negative macroeconomic repercussions.

Regulatory authorities, given the still existing 'natural monopoly' features of most of the networks should somehow check prices and charging rules. That is why rules governing the use of network infrastructures are as important for industry as the quality of these infrastructures itself. These rules have recently changed, also as a result of European policies. Positive consequences for downstream industries were immediately visible, as well as positive macroeconomic consequences in the form of falling prices for these services, having a dampening effect on consumer prices and wage claims as well.

Technical innovation and liberalisation of network services over the last decade have not only led to falling prices for traditional services, but they also triggered new markets on a large scale, for example, mobile phones and e-commerce. Sometimes this has resulted in a partial crowding out of traditional services, for example, electronic mail substituting traditional postal services. However, quite often it has also created totally new markets, or was even at the root of a revival of traditional services, for example, Internet shopping re-launching parcel delivery services.

Most technical progress is to be expected with respect to the use of communications networks. On the one hand, this will result in an information society where everybody will have easy access to the information he needs to make well-informed choices. This will bring us closer to a perfect market, where competition is no longer hampered by high information costs for consumers. This will, however, also ask for a more important role for those services providing education and qualifications, as the trend towards better informed consumers also asks for better informed suppliers and a better qualified labour force. On the other hand, new service industries might evolve which are hardly to be foreseen. In any case, striving for modern, reliable, fast and safe trans-European networks will definitely bring us closer to a service economy with many more jobs in the tertiary sector, while employment in the primary and secondary sector will become less important.

5.4 SUMMARY AND OUTLOOK

The instruments for getting the networks and their use to be more efficient and competitive have been a support for projects which link and upgrade the physical infrastructure, the approximation and liberalisation of regulations, and the prohibition of discrimination against foreign service providers. With the help of these instruments a trans-European infrastructure and TENs is about to be shaped, and an internal market for service providers to be established. In consequence, competitive forces will be freed by allowing for intensive international competition within and between different modes and technologies, and by liberalising relevant markets and privatising publicly owned service and infrastructure providers.

With respect to the transport networks, all these measures will make transport faster, more reliable and safer. Investing in a European TENs policy will secure jobs and create new ones. It will bring the regions of Europe closer together, and it will reduce congestion, by making transport faster. These improvements will mainly benefit traditional industry, be it through increased demand, for example, for the European car industry or machine building industry, or be it through reduced transport costs for downstream industries. The vision of this enhanced Common Transport

Policy is to transform the patchwork of national networks into a pan-European one, and to make mobility economically, socially and environmentally sustainable. By this, the trans-European networks could really work as a catalyst of a competitive European industry and economy as a whole.

However, what holds for most of the transport networks in general does not yet hold for the railway system. Its decline in importance is to a large extent related to its national and bureaucratic structures. Were it not for environmental and social reasons, one could neglect this problem and categorise railway services as an outdated technology for which one should not be too much concerned if it were completely marginalised. However, for the above reasons both Member States and the European Union have launched important initiatives to revitalise railway services, both for goods and for passenger transport. If these initiatives were successful Europe could rely on a modern and well-integrated network of interoperable transport modes, in which every mode serves the function it is best suited for.

European energy networks still suffer from too weak interconnections among some Member States, and some rather isolated networks, namely in peripheral regions. These missing connections might in the end serve as the most important stumbling blocks for exploiting all the economic benefits from the recent liberalisation of energy markets. Nevertheless, the recent liberalisation initiatives have covered a lot of ground in providing European industry with cheaper energy, thus supporting its international competitiveness.

Telecommunications networks in Europe can be characterised as being up-to-date and modernised according to the state of technology. Supported by liberalisation and privatisation at both the European and the national level, vertically integrated operators as well as newly emerging entities immediately respond to market needs. If this tendency were sustainable – and presently there are no indications to doubt this – no bottleneck or rigid structures could be blamed for weakening European industry's international competitiveness.

All in all, the patchwork of national infrastructure networks is gradually being transformed into an integrated system of trans-European infrastructure networks. This process got a late start, hindering European industry from adequately exploiting the economies of scale potentially to be reaped through the gradual establishment of the Single Market and the integration of the economies. In the end, however, it is now moving in the right direction, and it is gaining pace. This is also thanks to an emerging consensus among Member States that the era of national economies has come to an end, being replaced by an increasingly global economy, and to a vigilant European downstream industry that has always pushed for these improvements. Seeing competitors in other regions of the world enjoying different (and better) models of network structures and rules governing their use, European industries never paused in pushing for beneficial reforms and liberalisation at home. The reward for this has been the newly emerging efficient and modern trans-European networks.

However, this is not yet the end of the story. The integration of central and Eastern Europe into pan-European networks is still to come. The changes this may imply for western European industries and societies can not yet be overlooked, but they might be quite dramatic. In consequence, decisionmakers in industry and politics may not rest upon past achievements, but may have to remain vigilant and attentive to adequately react to this new challenge.

BIBLIOGRAPHY

Bergman, Lars et al. (1998), General Principles and European Deregulation, in Romesh Vaitilingam (ed.), *Europe's Network Industries: Conflicting Priorities - Telecommunications,* CEPR, London.

Bergman, Lars et al. (1999), *A European Market for Electricity?,* London.

BIPE Conseil (1997), Effects on Employment of the Liberalisation of the Telecommunications Sector, study prepared for the European Commission.

European Commission (1994a), *Europe and the Global Information Society,* Recommendations to the European Council, Bangemann Report, Brussels.

European Commission (1994b), *Growth, Competitiveness, Employment. The Challenges and Ways Forward into the 21st Century,* White Paper, Luxembourg.

European Commission (1995a), *For a European Union Energy Policy. Green Paper,* Supplement to *Energy in Europe,* Brussels, Luxembourg.

European Commission (1995b), *Trans-European Networks,* Group of Personal Representatives of the Heads of State or Government, Report, Christophersen Report, Brussels.

European Commission (1995c), *The Trans-European Transport Network. Transforming a Patchwork into a Network,* Brussels, Luxembourg.

European Commission (1996a), *Green Paper Living and Working in the Information Society: People First,* COM(96) 389 final, Luxembourg.

European Commission (1996b), *The Trans-European Transport Network. Fact Sheets, State of Progress of the 14 Priority Projects,* Directorate General for Transport, Brussels.

European Commission (1996c), Towards Fair and Efficient Pricing in Transport. Policy Options for Internalizing the External Costs of Transport in the European Union. Green Paper, in *Bulletin of the European Union,* Supplement 2/96, Luxembourg.

European Commission (1996d), *A Strategy for Revitalising the Community's Railways.* White Paper, COM(96) 421 final, Luxembourg.

European Commission (1997a), *Connecting the Union Transport Infrastructure Network to its Neighbours,* COM(1997) 172 final, Luxembourg.

European Commission (1997b), *The Likely Macroeconomic and Employment Impact of Investments in Trans-European Networks,* Commission Staff Working Paper, SEC(97) 10, Brussels.

European Commission (1997c), *Panorama of European Industries, Vol. 2: A Complete Analysis of the Recent Situation and the Outlook for Manufacturing Industries and Service Sectors within the European Union,* Luxembourg.

European Commission (1998b), *The Common Transport Policy. Sustainable Mobility: Perspectives for the Future,* COM(1998) 716 final, Luxembourg.

European Commission (1999a), *EU Transport in Figures, Statistical Notebook,* Luxembourg.

European Commission (1999b), *Fifth Report on the Implementation of the Telecommunications Regulatory Package,* COM(1999) 537 final, Luxembourg.

OECD (1999a), *OECD Communications Outlook 1999*, Paris.

OECD (1999b), *Energy Statistics of OECD Countries (1960–1997),* Paris

Ilzkovitz, Fabienne, Meiklejohn, Roderick and Mogensen, Ulrik (1999), Liberalisation of network industries. Economic implications and main policy issues, *European Economy, Reports and Studies*, No. 4/1999, 11–55.

Institut d'Economie Industrielle (1999), Network industries and public service, *European Economy, Reports and Studies*, No. 4/1999, 57–215.

The EU Committee (1999), *EU Transport and Logistics Guide,* The American Chamber of Commerce in Belgium, Brussels.

6. EU Environmental Policy – a Constraint or an Opportunity for Business?

Kevin Flowers

Environmental policy and industry have often been uncomfortable bed fellows. EU industry complains that the strict environmental standards it faces compared to its competitors imposes costs and restrictions on their activities that have significant implications for their competitive position in the marketplace. With over 200 pieces of EU environmental legislation currently in force, the focus of much of industry's complaints has been the EU Commission. Yet there are companies who claim to have turned the requirements of environmental legislation to their advantage by reducing costs and improving market shares via environment-inspired process and product innovations.

The importance of environmental policy for industry goes beyond just the issue of costs and competitiveness. There are laws that influence site location and permitting, product design and R&D, international trade, corporate and site management systems, disclosure of company performance to stakeholders, company liability, and so on. This chapter starts by considering the rationale behind environmental policy and why we need policies at the EU level. A brief overview of the history and basic structure of current EU environmental policy is given before examining the main policy measures and their influence on different aspects of business activity. The chapter then examines the effect of environmental policy on overall EU business competitiveness and finishes with a look at the direction of future EU environmental policy and its implications for industry.

Why an EU Environmental Policy?

The quality of our environment affects the quality of our lives. Pollution causes ill-health, damages buildings and crops and, together with land-use planning and construction activities, can damage natural habitats thereby reducing biodiversity. There is also a tendency for society to overexploit natural resources such as fish stocks, tropical rainforest timber, groundwater supplies and hydrocarbon reserves which raises issues of fairness and equity both between this generation of people and future generations as well as between the developed and less-developed nations of the world.

Environmental policy aims to correct these market and social failures so that we can all enjoy a high quality environment and make wise use of our limited natural resources. The need for, and implementation of, environmental policies began in earnest in the 1960s when efforts to tackle air, water and waste disposal problems were initiated. The whole debate was put into a wider framework and given new impetus in the late 1980s when the concept of sustainable development was coined (see Box 6.1). This highlighted the interdependence of policies in the economic, social and environmental areas and the fact that current policies, particularly in the economic field, seemed to be pushing society down a number of unsustainable environmental pathways.

Box 6.1   Sustainable development

Everybody talks about it yet when asked to define it in concrete terms, everybody seems to have a slightly different understanding of what it actually means. The term sustainable development gained international currency following the 1987 report of the World Commission on Environment and Development (Brundtland Commission). It defined sustainable development as 'development that meets the needs of the present generation without compromising the ability of future generations to meet their own needs'. The focus at this time was very much on the environmental and resource-carrying capacity of the planet.

The 1992 United Nations Conference on Environment and Development (UNCED) that was held in Rio de Janeiro added new impetus to the debate on sustainable development but also widened the concept to include the notions of economic and social sustainability. It culminated in the Agenda 21 declaration that was signed by heads of state from around the world. Under this framework our policies have to be economically and financially sustainable in terms of growth, capital maintenance, and efficient use of resources and investments. But they also have to be ecologically sustainable meaning ecosystem integrity, carrying capacity and conservation of natural resources including biodiversity. However, equally important is ensuring the social sustainability of our policies for example in terms of equity, social mobility, social cohesion, participation, empowerment, cultural identity and institutional development

Deciding what level of environmental quality to achieve also involves recognising and dealing with a number of tradeoffs. A good illustration of this is urban air pollution. The situation in most cities is generally not unsustainable in the sense that if we continue with today's levels of pollution everybody will die prematurely, society will collapse, and so on. It is much more a question of deciding what level of air pollution-induced health impacts we are willing to tolerate and what we are willing to 'sacrifice' (that is, the 'costs') to achieve the desired reductions in air pollution – will it mean we have to use our cars less, pay more for better technology (and thus forego benefits of some other service or good that could otherwise have been purchased), and so on?

At the same time, many policy and business decisions made in areas such as transport, agriculture and energy are done without taking full account of the wider environmental and health costs. For example, when the decision is made to build a new oil- or gas-fired power plant this has probably been done without assessing the costs and risks to society of the acidifying and greenhouse gases that will be emitted by the plant. If these costs were explicitly recognised and internalised into the decision process, then perhaps more expensive but cleaner forms of energy production such as wind and solar power would become a more attractive and financially viable choice. This need for identifying the hidden costs and benefits of environmental policies is explicitly recognised in the EU Treaty.[1]

There is little dispute, therefore, about the basic need for environmental policy. However, a more interesting question is what is the justification for action at the EU level? Why not just let the Member States get on with deciding what sort of environmental quality and policies they want? Essentially, we can identify four arguments for developing EU-level environmental policies.

First, and from a somewhat altruistic perspective, the Community has been mandated by its Member States (Article 2 of the Treaty) to aim at a high level of protection and improvement of the quality of the environment. This rests on the notion that nature has intrinsic value that should be respected and protected – that we must act as stewards for the planet rather than its exploiters. Secondly, a number of environmental issues, such as climate change, are transboundary in nature and require tackling at the EU. Furthermore, where there is a significant international dimension to the problem, Community competence is desirable in order to strengthen the EU's negotiating position. Thirdly, from a more pragmatic angle, there may be a need to harmonise environmental standards and policy measures between Member States to avoid internal market trade barriers. Finally, there is the idea that if some Member States are allowed to impose much less strict environmental requirements on their companies than other Member States this will amount to an unfair competitive advantage which is not consistent with the fair trading principles of the Single Market.

Within this framework, the Commission had produced over 200 pieces of environmental legislation by the end of the 1980s. However, during the early 1990s, and with the EU facing economic recession, divisions between Member States over what direction the European project should take began to surface. A number of influential Member States questioned the need and justification for certain policy actions to be taken at the EU level. The

---

[1]   Article 174 of the Treaty stated that the preparation of environmental policy 'shall take account of the potential benefits and costs of action or lack of action'.

principle of subsidiarity[2] was promulgated and it forced the Commission into providing much clearer justifications for its policy initiatives. Environmental policy was at the centre of this debate and it resulted in the repeal of a number of existing or proposed environmental Directives. However, irrespective of these developments, it is clear that EU environmental policy, in one form or another, is here to stay and that the pressure on business to deal with the environmental impacts of its production processes and products is going to intensify.

6.2   A BRIEF HISTORY OF EU ENVIRONMENTAL POLICY

The Treaty Basis for EU Environmental Policy

Until 1987 and the entry into force of the European Single Act, there was no legal provision in the Treaty for elaborating a common EC environmental policy. This, however, did not prevent the EC institutions from proposing and agreeing upon a number of environmental policy measures. The Paris Summit held in October 1972 called for the development of a policy in this area and early legislation was introduced either under what is now Article 94 of the Treaty – the basis for harmonising laws that affect the establishment or functioning of the EU common market – or under what is currently Article 308 which allows the Community to take measures to achieve one of its objectives even when the Treaty does not explicitly give it the necessary powers.

It was the entry into force of the Single European Act in 1987 that finally put EU environmental policy formally on the map. For the first time there was an explicit treaty basis for environmental action and, furthermore, there was the inclusion of environmental protection as a Community objective in itself. The Maastricht and Amsterdam amendments to the Treaty further strengthened the legal basis for EU environmental policy by introducing the basic objective of achieving a 'balanced and sustainable development …[and]… a high level of protection and improvement of the quality of the environment' into Article 2 of the Treaty. Following the Amsterdam amendments, environment was placed under Title XIX of the Treaty which comprised Articles 174–176. Among other things, these articles state that the primary objectives of the EU's environmental policy are:

---

2   The principle of subsidiarity means that political responsibility for a given policy should be exercised at the most 'appropriate' level of government. Article 5 of the Treaty states '.the Community shall take action, in accordance with the principles of subsidiarity, only if and insofar as the objectives of the proposed action cannot be sufficiently achieved by the Member States and can therefore, by reason of the scale or effects of the proposed action, be better achieved by the Community.'

- preserving, protecting, and improving the quality of the environment;
- protecting human health;
- prudent and rational use of natural resources.

They also state that 'Community policy on the environment shall be based on the precautionary principle and on the principles that preventive action should be taken, that environmental damage should as a priority be rectified at source and the polluter should pay.' These principles are examined in more detail below. Also required was the need to take into account the 'potential benefits and costs of action or lack of action' during the preparation of environmental policy. EU legislation based on Article 174 allows Member States to apply more stringent environmental requirements provided they were compatible with the Treaty.

The Single Act of 1987 also introduced Article 100a (which became Article 95 following the Maastricht and Amsterdam amendments), that aimed to harmonise conditions of trade and competition within the single EC market and ensure that the Commission 'take as a base a high level of protection' in proposals concerning health, safety, and the protection of consumers or the environment. Although an instrument of harmonisation, Article 100a included a 'flexibility' clause (see Box 6.2), that allowed Member States the possibility of maintaining more stringent national measures than the harmonised rules agreed at Community level. Member States could keep these on the grounds of 'major needs', or protection of the environment or working environment, on condition that the European Commission did not consider them discriminatory or a non-tariff barrier to trade. In the environment sphere, this Article has been used mainly where the measure in question sets uniform standards for traded products (for example, Directive 91/57/EC on waste batteries). Since then, however, the European Court of Justice has pronounced that any EU legislation whose primary aim is to protect the environment should be proposed under what is now Article 174 of the Treaty.

Also significant was the inclusion of a clause on 'integration' in the first section of the Treaty that covers the basic principles and objectives of the Community. It reads 'Environmental protection requirements must be integrated into the definition and implementation of the Community policies and activities referred to in Article 3 [all the main policy areas of the Community including commercial and industrial policy] ... in particular with a view to promoting sustainable development.'

Box 6.2 The 'flexibility' clause

The issue of allowing Member States to apply stricter environmental standards than those agreed at the EU level can be contentious. The fear is that it can lead to unjustified trade barriers and disruptions of the Internal Market. One much publicised case is that of the so-called 'Danish can ban'. In 1989 Denmark issued a decree banning the use of metal cans for soft drinks and the use of non-returnable packaging for beer and carbonated drinks. This sat uneasily with the harmonised standards and requirements of the Commission's packaging and packaging waste Directive (94/62/EC) issued in 1994, but Denmark maintained that its stricter measure was justified on environmental grounds, specifically in terms of waste prevention.

However, given the logistical problems of collecting and re-using bottles over long distances, several EU industry associations complained that it amounted to a trade restriction that was unjustified on environmental grounds. Although at the time of its introduction Denmark might have been able to make a case on the basis of waste prevention, by the mid-1990s the case began to look rather weak, as countries including Denmark set up comprehensive systems for the separate collection and recycling of packaging waste. In other words, the can ban measure was no longer proportionate to its goal since the same level of environmental protection could be achieved by other non-discriminatory measures such as setting up a collection and recycling system for used cans and non-returnable packaging. The Commission supported this position and, after issuing a 'reasoned opinion' to Denmark in 1998, has recently followed this up by making an application to the European Court Justice against Denmark on the issue.

The successive amendments to the Treaty meant a number of changes to the voting procedures used by the European Council of Ministers when dealing with environmental legislation proposed by the Commission. It also changed the power and influence of the European Parliament in this process. Under the Single European Act, environmental measures had to be adopted by unanimous voting procedures in the Council of Ministers unless they were adopted on the basis of Article 100a (now Article 95) in which case qualified majority voting procedures applied. In both cases, however, the European Parliament had very little real power to require amendments of the legislative texts proposed by the Commission.

As the subsequent revisions of the Treaty took effect after Maastricht and Amsterdam this changed rather radically. The European Parliament has become an equal partner in the decision-making process under the co-decision procedure and in the Council, qualified majority voting procedures now apply for the majority measures proposed whether this be under what are now Articles 95 or 174–176. The European Parliament has been notorious for its strong support and demand for environmental policy measures and its new-found powers mean the Council will often find itself being pushed by the European Parliament to agree to tougher environmental legislation than desired.

The Environmental Action Programmes

The lack of a specific legal provision for environmental policy in the Rome Treaty until 1987 did not prevent the Commission from elaborating Environmental Action Programmes. The first four Environmental Action Programmes (EAP) stretched from 1973 to 1992 and evolved from being essentially a shopping list that addressed the most immediate problems (atmospheric pollution, waste disposal, and so on) to a more cohesive strategy for protecting the environment.

In 1992, the Commission presented its fifth Environmental Action Programme under the title 'Towards Sustainability.' This was an ambitious document that was, in part, the Commission's answer to the challenge laid down in the Agenda 21 document.[3] This was bolstered by the White Paper on Growth, Competitiveness and Employment presented by the Commission in 1993. The last chapter of the paper called for a 'new development model' based on the sustainable development concept which included the idea of shifting the tax burden from labour to natural resource inputs. This, it claimed, would produce a double dividend – a reduction in the level of unemployment coupled with a reduction in the levels of resource use and associated pollution.

The fifth EAP moved beyond the traditional approach of tackling the environment question on an issue-by-issue basis (air, water, waste, and so on) and focussed on the underlying driving forces of environmental degradation. It stressed the need to integrate environmental criteria into other policy areas and singles out industrial, transport, agricultural, energy and tourism policy as areas for priority attention. The traditional approach was, however, not entirely abandoned and seven priority issues were singled out for action – climate change, air quality and acidification, biodiversity, water management, the urban environment, coastal zones and waste management. Emphasis was also given to industrial and nuclear risk management.

The other important focus of the document was on the need to broaden the range and types of policy instruments used to achieve the EU's environmental objectives. Market-based instruments such as taxes, tradeable emission permits and deposit–refund systems are strongly favoured but mention is also made of other instruments including voluntary agreements (now referred to as 'environmental agreements'), environmental management system standards, eco-labels, the creation of an environmental liability regime, and so on.

Yet despite its visionary character and the broad welcome it received by the various stakeholders many would argue that the visibility and influence of the document has been much too low. This partly reflects that fact that the document, as a Communication from the Commission, had no legal standing

---

[3]   Agenda 21 had just been endorsed by Heads of State from around the world at the Earth Summit in Rio in June 1992.

or impetus. The Council, the European Parliament and Member States were in no way bound or obliged to take up the objectives or recommended policy actions proposed in the programme. Ironically, a mid-term review[4] of the 5EAP published in 1998 by the Council and the European Parliament confirmed their commitment to the general approach and objectives of the 5EAP but concluded that progress towards achieving the objectives was disappointing.

The situation with the 5EAP resulted in demands by the European Parliament that the Sixth Environmental Action Programme (6EAP) be subject to the co-decision procedure and that it contain specific quantified targets against which progress can be measured. Although it is unclear at the time of writing whether the 6EAP will be a five- or ten-year programme, it will probably be adopted in the course of 2002. Subjecting it to the co-decision procedure, however, will change the rules of the game.

The European Parliament tends to be a stronger supporter of environmental policy and its demand for the inclusion of targets will sit uncomfortably with the Council which would prefer not to have its hands quite so tightly bound. In any case, the process will greatly raise the profile of the 6EAP and will make it legally binding on Member States. This will be further enhanced by the development of a Community strategy for sustainable development which was demanded by EU Heads of State at the December 1999 meeting of the European Council in Helsinki.

Finally, but not least, the launch of the fifth Environmental Action Programme was followed very shortly by the establishment of the European Environmental Agency (EEA) in Copenhagen in October 1993. Its task is to provide objective, reliable and comparable information to help improve environmental policy development and information to the public. One of the original ideas was for the EEA to monitor implementation of EU environmental legislation in Member States but this has yet to be endorsed by the Council.

6.3 OUTLINE OF CURRENT EU ENVIRONMENTAL POLICY AND ITS UNDERLYING PRINCIPLES

The Basic Structure and Main Pieces of EU Environmental Legislation

Most of the existing EU environmental legislation has been developed on an issue-by-issue basis (air, water, waste, biodiversity, and so on) and typically either specifies environmental quality standards and emission limits for selected pollutants or sets out performance and design standards for certain

---

[4]   Decision No 2179/98/EC of the European Parliament and of the Council of 24 September 1998 on the review of the European Community programme of policy and action in relation to the environment and sustainable development 'Towards Sustainability'.

products and processes. This section gives a very brief summary of the main structure of EU environmental legislation.[5]

There is no one clear and simple way to structure and classify EU environmental legislation. This reflects, in part, the somewhat ad hoc basis on which many policy measures were initiated in the early days of EU environmental policymaking. It is also the result of a shift in policy focus from symptoms such as air pollution, waste, and so on, to underlying causes such as transport use, energy production, agriculture and industrial activity. So at the end of the second millennium, EU environmental legislation covers a whole range of issues and business activities. The main elements include legislation aimed at tackling:

- *air pollution, climate change, the ozone hole problem, and noise* including emission standards for industrial facilities and energy generators, general air quality standards, various bans on the use of ozone-depleting substances, fuel and vehicle performance standards, noise standards for certain types of machinery, and so on;

- *water quality and use* including standards for drinking water, waste water treatment, and for effluent discharges from industrial facilities and a proposal for framework legislation to cover the ecological quality of surface water bodies;

- *waste management* issues including general waste management requirements (permits, reporting obligations, control and inspection procedures, and so on), operating standards for treatment facilities such as landfills and incinerators, separate collection and recycling obligations for specific waste streams such as batteries and packaging waste, and strict controls on the shipments of wastes between, into and from EU Member States;

- *chemicals and risk management* issues – this includes restrictions and bans on the marketing and use of certain dangerous substances and preparations as well how these should be classified, packaged and labelled for use in the EU. There are strict rules on the import from and export to third countries of certain dangerous chemicals that have been banned or severely restricted within the EU. It sets out requirements for conducting risk assessments of existing and new substances;

- *industrial installations and public sector projects* – this includes permitting requirements for all large industrial installations, the obligation to undertake an environmental impact assessment for certain types of planned facilities or public sector projects and a voluntary

---

[5] Readers interested in obtaining more detailed information about EU environmental legislation might consider either searching the EU Commission's 'EUR-lex' website or obtaining the seven volumes on 'European Community Environmental Legislation' last updated in 1996.

environmental management and auditing standard that includes the requirement to publish regular environmental performance reports;

- *product standards* – this includes, for example, the elaboration of environmental standards for packaging as required by the Packaging and Packaging Waste Directive 94/62/EC, fuel quality standards, vehicle emissions standards, Eco-label, and so on.
- *nature and bio-diversity degradation* – based primarily on requirements for Member States to designate protected areas and establish management plans for these areas.

The Commission is also responsible for developing legislation on nuclear safety and radiation protection.

The Key Principles Underpinning EU Environmental Legislation

EU environmental policy is underpinned by a number of principles that have important implications for business activity. Many of these principles are now enshrined in the Treaty. For example, Article 174, section 2, states 'It [community policy on the environment] shall be based on the precautionary principle and on principles that preventative action should be taken, that environmental damage should as a priority be rectified at source and that the polluter should pay.' In part, these principles are designed to help ensure the proper checks and balances are introduced into other areas of EU policy especially where these policies have the potential to create significant pressures on the environment.

The Precautionary Principle

The precautionary principle (see Box 6.3) is one of the most hotly debated yet least well defined principles affecting both EU environmental and consumer policy. It is not a principle that is easy to submit to a set of black and white application criteria and is open to many different interpretations. Its implications for business are many. It can be invoked, for instance, to justify a ban on the use of certain substances suspected of causing a specific problem but where the actual risks are not known. A good example of this is the debate over the use of plasticisers[6] in plastic toys and children's dummies. Suspected of being carcinogenic, the Commission instigated an emergency ban on the marketing of these products at the advice of the EU Scientific Committee, whilst more research is done to find reliable ways of testing whether or not the plasticisers leach out of particular toys when

---

[6]   Plasticisers are a certain class of chemicals added to plastics, primarily PVC, to make them soft and more flexible so that they can be used for things like medical tubing, plastic bags, raincoats, toys, and so on.

chewed on by children and whether or not this presents a potential health risk.

Box 6.3 *The precautionary principle*

As the term itself suggests, the idea is that action can be taken, as a precaution, where (i) potentially serious health or environmental impacts are suspected but have not yet been proven with any degree of certainty due to gaps in our scientific understanding of the issue or (ii) where a particular problem exists but its causes are only suspected and are not known with absolute certainty.

The precautionary principle captures a simple truth. It tells us we should not necessarily wait to establish the likely effects of pollution with certainty, as by delaying action we might expose ourselves to an unacceptably high risk of damage to the environment and human health. However, per se, it does not tell us how much evidence we require before we act nor what sort of action should be taken. Examples of its application include the BSE crisis, climate change, and the current concerns about the use of genetically-modified organisms (GMOs).

The plasticisers case raises some interesting issues. The independent American Council on Science and Health recently convened an expert panel to look at the issue. After an exhaustive review of existing literature and risk data on the issue, it concluded the risks were minimal and declared the products concerned as safe. Indeed, it seems we are more at risk from drinking orange juice or eating broccoli because of the natural carcinogens these contain. Many would argue, however, that the latter is somewhat unavoidable whereas the risk from plasticisers can be avoided. Yet they confer numerous benefits to society, especially in the medical domain. So it comes down to the difficult question of balancing potential but, as yet, unquantified risks, against the benefits of using plasticisers. Not something that is easily handled by a set of black and white rules for applying the precautionary principle.

The application of the precautionary principle can also lead to trade disputes (see Chapter 7), as witnessed during the BSE crisis and with the EU ban on beef produced from cattle reared using growth hormones (see Box 6.4). The latter provoked the US to take the EU to WTO on the grounds that there was no scientific evidence that beef produced this way was harmful to humans. The WTO dispute panel ruled that the scientific methods used by the EU to arrive at its position were not satisfactory. As a result, the ban remains in place whilst the EU revisits its scientific assessment of the issue. The outcome of this will determine whether the EU can maintain its ban on the basis of precautionary arguments.

Box 6.4   The precautionary principle and the biotechnology sector

The development and marketing of foods based on genetically-modified organisms (GMOs – mostly crops but also livestock) has led the fast-growing biotechnology sector into a number of precautionary principle and trade-related problems. There is once again a heated debate between the US and the EU. Although the EU agreed to the first applications by companies to market foodstuffs made with certain GMO crops, it has now imposed a moratorium on all new applications pending further research and risk analysis.

Most of the applications have come from US firms where the rules and regulations governing the development and use of GMOs are less onerous. Everything points to another trade dispute and the EU being challenged on its right to apply as well as its interpretation of the precautionary principle. There are also concerns that the EU approach is causing the migration of the biotechnology industry to the US giving the latter another important head-start in a fast-growing high-tech industrial sector. In the meantime, the Commission has recognised the need to clarify its position and is preparing a Communication that aims to give guidance on the interpretation and practical application of the precautionary principle in EU and Member State policymaking.

Preventative Action and the Polluter Pays Principle

The exigency that environmental policy should base itself on the principle of preventative action reflects the shift in focus from trying to deal with pollution after it has already been produced to trying to encourage the adoption of practices and processes that simply do not produce pollution or other environmental impacts in the first place.

That the polluter should pay now seems a self-evident principle, but at the time of its conception and inclusion into the Community's treaty, the case was less obvious and was strongly debated by industry and other interested parties. The principle provides that the 'agent' responsible for the pollution should pay for the costs of reducing the pollution to acceptable levels. Forcing the polluters who are actually directly responsible for environmental damage to face the costs of dealing with it incites them to change their behaviour and to research technologies and products that are less damaging to the environment.

In practice, the polluter pays principle can be difficult to implement. When a car is driven and its exhaust fumes pollute the atmosphere who is the polluter – the car manufacturer or the consumer who drives the car? This has led to the somewhat conflicting notions of shared responsibility and producer responsibility. Shared responsibility rests on the idea that the various actors along the chain of manufacturing, use and disposal/recovery should accept joint responsibility for the costs of mitigating the environmental impacts across the product life cycle and that of the producer of the product. By contrast, producer responsibility works on the concept that the producer should accept responsibility for the environmental impacts that occur during the normal use and disposal of its products. The idea of producer responsibility had significant influence on recent EU waste legislation whereby producers of specific products (for example, batteries, packaging, end-of-life vehicles) have been made responsible for the separate collection, treatment, and recycling of their products once they become wastes. The idea is that this will incite the producers to design products that are less hazardous and easier to recycle when they become wastes.

6.4 THE IMPLICATIONS FOR BUSINESS

A brief review of existing EU environmental legislation shows that EU environmental policy influences business across the board from site-permitting through to product marketing and corporate image. How companies actually respond to these regulations can vary considerably. Some may adopt a more reactive approach and concentrate on installing the necessary pollution abatement equipment to meet the minimum requirements whilst other companies may decide to address the problems at a more fundamental level and try to incorporate environmental criteria into the core of their business management systems so that they succeed in designing environmental problems out of their processes and products.

It is not just an issue of costs or restrictions. Environmental policy also presents opportunities for business to develop new, innovative processes and products that allow them to gain first-mover advantages, reduce operating costs, and so on. In addition, environmental standards and requirements rarely get weaker, and inevitably, all companies are forced to meet the higher standards. Those that respond in the right way at the right time are more likely to reduce the costs of structural adjustment.

The degree to which the different pieces of EU environmental legislation influence business can vary considerably. At the same time, one particular piece of legislation can have significant implications for one industrial sector and virtually none for others. With all these issues in mind, the following section considers each of the main aspects of business activity and how they are influenced by EU environmental policy and legislation and then finishes with an assessment of the implications for the competitiveness of business in general.

Site Selection and Permitting

Industrial facilities have the potential to pollute their surrounding water, soil and air resources. They also require space and can disturb sensitive habitats as land is cleared and roads are constructed to accommodate new facilities.

As a result, the EU has produced legislation[7] to ensure that industrial activities and facilities, as well as public sector projects, with a significant potential to pollute, or otherwise damage the environment, are subject to an *ex ante* analysis that identifies the potential environmental impacts and possible mitigating measures. The sorts of facilities covered include crude oil refineries, +300MW power stations, foundries, nuclear fuel reprocessing facilities, chemical plants, motorways and major roads, long distance railways, airports, waste treatment facilities, and so on.

Managing the whole environmental impact assessment (EIA) process is important for a company. Whilst EIAs are necessary and useful, they can also be time-consuming and lead to significant design changes for the project. For example, the selection of the route for the high-speed rail link from the Channel Tunnel to London in the United Kingdom involved three EIAs of three separate routes before an acceptable compromise could be found. The final solution could only be arrived at after it was agreed that substantial portions of the line would be built underground adding quite significantly to the project's expected investment costs. At the same time, when the EIA process is well managed and its findings are taken seriously by the company involved, it can greatly ease the permitting procedure and build goodwill and trust with the local authorities and citizens.

Site permitting is also something that is subject to EU legislation – unless the company is an SME in which case it is exempted. Proposals for new facilities or for significant extensions to existing sites are subject to the requirements of the Integrated Pollution Prevention and Control (IPPC) Directive (96/61/EC). The Directive aims to encourage a comprehensive, 'one-stop-shop' permitting system for industrial installations. It requires that Member State authorities establish emission limit values, across all media (air, surface waters, groundwaters, and so on) for each industrial installation by taking into account statutory environmental quality standards, the carrying capacity of the local environment, and what can be achieved using Best Available Techniques (BAT).

Because the process of setting emission limits takes account of the carrying capacity of the local environment, similar facilities in different locations can end up facing different standards. The net result, however, for most cases will be a tightening of emission limits with consequent implications for investment and operating costs. Yet, on the other hand, IPPC brings the whole environmental permitting process under a more coherent roof which should help to simplify matters for many facilities currently faced with multiple environmental permits (for example, for atmospheric emissions, effluent emissions, waste management, and so on) issued by a number of different competent authorities. It will also help simplify monitoring and reporting procedures with consequent opportunities for cost savings.

---

7   Directive 85/337/EEC as amended 91/11/EC on Environmental Impact Assessment.

Investment and Operating Costs

Recent initiatives launched by the EU Commission via Eurostat will require Member States to collect and report data on end-of-pipe pollution control investment costs on regular basis. The EU Commission is also exploring options for requiring companies to report certain pollution control costs in their financial statements and accounts. Getting a handle on how important these costs are for companies and industry sectors is difficult. Many companies do not have accounting systems in place to distinguish these types of costs separately from more general investment and operating costs, and even where they do, it is in itself not always an easy task.

Despite its current limitations, existing data on pollution control costs tell an interesting story. At the aggregate level, data collected and presented by Eurostat[8] suggests that the costs to industry of meeting current pollution control requirements in the EU are on average about 0.6 per cent of GDP. Looking at average costs, however, masks some important variations between sectors. Analysis done in the United States,[9] where fairly detailed times series of pollution abatement costs have been collected, shows that these costs can go up to 3.8 per cent of turnover for industry sectors such as petroleum refining and down to 0.2 per cent of turnover for sectors such as publishing and printing.

In the EU, the main source of these costs is air, water and waste management legislation – the majority of which is based on EU directives and regulations. For example, a 1999 survey[10] done in the UK found that industry spent approximately €6.2 billion; equivalent to about 0.5 per cent of the UK's GDP, on pollution abatement control. Nearly three-quarters of this is accounted for by operating costs arising mainly from waste water treatment and air emission requirements. The survey also found that two-thirds of the total expenditure was accounted for by companies with over 250 employees and that just ten industry sectors accounted for 80 per cent of total spending. Finally, the survey found that 29 per cent of the total capital spending went on process improvements (clean technology) rather than conventional end-of-pipe pollution controls but, despite trying, was unable to identify spending on cleaner products.

Despite its repeated efforts to launch a CO_2 tax and now a more general energy tax, the EU has yet to adopt any Community-level environmental taxes (see Box 6.5). This, however, has not stopped Member States from

---

[8]   Environment Monograph, 'Pollution Abatement and Control Expenditure in OECD countries, 1996 (OECD/GD(96)50).

[9]   Current Industrial Reports, 'Pollution Abatement Costs and Expenditures, 1994', US Department of Commerce, Economics and Statistics Administration.

[10] 'Environmental Protection Expenditure by UK Industry: A Survey of 1997 Expenditure', Department of Environment, Transport and the Regions, United Kingdom Government.

taking action. Recent surveys[11] by the EU Commission and the OECD suggest a proliferation in the use and types of economic instruments in place across the EU covering everything from CO_2 taxes to levies on the use of plastic bags. Total revenues from environmental taxes in the EU15 were estimated to amount to €204 billion in 1997 and represented 6.7 per cent of the total revenues from taxes and social contributions. Over 90 per cent of this is accounted for by energy and transport taxes. Although many Member States have promised industry that they will make their main environmental taxes neutral by offsetting them with decreases in other taxes faced by companies, such as social security contributions, it remains to be seen whether this promise is actually kept.

Box 6.5   Economic instruments

One way of encouraging 'polluters' to minimise their impacts on the environment is to use economic instruments such as pollution taxes, tradeable emission permits, and tax differentiation. Used wisely and in the right circumstances, these can be very efficient and effective alternatives to more traditional 'command-and-control' legislation (which stipulates what has to be achieved and how it is to be achieved). For example, the EU used tax differentiation to encourage motorists to switch from leaded to unleaded petrol by lowering the VAT rates on the latter. This was highly successful and has led to significant decreases in ambient air concentrations of lead in urban areas.

Offsetting environmental taxes with decreases in other taxes on business may seem perfectly reasonable when examined at the aggregate level but closer examination at the sector level reveals some potentially worrying distortions. Consider, for example, a tax on air pollution arising from industrial facilities which is offset by a general reduction in social security contributions from all business. The sorts of sectors likely to pay the highest levels of the tax are capital-intensive industries such as the energy, petroleum refining, steel and chemicals sectors. Yet these sectors have relatively lower levels of labour intensity so will not benefit as much as say the retail or other service sectors from the general reduction in social security contributions.

R&D, Product Design and Marketing Activities

In the early days of environmental policymaking the focus was very much on controlling and reducing pollution that occurred at the manufacturing stage,

---

[11] 'Database on Environmental Taxes in the European Union Member States, Plus Norway and Switzerland – Evaluation of Environmental Effects of Environmental Taxes', European Commission, August 1998; 'Economic Instruments for Pollution Control and Natural Resources Management in OECD Countries: A Survey', OECD, 1999; 'Environmental Taxes in the EU, Eurostat, November 1999.

that is, from the industrial facilities themselves. However, despite the many and often significant improvements made at the level of industrial facilities, the growth in consumption levels seemed to be working in the opposite direction with society releasing growing quantities and different types of pollutants into the environment as a result of product use and disposal. Environment policy, therefore, began to broaden its focus to look at ways of influencing consumer demand and product design with the idea of encouraging the development and sales of 'environmentally sound' products. This meant policies aimed at influencing the R&D, product design and marketing activities of businesses.

In terms of R&D, for example, the EU Commission's Fifth Framework Programme for research and development (see Chapter 11), which runs from 1998 to 2002 and has a total annual budget of €14.96 billion. Approximately 37 per cent of this is devoted to environment related programmes such as 'Quality of Life and Management of Living Resources' and 'Energy, Environment and Sustainable Development' for its 'Quality of Life' programme which includes the support of research on environmentally sound technologies and products. At a somewhat less ambitious scale but nevertheless important is the LIFE programme run by the Commission. This aims to support both private and public sector pilot project initiatives related to environmentally-sound technologies and products. It had a total budget of €450 million for its second phase between 1996 and 1999 and the budget proposed for the third phase covering 2000–2003 was €700 million.

Product design and the rules governing the placement of products on the market are both directly and indirectly affected by EU environmental policy. Regulations such as the Directives on the marketing and use of certain dangerous substances and preparations, on how dangerous substances and preparations should be classified, packaged and labelled for use in the EU and on plant protection and biocidal products all have a direct influence on product design and placement on the market.

The EU Commission's 'Priority Waste Streams' strategy that targets specific waste streams such as batteries, cars and electronic equipment has produced regulations that include product design criteria. The Packaging and Packaging Waste Directive (94/62/EC), sets out a number of 'essential requirements' regarding the design of packaging that includes such things as limitations on the use of heavy metals in packaging. The proposed Directives on End-of-Life Vehicles, on Waste from Electrical and Electronic Equipment and on Batteries and Accumulators[12] all contain requirements that will affect the design of these products both directly and indirectly including strict · limitations or bans proposed for the use of certain hazardous substances.

Underpinning the European Commission's approach to waste management is the notion of producer responsibility or what is sometimes referred to as extended producer responsibility. The idea is that by making

---

[12] Internal Commission draft proposals and likely to be subject to change.

producers responsible for their products when they become wastes, this will encourage them to design their products in ways that are less hazardous and make them easier to recycle. Thus the current and proposed Priority Waste Stream directives all, in one way or another, make the producers responsible for the separate collection and recycling of their products when they become wastes.

But what seems nice in theory may not always be so perfect in practice. For example, industry has responded to a number of producer responsibility initiatives in the waste domain by setting up centralised organisations responsible for ensuring the necessary separate waste collection and treatment systems are established. The costs of the system are either covered by charging members a fee according to the amount of products they place on the market each year or by passing on the costs to consumers via the product price as is done under the 'Green Dot' packaging waste system set up by industry in Germany. Such systems seem to provide little incentive to companies to redesign their products. Furthermore, the costs can be significantly higher than the alternative systems for dealing with these wastes.

Other EU environmental policy developments aimed at influencing product design include the eco-label initiative. Although the EU scheme has been slow to get off the ground, national and regional initiatives such as the Blue Angel scheme in Germany and the Nordic Swan system operated by the Nordic countries have achieved significant market penetration.

The schemes all operate on a voluntary participation basis and the criteria for each product group is regularly reviewed and updated so that only the top performing products make the cut. This, in part, explains the tail-off in the number of products participating in the Blue Angel system (see Figure 6.1). Companies that wish to participate apply for eco-labels on a product-by-product basis and must prove that their products meet a stringent set of environmental criteria that have been selected by an independent panel of experts and cover relevant issues across the whole life cycle of the product from manufacturing through to recovery or final disposal. At the same time, increasing numbers of public administrations are adopting green purchasing policies that often require that eco-labelled products be favoured over non-eco-labelled ones. Since government-driven consumption of products and services accounts for anywhere between 8 to 25 per cent of total GDP expenditures in OECD Member Countries, the influence of these developments on product design are likely to grow significantly.

Figure 6.1 Number of products labelled with the Blue Angel

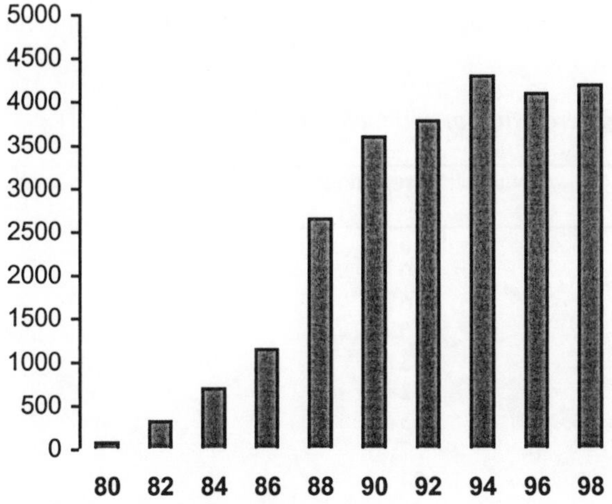

Source: RAL, Umweltbundesamt (1999)

Corporate Activities, Management Systems and Public Relations

As the pressure on companies from EU environmental legislation has grown over the last two decades so has the need for them to develop coherent business strategies and management systems that address the environmental aspects of their activities. Poor management of the latter can have serious business implications as experienced by Shell when huge numbers of EU citizens boycotted their petrol stations during the crisis sparked by Shell's proposal to dispose of one of its North Sea oil platforms by dumping it in the North Atlantic.

The implementation of corporate environmental management strategies and systems has been further encouraged by the EU's Environmental Management and Audit Scheme (EMAS) as well as the ISO 14000 series of environmental management standards. Participation in these two schemes is voluntary, but to be certified under either scheme a company must have a number of specific elements in place including an environmental mission statement, clear performance targets, comprehensive management systems, an environmental auditing system and, in the case of EMAS, the publication of regular reports available to the public on the company's environmental performance.

Uptake of the EMAS (see Table 6.1) and ISO 14000 standards has, not surprisingly, been dominated by multinational or large national companies. The limited resources and lack of environmental know-how of SMEs at the corporate level makes participation in schemes such as EMAS seem costly and difficult. Nevertheless, as multinationals put pressure on their suppliers to meet the same strict environmental standards they have imposed on themselves many SMEs are adopting tailored versions of environmental management systems.

Table 6.1   EMAS-registered sites at end October 1999

Member State	Number of registered sites
Germany	1786
Austria	200
Sweden	146
Denmark	110
UK	73
Spain	42
France	33
Finland	27
Netherlands	24
Italy	21
Belgium	9
Ireland	6
Luxembourg	1
Greece	1
Portugal	0
EU15	2537

Source: European Commission

But the pressure on companies to adopt corporate level environmental business strategies and associated management plans is not only coming from pure environmental regulation or management standards. Increasing awareness of environmental issues, both in terms of their affects on company performance as well as from a liability perspective, in the banking and investment community is leading to demands for certain types of environmental performance criteria. This has even led the Commission into considering a proposal that would require EU companies to disclose selected information on environmental costs and investments in their annual financial reports.

Trade

The relationship between trade (see Chapter 7) and the environment is a subject of much debate and, with the trend toward economic globalisation, of growing concern. Key issues are the extent to which trade liberalisation is compatible with environmental protection and the effect that environmental policy has on competitiveness.

From a business perspective, the main concerns are:

- the relationship between environmental measures and market access;
- the potentially restrictive effect of the Agreement on Trade-Related Aspects of Intellectual Property Rights (TRIPS) on the transfer of environmental technology;
- the development of eco-labelling programmes, technical regulations; systems where producers are made responsible for waste collection and recycling schemes aimed at specific products categories;
- the application of the precautionary principle;
- environmental charges and taxes;
- the issue of exports of domestically prohibited goods;
- the trade-restrictive elements included in multilateral environmental agreements (MEAs) such as the UNEP Basel Convention restricting the trade of hazardous wastes · and the UNEP CITES convention (Convention on the International Trade of Endangered Species) that restricts the trade in endangered species.

The EU Commission is committed to addressing the issues of trade and the environment. It takes the view that both are equally important and argues that trade liberalisation and environmental protection can play a mutually supportive role. An improved trade regime is likely to encourage a more efficient use of natural resources. At the same time, however, a more open trading system is also likely to lead to increased economic activity, which, without the appropriate controls, could place additional burdens on the environment. In its Communication of 1996 (COM(96) 54, 28 February) and since, the EU Commission has identified a number of priorities that have been proposed for rule-making negotiations in a future World Trade Organisation (WTO). Many of these issues have been addressed by the WTO Committee on Trade and Environment, established in 1994. Key elements include:

- the ability to use trade restrictions in multilateral environmental agreements where justified and considered necessary;
- the need to clarify the relationship between new instruments of environment policy (especially eco-labels) and trade rules;
- the need to reinforce the sustainability objective in WTO, and to more fully integrate the Precautionary Principle into the rules and dispute settlement processes of the WTO;
- the need to ensure the proper inputs and co-operation of both trade and environmental experts in dispute settlement cases.

Progress has been very slow because developing countries fear that the agenda is a bid to cover protectionist policies aimed at their exports and because the US and some other developed countries seem less sure that the greening of WTO can be in their own long-term interests. On the other hand, it is clear that European public opinion wants stronger WTO guarantees that trade-led globalisation can be allowed to go forward without despoiling the planet.[13]

To date, most environment–trade disputes have centred around product-related issues such as the Danish ban on the sale of certain beverages in metal cans. The proposed Directives on Waste from Electrical and Electronic Equipment and on End-of-Life vehicles contain bans on the use of lead on solder which has already led to warnings from US business and government that they consider this would represent an unjustified barrier to trade.

More contentious, however, is the debate on whether trade restrictions based on *how* products are manufactured can, and should, be allowed. The US ban on imports of tuna caught using 'purse-string fishing net' methods (a method that inadvertently kills many dolphins) was perhaps the first case of this kind to go to a GATT dispute settlement panel. In the end the case was lost with the dispute panel ruling the rules do not permit signatory nations to 'restrict imports of a product merely because [the product] originates from a country with environmental policies different from its own'.[14] However, this general issue is far from having been resolved.

At the moment, the conventional reading of the rules of the GATT/WTO Agreements is that a country must not discriminate between the imported products from one country as compared with 'like products' from another country. One of the main requests made by environmental groups in advance of the Seattle WTO Ministerial meeting in December 1999 was to redefine the concept of 'like products' to permit discrimination not only with respect to product performance characteristics but also in terms of the environmental performance of the production facility that manufactured the product – often referred to as the product's 'process and production methods' (PPMs). Under this system, a country could impose trade barriers on products deemed to have been *produced* in an environmentally unsound manner. This issue has already become a point of discussion between trade and environmental experts because eco-labels represent an indirect form of discrimination on the basis of PPMs. Eco-labels are awarded on the basis of performance criteria across the whole life cycle of a product and they influence demand for a product in the market.

Industrial Competitiveness

There is much debate on how and to what extent the requirement to meet strict environmental standards affects the competitive performance of

---

[13] On the role of business in calming these fears, see also Chapter 7.
[14] Quoted in Robert Housman and Durwood Zaelke, 'The Collision of the Environment and Trade: The Gatt Tuna/Dolphin Decision', *Environment Law Reporter*, April 1992.

industry. The general perception is that EU industry faces a competitive problem relative to both high technology rivals (for example, US and Japan) and low-cost competitors (that is, newly industrialised countries).

Analysis at the aggregate level, however, provides little convincing empirical evidence that the relative stringency of environmental regulations in different countries has had any significant effect on industrial competitiveness. A preliminary analysis made recently by the World Bank (see Figure 6.2), found that industries most affected by higher environmental standards have performed relatively well in international trade terms over a period (1970–90) in which environmental compliance costs were rising. Industries covered by the analysis included pulp and paper, petroleum products, chemicals, coal mining, fertiliser, cement, ferrous and non-ferrous metals, metal and wood manufacturers. In fact, it would seem that industrial countries with strict environmental standards have had more export success in these environmentally sensitive industries than they have had in their manufacturing sector as a whole.

Figure 6.2 Percentage share in total world exports of manufactures and of environmentally sensitive goods, industrial countries 1970–90

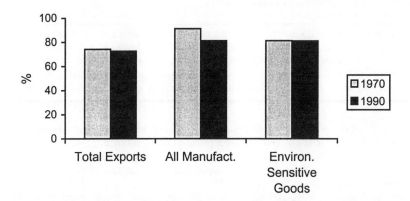

Source: Piritta Sorsa, World Bank

At the sector level, a recent study[15] completed for the EU Commission concerning the impact of EU environmental regulation on the competitiveness of the EU chemicals industry produced similar findings. It concludes that empirical data on the evolution of production, trade shares, and productivity of the EU chemical industry strongly suggests that the

---

[15] Study on the Impact of EU Environmental Regulation on Selected Indicators of the Competitiveness of the EU Chemical Industry, Volume 1: Synthesis, May 1998, European Commission, Directorate-General Environment, Nuclear Safety and Civil Protection.

relative strictness of environmental regulation is not a significant determinant of the sector's competitiveness. It would seem, therefore, that differentials in elements such as infrastructure, labour costs, management and labour skills, the fiscal regime, raw material costs, proximity and access to relevant markets, and so on, overwhelm any environmental compliance cost differentials when it comes to considerations of industrial competitiveness and productivity.

Case study analysis at the level of the firm points to a slightly more heterogeneous picture with evidence of some sectors and companies suffering adjustment costs following the introduction of high environmental standards. This, however, tends to be limited to more mature industry sectors such as the cement and steel manufacturing. Yet, the literature abounds with an equal if not greater number of well-documented case studies of sectors and firms that have been able to turn the imposition of strict standards to their advantage. This has usually been achieved by process and product innovations that resulted in cost reductions, resource efficiency improvements, market share increases or the development of new products and markets (see Box 6.6).

Box 6.6   Environment and innovation

One of the better known illustrations of how environment policy can drive innovation and give companies a competitive edge is that of the Swedish pulp and paper industry. In the United States, water discharge regulations were imposed on the pulp and paper sector during the 1970s without adequate phase-in periods, forcing companies to adopt existing best available technologies quickly. At that time the requirements usually meant installing costly end-of-pipe water effluent treatment systems.

In Scandinavia, a more flexible regulatory approach was adopted involving the initial use of loose standards and adequate phase-in times coupled, however, with a clear signal that tighter standards would follow. This enabled Scandinavian companies to focus on the production process itself, and not just of the secondary treatment of wastes.

Scandinavian companies developed innovative pulping and bleaching technologies (so-called 'clean technologies') that not only met emission requirements but also lowered production costs. Spurred by Scandinavian demand for sophisticated process improvements, local equipment suppliers ultimately made major international gains in selling innovative pulping and bleaching technologies. In addition, the Scandinavian pulp and paper industry reaped spill-over advantages as they were able to meet the growing niche market of the late 1980s and early 1990s for totally chlorine-free paper, whilst its competitors lagged behind, and thus were able to charge premium prices.

But what of SMEs? The general perception is that SMEs can be disproportionately burdened by regulations if account of their size and scarce financial and human resource is not taken. Environmental regulations designed with large companies in mind and applied without due consideration of the specific characteristics of SMEs, might impose significant and excessive costs on SMEs. Once again, however, empirical evidence does not seem to bear this out. A detailed analysis[16] of the European food processing sector that compared responses and performance of 67 firms in Germany (east and west), Ireland, Northern Ireland and Italy (north and south) found 'no evidence that existing levels of environmental regulations hindered any company from achieving internationally competitive performance.' Indeed, the findings tended to suggest that those firms that were the most competitive were often those that had also put the most effort into improving their environmental performance.

On a slightly different but related front, environmental legislation has also been an important driver behind the creation of the so-called 'eco-industry' sector. Europe has witnessed significant growth of its eco-industry which includes, amongst others, the wastewater treatment, waste management, air quality control, environmental consultancy and monitoring sectors. Because of a lack of common definitions and methodologies, most data concerning the size and growth of the industry are estimates and need to recognised as such.

Figure 6.3   Estimated market size of eco-industry in 1990

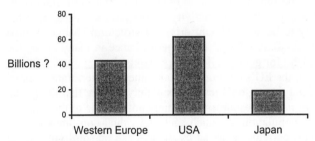

Source: OECD

The OECD estimates that the market size of the western European eco-industry in 1990 was approximately 43 billion ECU with an predicted growth rate of 4.9 per cent per annum between 1990 and 2000. This compares to €62 billion and 5 per cent for the United States and €19 billion and 6.7 per cent for Japan (see Figure 6.3). The next stage is likely to see industry internalising the management of these requirements and shifting to resource efficient clean technology solutions.

---

[16] 'The Firm, Competitiveness and Environmental Regulations: A study of the European Food Processing Industries' by David Hitchens, Esmond Birnie, Angela McGowan, Ursula Triebswetter, and Alberto Cottica (published by Edward Elgar).

6.6   CONCLUSIONS AND OUTLOOK FOR THE FUTURE

In the grand scheme of things, EU environmental policy is clearly not the most important policy area in terms of its influence on business activities, at least not in terms of costs and competitiveness. Empirical evidence suggests that differentials in factors such as labour costs, access to infrastructure, management skills and raw material costs far outweigh environmental factors. But the importance of environmental policy for industry goes beyond just the issue of costs and competitiveness. There are EU laws that influence site location and permitting, product design and R&D, international trade, corporate and site management systems, disclosure of company performance to stakeholders, company liability, and so on.

Although much of industry would view EU environmental policy as a cost burden or a restriction on their freedom to operate, it can also present business with important opportunities. These range from resource efficiency improvements and associated cost savings to the development and sales of clean technologies and eco-products. A number of indirect benefits can also accrue to companies that implement proactive environmental management strategies including, for example, the ease and speed with which such companies are granted permits to build new facilities because of their good reputation with the authorities.

When we look to the future, one can only conclude that the influence of EU environmental policy on business activity is going to increase and, in the longer-term, is likely to be an important driver of structural change. Whilst EU industry has successfully cleaned up its performance in many areas, the sheer growth in demand for goods and services is outstripping many of these gains and the status of the EU's environment continues to deteriorate across a number of fronts. On a more global level, it is plainly evident that the planet and its endowment of natural resources are simply not capable of meeting the demands of a world population in which each individual consumes natural resources at the levels currently enjoyed by the average person living in the industrialised countries.

Society and business will have to find new ways of meeting our demands for goods and services that are hugely less resource-intensive and that give rise to environmental impacts that are within the carrying capacity of earth's eco-systems and that are tolerable from a quality of life perspective. The focus, therefore, is now on integrating environment into the other policy areas such as energy, transport, industrial and agricultural policy. One manifestation of this is the initiation of the so-called Cardiff Process whereby various formations of the Council of Ministers have been mandated by EU Heads of State to prepare strategies for integrating environmental criteria into each policy area.

This includes the Councils on Transport, Agriculture, Energy and Industry. They are also required to develop a set of indicators that can be used to measure the progress of the integration strategies. If successful, the implications of this process for industry will be significant. For example, it would almost certainly mean important changes to the way in which transport services and energy production are structured and provided. As environmental externalities (the costs of pollution that are borne by society as a whole but not directly by the polluter) of transport and agriculture are internalised, costs per unit of service provided are likely to increase. The challenge to business will be to find more transport and energy-efficient ways of manufacturing goods and providing services so that overall costs and productivity are not adversely effected.

At a more general level, the focus on underlying driving forces is leading to new policy initiatives such as the implementation of producer responsibility (for example, for collecting and recycling their products when they become wastes as witnessed by the proposed Directive on end-of-life vehicles), the development of integrated product policy and the use of associated instruments such as the EU eco-label scheme, and a greater focus on market-based instruments, particularly taxes, in an effort to change the behaviour of consumers via price signals in the market place. The latter is being coupled with the wider notion of shifting the tax burden from labour to resource use – taxing the 'bads' instead of the 'goods'. Furthermore, if the EU commitments to reduce the emissions of greenhouse gases (GHG) are to be met, as required under the Kyoto Convention, then significant investments as well as changes to how things are done will be needed in many sectors of industry.

Behind all this lies the increasing demand from the citizens, NGOs and even Member States for the EU to clarify its vision and strategy for achieving sustainable development – hence the creation in 1999 of a high-level EU Commission task force on Employment, Growth, Competitiveness and Sustainable Development. Environmental objectives and policy represent one of the main pillars of the sustainable development concept. If the EU decides to take this challenge seriously, then environmental policy will move towards the centre stage and greatly influence how we organise our society and the framework within which the market and business activity operates.

In the end, the winners will be those companies and countries that understand the importance of all this and make the right decisions at the right time so that they minimise the risks and costs of the inevitable structural changes that will occur. At the same time, the EU environmental policymaker has a duty to ensure the environmental targets and objectives are achieved at least cost to society and to EU business. He also has a duty to ensure the costs are reasonable when compared to level of impact or risk reduction that is likely to be achieved by the policy measures. But perhaps the biggest challenge to both the policymaker and industry is that of identifying and encouraging opportunities for efficiency improvements, new product and service innovations and changing consumer behaviour.

BIBLIOGRAPHY

Arthur D. Little (1996), *Sustainable Industrial Development – Sharing Responsibilities in a Competitive World.*

Council (1993), Council Regulation (EEC) No. 1836/93 of 29 June 1993 allowing voluntary participation by companies in the industrial sector in a Community eco-management and audit scheme, OJ L168/1.

EC Committee of the American Chamber of Commerce (1998), *EU Environment Guide*, Brussels.

Ecotec Research and Consulting Ltd. (1996), *Data Collection on Eco-Industries in the European Union.*

Ecotec Research and Consulting Ltd., Ivam Environmental Research, Zenit GmbH (1996), *New, Clean and Low Waste Practices and Ways of Promoting their Diffusion*, Brussels.

European Commission (1992*), Towards Sustainability – A European Community Programme of Policy and Action in Relation to Environment and Sustainable Development,* COM(92) 23.

European Commission (1997), *Environmental Taxes and Charges in the Single Market,* COM (97) 9 final, Brussels, 26.03.1997.

Eurostat (1999), *Environmental Protection Expenditure in Member States 1988–96*, first edition, Luxembourg

KPMG Environmental Consulting (1997), The Environmental Challenge and Small and Medium-sized Enterprises in Europe, Amsterdam.

OECD (1999) *Greener Public Purchasing: Issues and Practical Solutions,* doc. ref. ENV/EPOC/PPC(pp)3/REV1, OECD, Paris.

Parry, I. and Oates, W. (1998), Policy analysis in a second-best world, Discussion Paper 98-48, Resources for the Future, Washington.

Vogel, D. Haas School of Business, University of California, Berkeley, EU Environmental Policy and the GATT/WTO, a paper prepared for a conference on 'Regulatory Reform and EU Environmental Agreements', European University Institute, Florence, Italy.

7. Trade Policy – Opening World Markets for Business

Robert Madelin

In the global economy, when the smallest company can be a world player, why do European industrialists need to worry about EU trade policy? European exports to the US of cashmere sweaters and scented candles were threatened in 1999 by the fall-out from transatlantic disputes about trade in beef and bananas. This is just one proof that, in an increasingly complex world, Europe's foreign trade relationships matter because, however remote they may appear to be from industry interests, their impact can turn out to be direct and damaging.

More generally, global economic interdependence[1] requires all business operators to interpret trade as a broad concept. Trade is no longer limited to questions of import duty and import quota on manufactures and commodities. It applies also to internationally traded services, foreign direct investment and intellectual property rights. Nor do trade policy concerns stop at the border. It is increasingly likely that effective access by exporters in one country to the market of a second country depends not only on border measures but also on the effects (discriminatory or otherwise) of that second country's rules and regulations.

Box 7.1   Trade and business: the key points

Europe has an open trade policy of long standing and has made particularly rapid progress in the last decade in eliminating exceptions to this policy. Europe makes no attempt to fit all issues into a rigid straitjacket, so exceptions will not all be swept away, nor is there any prospect of full free trade becoming the objective, in Europe or anywhere else in the world. But Europe's openness compares well with that of other benchmark world economies and Europe is playing a leading role in the strengthening and extension of the worldwide, rule-based trading system. Business can and should both take advantage of the present opportunities offered by trade policy achievements and regard the defence of an open economic model in the trade field as a priority in the years ahead.

---

[1] The Commission's 1993 assessment of the trade/globalisation interface is still the best short study.

7.1   THE FRAMEWORK FOR EU TRADE POLICY

The authors of the Treaty of Rome already realised that any group of countries pooling policy to create an internal common market would also require a coherent policy for trade with third countries who wanted access to that market. So a 'common commercial policy' constitutes one of the core elements of the founding Treaty of the European Union. International trade is not an end in itself, but a means of enhancing economic welfare. The Treaty sets for Europe the objective of progressively abolishing trade restrictions, lowering barriers and facilitating the 'harmonious development of world trade' (Article 131 of the Treaty).

Why should that be? There are a variety of reasons. The classic economic reason, known to the 'Founding Fathers of the Treaty', is that to lower Europe's barriers to imports would bring economic benefits to Europe: even if import liberalisation brought job losses or reduced sales for some, the continent as a whole would be better off. This vision was enough to persuade the six original Member States to aim at fully free trade among themselves, and to persuade them of the benefits of progressively more open trade with the rest of the world. More pragmatically, they also expected that, on the export front, European companies operating from the enlarged domestic base of a single market would be competitive enough to reap the benefits of an open world trading system.

Trade policy covers trade in agriculture products, commodities and manufactured goods, including nuclear, coal and steel products. Services provided across borders are also covered by the common commercial policy. In addition, common policy applies to areas where internal European policy has already been made in a way, which transfers decision-making power ('competence') to the Community institutions. What all this means is that, as a practical matter, the vast majority of trade policy negotiations fall essentially but not exclusively to the competence of the Community rather than to the national competence of Member States. While ad hoc decisions in areas such as dumping, textiles or agriculture can therefore be taken by a 'qualified majority' vote of Member States in the Council, policy on any broader trade agenda, of the sort that arises in a round of WTO negotiations, will fall under 'shared competence' and must therefore be decided by unanimity among the States.

In theory, such a policymaking process could produce inertia and sometimes it does, not least because the process tends to seek consensus even where a qualified majority vote would suffice. In practice, however, Europe's natural leading role in the development of international economic relations creates a sufficient impetus in Council debates that Member States usually produce a clear line in a timely manner. The difficulty in co-ordinating positions is in any case a cloud with a silver lining: intense internal peer review means that positions adopted will have been thoroughly debated and are usually capable of withstanding further scrutiny during negotiations. By contrast, unitary trade policy administrations produce simpler proposals more quickly, but need to adjust them thereafter to take account of considerations not raised during internal debate.

The Commission, the Council of Ministers and the Parliament all have an interest in the formation of trade policy. Broadly, the Commission initiates trade policy and is the sole voice of the Community in negotiations with the rest of the world, the Council gives the Commission the necessary mandate to negotiate and follows the course of the talks, the Parliament works from a position of relative constitutional weakness to influence the mandate to the Commission and joins with the Council to ratify the results. With so many players in the policymaking process, businessmen (or other stakeholders) seeking to make their interests and views known can easily get access to some of them but will have to devote considerable effort to making sure that they have covered all the potential players: the European decision-making process is as transparent as any, but its complexities make it a time-consuming target for the lobbyist.

Policy in Practice

The Treaty's basic choice in favour of open[2] trade has been fully matched by Europe's leading role in the explosion of the world economy since the Second World War. 25 per cent of global output is now traded internationally, and the European Union makes a considerable contribution to that trade.

The EU is the world's largest trader; accounting for 20 per cent of merchandise exports (the US represents 16 per cent and Japan 9 per cent). The EU is also the world's largest exporter of commercial services, with a 24 per cent share of the world market in 1997 (US, 19 per cent; Japan, 9 per cent). These figures are no longer generated by the interplay of distinct national economies. We no longer know which are 'our' companies, 'our' cars, and 'our' aircraft.[3] The volume of foreign direct investment (FDI) has been growing three times as fast as world trade during the last decade. Both FDI and visible trade are driven to an increasing extent by so-called transnational corporations (TNCs), such that 25 per cent of world trade is estimated to be intra-firm trade, and the gross product (total as opposed to internationally traded output) of the world's almost 300 000 foreign affiliates accounts for 6 per cent of world GDP, and almost 10 per cent in developing countries.[4]

---

[2] 'Open' trade but not, as explained in Chapter 1, 'free trade'.

[3] Nobody, for example, regards a Ford or an Opel as a non-European car. When some Europeans argued in the 1980s that a UK-built Nissan Bluebird was Japanese rather than European, the Commission was swift to rule that these Nissans too had become European cars.

[4] The annual UNCTAD studies of international investment activities are unparalleled sources of data and analysis in this field.

Table 7.1   EU trade in goods (1998)

	The major import partners				The major export partners		
Rank	Partners	€ M	%	Rank	Partners	€ M	%
	World	709.227	100.0		World	729.236	100.0
1	US	150.756	21.3	1	US	159.807	21.9
2	Japan	65.511	9.2	2	Switzerland	56.934	7.8
3	Switzerland	49.229	6.9	3	Japan	31.418	4.3
4	China	41.788	5.9	4	Poland	28.066	3.8
5	Norway	29.023	4.1	5	Norway	24.887	3.4

	The major import products				The major export products		
Rank	Products	€ M	%	Rank	Products	€ M	%
	Total of which	709.227	100.0		Total of which	729.236	100.0
1	Electrical machinery	53.565	7.6	1	Road vehicles	68.026	9.3
2	Office mach. (PC)	52.204	7.4	2	Electrical machinery	52.558	7.2
3	Oil	46.859	6.6	3	General ind. machinery	47.145	6.5
4	Articles of apparel	40.762	5.7	4	Specialised machinery	43.955	6.0
5	Road vehicles	36.632	5.2	5	Other transp. equipments	40.809	5.6

Source: European Commission (1999)

Treatment of foreign affiliates investing in Europe is as open as treatment of imports. Under a principle laid down from the first draft of the Treaty of Rome, foreign (non-EU) investors established in any of the European Member States must be treated in all the other member countries just like any home-grown European company. Setting up a shell company or a branch in Europe will not enable a foreign corporation to meet this 1957 establishment test, but all free-standing companies and subsidiaries genuinely operating in Europe will benefit. Despite these figures, Europe is not a free trade economy. There are no such economies in the world today, if there ever have been. 'Free trade' is a widely used shorthand for broadly liberal policies, but genuine free trade is too simple a policy prescription for a world where there exists a widespread desire to resist international co-operation among Mafiosi, producers of pornography and drugs, illegal arms dealers and terrorists. It is also too simple an approach for a world where competition is imperfect, to say the least. Nor is there consensus in Europe or anywhere else to abandon all potential defences against even legitimate competition from foreign economies that public opinion often feels are less open to 'our' exporters or investors than we are to theirs.

Short of free trade, then, the European trade policy stance (reflected in numerous specific decisions but not set down in a single instrument or document) is of leadership and support for the multilateral 'open' (not free) trading system established in 1947 under the aegis of the General Agreement on Tariffs and Trade (GATT) and maintained since 1995 by the World Trade Organisation (WTO).

Within WTO, Europe has progressively liberalised import protection in parallel with liberalisation by others.[5] Europe maintains current protection in conformity with WTO rules. Europe develops its network of preferential trade relationships within the WTO rules for such special arrangements. Each of these aspects of trade policy are dealt with in the remainder of this chapter. This is not the place for a detailed description of WTO policies,[6] but some key WTO rules should be borne in mind (see Box 7.2).

Box 7.2   Some key WTO principles

Non-discrimination among foreigners (the so-called most favoured nation clause) so that the European Union should apply the same policy to imports of a given product from all sources.

- National treatment, so that foreign products are treated like local products on the domestic market.
- The right to regulate for public policy purposes, such as consumer or environment protection, but the duty to do so transparently, and without placing unnecessary burdens on business.
- Peaceful dispute settlement, so that conflicts over access to each other's markets are dealt with under international rules and not by the use of force, whether military or economic, naked or covert.

---

[5] And, in practice, the EU economy has become considerably more open since the completion of the single market in 1992, with imports of goods and services now taking 12 per cent of the market as opposed to 10 per cent before its completion. This compares with the US at 13.5 per cent and Japan at 9 per cent. More comparative analysis of EU openness can be found below.

[6] The WTO's own publications and website are essential for any student of trade issues.

7.2   WHAT ARE THE MAIN IMPACTS OF TRADE POLICY ON INDUSTRY?[7]

This section highlights key areas where trade policy can affect:

- Imports
- Exports
- Access to new markets

Modest Protection at Home

Import duties are the normal and legitimate means of imposing border protection under WTO.

The creation of a common customs tariff, and common import duties, was the fundamental first step towards creating a common trade policy for the European Community. At the time of its creation, average duty/tariff rates differed sharply, from around 6 per cent for Germany to 19 per cent for Italy in 1958. Ten years later, a common external tariff existed at an average of 10 per cent. This has been reduced step by step since then in successive GATT negotiations, and on the basis of all deals done to date, the average import duty in manufactures stands at 3 per cent. Most manufactures face not even this level of import duty. Roughly one-third of manufactured imports enter duty-free, either because they come from near neighbours with whom preferential duty-free arrangements exist or because they come from developing countries which benefit from duty-free access on a non-reciprocal basis. Another third of imports enter at preferential rates below the bound tariff, leaving imports from essentially non-European developed countries facing the 3 per cent average (see Box 7.3).

Duties are the norm today. In Europe, however, quantitative restrictions on trade were very widespread in the immediate aftermath of the Second World War, largely on balance of payments grounds. Their removal was one of the key elements of the post-war recovery plan. Yet, in the early 1990s, there remained roughly 10 000 quotas, maintained by individual Member States largely on imports from State-trading countries. There are now only a handful of quotas on footwear, porcelain and ceramics from China, and these are on the table in the WTO accession talks.

---

[7]   This section draws essentially on independent assessments by the WTO Secretariat and OECD, which together provide more detailed and comprehensive accounts than is possible here.

Box 7.3   Import duties: issues for business

Whether you buy goods from a non-EU supplier for an EU operation or import your own products from a non-EU subsidiary, the import duty levied will hit your cost structure. How to minimise costs?

If the product is available from several sources, you might choose a source whose exports enter duty-free (Switzerland, Poland, Turkey) or at reduced rates (Brazil, Thailand).

If the product can be imported as a finished good, a semi-manufacture or as a raw material, one of these options might be cheaper than others. Example: the duty on raw aluminium and finished products is 6 per cent, but it is 7.5 per cent on semi-manufactures. For leather, raw hide is duty-free, prepared leather is 3.7 per cent while finished goods are 5.5 per cent.

If the product cannot be found in Europe, an ad hoc duty waiver can be granted.

In the next Round of WTO negotiations, you can argue that EU duties on the product should be reduced as part of the overall deal.

These cases apart, quantitative restrictions also apply in the textiles and clothing field. Here, a general WTO regime, the Multi-Fibre Arrangement (MFA), has allowed developed countries to maintain quantitative protection in a sector where employment and production in the developed world has been falling rapidly over the past three decades, while developing country production and market share have increased. It is now agreed that MFA protection will be phased out, the final disappearance of all quotas for WTO members being set for January 2005. Already, three-quarters of textiles and clothing imports enter Europe free of quota, and the regime is adjusted by a process of continual bilateral negotiations with the principal supplier countries, which ensures that barriers are further lowered wherever opportunities arise. Paradoxically, many supplier countries support the maintenance of quota regimes for the time being, because they fear that their own industry will lose out to more efficient production in other developing countries once a free market is in place (see Box 7.4).

Another form of non-tariff restriction is the voluntary restraint agreement (VRA). Such informal, usually industry-run restraints on levels and/or prices of exports were applied particularly in the 1970s and particularly (in the case of Europe) to trade with Japan. A major achievement of the Uruguay Round was to prohibit the use of such inter-industry arrangements, and to require their phase-out. The single market programme had already set the scene for their disappearance in Europe by the early 1990s, and the high-profile restraint arrangement on trade in cars between Japan and Europe has now expired at the end of 1999.[8]

---

[8]   The creation in 1981 of a common EU quota regime for Japanese car imports marked the start of good trade relations with Japan. It required a complex deal whereby markets traditionally free of restrictions could continue to obtain the supplies needed, while markets protected till then by national quotas (for example UK and France) enjoyed degressive residual protection to the end of the century.

Box 7.4   Quotas: issues for business: the textile example

Quotas are a tool on the verge of extinction. Their costs to the protected economy and its consumers always outweigh the value to workers of the jobs preserved in the sector.

Yet quotas have not been capable of producing lasting or decisive competitive advantage for those protected. Quotas have controlled EU imports of textiles and clothing for over 50 years.

During that period, employment in the industry has declined inexorably: it has dropped by 25 per cent in the decade 1988–99. Output has held up better, thanks to improving technology. Profitability of the industry as a whole has been maintained by a mix of outward investment and outward processing, to transfer low-skill parts of the production process to low-cost offshore plants, while retaining design and finishing operations largely in Europe. The latest technology is further reducing the impact of labour costs on competitiveness while market needs require ever-increasing speed and flexibility in production. This is now driving the repatriation to some parts of Europe of a broader range of activities.

Conclusion: quantitative protection has been a palliative for the pressure of competition in a sector undergoing painful change; protection has not been cost free; it seems now less than ever the driver of a viable EU industry in the textiles sector.

How does this import regime compare with those of Europe's major trading partners? According to recent independent analysis (OECD Economics Working Paper), while US and Japan have somewhat lower levels of overall tariff protection (mainly because of high EU agricultural tariff equivalents) their tariff structures are more variable and more 'distorting' than that of the EU. As to non-tariff barriers, those being applied in 1996 in the EU covered just over 6 per cent of EU imports, as compared with 7 per cent in Japan and the US.

All these indicators should be taken as general guidelines, bearing in mind that the situation can vary over time and from sector to sector. But they clearly lend some weight to the European Community's own assessment that its market is, in trade terms, easily as open as those of comparable world economies.

Protection Against Unfair Competition: Anti-dumping and Anti-subsidy Policy

Arguably the most famous weapon of defence against imports in the world today is the imposition of duties, additional to normal WTO duties, on goods which are found by importing countries to be 'dumped' (that is, sold at below the price prevailing in the home market of the exporter) and to be causing injury to local industry.

There is no place for the concept of dumping in the classic economic model, where markets are open, knowledge is perfect and employment is full. Alas, the classic model has no place in the real world markets of today.

Dumping occurs where markets are distorted, for example where the exporting market is sufficiently protected against imports that the prices charged there can be artificially high, allowing industry to sell at a loss on export markets, thus expanding volume and increasing profit overall.

In economies where strong and uniform competition rules exist to guard against this sort of market distortion, dumping is a symptom of a competition problem, not a problem requiring treatment in its own right. Thus, the existence of a fully developed European competition law precludes the need for anti-dumping action on trade within the single market. But there is no scope in the foreseeable future that current moves for better competition policy co-operation worldwide will match Europe. On a worldwide scale, no such uniform pro-competitive guarantees exist, nor is there much appetite to create them, since they would imply a high degree of supranational intervention in national economic policies. So the founding fathers of the GATT recognised from the first that Member Countries would require continuing rights to impose protection against dumped imports.

Systemically, this makes sense because of the failure of worldwide competition rules just outlined. Politically, it makes sense too. Open trade policies are not understood or supported by public opinion: it has, however, been possible to use the GATT and now the WTO for a 50-year process of sustained trade liberalisation, because the existence of adequate rules against dumping and (see below) subsidy has demonstrated even to the most sceptical or protectionist constituencies that liberalisation under the WTO is fair to their competitive needs on world markets, as well as being a trade-liberalising endeavour.

The current European anti-dumping regime is based on the improved WTO rules adopted at the end of the Uruguay Round. In order for anti-dumping action to be taken, four conditions must be met: dumping must be shown to have occurred, the domestic industry must be shown to have suffered injury, dumping must have caused that injury and (a more qualitative judgement) the anti-dumping action must not overall be against the public interest. The final public interest hurdle is a self-imposed constraint unique to Europe, not required by WTO and not maintained elsewhere.

Measures can take the form of either import duties or undertakings by the exporters to respect minimum prices. In order to impose as little disruption as possible on international trade, anti-dumping investigations are subject to the tightest feasible time-limits: investigations must be concluded with a decision one way or another within 15 months from initiation. Where it becomes clear mid-way through an investigation that one or more of the conditions is not met, investigations are closed at that stage.

The parties concerned (both exporters and importers) have extensive rights and are generally represented during the investigative process by highly specialised legal advisers. Decisions are ultimately the responsibility of the Commission and the Member States acting together, and are subject to judicial review in the European Court of Justice and, ultimately, to WTO dispute settlement (see Box 7.5).

Equally, in a global economy, EU-based firms need to think ever more carefully whether dumping duties, if imposed, might not catch the exports to Europe of their own sister companies (as was almost the case for colour TVs in recent years!).

Parallel to the dumping provisions are those dealing with *subsidies*. The Uruguay Round rules on subsidies prohibit subsidies granted on exports and subsidies granted in return for the achievement a certain level of local content in production: these are the subsidies deemed to distort trade the most. Subsidies in support of research, regional development and environmental protection are guaranteed freedom from WTO sanctions. All other subsidies are permitted but subject to countervailing duties at the border of the importing country, where the subsidy can be shown to have caused injury to the competing industry in the import market.

These rules are much clearer than any which existed before 1994. Their entry into force coincided with a time when European industry has itself been subject to increasingly restrictive rules on the granting of subsidy, especially in sectors such as steel and synthetic fibres. In fact, outside the categories approved by WTO, only very limited rescue and restructuring aid for troubled sectors has been available to Community industry. In the absence of high subsidies for manufactures in Europe, there have been many more requests than in the past for countervailing duty against subsidised imports from the rest of the world. Between 1987 and 1994 only two anti-subsidy investigations were initiated by the European Commission. Between 1995 and 1999 there have been new investigations concerning 11 products from 17 countries. But EC levels of anti-subsidy action are still well below those shown by the US administration, traditionally a strong opponent of anything they judge to be subsidised imports.

For dumping and subsidy, as for other aspects of trade policy, it is appropriate to benchmark European policy against practice in major partners. In terms of import coverage, the 1998 OECD survey finds that, if anti-dumping duties, anti-subsidies measures and export price undertakings were considered together, they covered about 5 per cent of US imports in 1996 as compared to 0.2 per cent for EU imports in the same period. This particularly large discrepancy may reflect the increasing use of export price restraints in steel by the US administration, but serves to illustrate that any caricature of Europe as being more protectionist than other major economies in its use of trade defence instruments would be very far from the mark.

Box 7.5   Anti-dumping: common sense for business

Anti-dumping is an extremely complex issue and it is absolutely essential that companies, even SMEs, are assisted by lawyers if subject to an investigation. Generally, the use of specialised lawyers rather than the general business lawyers of the firm is preferable. It is also essential that the company acts as soon as the notice of opening of an investigation is published in the EC Official Journal: the deadline for completing the questionnaire is quite short (37 days) and is followed by an on-site investigation: the advice of specialised lawyers is necessary at the earliest stage as initial errors in presenting one's case can be extremely costly.

Defensive:
Businesses supplying the European market, as EU importers of their own or others' non-EU goods, or as exporters of those goods, need to be as aware of the Anti-dumping Regulation as of any other piece of directly applicable commercial law. Like all democratically adopted laws, businessmen infringe this one at their peril.
If an established flow of goods into Europe is subjected to an investigation, the record shows that a co-operative attitude towards the Commission officials investigating the allegations is essential: lots of data are needed on the cost structure of your enterprise: in the absence of full disclosure, the Regulation requires the Commission to make a best guess at the facts.
Where the allegations affect a state-trading economy, exporters need to demonstrate where possible that the exporting facilities operate in market conditions and at arms' length from government before their books can be accepted as evidence of cost structure.

Offensive:
Investigations are equally thorough for EU companies alleging that they are victims of dumping. Unless it is proved that the industry is suffering injury (job losses, capacity under-utilisation, price declines and so on) and that dumped imports are the cause, the case is closed automatically. So the burden of providing the data and the strength of the evidence has to be carefully weighed before industries embark on the allegation in the first place.

A Minimum of Restrictions on Exports

The economics of border controls is symmetrical: export restrictions impose costs in the same way as import restrictions. But, perhaps under an unacknowledged mercantilistic influence, most businessmen accept modest import barriers but find it surprising that a market economy interferes with the business of exporters. Surprising or not, there remains in Europe, as in other market economies around the world, a range of barriers to exports: these fall on a small proportion of export business, but can prove very costly to those affected.

The most widespread controls relate to so-called *dual-use goods*. These are goods which are traded, sometimes very widely, for perfectly legitimate civilian uses, but which also have military applications, and whose export to potentially unfriendly countries has therefore been controlled, very widely during the Cold War and on a somewhat narrower basis today.

The Treaty aims to ensure that exporters from different Member States enjoy an equivalent competitive environment not only at home but on third markets.

The application of this principle to the field of dual-use control has been long in coming, and it was only in 1994 that a common regime was first adopted. Even then, a large proportion of the judgements as to which goods should be controlled for exports to which countries remained with Member States. A revised and much more even-handed regime has now been concluded.

It establishes full harmonisation of controls on less sensitive products for friendly countries, while allowing controls even on trade within the single market on the most sensitive (typically cryptographic and nuclear) equipment. The issues for business in this field are clear: first, it is essential to establish whether potential export products are on the controlled list, and if so to seek the necessary license. Second, it is important to tell European public authorities about export opportunities existing in controlled products, particularly if other partners are releasing products from their controlled list in order to secure an unfair advantage over European traders.

A second category of export control relates to *political sanctions*, which have been increasingly attractive to governments around the world since the end of the Cold War. Such sanctions are more widespread than a casual glance at the news may suggest: in mid-1999, for example, the EU was applying economic sanctions of its own to several countries, notably Burma, Togo and Serbia. UN-mandated EU sanctions were also in force against the UNITA of Angola, with sanctions against Libya suspended but still formally in place.

Outside these sanctions, European firms are legally free to trade, but have in the past found themselves falling foul of other countries' *extraterritorial sanctions policy*. This has been the case particularly in recent years with the US administration's attempt to apply outside its own territory and to non-US companies its own policies concerning business with, for example, Cuba or Iran. US extraterritorial claims of jurisdiction have been resisted by the European Union and its Member States as a matter of principle. In order to help European companies to resist extraterritorial requirements, the EC passed in 1996 a so-called Blocking Statute. This law forbids European companies from complying with specified extraterritorial requirements, notably US requirements in respect of Cuba. The legislation not only makes operational European rejection of others' claims to exercise jurisdiction over its companies and nationals, but enables a European company arraigned before a foreign court to defend its non-compliance with that country's requirements by pointing to its countervailing obligations under the Blocking Statute. Courts in the US, as in some other countries, accept such a 'foreign sovereign compulsion' defence.

At the other end of the scale from trade, which may enhance an unfriendly power's military potential, come restrictions on *trade in waste products*. Trade in waste products has become one of the key issues for environmental protection in the global economy. In the past, countries have exported waste to other, usually poorer, countries where the costs of storage were low and where sometimes the level of awareness of waste-related environment problems was also lower than in the country producing the waste in question. The Basel Convention[9] bans trade in any waste that is deemed to be hazardous. OECD countries have also agreed that they will export other, non-hazardous waste to non-OECD countries only if it is intended for recycling and if the intended importing country formally notifies that it wishes to accept that waste.

The resulting EU export control regime covers a wide range of economically significant trade, from the export of ships for scrapping to the export of clothes for treatment as a basic input for paper-making. For customs officers, there can be difficulties distinguishing an old ship from a ship on its way to the scrapyard, or clothes sold as rags from second-hand clothes being sent to countries where there is a humanitarian need for them. This apart, potential exporters find difficulty in establishing whether or not an importing country wants to accept a given category of waste, and whether that desire has been notified formally in accordance with Community regulations.

The potential for interfering in trade that both importer and exporter want to take place is considerable. The Commission endeavours (increasingly through the Web), to ensure that up-to-date information is available to all exporters. Nonetheless, exporters of non-hazardous waste have repeatedly been surprised to find that their trade with a particular country is subject to a ban or to controls, and sometimes only discover this at a stage when costly initial steps to export given consignments have already been taken. This is a final illustration of the way in which costs and benefits of some little known areas of trade policy merit continued attention not only by policymakers but also by business.

A Network of Special Relationships

The European Union has been built on the apparently mundane foundation of economic co-operation. In the same spirit, Europe has from the first used trade as the foundation for its special relationships worldwide.

These special relationships are not all 'preferential', in the sense of giving the partner country better access to European markets than would membership of WTO. Non-preferential economic arrangements span much of the world, notably countries of Asia and of the former Soviet Union.

---

[9]   The Basel Convention on the Control of Transboundary Movement of Hazardous Wastes and their Disposal, with 130-plus signatories, administered by UNEP.

Significant preferences, whether unilaterally granted by the EU[10] or applying to trade in both directions, exist between the EU and the African, Caribbean and Pacific (ACP) developing countries; between the European Union and all European neighbours; between the European Union and its neighbours in the Mediterranean basin; between the European Union and Latin America.

From the first, GATT provided an exemption from the non-discrimination rule to allow this sort of agreement (which the WTO terms Free Trade Areas, or Customs Unions).[11]   However, in order to ensure that such agreements remain open to the outside world and create opportunities for all, certain criteria must be respected, notably that agreements must free 'substantially all trade' and that trade barriers with respect to third countries must not be higher overall than those that exist prior to the agreement.

Box 7.6   Preferential trade: future developments for business to watch

Future negotiations offer opportunities to create new export market opportunities, if business gives negotiators timely guidance as to its priorities.

The main EU negotiations in prospect for the immediate future are with the Mercosur bloc (Brazil, Argentina, Uruguay and Paraguay). The precise timetable will depend on political judgements to be made in the coming months and years both in Europe and among the Mercosur countries. But it is clear that on both sides there is a desire to cement a strong relationship, not least to balance the increasingly strong drive towards economic integration among all the countries of the Americas. Businessmen interested in the South American market should therefore take a close interest in this issue in the coming years.

Similarly in Asia, the Asia–Europe meetings initiated in 1996, while targeted at economic co-operation in more general terms, rather than any formal or preferential agreement, should improve co-operation in fields such as standards that will be of direct relevance to business in the coming years: those interested in the markets of Asian, Japan, the greater China, or Korea would do well to keep an eye on developments there.

Last but not least, negotiations to update the relationship with ACP countries, currently encapsulated in a single convention, will set the scene for Europe's contribution to the emerging economies of Africa, the Caribbean and the Pacific over the next decade: these are without exception small markets but in many cases markets with considerable potential.

---

[10]   Developing countries benefit in any case from a basic set of unilateral EU tariff preferences under   the Generalised System of Preferences or GSP.

[11]   In a Free Trade Area, zero duties apply between participating countries, but each country sets duties on other imports at whatever rate seems suitable; in a Customs Union, all participating countries apply the same import duties on trade with the rest of the world.

It is fair to say that Europe is recognised to be doing a good job,[12] certainly in its latest waves of agreements, in meeting the spirit and the letter of WTO requirements. The agreements concluded in the last decade with Central or Eastern European and with Mediterranean partners, for example, provide for reciprocal industrial free trade over a short transition period (shorter in the European than the Mediterranean cases), cover agriculture (albeit in a less ambitious way) and in many cases also provide for progressive liberalisation of trade in services. In parallel with bilateral agreements themselves, Europe is active in encouraging regional co-operation among its partners (for example in the Mediterranean) and in encouraging all its preferential partners to join the WTO and to participate actively (see Box 7.6).

Increasing Access to Export Markets

Today's world economy creates many opportunities worldwide for new export business. The biggest challenge for a potential exporter is to identify those opportunities. The chances are that government policy in the target market poses no insurmountable obstacle to the exporter. But there can be a role for European administrations in guiding the exporter towards new opportunities. Much of this task of export promotion falls on the European Member States. But there is a role for Brussels in three fields: informing exporters, co-operating to help third countries become more open, and using WTO dispute settlement where all other attempts to remove obstacles fail. With all this in mind, the Commission has been running a new market access strategy since 1996, with very heavy reliance on information technology.

The Market Access Database[13] is designed to provide, over the Web, up-to-date information on the import duties and import documentation required for specific products in specific markets. The database not only provides information but enables those working with it to contribute their own additional data whenever an exporter has experience that suggests Commission knowledge is incomplete, or inaccurate. In compiling and maintaining the database, the Commission has also worked closely both with Member State trade experts and with the administrations of the countries covered. As a result, the database lists an increasing number of specific market access problems encountered in an increasing number of countries analysed so far: currently, the list of market access obstacles runs at over 1000 targets.

The market access strategy has moved, since mid-1999, into the second phase, consisting of a barrier removal programme. The programme is designed to concentrate the Commission's limited resources on priority cases

---

[12]   See the WTO's Trade Policy Review of the EU.
[13]   http://mkaccdb.eu.int

where market-opening results can be achieved in reasonably short order and with the maximum possible economic benefit.

The main elements of the programme are as follows:

- The establishment of priority cases for WTO dispute settlement (see below);
- The establishment of market opening objectives for the new WTO negotiations (see below);
- The pursuit of bilateral consultations on important non-WTO issues with major market partners (especially the US, Japan, Korea, ASEAN, Mexico, Mercosur and South Africa) and with countries currently negotiating WTO membership, for example China, Russia and Ukraine.

As the key elements of this programme make clear, the essential tool for creating effective market access worldwide is to secure compliance by partner countries with the obligations they have voluntarily undertaken, either in WTO or bilaterally by agreement with the EU.

Settling Disputes

When an obstacle to trade is maintained contrary to existing WTO obligations, and the country maintaining the restriction has no excuse, such as a lack of administrative capacity to fulfil its WTO obligations, how is such a problem settled under WTO rules?

The first step in the 'Dispute Settlement Procedure' is always consultation between the EU and the partner whose measure is affecting EU exports. Bilateral consultations first begin informally, through normal diplomatic contacts, and then shift to formal consultations under the aegis of WTO. If such formal consultations fail to produce a mutually agreed solution to the problem, it is open to the EU to request the WTO to set up a dispute settlement panel.

The rules concerning such panels were considerably strengthened during the Uruguay Round of negotiations, the results of which came into force in 1995. Until that date, a panel finding could only be made operational when it had been approved by all WTO Members, including the defendant party. Very frequently, the defendant party (even in some cases the EU) blocked adoption of the panel findings, so that the Dispute Settlement procedures produced no result. Since 1995, panel findings have not been subjected to consensus in order for them to enter into force. They have become 'semi-automatic': the finding is adopted subject to appeal (see below), but the member country has discretion as to how it changes policies in order to comply with the finding.

It is possible for either the plaintiff or the defendant in a panel case to take some aspects of a panel finding to the WTO Appeals Body, typically on the grounds that the panel has misinterpreted the relevant agreement or applied flawed legal reasoning. This only has the effect of delaying the implementation of the panel finding until it can be confirmed or adjusted by the Appeals Body, whose decisions are final (unless set aside by a unanimous decision of all WTO members, including the party who has won: a difficult thing to achieve!). Thereafter, there is a clear judgement and a deadline, in principle of no more than 15 months, for the implementation of the finding. If the country fails to implement the WTO dispute settlement ruling, it lays itself open to retaliation, in the form of a withdrawal by the party who won the case of a part of the WTO benefits enjoyed by exports of the non-complying country. Such withdrawal of benefits typically takes the form of the imposition of punitive import duties on a range of products: it was the threat of such import duties that drew the attention of the cashmere industry to transatlantic difficulties in the banana trade during 1999.

No legal system can be described adequately in a few paragraphs: the WTO's is no exception. The new system has been in operation for only a few years and is already up for review and refinement. What it is important to keep in mind, however, is that a system does exist whereby member governments have, within areas of policy covered by WTO, subjected their actions to international oversight.

As a major trading partner and a leading player in WTO, the EU has been a major user of the Dispute Settlement System. The EU has been actively involved in over half of the almost 200 dispute settlement cases which have been processed by the WTO in the last five years and, contrary to the impression created by various *causes célèbres* in the field of agriculture, it has been the complainant party roughly twice as often as it has been the defendant party.

Expanding WTO Membership

The efficiency of the Dispute Settlement System is the most widely acknowledged feature of WTO's many strengths, as it emerged from the Uruguay Round[14]. The birth of WTO, coinciding with the collapse of communism, has seen an unprecedented queue of non-member countries seeking to join. The GATT, when it began life in 1947, mustered barely two dozen members. WTO today accounts for over 130. And most of the non-members in the world are in the queue for membership.

The accession process includes at the time of writing some very significant participants in the world economy, notably, China, Taiwan, Russia, Ukraine and Saudi Arabia. Negotiations with some accession

---

[14] The Uruguay Round was the biggest trade-liberalising package ever, with over 120 participating countries: its effect on the world economy has been variously assessed, but overall seems to have generated around 1 per cent additional growth. Paemen and Bensch (1995) and Schott and Buurman (1997) both provide very readable accounts of the details; the former with the advantage that they write as negotiators of the deal.

candidates have dragged on for many years; over 13 in the case of China. Some argue that the requirements for membership in what is meant to be a global organisation should be more straightforward, and not require lengthy negotiations. But, while WTO is a world organisation, it is also an organisation whose members undertake extremely onerous obligations towards all other members. The delay in accessions largely reflects the reluctance of current members to accept potentially powerful economies such as China or Russia without some guarantee that those economies, through WTO tariff and other access commitments, will be as open to existing WTO members' exports as the new members will expect current members' markets to be for their own goods and services. Given these uncertainties, it is not clear how quickly the accessions backlog can be cleared.

Strengthening the System: the New WTO Round

GATT traditionally developed its rulebook and advanced the cause of trade liberalisation by major 'rounds' of negotiation covering a full agenda of trade issues of concern to member countries. Between 1947 and 1993, GATT held eight of such sets of talks. Negotiations dealt at first only with import duties and import quotas. But the last GATT round, the so-called Uruguay Round (1986–93) addressed also such hitherto taboo issues as agricultural subsidy and textiles liberalisation, as well as wholly new items such as services,[15] intellectual property and investment.

Since 1966, the Commission has been calling for the launch of a new round, the first under WTO auspices, in order to cover not only the issues of the Uruguay Round, but also new subjects such as investment or social standards, and the needs generated by new technological developments in fields such as electronic commerce and biotechnology.

Opposition to an ambitious negotiation on these lines has come from several quarters. Developing countries have argued that they still have to digest the new obligations created for them by the Uruguay Round (which entered into force only in 1995, with up to ten-year transitional periods for developing countries to implement the results). The US has shown scepticism at the idea of multilateral rules for investment and competition (where the US is quite capable of imposing its own rules on developing countries in bilateral negotiations); while supportive of a social agenda for WTO, the US has also been suspicious that environmental rules would accommodate European needs while creating obstacles to US exports. In Europe itself, business has supported a new round of negotiations, but non-government organisations have in general argued that the WTO must move at a slower pace, in order to

---

[15] The services economy, accounting for two-thirds of EU GDP, a quarter of exports and half of outward investment, merits a chapter to itself, but the interested reader will find a good starting point in the referenced Commission work on GATS 2000, the current WTO services negotiation.

be sure that the world's trade rules genuinely contribute to sustainable development.

In order to address the concern of civil society relating to sustainability, the Commission has set up a 'Sustainability Impact Assessment': this tool, the first of its kind, is designed to assess the effect of new trade rules on the pursuit not only of economic growth but also of social equity and environmental efficiency. Its creation has been welcomed by civil society, and has set the pace for similar developments in other developed countries. But this alone has not been enough to allay fears that the WTO was an instrument set towards unsustainable objectives of primary interest to corporate Europe and contrary to the interest of developing countries or the global environment.

In these circumstances, it seemed likely that the negotiations due to be launched at the third WTO Ministerial meeting in Seattle in December 1999 would have an agenda somewhat short of European ambitions. Few commentators, however, predicted that the Ministerial meeting would close without agreement on any negotiations at all. This, however, was the result.

The consequence is that the 'Built-in Agenda' of WTO negotiations, notably on agriculture and services, begin on time in the year 2000, but that decisions on a broader package will most certainly have to await the Fourth Ministerial meeting, in mid-2001, by which time there will be a new US President with a fresh mandate, on trade as on other matters.

It is somewhat early to predict whether or not a Round will be launched in 2001, and what precisely the negotiating agenda might look like.

One thing is clear from recent months of discussions, and it is the need to give a greater voice to developing country negotiators in setting the WTO agenda. In the early days of GATT, developing countries were members (largely for political reasons during the Cold War) but were under very few obligations and as a result enjoyed little weight in setting the direction of the organisation. Since the end of the Uruguay Round, developing countries play a growing role in the world economy: the legitimate expectation of developing countries to enjoy in consequence a louder voice in WTO affairs has not yet been met. It was clear as never before at Seattle that developing countries are not prepared to endorse agendas which fail to give due weight to their needs, above all to their need for real improvements to access for basic products, such as textiles, to key markets such as the US and Europe.

Less clear is how to interpret the message from Seattle concerning the fears of some parts of European and North American society that WTO is bad for their social agenda or bad for the planet. This question is addressed in greater detail in the next section. We need to work both on the substance of so-called civil society criticism of the open trading system, as well as on procedural questions such as the need for WTO to operate in a more transparent manner.

In short, the new millennium ushers in not the launch of a set agenda of trade negotiations, but a period of considerable uncertainty and creativity concerning the role of open trade policies in the global economy. This period of flux creates a considerable opportunity for business to reconsider the trade agenda and work to ensure that it meets business needs.

7.3   WHAT IMPACT CAN INDUSTRY HAVE ON EUROPEAN TRADE POLICY?

Broadly, business can relate to trade policy in three ways. Business can use the trade policy network that exists in Europe as a tool for creating new opportunities. Business can become actively involved in ensuring that the trade policy tool develops in line with business priorities. Finally, if the current business-friendly policies are going to be preserved and extended, business must devote some attention to defending the underlying principles of open trade.

Using the Tool

EU trade policymaking is open to direct business influence. In addition to the Market Access Database, the Commission maintains close contacts with the European business federations (UNICE and ERT) as well as with the more specialised European Services Network. It is now possible for even the smallest company to lobby directly letting both Member State governments and the European Commission know where problems exist that may be amenable to government action.

Helping to Make the Policy

Since trade policy is formally made by agreement between the European Commission and the Member States, both the Commission and businessmen's national trade policy experts need to know what the company needs. This is particularly important when a major negotiation is underway, whether at the WTO or elsewhere, and choices have to be made as to which particular objectives to pursue in which priority country. In the absence of clear business advice, national administrations and the European Commission will make their best guess as to what priority shopping list is in Europe's interest. Nor will individual business views be taken as necessarily reflecting the broader interest. But objectives tend to be better when they are formulated on the basis of considered advice from those whom the policy is meant to help.

Business can also contribute to trade policy by creating its own international business dialogues (many examples exist already, with the US, Japan, Mercosur) and by increasing business contact with other stakeholders, such as citizens groups and trade unions.

Supporting the Case for the Open Economy

Finally, trade policy needs sustained, active business support and advocacy, at home and abroad.

Abroad, the key audience lies in the administrations of developing countries and emerging economies who participate in trade liberalisation talks but remain unsure of their own national interest in the matter. Foreign business leaders often have good connections and real credibility in developing countries. In past WTO negotiations, for example in the field of banking and insurance, 'good news' stories from the real world of business have been critically important in convincing developing country governments that it is in their own economic interest to make the final additional contributions necessary to clinch a deal. Businessmen should think of themselves as diplomats for open trade. At home, as well, there is a need for advocacy.

In Europe, as in North America, public opinion has taken fright at the (exaggerated) prospect of a world without frontiers and therefore, some fear, without protection for the weak, punishment for the wrong-doer,[16] or respect for the citizen's values. These fears have in recent years had an influence on the openness of the world economy. Popular opposition has made it difficult for the North American Free Trade Agreement (between the US, Canada and Mexico) to come into force, has hampered the participation of some liberal and democratic European countries in the EU endeavour and has contributed to the abandonment, after five years of expensive effort, of the talks on a 'Multilateral Agreement on Investment', a negotiation among OECD countries to create a freer (not a free-for-all) framework for foreign investors.[17]

This opposition was vividly demonstrated by the rioting that accompanied (but only partly disrupted) the Third Ministerial Meeting of WTO in Seattle, USA, in December 1999. The rioters were not the cause of any of the failures of that meeting. Nor were they representative of any single school of thought. But it is clear that if the WTO is to operate as intended, the discomfort felt by the demonstrators with the work of trade liberalisation has to be dealt with in future more effectively than in the past.

Popular opposition to open trade is diverse. Three main schools of thought can be distinguished, and business has messages for each. First, there is what I will term the fundamentalist opposition of those who believe that EU leadership in the WTO seeks to globalise a Western model of consumption,

---

[16] Lankoski and Lankoski (1999) offer the best short summary of the linkages between globalisation, liberalisation and sustainable development. Goldsmith and Mander's (1997) compilation of essays is the most complete account of the case currently being made against global economic interdependence: the 'globaphobia' study, although focussed on the US case, makes clear the main thrust of the counterarguments.

[17] See Henderson (1999) for a good assessment so far of the failure of the 'MAI' negotiations, albeit from a viewpoint contrary to that of the anti-MAI lobbies.

which cannot be extended much further without destroying the planet as a whole, while Europeans should certainly worry that their ecological impact on our economy is so big that if the rest of the planet grew to the same size without continued dematerialization or increased eco-efficiency of production, the world's resources would be exhausted. But to act to resolve that problem through the trade instrument is to focus on international symptoms of an issue, which has to be addressed first at home.[18] Would the fundamentalists be more inclined to leave open trade policies free to develop if they were engaged in a dialogue with European business, and if that dialogue created confidence that the fundamentals were being taken into account? If business needs an open world economy, it should consider devoting some resources to this sort of dialogue.

A second segment of opposition believes that trade policy is amoral, because we do not discriminate between imports from countries where European values prevail and those where child labour is tolerated, unions are suppressed and working conditions ignored.

This is where the Global Village meets the Law of Nations: international law since the Middle Ages has sought to encourage peaceful co-operation amongst sovereign nation states by advocating the respect of national sovereignty for matters within national borders. The core UN instruments and other great international conventions since World War II amount to no more than the pooling of that sovereignty to impose common constraints on the exercise of domestic territorial power. But attempts to force compliance with such commitments frequently run foul of one or another country's predilection for the principle of non-interference by others in its domestic affairs. Europe's willingness to go to war in Kosovo in the name of human rights is one of the more recent illustrations of the continuing evolution of the balance between the respect of national sovereignty and the protection of international values. In the trade policy field, the question is whether Europe should get ahead of the consensus and sometimes impose some of its own values through trade sanctions. The issue for business is whether they can work with those expressing such concerns to develop an approach case-by-case, which leaves open trade essentially intact.

A third segment of opposition believes that trade liberalisation under WTO auspices is pushing the process of world economic integration at a pace too hectic for most countries' administrative or social systems to cope. These critics want developing countries to be able to implement open trade principles in their own time, and believe that meanwhile new requirements should not be laid upon them. It is unlikely that the market will allow developing countries to delay reform and liberalisation without imposing on them a considerable penalty in terms of lost opportunities for trade and investment. Almost all developing countries indeed are busy opening their markets to goods, services and investment faster than WTO can negotiate.

---

[18] The trade and environmental policy link is studied in greater detail in Chapter 6.

They do so not only to attract foreign capital but also because they believe sound development requires a move away from discretionary and often corruption-prone systems and towards the rules-based transparency of the WTO.

So a moratorium on trade liberalisation is unlikely. It is, however, equally unlikely that WTO trade talks can meet business desires for increased market access worldwide if fears persist concerning LDC lack of capacity. Government-financed technical assistance to developing countries can be a major part of the response to concerns such as this. But businessmen could ask themselves two questions: whether they are prepared to support a significant shift in international public development aid towards the objective of coping with globalisation; and whether, in the private field, business could not make a more effective and sustained contribution itself to helping developing countries to cope more rapidly.

7.4 CONCLUSION

There can be very few companies in Europe whose interests are not affected by Europe's place in the broader world economy. Most of the policies relevant to the international trading relationship are set by Member States and the Commission, working together through Brussels-based institutions. While the policies in place are broadly open and business-friendly, there are opportunities for the alert, and traps for the unwary, that make trade policy a worthwhile subject of at least brief study for serious business planners. Trade is in any case a policy area where European society's difficulties in relating to the world of today come into sharp focus: business needs to concern itself with society's concerns, so that policies continue to evolve in a direction that reconciles Europe's broader value system with the needs of business. Now is a particularly good time for European business players to get involved in trade policy debate.

BIBLIOGRAPHY

Aga Khan, Prince Sadruddin. (1998), *Policing the Global Economy*, Cameron and May, London.

Barth, D. (1999), *The Prospects of International Trade in Services*, Friedrich Ebert Stiftung, Bonn.

Brittan, L. (1994), *The Europe we Need*, Hamish Hamilton, London.

Burtless, G. Lawrence, R. Z. and Litan, R.E. (1998), *Globaphobia, Confronting Fears about Open Trade*, Brookings Institute, Washington.

Shapiro, R.J. (1998), *Globaphobia, Confronting Fears about Open Trade*, Brookings Institution, Washington.

Croome, John (1995), *Reshaping the World Trading System: A History of the Uruguay Round*, Geneva, World Trade Organization.

European Commission (1993), International economic interdependance, a discussion paper, Brussels.

European Commission (1998), *GATS 2000: Opening Markets for Services*, Office for Official Publications, Luxembourg.

European Commission (1999a), *The EU Approach to the WTO Millenium Round*, COM (1999) 331 final, Office for Official Publications, Luxembourg.

European Commission (1999b), *World Trade Information Pack*, Office for Official Publication, Luxembourg.

Goldsmith, E and Mander J (1997), *The Case Against Globalisation*, Sierra Club Books, San Francisco.

Henderson, D. (1999), *The MAI Affair*, Royal Institute of International Affairs, London.

Johnson, Michael (1998), *European Community Trade Policy and the Article 113 Committee*, Royal Institute of International Affairs, London.

Krueger, Anne O. (ed.) (1998), *The WTO as an International Organisation,* Chicago University Press, Chicago and London.

Lankoski, L. and Lankoski, J. (1999), *Economic Globalisation and the Environment,* Edita Ltd, Helsinki.

OECD (1998a), *Open Markets Matter: the Benefits of Trade and Investment Liberalisation*, OECD, Paris.

OECD (1998b), The European Union's trade policies and their economic effects, Economics Working Paper N° 194, OECD, Paris.

Paemen, H. and Bensch, A. (1995), *Du GATT à l'OMC: la Communauté européenne dans le Cycle d'Uruguay*, Leuven LLP.

Schott, J.J. and Buurman, J.W. (1997), *The Uruguay Round, An Assessment*, Institute for International Economies, Washington.

Schott, J.J. (ed). (1998), *Launching New Global Trade Talks*, Institute for International Economics, Washington.

UNCTAD, *World Investment Reports*: for 1996, 1997, 1998, 1999. UNCTAD, Geneva.

WTO (1997), *Trade Policy Review: European Union,* Report by the Secretariat, WTO, Geneva.

PART THREE

The Industrial Policy of the European Union

8. Competition Policy – Controlling the Market Power of Business

Svend Albæk

Article 3 of the Treaty of Amsterdam establishes that 'the activities of the Community shall include', among other elements, 'a system ensuring that competition in the internal market is not distorted'. The system implementing the competition policy of the Community gives the Commission extensive powers. Competition policy is one of the few areas where the Commission has been given the exclusive competence in an important policy field. In most policy areas the Council takes the decisions based on proposals made by the Commission. But in the field of competition policy, the Commission decides in the individual cases. The Member States are consulted, but the Commission does not have to follow the opinion of the Member States. The basic framework is, of course, laid down by the Member States through the Treaty and Council Regulations. However, the Commission takes the decision in individual cases.

Hence, in the field of competition policy, the Commission takes important decisions that directly influence companies. It may also fine companies that have breached the competition rules.

Within the European Commission, competition policy is usually taken to cover four areas: antitrust, merger policy, state aid and liberalisation. This chapter will occupy itself with the first two of these areas, that is, antitrust and merger policy. A common denominator for these two areas is that the rules are directed toward companies, prescribing what companies can and cannot do. Both the rules on state aid and on liberalisation are instead directed toward the Member States.[1]

The chapter is organized as follows. Section 1 will deal with the legal basis and the institutional framework for EU competition policy. Section 2 briefly explains the central concept of 'relevant market'. Section 3 describes the rules governing restrictive practices (cartels, vertical and horizontal agreements, and so on) while Section 4 covers the policy towards the abuse of a dominant position. In Section 5 the system of EU merger control is described. Section 6 contains some indications of the likely future

---

[1] The State aid rules are the subject of the next chapter.

development of the EU competition policy while Section 7 concludes the chapter.

8.1   LEGAL BASIS AND INSTITUTIONAL FRAMEWORK

The legal basis for the Commission's activities in the area of competition policy is found in Title V of the Treaty, 'Common rules on competition, taxation and approximation of laws'. Articles 81–89 have the heading 'Rules on Competition', including the rules on State aid and liberalization. The two central rules on competition, as understood by this chapter, are Articles 81 and 82.[2] The full text of these two articles will be given in Sections 3 and 4. In this section their content will, however, be mentioned briefly in order to give an overview of the system.

First of all, it should be understood that EU competition law is concerned with 'trade between Member States'. The national competition authority in a Member State should normally deal with a restrictive practice or a merger which only has effects in that Member State. The Commission and the European Courts have, however, taken what some outsiders have considered a quite wide interpretation of 'trade between Member States'. Thus this trade need not be actual trade but could also be 'potential trade'. A practice, which would seal off a market in a Member State and prevent imports in the future, could well be attacked under EU competition law, even if the practice only directly affected firms in one Member State and there were no present imports from another Member State.

Article 81 is concerned with restrictive practices, for instance agreements between undertakings.[3] It covers both 'horizontal' agreements by firms in the same industry to fix prices or share markets and 'vertical' agreements such as dealership contracts, and so on. Article 81(1) basically prohibits all restrictive practices which may affect trade between Member States and which restrict or distort competition. This is, of course, a very drastic statement which, on its own, seemingly would prohibit many normal business practices such as exclusive dealing, and so on. Article 81(3) therefore gives the possibility that certain such restrictive practices may anyway not be prohibited if they are deemed to have overall positive effects and give consumers a 'fair share' of these.

Article 82 establishes that dominant positions may not be abused. Any such behaviour is therefore prohibited if it may affect trade between Member States. Examples of such abuse of dominant position are: imposing unfair

---

[2]   These were Articles 85 and 86 until the Treaty of Amsterdam came into force on 1 May 1999. In this chapter these two articles are referred to as 81 and 82, even when discussing decisions made when the articles were still numbered 85 and 86.

[3]   The legal term 'undertakings' used in EU competition law covers what is usually called 'companies' or 'firms' in daily language.

prices or other unfair trading conditions; limiting production, markets or technical development to the prejudice of consumers; applying price discrimination or other types of discriminatory behaviour; tying the sales of otherwise not related products.

The Treaty of Paris which established the European Coal and Steel Community (ECSC) in 1951 also contains rules on competition. Article 65 of that treaty is clearly the predecessor of Article 81 of the Treaty of Amsterdam. Articles 60–64 of the Treaty of Paris deal with prices. In particular, Article 60 prohibits predatory and discriminatory pricing. It can therefore be seen as an inspiration for Article 82 of the Treaty of Amsterdam along with the last paragraph of Article 66 which, in more general terms, is concerned with abuse of a dominant position. In the Treaty of Amsterdam, there is, however, no counterpart to the remainder of Article 66. The first six paragraphs of Article 66 establish merger control for companies producing ECSC products. Merger control was not mentioned in the Treaty of Rome and it took 32 years before an explicit merger control regime was established in the EEC. In the meantime the Commission tried, with some help from the Court of Justice, to interpret Articles 81 and 82 in ways that allowed it to control mergers. And, finally, the Member States agreed to pass a Council Regulation in December 1989, No. 4064/89[4] (the Merger Regulation). This is the last piece of legislation to look at in order to have a first idea of the Rules of Competition in the Community.

The Merger Regulation establishes in Article 2(3) that 'a concentration[5] which creates or strengthens a dominant position as a result of which effective competition would be significantly impeded in the common market or in a substantial part of it' shall be prohibited. In line with the other elements of EU competition law the Merger Regulation only applies to concentrations which affect trade between Member States. To avoid uncertainty among companies this is defined explicitly in the Merger Regulation, as will be explained in Section 5.

Finally, it is useful to briefly consider the institutional settings of the EU competition policy. As mentioned above, the Commission – and *not* the Council – decides in individual cases. The Commission is a 'collective' body. This means that, in theory, all twenty commissioners together take the decisions. In practice, some cases, most importantly merger cases which do not need a full investigation, are delegated to the commissioner responsible for competition, for the moment Mario Monti. But in most other cases, the decision actually goes before the entire Commission.

---

[4]   Published in Official Journal (OJ), L 395, 30.12.1989; corrected version OJ L 257, 21.9.1990. Amended in 1997 (OJ L 180, 9.7.97; corrigendum in OJ L 40, 13.2.1998).

[5]   The generic term used in the Regulation is not 'merger' but 'concentration'. This is because the Merger Regulation covers not only what is normally understood by mergers, but also acquisitions, certain types of joint ventures, and so on. In this chapter the term 'merger' will, however, in general be used as a synonym for 'concentration'.

Although the Member States do not decide on the cases, they are involved in the procedure, and they do give their opinion on the cases – at least the most problematic ones. Representatives from the Member States therefore come to Brussels to two kinds of meetings. One is the 'hearing' where the undertakings involved in a case get the chance to present orally their view of the case – and where so-called third parties, for instance competitors and customers, can also present their views. The other type of meeting is the Advisory Committee meeting, where representatives of the Member States give their opinion on a draft decision presented by the Commission. The Commission is, however, not bound to follow the opinion of the majority of the Advisory Committee.

This description of the involvement of the Member States in the decision process in the individual cases does not give a full picture of the role of the Member States in the EU competition system. The Commission is operating within a framework laid down by the Member States. For instance, an explicit EU merger control system was only established when the Member States through a Council decision agreed upon the Merger Regulation in 1989. Major changes to the system can only be made by the Member States. Within the framework laid down by the Member States, the Commission does, however, have a larger room for maneuver than in most other policy areas.

The decisions taken by the Commission can be appealed to the European Courts. The Court of First Instance hears competition cases appealed by companies. Its decisions can be further appealed to the Court of Justice.[6]

8.2   THE RELEVANT MARKET

Before describing in more detail the way these various pieces of legislation have been transformed into practical competition policy, it is useful to mention the fundamental concept of the 'relevant market'. To understand whether a certain agreement, restrictive practice or merger is harmful or not, it is necessary to know which market(s) will be affected and who the competitors and the customers are. The technical term in competition policy is a 'relevant market', relevant in the sense of being relevant for the analysis of the competition effects in a specific case. The relevant market is thus an analytical tool that helps competition authorities to assess the effects of, for instance, a merger.

The relevant market is not necessarily the same 'market' as a businessman has in mind. It is a very specific term used in competition policy analysis. A businessman may take as his starting point whether he is competing with more or less the same competitors in various product or geographic markets. He may, for instance, be of the opinion that his company is competing on a

---

[6]   National courts can also be involved in competition cases based on EU competition law.

world market because all his major competitors are following a strategy of being present in all parts of the world. He may also be thinking of his company as competing in a broad product category such as paper production, agrochemicals, banking, and so on, because those are the categories that he typically uses in his strategic thinking.

The starting point for a definition of a relevant market in competition policy is, however, the consumer and not the producer.[7] The basic idea is therefore to look at various products (for instance those produced by the merging parties in a merger case) and ask what the realistic alternatives are for the consumer. This can lead to much narrower markets than a businessman would expect, both with regard to product and geographic market definitions. For instance, there may be a separate relevant market for 'insecticides for beans and peas used as cattle fodder in France'.[8]

8.3 RESTRICTIVE PRACTICES

The text of Article 81[9] of the Treaty, which covers restrictive practices, is given in Box 8.1. The first paragraph is actually a quite sweeping statement: 'all agreements between undertakings... which have as their object or effect the prevention, restriction or distortion of competition within the common market' are prohibited.

At the time the Treaty of Rome came into force, this meant that thousands of contracts involving perfectly normal, and from a competition point of view relatively innocuous, business practices in theory were illegal, at least until they got an exemption under Article 81(3).[10] In particular a lot of so-called 'vertical restraints' seemed to be perfectly reasonable agreements but were nevertheless at face value illegal. The problem can be illustrated by the way franchising systems operate. Typically, the franchisor does not own the individual shop. Rather, it is owned by a franchisee. However, the franchisor imposes restrictions on what the franchisee can and cannot do. Common examples are that the franchisee may not sell the products of competing companies, that he may not advertise in ways that damage the image of the products of the franchisor, and so on. Such restrictions are, according to 81(1), illegal, but they may be exempted under 81(3). Also the widespread practices of exclusive distribution and purchasing agreements and selective distribution systems were in need of exemptions under 81(3).

---

[7]   The Commission has explained its approach in its *Notice on the definition of relevant market for the purposes of Community competition law*, OJ 97/C 372/03.

[8]   Case No. IV/M.737 *Ciba-Geigy/Sandoz* (1997).

[9]   Remember that this was Article 85 until the Treaty of Amsterdam came into force on 1 May 1999. Hence, most decisions and literature refer to Article 85 and not to Article 81.

[10] Council Regulation 17 of 6 February 1962 established that the Commission has the exclusive right to grant exemptions under Article 81(3). See however Section 7 on how the Commission proposes to change this.

Box 8.1   Article 81

1. The following shall be prohibited as incompatible with the common market: all agreements between undertakings, decisions by associations of undertakings and concerted practices which may affect trade between Member States and which have as their object or effect the prevention, restriction or distortion of competition within the common market, and in particular those which:

(a)   directly or indirectly fix purchase or selling prices or any other trading conditions;

(b)   limit or control production, markets, technical development, or investment;

(c)   share markets or sources of supply;

(d)   apply dissimilar conditions to equivalent transactions with other trading parties, thereby placing them at a competitive disadvantage;

(e)   make the conclusion of contracts subject to acceptance by the other parties of supplementary obligations which, by their nature or according to commercial usage, have no connection with the subject of such contracts.

2. Any agreements or decisions prohibited pursuant to this Article shall be automatically void.

3. The provisions of paragraph 1 may, however, be declared inapplicable in the case of:

– any agreement or category of agreements of concerted practices;
– any decision or category of decisions by associations of undertakings;
– any concerted practice or category of concerted practices;
which contributes to improving the production or distribution of goods or to promoting technical or economics progress, while allowing consumers a fair share of the resulting benefit, and which does not:

(a)   impose on the undertakings concerned restrictions which are not indispensable to the attainment of these objectives;

(b)   afford such undertakings the possibility of eliminating competition in respect of a substantial part of the products in question

The consequence was that the Commission was completely swamped with registrations of agreements. By 1967 it had accumulated 37 450 registered agreements that it, in theory, had to decide upon. The vast majority of these were bilateral agreements, that is, between two companies only, and the majority of these were vertical agreements. It was clear that the Commission could not and should not look at each of these individually. It therefore 'invented' what is known as 'block exemptions'.

Before looking closer at the block exemptions, it is useful to mention that collusion, for instance in the form of cartels, obviously is not allowed. Article 81 prohibits fixing prices (directly or indirectly), limiting or controlling production, markets, and so on, and sharing markets. These types of agreements are normally so detrimental to competition and without redeeming features that they cannot be exempted under Article 81(3). Box 8.2 gives an example of a recent cartel case.

Box 8.2 The pre-insulated pipe cartel

In October 1998 the Commission fined several companies in the pre-insulated pipe industry for having fixed prices and shared markets via quota systems. Pre-insulated pipes are mainly used in district heating systems which are commonly employed in Northern and Eastern Europe where the climate is severe. The cartel had started in Denmark in 1990–91 but the price increases also applied to export markets. The cooperation on market-sharing was later extended to Germany and German producers were brought into the cartel. From 1994 a Europe-wide cartel was in place. The cartel also engaged in activities to eliminate a Swedish competitor who did not participate in the cartel. The Commission decided that ten companies had infringed Article 85(1) and imposed fines ranging from €400 000 to € 70 million. The €70 million fine applied to ABB Asea Brown Boveri which was found to be the ringleader and instigator of the cartel. ABB and eight of the other nine companies have appealed against the Commission's decision to the Court of First Instance.

Source: Case No IV/35.691/E-4, Pre-Insulated Pipe Cartel

Block Exemptions

Block exemptions are exemptions of certain categories of restrictive practices, provided that they fall within certain limits. Typically, a block exemption has a description of what is allowed in an agreement, and of what is not allowed. Companies then do not have to register individual agreements as long as they fall within the limits set out in a block exemption.

Within the block exemptions a distinction is made between horizontal and vertical agreements. Horizontal agreements are between companies at the same level of the production chain. An example could be an agreement between two car manufacturers to develop a common gear box. Vertical agreements are between companies/parties at different level of the chain, for instance, between a car manufacturer and its dealers or between a franchisor and his franchisees. Clearly, there is a fundamental difference between horizontal agreements and vertical agreements. Horizontal agreements are, by definition, between companies that 'ought' to be competing. The practices listed in Article 81(1) sound quite anti-competitive if engaged in between competitors, for example, agreeing on prices. The same practices do not necessarily sound anti-competitive if engaged in between companies at different levels of the chain. After all, they are not competing against each other, rather they are together competing against other supply chains. Why should competition authorities bother about, for instance, what a franchisor agrees with its franchisees? Several of the block exemptions are exactly concerned with establishing what types of vertical restraints are allowed in contracts between companies at different levels in the supply chain. However, some types of horizontal agreements are also covered by block exemptions as will be explained below.

Vertical Restraints

Recently five block exemptions toward certain types of vertical restraints have been in place:

- Regulation 1983/83 on exclusive distribution agreements.
- Regulation 1984/83 on exclusive purchasing agreements.
- Regulation 4087/88 on franchising agreements.
- Regulation 1475/95 on distribution systems for motor vehicles.
- Regulation 240/96 on technology transfer agreements.

The first four of these regulations are basically concerned with establishing what types of clauses contracts between suppliers and resellers can contain, in particular what types of constraints such contracts can place on the behaviour of the two parties to the contract. They explain how the supplier can allot a defined territory to one reseller and how a reseller can agree not to buy certain types of goods from other suppliers. Certain restrictions aimed at preserving quality, image, and so on are also allowed.

The final block exemption is the most recent one, Regulation 240/96 on technology transfer agreements. It unified what was earlier two exemptions, one on patent licensing and another on know-how licensing. The basic idea behind this block exemption is that licencing intellectual property rights is a tricky transaction which needs to impose certain ties on what the licensee can do with the transferred technology. The exemption therefore gives a framework for which types of obligations the (two) parties to a contract can safely include and be sure that the agreement falls under Article 81(3).

An element of EU competition law which distinguishes it from other systems is the particular emphasis on market integration. The block exemptions covering vertical restraints therefore always contain clauses which prohibit absolute territorial segmentation. One market where this has often been discussed in the general public is the new car market. The Commission's recent case against Volkswagen, which is described in Box 8.3, is an interesting illustration.

Box 8.3 Volkswagen and parallel imports

Around 1995 the Commission started investigating whether Volkswagen had infringed Article 81(1) by entering into agreements with the Italian dealers in its distribution network in order to prohibit or restrict sales to final customers coming from other Member States. The customers were mainly Austrian and German who sought to benefit from significantly lower prices on new VW and Audi cars in Italy. Prices in Germany had at times been up to almost 50 per cent higher than in Italy, although differences in the range 15–30 per cent were more normal. It was also quite normal that prices in Austria were 15–30 per cent higher than in Italy. Volkswagen, and its subsidiaries Audi and Autogerma (the Italian importer), very actively tried to discourage its dealers from selling to foreigners. A system was put into place to try to trace cars coming into Germany and Austria back to the Italian dealers that sold them. Dealers suspected of selling to foreigners had orders withheld and some in the end lost the dealership. In January 1998 the Commission imposed a fine of € 102 million on Volkswagen. Volkswagen has appealed against the Commission's decision to the Court of First Instance.

Source: Case No IV/35.733 VW

The system of control of vertical restaints just described is in the process of changing. The system has often been criticized for focusing too much on the (legal) form of contracts instead of on their effects. As discussed above, vertical agreements are fundamentally different from horizontal ones in that vertical agreements are often meant to increase efficiency in, for instance, distribution. They may also be used to prevent competition, but most often attempts at such prevention would only be successful if the companies involved have some degree of market power. Many economists have therefore argued that there is no reason to worry about vertical restraints if the companies involved have no market power. Some of these economists would claim that even resale price maintenance ('vertical price fixing') and complete geographical separation should not be considered problematic as long as the companies have no market power (and as long as there are no signs that they are used as a means of achieving collusion).

The Commission has partly accepted this criticism. It has also realised that valuable resources are being used to control vertical agreements between firms which have no market power. At the same time, the Commission would like to increase the resources used to investigate, for instance, cartels. A new block exemption regulation ((EC) No. 2790/1999) on vertical restraints was therefore adopted by the Commission in December 1999. The new regulation enters into force in June 2000, by which time the block exemptions on exclusive distribution agreements, exclusive purchasing agreements and franchising agreements will no longer apply.[11]

---

[11] Except for agreements which are already in force on 31 May 2000 for which a prolongation until 31 December 2000 is given.

The new block exemption covers agreements between undertakings at different levels (but only one at each level) of a production or distribution chain as long as neither seller nor buyer has more than a 30 per cent market share as a seller/buyer.[12] [13] A few 'hardcore' vertical restraints will, however, still not be permitted, even with market shares below 30 per cent. One such restraint is resale price maintenaince, in that the seller is not allowed to impose a fixed or minimum resale price on the buyer. Absolute territorial division of markets is also not allowed. Furthermore, there are some provisions regarding selective distribution systems and non-compete obligations. Finally, the Commission conserves the right to withdraw the benefit of the new regulation if it finds that certain agreements have nevertheless such negative competition effects that they cannot be allowed. Article 8 covers 'cumulative' effects in that the Commission may declare that the regulation does not apply to a situation 'where parallel networks of similar vertical restraints cover more than 50 per cent of a relevant market'.

Companies with market shares below 30 per cent will in the future have much freer hands in deciding their vertical agreements. Companies with market shares above 30 per cent will, however, have to apply individually for exemption under Article 81(3). Until now it has been the legal form of an agreement that has determined whether it fell under a block exemption. Now it will largely be the market positions of the companies that determine this. Note, however, that this also puts a burden on companies to evaluate their market position. In this respect companies have to keep in mind that a market means a 'relevant market' as described in Section 2.

Horizontal Co-operation Agreements

The two important (general) horizontal co-operation agreements are both from December 1985.[14] One is a block exemption for certain types of specialization agreements (Regulation No. 417/85). This regulation allows companies, under certain conditions, to each agree to specialize in production to a certain (different) segment in a market. Furthermore, the companies can also agree to joint specialized production where they both agree to specialize (together) in a certain segment. They are now also allowed to extend the co-operation to joint sale of the products. These specialization agreements are, however, only allowed for companies which together have less than 20 per cent of the relevant market and have rather limited turnover (together €1000 million in 1993).

---

[12] Hence, the buyer's share is measured on its input, and not output, market.
[13] The Regulation also have some rules concerning vertical restraints concerning associations, intellectual property rights and (small) competing companies.
[14] There is furthermore a special block exemption for the insurance sector (Regulation 3932/92).

The other horizontal block exemption concerns research and development agreements (Regulation No. 418/85). It sets out the circumstances under which companies, without running foul of Article 81, can do research and development together and jointly exploit the results.

By adopting the new regulation on vertical restraints the Commission has responded to the criticism that its practise in this field did not take sufficiently into account the market power of companies but rather concentrated on the legal form of the agreements. This is part of a greater overall tendency of the Commission to rely more on economic arguments in its competition policy. The Commission is now in the process of reviewing its policy on horizontal co-operation agreements and the related block exemptions.

8.4 ABUSE OF DOMINANT POSITION

Article 82 which covers abuse of dominant position is not used to the same extent as Article 81. Article 81 gives rise to a lot of 'reactive' work where the Commission has to decide whether agreements, that have been notified to it, fall under Article 81 or, for those that do, whether they can be given an exemption under Article 81(3). The text of Article 82 is given in Box 8.2.

Box 8.4   Article 82

Any abuse by one or more undertakings of a dominant position within the common market or in a substantial part of it shall be prohibited as incompatible with the common market in so far as it may affect trade between Member States.
Such abuse may, in particular, consist in:

(a)   directly or indirectly imposing unfair purchase or selling prices or other unfair trading conditions;

(b)   limiting production, markets or technical development to the prejudice of consumers;

(c)   applying dissimilar conditions to equivalent transactions with other trading parties, thereby placing them at a comparative disadvantage;

(d)   making the conclusion of contracts subject to acceptance by the other parties of supplementary obligations which, by their nature or according to commercial usage, have no connection with the subject of such contracts.

To use Article 82 the Commission has to do a lot of work. To attack a certain behaviour by one or more companies it has to prove not only that a dominant position exists but also that it is being abused. Notice that it is not the dominant position per se that is illegal; the illegality concerns the abuse of the dominant position. A small aside: there is no provision in European competition law for splitting up dominant firms as there is in the US, last used for splitting up the old AT&T, but also discussed as a possible solution in the case against Microsoft.

Before looking at what types of behaviour can be considered abuse, it is useful to examine the concept of a dominant position. This will also be relevant in the next section on merger control. The accepted case law definition of dominant position can be found in the Court of Justice's decision in 1979 in the *Hoffmann-la Roche* case. Hoffman-la Roche had very large market shares in several markets for bulk vitamins. The Court first explained what is meant by a dominant position, as shown in Box 8.5.

Box 8.5　Dominant position

The dominant position ... relates to a position of economic strength enjoyed by an undertaking which enables it to prevent effective competition being maintained on the relevant market by affording it the power to behave to an appreciable extent independently of its competitors, its customers and ultimately of the consumers. Such a position does not preclude some competition which it does where there is a monopoly or quasi-monopoly but enables the undertaking which profits by it, if not to determine, at least to have an appreciable influence on the conditions under which that competition will develop, and in any case to act largely in disregard of it so long as such conduct does not operate to its detriment.

... The existence of a dominant position may derive from several factors which taken separately are not necessarily determinative but among these factors a highly important one is the existence of very large market shares.

Source: Case 85/76 (ECJ 1979) *Hoffmann-La Roche v. Commission*

The Court went on to state that 'the view may legitimately be taken that very large market shares are in themselves, and save in exceptional circumstances, evidence of the existence of a dominant position'. The Court held that market shares above 75 per cent are 'so large that they prove the existence of a dominant position'. The issue in the case was contracts between Hoffman-La Roche and its clients which contained so-called 'fidelity' rebates, in which the clients would get extra large rebates if they only procured vitamins from Hoffman-La Roche. The Court held that for a dominant firm to engage in contracts containing this type of rebates constitutes an abuse of a dominant position.

Notwithstanding the Court's position in *Hoffman-La Roche* there can be markets where shares over 75 per cent do not necessarily mean that there is a dominant position. This could, for instance, be the case in a newly developed market where new entrants are expected shortly; in markets where market shares fluctuate wildly because of infrequent large orders; or where there is very strong buyer power, as is the case for defence products, where the buyers are almost exclusively national governments.

In the *Akzo* decision[15] the Court said that a 50 per cent market share would establish a presumption of a dominant position, quoting the *Hoffman-La Roche* decision about the importance of very large market shares. The Court agreed with the Commission that Akzo had abusively exploited its dominant position in the organic peroxides (specialty chemicals used in the plastics industry) by endeavouring to eliminate a new competitor from this market by massive and prolonged price-cutting in the flour additives sector where the competitor had its primary business. The Court defined predatory pricing by stating that

> prices below average variable costs ... by means of which a dominant undertaking seeks to eliminate a competitor must be regarded as abusive. Moreover, prices below average total costs ...must be regarded as abusive if they are determined as part of a plan for eliminating a competitor.

The Court found that Akzo had indeed priced below average total costs in the flour additives sector with the aim of damaging the competitor's viability and that this was an abuse of its dominant position.

What about lower market shares? In merger proceedings market shares of 40 per cent have developed into an important *de facto* threshold for when there is a presumption of a dominant position. Finally, according to the preamble of the merger regulation, a company with a market share below 25 per cent can be presumed not to have a dominant position.[16]

What other types of behaviour can be considered abuse of dominant position? One starting point is the list of practices mentioned in Article 82 itself: unfair prices or other trading conditions; limiting production, markets or technical development; applying dissimilar conditions to equivalent transactions; and tying. In the very early cases, the issue was often refusal to deal. In the *United Brands* case,[17] the Commission claimed that United Brands, when selling its Chiquita bananas to wholesalers in various countries in Europe, had used four practices which infringed Article 82:

1. the prohibition of the resale by distributors of green, that is, unripe bananas;
2. the refusal of supplies on certain occasions to a Danish distributor which had offended United Brands by promoting a competitive brand of banana;
3. pricing that showed discrimination between the markets of different Member States;
4. excessive pricing.

The Court went along with the Commission in the first three counts. On the fourth point, the Court did not accept the analysis of the Commission. The Commission relied on the lowest prices in the EEC as a benchmark and

---

[15] Case C 62/86 (ECJ 1991), *AKZO Chemie v. Commission*.

[16] Such a company could, however, still be considered to be part of a group of companies holding a 'collective dominant position'; this will be discussed in Section 6.

[17] Case 27/76 (ECJ 1978), *United Brands v. Commission*.

argued that relative to this benchmark some of the other prices were excessive. The Court did not accept that the Commission to a sufficient degree had established that the prices charged by United Brands were excessive.

To sum up Article 82, once a company reaches about a 40 per cent share of the market, it has to start being a bit careful about what it does. The easiest way to run into trouble is probably by refusing to supply, tying the sales of products and so on. However, other practices such as using rebates to tie down customers and charging excessive prices (or engage in predatory behaviour) may also be attacked under EU competition law.

8.5 MERGER CONTROL

As mentioned earlier, there was no explicit mention of the regulation of mergers (or 'concentrations', which is the official legal terminology) in the Treaty of Rome, while merger control is covered in Article 66 of the Treaty of Paris (establishing the ECSC). Many considered this a problematic omission, including the Commission which first proposed a merger regulation to the Member States in 1973. The Member States did not, however, at the time agree to passing such a regulation. Some of them were afraid that merger regulation at the Community level could prevent European companies from reaching the scale necessary to compete with American companies. The Commission tried instead to explore to what extent it could use Articles 81 and 82 (then Articles 85 and 86) and had some success in this as the Court of Justice supported such an interpretation on two occasions.[18] This was helpful in eventually convincing the Council that a proper sort of merger regulation was needed. The coming of the Single Market which was expected to lead to a wave of concentrations also pushed in this direction.

---

[18] In Case 6/72, *Continental Can v. Commission* (1973), the issue was whether the Commission was correct in applying Article 82 to prohibit Continental Can from acquiring the majority of the shares in a competitor in the business of producing cans and lids for food packaging. The Court agreed with the Commission it could be considered an abuse of a dominant position under Article 82 if a firm having a dominant position strengthened this position through an acquisition or a merger. However, the Court annulled the Commission's decision as it found that the Commission had not convincingly defined the relevant markets nor analysed potential competition in sufficient detail. In Cases 142/84 and 156/84, *BAT and RJ Reynolds v. Commission* (1987), BAT and RJ Reynolds contested a decision by the Commission to allow Phillip Morris to acquire a minority shareholding in Rothman International, all four companies being competitors in the cigarette market. The Court stated that the acquistition of an equity interest in a competitor could fall under Article 81(1) but that the Commission was right in its assessment that this was not so in the case in question.

The Merger Regulation was passed in December 1989 and came into force on 21 September 1990.

The Merger Regulation establishes that it is the duty of the Commission to prohibit mergers which have anti-competitive effects. The exact wording of the central Article 2(3) is found in Box 8.6.

Box 8.6 Merger Regulation, Article 2(3)

A concentration which creates or strengthens a dominant position as a result of which effective competition would be significantly impeded in the common market or in a substantial part of it shall be declared incompatible with the common market.

The Merger Regulation is structured around the idea that the Commission should only deal with large mergers which seriously affect more than one Member State. There are therefore various thresholds which have to be met before a merger (or a joint venture, or an acquisition, or whatever falls under the term concentration) has what is called 'Community dimension'. These are given in Article 1 of the Regulation. Article 1(2), see Box 8.7, is the original formulation, which is still the one by far most frequently used.

Box 8.7 Merger Regulation, Article 1(2)

For the purposes of this Regulation, a concentration has a Community dimension where: (a) the combined aggregate worldwide turnover of all the undertakings concerned is more than €5000 million; and   (b) the aggregate Community-wide turnover of each of at least two of the undertakings concerned is more than €250 million, unless each of the undertakings concerned achieves more than two-thirds of its aggregate Community-wide turnover within one and the same Member State.

If a concentration meets the thresholds in Box 8.7, according to the so-called 'one-stop shop' principle the concentration does not also have to go through approval by national competition authorities within the EU. If, however, a concentration does not meet the thresholds, the parties may have to notify the concentration to the authorities in several Member States. This can become a rather complicated matter for large mergers where sometimes more than ten national authorities will have to give permission for the merger to proceed. Many companies would then prefer to have to notify only the Commission. When the Merger Regulation was amended in June 1997, with effect as of 1 March 1998, one of the changes was a new Article 1(3), see Box 8.8.

Box 8.8   Merger Regulation, Article 1(3)

For the purposes of this Regulation, a concentration that does not meet the thresholds laid down in paragraph 2 has a Community dimension where:

(a) the combined aggregate worldwide turnover of all the undertakings concerned is more than €2500 million;
(b) in each of at least three Member States, the combined aggregate turnover of all the undertakings concerned is more than €100 million;
(c) in each of at least three Member States included for the purposes of point (b), the aggregate turnover of each of at least two of the undertakings concerned is more than €25 million; and
(d) the aggregate Community-wide turnover of each of at least two of the undertakings concerned is more than €100 million;

unless each of the undertakings concerned achieves more than two-thirds of its aggregate Community-wide turnover in one and the same Member State.

While paragraph 2 of Article 1 is quite easy to read, paragraph 3 is slightly more complicated. The total worldwide threshold is €2500 million (half of that in paragraph 2) while at least two of the companies involved have to each have an aggregate Community-wide turnover of €100 million (€250 million in paragraph 2). Again the two-thirds rule apply: if each of the companies involved has more than two-thirds of its aggregate Community-wide turnover in the same Member State, the concentration does not have a Community dimension. It is left to the competition authority of that Member State to deal with the concentration.

Thus (a) and (d) establish lower turnover thresholds than those of paragraph 2. However, (b) and (c) complicate the picture so that paragraph 3 is not simply a lowering of the thresholds. They ensure that the merger would really have effects in (at least) three Member States – and hence probably would have to be dealt with simultaneously by the competition authorities of several Member States, if it were not dealt with by the Commission. Therefore, there have to be at least three Member States in each of which it is true that (b) the total aggregate turnover of all the companies involved exceeds €100 million and (c) at least two of the companies involved each have a turnover exceeding €25 million.

The Commission has to decide whether a notified concentration 'creates or strengthens a dominant position as a result of which effective competition would be significantly impeded in the common market or in a substantial part of it'. The notification has to be submitted within one week of the final signing of a merger agreement or a public bid.[19] The operation cannot be

---

[19]   The Commission can impose fines if a merger is not notified in time.

executed before the operation has been finally cleared by the Commission.[20]

The Merger Regulation gives tight deadlines within which the Commission has to make its decision. Most often the Commission has already been approached by the lawyers of the merging companies to discuss the case before the notification, so that everything can go smoothly once the formal procedure starts. However, the deadlines are measured from the date of the notification. From that date the Commission has one month to decide whether the operation does not raise any competition concerns or whether the operation raises 'serious doubts as to its compatibility with the common market'. If the former is the case, the Commission declares the operation compatible with the common market, and that is the end of the story. If the latter is the case, the Commission will 'initiate proceedings', that is, go into a more detailed examination of the case. The first month is known as a 'Phase I investigation', while the detailed examination is a 'Phase II investigation'. The Commission has another four months for a Phase II investigation. Or rather, it has four months to make a decision after a Phase II investigation. Because there are many adminstrative steps that have to be followed in the procedure, the time for the real investigation is considerably less.

There are two ways in which the time limit of one month for a Phase I investigation can be extended to six weeks. The most important one is that the companies during the Phase I investigation offer to do something, typically to sell off a part of their business, in order to remove the 'serious doubts' that they understand the Commission has. In that case, the Commission gets another two weeks to investigate this new development. The other way is that a Member State asks the Commission that a case be transferred to the competition authority of that Member State instead of being dealt with by the Commission. This can be reasonable if all the effects of a case will be on local markets in that Member State, but that for some reason the thresholds for the case having a community dimension have been met. Also in this situation the Commission gets another two weeks to assess whether the case can indeed be transferred. This second extension was already included in the original Merger Regulation, while the first extension was only introduced starting 1 March, 1998. This important change was made in order to give firms a chance to avoid the full four month procedure, if they have already decided not to 'fight' the Commission.

The total number of cases notified to the Commission from 21 September 1990, when the Merger Regulation came into force, until 31 October 1999 is 1168. The number of cases has been increasing over the years, especially since 1993 (see Table 8.1).

---

[20]   In certain special cases, the Commission may, however, allow it to go ahead earlier. The Commission can impose fines if an operation has been put into effect without prior approval or permission.

Table 8.1   Number of notified cases

1990	1991	1992	1993	1994	1995	1996	1997	1998	1999
12	63	60	58	95	110	131	172	235	292

Note: The data for 1990 cover only the period 21.09.90–31.12.90, since the Merger Regulation only came into force on 21 September 1990.

Until 31 December 1999, 11 mergers have been prohibited. This relatively small number is sometimes used as an argument that the EU merger control has little effect or 'bite' because very few cases have actually led to a prohibition decision. This is, however, a superficial argument. First, a further 36 cases which went into Phase II were cleared only after the parties offered remedies, that is, changed the operation in a such a way that there were no competition problems. This can, for instance, be done be selling off certain assets so that the combined market share of the merged companies is reduced. Another 11 cases were withdrawn in Phase II. Presumably, these mergers would have run a quite high risk of being prohibited if undertakings had not been offered. Second, a further 45 operations were cleared after Phase I remedies and 40 withdrawn in Phase I. A large part of these mergers would presumably also have been 'high risk' cases. Although adding these cases may not be completely correct, one could argue that the merger regulation has directly had a full or partial 'prohibitive effect' on a total of 143 cases out of the 1228 notified cases. Third, there are also indirect effects. Some operations are modified from the outset, because the parties know that otherwise there would be competition problems. Hence, some operations have incorporated changes – mostly divestitures – already as part of the notification. These cases do not show up in the statistics as anything else than cases cleared after Phase I. Finally, there are probably transactions which are never consumed since the companies know that they would never get the operation cleared. To sum up, although it is hard to measure exactly what the effects of the EU merger control system are, it is clearly superficial to focus only on a low number of prohibition decisions.

Most decisions in the EU have been based on what is called 'single dominance', that is, the idea that a single firm after the merger can 'dominate' in the way discussed in Section 4. Typically, a market share of 40 per cent has been considered a guideline threshold for when the 'bells start ringing' and the Commission will pay extra attention to the situation in such a market. However, there is no automatic way of translating a high market share into a dominant position. The particular circumstances in each market will have to be investigated.

In March 1998 the Court of Justice confirmed[21] that the Merger Regulation covers not also single dominance but also 'collective dominance'. This had

---

[21]   Cases C 68/94 and 30/95, *France and Others v. Commission* (1998).

been a hotly debated issue ever since the birth of the merger regulation. Article 82 clearly talks about the 'abuse by one or more undertakings of a dominant position'. The Merger Regulation does not explicitly mention that a dominant position could be held by more than one firm. This would have been an important hole in the EU competition system. The Court's decision 'closed' this hole. The full importance of this will only become clear once a sufficient body of case law has evolved and the Commission has established its practise in this field. A good indication about what is to be understood by collective dominance[22] can, however, be found in the decision by the Court of First Instance (CFI) in March 1999 in *Gencor v. Commission* where it upheld a Commission prohibition decision based on collective dominance. A further description of this case is found in Box 8.9.

Box 8.9   The Gencor/Lonrho case

In April 1996 the Commission prohibited a merger between the South African company Gencor and the British company Lonrho. Gencor appealed the decision to the Court of First Instance which gave its judgment in the case in March 1999. Gencor and Lonrho were both active in the platinum group metal (PGM) sector. In this sector only two other significant players were present on a world scale, the South African company Amplats, owned by the Anglo American Company, and the Russian state. The Commission found in its decision that the merger would have led to the creation of a duopolistic dominant position between the new entity and Amplats on the world platinum and rhodium markets. As platinum is by far the most important of these two products, both the decision of the Commission and the judgment of the Court focus on this market. After the proposed merger the new entity and Amplats would together have had a market share of around 70 per cent of the world market for platinum. The Commission estimated that this share would increase to around 80 per cent as Russia was selling from its stocks in a manner that could not be sustained. The new entity and Amplats would control approximately 89 per cent of the world PGM reserves. The Commission had in its decision explained that the platinum market had many characteristics that made it prone to duopolistic dominance, for instance, price transparency, a homogeneous product, slow market growth, inelastic demand, insignificant countervailing buyer power, mature production technology and high entry barriers. The Court of First Instance concurred with the Commission's analysis and dismissed the appeal by Gencor.

Source: Cases IV/M.613 *Gencor/Lonrho* and T-102/96 (CFI 1999) *Gencor v. Commission*

The CFI wrote that collective dominance may arise in the 'market structures of an oligopolistic kind where each undertaking may become aware of common interests and, in particular, cause prices to increase without having to enter into an agreement or resort to a concerted practice'. Most observers have from this and similar phrases by the courts concluded that the courts

---

[22] The terms 'joint dominance' and 'oligopolistic dominance' are also sometimes used.

have so far identified collective dominance with what in economics is known as 'tacit collusion', that is, that companies may – without making 'formal' agreements – engage in behaviour which raises prices above the 'normal' competitive level in that market.[23]

Collective dominance is normally only an issue when a few companies have large market shares but none of them individually so large as to be able to exert 'single dominance'. Furthermore, certain features are generally thought to render a market more conducive to collective dominance.[24] The early cases concerned duopolistic dominance, that is, they involved only two companies.[25] However, in 1999 the Commission for the first time applied collective dominance to an oligopoly of three firms in a prohibition decision.[26] While this is perfectly logical from an economic point of view, this evolution of the use of the Merger Regulation has caused some debate in the legal community and the press. Collective dominance will therefore remain one of the most interesting areas of EU merger control for some time to come.

8.6   THE FUTURE

Competition policy has been one of the undisputed success stories of the Community. There is, however, a widespread recognition within the Commission that there is a need for modernisation of the entire system of EU competition policy.

One important theme of this modernisation is that 'the analysis of market structures and the assessment of a transaction's potential economics impact must now play a greater role than they have sometimes done in the past'.[27] This would also allow the Commission to concentrate on the most important cases. The new block exemption on vertical restraints is a prime example of this. There has also been a tendency to use more economic analysis in merger cases.

Another theme of the modernisation is the move to involve the Member States more in the application of EU competition law. The present system is in many ways quite centralised with the prime example being the exclusive right of the Commission to grant exemptions under Article 81(3). The

---

[23] The Commission seems to share this interpretation in its contribution to an OECD Roundtable on Oligopoly in May 1999. See also P. Christensen and P. Owen, *Comment on the Judgement of the Court of First Instance of 25 March 1999 in the merger case IV/M.619 - Gencor/Lonrho*, EC Competition Policy Newsletter, June 1999.

[24] A description of the Commission's practice is found in the contribution to the OECD Roundtable on Oligopoly in May 1999.

[25] Besides the cases already mentioned the most important early case is IV/M.190 *Nestlé/Perrier* (1992).

[26] Case IV/M.1524 *Airtours/First Choice* (1999).

[27] Alexander Schaub, Director General for Competition, in a speech given at the Second Oslo Competition Conference in June 1998.

Commission published in 1999 a 'White Paper on the Modernisation of the Rules Implementing Articles 85 and 86 of the EC Treaty' describing its views on how this could be changed. The Commission in that paper recalled why a centralised system was seen as necessary in the early years of the Community. First, an authorisation system which normally requires the Commission to be informed in advance provided the Commission with useful information in order to establish its practice. Secondly, the coherent development of the interpretation of Article 81(3) initially required a certain degree of control. Thirdly, the system gave legal certainty to businesses at a time when competition policy was not firmly established, neither in the Community as a whole, nor in most of the Member States.

The Commission takes the view that the three reasons mentioned above for introducing a centralised system are no longer important since they were primarily related to getting the competition policy of the Community off to a safe start. At the same time, the present system, which is designed to a Community with six Member States, is already now under strain and will certainly not be able to handle a situation with even more Member States.

Seen from the Commission, the ideal would be a 'seamless' network of competition authorities working on a similar set of rules in which the Commission would still be the overall responsible for the Community as a whole. A system of allocating cases between the Commission and national authorities would then be needed. Member State competition authorities and courts would be allowed to grant exemptions under Article 81(3) and the authorisation system currently in place would be abandoned in favour of a system of *ex post* control. This development would free resources and allow the Commission to concentrate on, for instance, large cartels.

The views of the Commission on modernisation have not been met with universal approval. Some – including both some of the larger Member States and industry organisations – fear that the EC competition law will run the risk of not being implemented uniformly throughout the Community and that some legal certainty will be lost in the new system. As the changes will take several years to be implemented, these issues will continue to be debated in the coming years.

8.7 CONCLUSION

This chapter has shown how the competition policy of the European Union has a direct influence on what choices large industrial companies operating in Europe can make. It sets limits for their behaviour toward competitors and customers, and it restricts what kinds of mergers can be allowed. Smaller companies may be affected as customers of larger companies.

Furthermore, there is a clear tendency for the competition policies of the EU Member States to converge to a model based on the EU competition system. Thus the decisions made by the Commission in Brussels or the Courts in Luxembourg may also have importance for industrial companies through the influence on national competition policies.

Competition policy is therefore a fact of life that has to be taken into account. It is a highly specialised field in which the normal businessman cannot be expected to be an expert. He should, however, be aware that there are rules to be followed and that he, in case of doubt, should seek expert advice from either in-house legal counsel, specialised competition lawyers, the Commission or national competition authorities.

BIBLIOGRAPHY

Amato, Giuliano (1997), *Antitrust and the Bounds of Power*, Hart Publishing, Oxford.

Bishop, Simon and Walker, Mike (1999), *The Economics of EC Competition Law*, Sweet & Maxwell, London.

Cini, Michelle and McGowan, Lee (1998), *Competition Policy in the European Union*, MacMillan Press, London.

European Commission, *Annual Reports on Competition Policy*, Office for Official Publications, Luxembourg.

European Commission, *EC Competition Policy Newsletter* (published three times a year, since 1994), Directorate-General for Competition, Brussels.

European Commission, *Merger Control Law in the European Union*, (published since 1990), Office for Official Publications, Luxembourg.

European Commission (1994), *Competition Law in the European Communities, Volume IA, Rules Applicable to Undertakings*. Office for Official Publications, Luxembourg.

European Commission (1999), *White Paper on the Modernisation of the Rules Implementing Articles 85 and 86 of the EC Treaty*, COM(1999) 101, Office for Official Publications, Brussels

Faull, Jonathan and Nikpay, Ali (eds) (1999), *EC Competition Law*, Oxford University Press, Oxford.

Goyder, D.G. (1998), *EC Competition Law*, 3rd Edition, Clarendon Press, Oxford.

Sauter, Wolf (1997), *Competition Law and Industrial Policy in the EU*, Clarendon Press, Oxford.

9. State Aid Rules for a Level Playing Field

Laurens Kuyper

The internal market requires free and undistorted competition, to create a level playing field 'where individual talent, effort and comparative advantage lead to victory, rather than an inclined pitch with moving goalposts, a biased referee and an opposing team full of steroids'[1]. Governments often feel pressed to influence this playing field, for instance, to ensure that domestic industries operate under conditions equivalent to their foreign competitors, in spite of the knowledge that unilateral matching of distortive practices often results in multiplication of distortions.

In many countries governments tended to protect industries by intervening in the industrial adjustment process, motivating this with the supposed need to compensate 'market failures' or correct 'market imperfections'. These interventions may have a positive effect on national industries, but may also cause injury to exporting companies from other countries. In both cases, industry has an interest in the application of European State aid rules: to defend itself against distortions that affect its competitiveness, as well as to be certain that the aid it receives from national governments is allowable under those rules.

In a completed internal market companies should be able to compete on the merits of their products and services. Government interventions that distort this competition, such as favouring domestic products to the detriment of imported ones, all forms of trade barriers, discriminating taxation, and preferential treatment, are not allowed; the Treaty prohibits them. The granting of State aid is a very visible government activity, which is not absolutely prohibited by the Treaty, because the prohibition only applies when the aid also distorts trade between Member States. And even State aids that distort trade may be allowed (by the Treaty, the Commission or the Council).

State aid control lies exclusively with the Commission; the Member States (the Council) have no such power and thus are directly limited in their national sovereignty. Member States are obliged to notify the Commission in

---

[1] Peter Sutherland, former Commissioner for Competition.

advance of any measure that could constitute State aid. The Commission decides in each case whether derogation can be granted.

The first section of this chapter gives an overview of the amount of State aid granted by the Member States, followed by a section concerned with the legal basics of State aid control and the possible derogations. The third section explains some of the different applications of State aid control by the Commission, and the fourth section addresses rule making by the Council.

9.1   STATE AID IN PRACTICE

Surveys of State aid measures of the Member States have been published since 1988,[2] showing a slight decline in the total amount of aid granted over the years. In general, total aid (agriculture excluded) has remained high. Averaged over 1988–90, they amounted to 2 per cent of the Union's GDP, with large differences between Member States, as can be seen from Table 9.1. For the period 1995–97, the average decreased to 1.2 per cent of GDP.

Table 9.1   Total amount of State aid (1995 prices in million €)

	Manufacturing 1992–94	Manufacturing 1994–96	Total 1992–94	Total 1994–96
Austria	–	448	–	1 104
Belgium	920	1 149	3 083	2 721
Denmark	539	671	1 162	1 207
Germany	19 851	16.639	39 976	34 039
Greece	722	662	976	978
Spain	1 311	2 101	4 601	5 024
Finland	–	365	–	416
France	4 931	3 740	14 218	12 755
Ireland	198	215	396	394
Italy	10 320	9 760	17 739	16 748
Luxembourg	55	46	258	131
Netherlands	694	686	1 827	2 062
Portugal	467	382	673	720
Sweden	–	318	–	1 404
UK	1 431	1 513	3 051	4 328
EUR15	41 439	38 695	87 961	84 032

---

[2]   There have been seven Surveys published: COM(88) 945, COM(90) 1021, COM(92) 1116, COM(95) 365, COM(97) 170, COM(98) 417 and SEC(99) 148; the first Survey covered the period 1981–86, the subsequent surveys were updated every two years. From the seventh survey onwards, the Commission intends to publish these reports annually.

Total national aid, excluding aid granted by the European institutions (for instance, from the Framework Programme, as explained in Chapter 11), amounts to figures that are even larger than those in Table 9.2.

Of total aid to manufacturing, regional aid represents almost 60 per cent; 12 per cent is aid to individual firms; and 10 per cent is aid in the area of research and development. Government objectives in the field of environment (1 per cent), SMEs (7 per cent) and energy saving (3 per cent) receive relatively low aid amounts, as compared to aid to particular sectors like shipbuilding (8 per cent). The bulk of ad-hoc aid is given for restructuring or rescuing companies, half of which is used in the steel and shipbuilding sector.

The data for these surveys do not give a complete picture of State aids: they only concern measures within the scope of the Treaty. This means that aid in the form of 'general measures' is excluded, because it is available for every firm in the Member State concerned, thereby not fulfilling the Treaty condition that aid must be specific (see below).

It is likely that the total amount of aid to industry is much higher in reality.

Table 9.2   National aid in Member States (in € million)

	1993–95 (EUR 12)	1995–97 (EUR 12)	1995–97 (EUR 15)
Manufacturing	42 882	36 365	37 680
Agriculture	10 772	9 658	13 129
Fisheries	333	240	252
Coal mining	11 487	7 646	7 646
Transport	34 843	31 855	33 655
Financial services	1 147	2 702	2 702
Total	101 464	88 466	95 064

State aid amounts of this magnitude undoubtedly have an influence on the competitive position of firms, enabling them to increase or maintain their market shares at the expense of others.

It would be unrealistic to suppose that governments would completely refrain from giving financial assistance to industry, in spite of the already realised integration of the Union's markets. Over the past years, State aid control by the Commission has been more actively – and stricter – enforced, as shown by the increase of State aid notifications: in the 1970s and 1980s the average was 100 newly notified cases per year. At the end of the 1990s that average was 1000; it must be noted that the different enlargements of the EU had no great impact on this figure.

The increase of State aid cases is partly caused by complaints from competing companies that are affected when their competitors are receiving

State aid; but also from concerned or angry citizens and opposing politicians, as well as from other Member States. The Commission's State aid control seems to have led to greater public confidence in the practical effects of Commission decisions.

Already in 1973, the Court of Justice[3] remarked that Commission decisions requiring the abolition or modification of an aid measure could include the obligation to repay any amounts granted. It took, however, another ten years before the Commission started to make use of this possibility.[4] The practice of ordering recovery – including interest – of State aids that are judged to be incompatible with the common market, was generalised in 1985.

At the same time the Commission warned potential recipients of State aid that any aid granted to them illegally (that is, without the Commission having reached a final decision on the aid in case), may have to be refunded. It is the Member State who has the obligation to recover such an illegal aid from the recipient. In recent times, however, companies that received such aid cannot defend themselves with the argument that were not aware of the illegality of that aid: a company has to make certain that the aid is granted in accordance with the European rules and, for instance, is duly notified to the Commission.

9.2 LEGAL BASIS

Basic Rule

The Treaty addresses State aid in a few Articles, of which Articles 87, 88 and 89 form the basic text.
This section analyses the main rule as contained in Article 87(1); the position of the Commission; and the derogations. Article 87(1):

> Save as otherwise provided in this Treaty, any aid granted by a Member State or through State resources in any form whatsoever which distorts or threatens to distort competition by favouring certain undertakings or the production of certain goods shall, insofar as it affects trade between Member States, be incompatible with the common market.

'Save as otherwise provided in this Treaty':
The start of the text of the Article refers to other places in the Treaty where State aid is mentioned. These are agriculture and fisheries, empowering the Council to make rules for that sector (Article 36); for transport, by allowing aids that meet the need of co-ordination of transport or if they represent payments connected with the concept of a public service (Article 73); for the

---

[3] Case 70/72, *Commission vs Germany.*
[4] Communication concerning aids granted illegally, 1983, OJ C-318.

services of general economic interest and the particular tasks assigned to such undertakings (Article 86,2).

'any aid granted ... in any form whatsoever':
The Treaty does not give a definition of aid. The case law of the Court of Justice and, since 1993, the Court of First Instance, expanded its meaning – and often created its content – in numerous cases. Aid should be understood broadly as all forms of specific transfers from the government sector which directly or indirectly benefit enterprises, for which the government receives no equivalent compensation in return and which are granted with the purpose of changing market outcome.

In most cases it is defined as 'any economic advantage that a firm would not have received in the normal course of business'. This is the so-called 'commercial investor principle'[5]: the provision of finance to an enterprise constitutes aid if that firm would not, in the given circumstance, be able to obtain the sums concerned on the private capital markets, or if it could do so only on terms less favourable to itself. This situation often occurs when the State participates in the capital of a company.

The Treaty makes clear that the form of the aid is irrelevant; it can be anything from subsidies or grants, soft loans, tax concessions, guarantees to the supply of goods and services at less than cost.

'by a Member State or through State resources':
State means all public bodies or agencies acting on their behalf, whatever their status, name or description[6]: 'there is no necessity to draw any distinction according to whether the aid is granted directly by the State or by public or private bodies established or appointed by it to administer the aid'[7]. It can even be a private body if it is entrusted by the State to distribute funds; or private funds if a public body distributes the money and the State has thus the final say about the way the proceeds of the levy are used.[8] If the resources are obtained by a compulsory levy on a sector ('parafiscal' levies are used in several Member States) and these proceeds are used for that sector only; this aid is deemed to be financed by the State.[9]

The Court also stated that a tax exemption constituted State aid, although it does not involve a transfer of State resources. Because the person exempted is placed in a more favourable financial situation than other taxpayers (Case C-387/92).

---

[5] Case 234/84 of 10 July 1986, *Belgium vs Commission*; Case 301/87 of 14 February 1990, *France vs Commission*.
[6] Case 248/84 of 14 October 1987, *Germany vs Commission*.
[7] Case 78/76 of 22 March 1977, *Steinicke and Weilig vs Germany*; Case 57/87 of 7 June 1988, *Greece vs Commission*.
[8] Case 259/85 of 11 November 1987, *France vs Commission*.
[9] Case 47/69 of 25 June 1970, *France vs Commission*.

'which distorts or threatens to distort competition':
In the Commission's practice, this sentence is interpreted almost automatically: as soon as there is aid, the Commission presumes that there is such a (potential) distortion if the beneficiary company is in competition with another company in the Union that produces the same sort of products.
The Commission assesses[10] the distortion by comparing the situation of the beneficiary firm on the market with and without, before and after the aid. The market in this case is always the Community market. There is no precise threshold to assess the existence of a distortion, neither is there a ceiling on the beneficiary firm's market share below which trade and competition are deemed not to be affected.

'by favouring certain undertakings or the production of certain goods':
This is the criterion of specificity; it excludes from the application of this Article in the Treaty all aids that benefit all enterprises, be they private or public, without any distinction. Such general measures are not State aid: if these create competitive advantages for firms in one Member State, for instance, arising from differences in general economic or fiscal policy, they should be tackled under Article 96 (harmonisation of national legislation which leads to distortions of competition arising from differences between legal or administrative provisions). Article 87 concerns the effects of a State aid measure; not the intention of the Member State.[11]

'insofar as it affects trade between Member States':
Given the present high degree of integration of the Union's economy, this paragraph is not a real limitation. It applies even when the beneficiary firm does not export any of its products to other Member States,[12] it is sufficient when that firm is in competition on its home market with producers from other Member States.

Aids for exports to non-member countries could also distort intra-Community competition,[13] because aid to the exporting firm gives it an advantage above its competitors.

Whenever aid fulfils the conditions mentioned above, the Commission could not refuse the aid.

Commission Competence

Member States are obliged to notify all aid measures prior to their implementation, as stated in Article 88(3): 'The Commission shall be

---

[10] Joined Cases 296 and 318/82, *Leeuwarder papierfabriek*; Case 323/82, *Intermills*.
[11] Case 173/73 of 2 July 1974, *Italy vs Commission*; 310/85 of 24 February 1987, *Deufil vs Commission*.
[12] Case 102/87 of 13 July 1988, *France vs Commission*.
[13] Case 142/87 of 21 March 1990, *Belgium vs Commission*.

informed, in sufficient time to enable it to submit its comments, of any plans to grant or alter aid'.

It is up to the Commission's discretion to approve the aid, taking into account economic and social assessment in a Community context. The aim is to determine whether the benefits to be expected from the aid may outweigh the disadvantages of distorting competition in the internal market.

As a general rule, the Commission does not allow export aid (by Member States in intra-Community trade) and is very hesitant in accepting operating aid (aid to cover the running costs of an enterprise).

The Philip Morris case[14] is one of the most clarifying judgements on the Commission's powers in State aid control. In this case, the Commission refused the granting of State aid by the Dutch government to the company for developing the production of cigarettes. The company appealed to the Court, stating that the Commission should only consider whether the proposed investment plan in question was in conformity with the objectives mentioned in Article 87(3) in order to grant a derogation. The Court supported the Commission's argument, emphasising that the aid should not serve to improve the financial situation of the recipient undertaking but be necessary for the attainment of the objectives specified in Article 87(3).

In this particular case it was established that the company had sufficient economic resources to carry out the proposed investment without state intervention. The Court also stated that Article 87(3) gives the Commission discretion ('may') to declare the aid compatible with the common market, and stated that the Commission's assessment of the unemployment situation in the proposed area of investment rightly was referring not to the national average in the Netherlands but in relation to the Community level.

So, under its assessment of a notified State aid measure, the Commission can also consider the economic strength of the beneficiary, as well as whether the investment would be in the firm's own commercial interests.

The need for fundamental restructuring is a sufficient justification for allowing aid, meeting increased competition is not. The obligation to restructure (as a 'counterpart' for receiving aid) may justify the grant of aid unless the Commission proves that the adverse effect of the aid on trading conditions is such that the beneficiary's closure would have been preferable to its rationalisation.[15]

The Commission also looks at the state of the sector concerned. For example, it denied authorising any aid that would lead to an increase in production capacity for man-made fibres, and requested the Member States to notify in advance any individual proposals to grant aid to firms in this sector. The Commission also introduced limitations to the granting of aid in the steel and shipbuilding sectors, in view of their situation of overcapacity,

---

[14] Case 730/79 of 17 September 1980, *Philip Morris vs Commission*.
[15] Case 323/82, *Intermills vs Commission*.

such as the limited use of environmental aid for the steel industry and the prohibition of regional aid for shipbuilding.

The only exception to the exclusive competence of the Commission in State aid, is Article 88(2), which allows the Council, acting unanimously, to declare a State aid compatible 'if such decision is justified by exceptional circumstances'. This possibility has only been used in the agricultural sector.

Derogations

The Treaty gives the Commission the discretion to consider aid to be compatible with the common market, as a derogation from the basic rule mentioned above. Such aid should be consistent with the objectives stated in Article 87(3):

(a)   aid to promote the economic development of areas where the standard of living is abnormally low or where there is a serious underemployment;

(b)   aid to promote the execution of an important project of common European interest or to remedy a serious disturbance in the economy of a Member State;

(c)   aid to facilitate the development of certain economic activities or of certain economic areas, where such aid does not adversely affect trading conditions to an extent contrary to the common interest.

Article 87(3)(a)
This Article means that the Commission must be satisfied that the areas concerned are experiencing difficulties which are serious enough, in a Community-wide comparison, to warrant the grant of aid at the level proposed, in other words, that the aid is necessary to ensure attainment of the objectives set out in Article 87(3). The assessment is made with the average Community per capita domestic product,[16] measured in purchasing power standards.

Regional aid aimed at reducing a firm's current expenses (operating aid) is normally prohibited; however, in the regions mentioned in this paragraph, it may be defendable. In any case, operating aid must be both limited in time and progressively reduced.

Article 87(3)(b)
The derogation for an important project of common European interest has rarely been used. Aid to the construction of Airbus, set up jointly by several companies from different Member States, and the project's technical and economic features, has been allowed under this provision. Other examples concern the formulation of industrial standards in an important area of business, such as a number of Eureka projects in the field of electronics or high-definition television.

---

[16]   For a region to be eligible, this should be less than 75 per cent of the Community average.

Serious disturbance in the context of this paragraph must concern the whole of the national economy and not just one region or sector, for example, the financial support measures Member States undertook immediately after the oil shock in 1974.

Article 87(3)(c)

This derogation is the one mostly used; it mainly concerns sectoral aid and regional aid, where facilitating economic development is more easily applicable. It concerns support for new investment or expansion of existing capacity, but also a restructuring operation involving closures, rationalisation and adaptation of production to new or more specialised market demand.[17]

The Commission has to assess whether trading conditions are affected: taking into account the amount of the proposed increased output or the percentage of the company's total production which will probably be exported to other Member States after the grant of aid. The Commission examines the existence of strong competition, of decline in demand and of surplus capacity.

In the opinion of the Commission, regional aid in this sense may only be allowed for a small part of the national territory of a Member State, and the aid must also form part of a coherent national regional policy. The selection of eligible regions, as well as the fixing of an aid ceiling for each Member State, needs the approval of the Commission; the result is put on a regional aid map, which will be applicable for a period of five years.

Coal and Steel

The ECSC Treaty is much stricter: subsidies or aids granted by Member States in any form whatsoever are incompatible with the common market and must be abolished and prohibited.

However, Article 95 of the ECSC Treaty gives the Commission the power to decide otherwise, with the unanimous consent of the Council. The difficulties in the coal and steel sector have been reasons for the Commission to make use of that power; the aid codex for the steel industry gives the conditions for granting aid. This has been used at the end of 1983, when steel companies in several Member States were allowed to receive aid, see Chapter 13.

Existing Aid

The Commission is obliged to monitor aid that already existed before the common market was created (or aid that it authorised before), as a check that compatibility with the common market is still in force (Article 88):

---

[17] Joined cases 296 and 318/82, *Leeuwarder Papierfabriek*, OJ 1983 C-16.

The Commission shall, in co-operation with Member States, keep under constant review all systems of aid existing in those States. It shall propose to the latter any appropriate measures required by the progressive development or by the functioning of the common market.

Whenever the Commission finds that the aid is not answering to the compatibility test, it proposes that the Member State abolishes or alters the aid.

9.3   APPLICATION OF STATE AID CONTROL

As the Treaty itself offers not much detail, it has been up to the Commission to fill in the practices for its control: in notices and letters to the Member States, it constructed a regulatory framework, explaining the ways and means for applying the Treaty. Since the mid-1990s Member States are consulted[18] on those frameworks and guidelines, which concern certain categories of aid such as: aids to the textile and clothing industry (SEC(71) 363); the synthetic fibres industry (1989, OJ C-173); the motor vehicles industry (1989, OJ C-123); shipbuilding[19], regional aid,[20] aids in environmental matters (1994, OJ C-72); research and development (1986, OJ C-83; 1996, OJ C-45); rescue and restructuring aids.[21]

Rescue and Restructuring Aid

In the Commission's practice of State aid control, rescue and restructuring aid always has had its special attention. It regards a company as being in difficulties where it is unable to stop losses occurring and almost certainly would be forced to go out of business. Rescue aids are allowed as a short term (in principle not longer than six months) transitional device preceding a restructuring operation.

Restructuring aid is subject to a series of conditions, such as the setting up of a restructuring plan, which restores the long-term viability of the enterprise within a reasonable timescale; and on the basis of realistic assumptions as to its future operation. Aid should not be higher than strictly necessary to enable the restructuring of the enterprise, nor should it be used for financing new investment that is not necessary for the restructuring.

In case of a structural excess of production capacity in a relevant market in the Community served by the recipient, the restructuring plan must make a contribution, proportionate to the amount of aid received, to the restructuring of the industrial sector involved, for instance, by irreversibly reducing or

---

[18]   In so-called Multilateral Meetings, chaired by the Commission.
[19]   By seven consecutive Directives.
[20]   1971, OJ C-111; 1979, OJ C-31; 1988, OJ C-212.
[21]   Guidelines, July 1994; renewed in 1999 (OJ 1999, C-288).

closing capacity. The beneficiary of the aid will be expected to make a significant contribution to the restructuring plan.

Such a 'counterpart' will normally not be required if there is no structural excess capacity; in that case, the Commission shall require that capacity will not be expanded during the implementation of the restructuring plan, except where that is essential for restoring the viability of the enterprise. A lower level of aid will logically lead to a smaller counterpart.

The Commission regards this 'counterpart' as an essential accessory of its State aid control, aimed not only at improving the overall structure of the market, but also at protecting competitors against distortion of competition. In case there is no overcapacity, this would mean that the 'counterpart' could very well be a reduction of market share.

One Time Last Time Principle

One of the first attempts to put a limit on the amount of State aid to a specific company appeared in the Council's conclusions (December 1993) that unanimously approved significant amounts of restructuring aid to a number of firms in the steel industry. At that time, Member States promised not to propose to the Commission new aids for this sector. For the Commission it was legally impossible to make a similar promise: the Treaty obliges the Commission to take a decision on any aid measure, even when such a measure is not notified to it.

The guidelines for rescue and restructuring aid originally made a careful reference to this concept: 'aid for restructuring should normally only need to be granted once'. In assessing an aid, the Commission will take all relevant element into account, one of them being the fact that the company has already been granted aid; in such a case, the Commission will not allow further aid, unless exceptional circumstances occur which were unforeseeable to the company in question.

Public Companies[22]

Public enterprises are not treated differently from private companies. The Treaty (Article 295) accepts that Member States have State-owned companies. However, these are not exempted from the Treaty obligations. Article 86(1) prohibits Member States from using public undertakings to go against the rules of the Treaty, especially those concerning the principle of non-discrimination, and those in Articles 81 to 89 (competition rules). Article 86(2) emphasises that undertakings entrusted with the operation of services of general economic interest or having the character of a revenue-producing monopoly are subject to the rules on competition, unless the application of

---

[22] Bulletin EC 9–1984.

these rules would obstruct the performance of the particular tasks assigned to them.

This paragraph is an exemption for public companies from substantive provisions of the Treaty, but nor from procedural provisions. In other words, Member States are obliged to notify all State aids, including aid to public undertakings.

The Commission is of the opinion that almost any action, in which the State, as owner, acts differently from a private investor, constitutes State aid. Such actions may include cash payments, debt write-offs and cases in which governments, for instance, accept a rate of return below the market rate on investments or waive dividend payments.

In practice, the application of the State aid rules to public undertakings presents political problems because of the close, intricate and confidential relationship between such undertakings and the State. For example, after long and difficult exchanges with the French government, the Commission allowed around €1.8 billion (FF12 billion) write-off of the debts of Renault. That company accepted to cut capacity and change its status as a State enterprise, but when the government delayed action, the Commission demanded the repayment of around €1.1 billion (FF8 billion). Political negotiations ended up in the compromise that Renault agreed to pay back not more than €900 million (FF6 billion).

The Transparency Directive[23]

In order to make it possible for the Commission to judge the State's influence in public companies, a *Commission* Directive (based on Article 86,3) was adopted that requires Member States to deliver information on their financial relations with such companies. Public undertaking is defined in this Directive as ' any undertaking over which the public authorities may exercise directly or indirectly a dominant influence by virtue of their ownership of it, their financial participation therein, or the rules which govern it'.

Member States have to inform the Commission about: the setting-off of operating losses; the provision of capital; non-refundable grants or loans on privileged terms; the granting of financial advantages by forgoing profits or the recovery of sums due; the forgoing of a normal return on public funds used; compensation for financial burdens imposed by the public authorities. The Commission intends to compare the behaviour of the public authorities with that of a private owner in a similar situation.

France, Italy and the UK challenged the Directive before the Court[24], claiming that it should have been a *Council* Directive under Article 89.

---

[23] Commission Directive 80/723/EEC (OJ 1980 L-195), amended by Commission Directives 85/413/EEC (OJ 1985 L-229) and 93/84/EEC (OJ 1993 L-254).

[24] Joined Cases 188 to 190/80.

Under Article 86(3) the Council is not involved. In view of the resistance among the Member States, the required qualified majority of Article 89 would probably not have been reached. The Court, however, recognised the Commission's competence to create, under Article 86(3), rules parallel to those possible under Article 89.

The Commission amended its Directive[25] to take account of the increased market liberalisation, where public companies progressively manifested themselves in the market as normal operators, thereby enlarging possible problems of competition (through cross-subsidisation).

The amendment requires Member States to create separate accounts in those companies, separating public from commercial activities. The Commission then could more easily ascertain that no unjustified aid is being used.

Framework for Aid to Research and Development

The Commission's White Paper on Growth, Competitiveness and Employment stressed the importance of general measures to promote R&D investment by firms. The emphasis is on 'general' measures, including favourable tax treatment and measures to enhance the effectiveness of research: 'shifting government intervention from direct support to indirect instruments.'

Traditionally, the Commission expressed a favourable view of State aid for R&D, because it accepts a role for governments in the promotion of research and development in the economy. It justifies this favourable attitude by taking into account the aims of such aid and the often considerable financial requirements and risks of R&D operations. Member States have to notify (by means of a standard form[26]) to the Commission their intention to provide State aid to R&D projects, as well as their general schemes to promote R&D. The Commission then examines in particular the type of research, the beneficiaries, the incentive effect, and the aid intensity.

Type of research
The closer R&D is to the market, the more significant may be the distortive effect of the State aid. In order to determine the proximity to the market of the aided R&D, the Commission makes a distinction between the following categories: fundamental research, industrial research and precompetitive development activity.[27]

---

[25] First proposed in March 1999.
[26] Letter to the Member States 22 February 1994, amended 2 August 1995.
[27] The framework: OJ 1986 C-83. Revised OJ 1996 C-45 and adapted to include research and development in the agricultural sector, OJ 1998 C-48.

Individual grants of aid under an R&D scheme that has been authorised by the Commission do not, in principle, need to be notified. However, prior notification is required of any individual research project costing more than €25 million and for which it is proposed to provide aid with a gross grant equivalent of more than €5 million.

Innovation does not qualify as a separate category of R&D. Aid for activities that could be regarded as innovative but do not correspond to the categories can only benefit from State aid if it conforms to the Commission's policy on investment aid.

The beneficiaries
R&D activities by public universities or research establishments are normally not covered as State aid by Article 87(1). Especially where the results of such projects are made available to Community industry on a non-discriminatory basis, the Commission assumes that no State aid is involved.

The Commission will likewise assume that collaboration between these establishments and industry to carry out R&D does not involve State aid, when they act as a commercial firm would. For example: in return for payment at the market rate for the services they provide; or when the industrial participants bear the full cost of the project; or when the results (outside intellectual property rights) may be widely disseminated and intellectual property rights are fully allocated to these public establishments; or when these establishments receive from the industrial participants compensation equivalent to the market price for these rights.

Public authorities may commission R&D from firms or buy the results of R&D directly from them. If there is no open tender procedure, the Commission will assume that there may be State aid. If these contracts are awarded according to market conditions, in particular after an open tender procedure, it will normally be assumed that no State aid is involved.

Incentive effect
The aid should serve as an incentive for firms to undertake R&D activities in addition to their normal day-to-day operations. It may also encourage firms not carrying out R&D to undertake such activities.

Where this incentive effect is not evident, the Commission may consider such aid less favourably than it usually does. In its considerations it takes into account: quantifiable factors (such as changes in the R&D spending, in the number of people assigned to R&D activities and in R&D spending as a proportion of total turnover), market failures, additional costs connected with cross-border co-operation and so on.

Member States have to demonstrate in their notifications that the aid is necessary as an incentive. The Commission assumes this is the case if the recipient is an SME.

The allowable intensity of aid

The Commission determines this on a case-by-case basis. Its assessment will take into consideration the nature of the project or programme, overall policy considerations relating to the competitiveness of European industry, the risk of distortion of competition and the effect on trade between Member States (see Box 9.1).

Box 9.1   Aid intensities

As a general rule, the gross aid intensity for industrial research must not exceed 50% of the eligible costs of the project.
Technical feasibility studies preparatory to industrial research may qualify for aid amounting to 75 per cent of study costs; for such studies preparatory to precompetitive development activities support may amount to 50 per cent of costs.
Commission practice concerning precompetitive development activities is that the permissible gross aid intensity is fixed at 25 per cent of the eligible costs.
These aid intensities may be exceeded:
Where the aid is given to SMEs – an extra 10 percentage points;
Where the project is carried out in a (c) region – 5 extra points;
Where the project fits in with the Framework Programme – 15 extra points (plus 10 if it also involves cross-border co-operation and dissemination of the results;
Where the projects involves cross-border co-operation plus wide dissemination – 10 extra points.
All these bonuses have to fulfil the total maximum of 75 per cent for industrial research and 50 per cent for precompetitive development.
Where the derogation of 87(3) (b) applies, the aid intensity must not exceed the WTO Subsidies Code (75 and 50 per cent).
Where State aid and Community financing are combined, total support may not exceed 75 per cent and 50 per cent.

Fundamental research and industrial research may qualify for higher levels of aid than precompetitive development activities, which are more closely related to the market introduction of R&D results and, if aided, could therefore more easily lead to distortions of competition and trade. To qualify as fundamental research, the work should not be linked to any industrial or commercial objectives of a particular enterprise, and a wide dissemination of the results of the research must be guaranteed.

Regional Aid

In order to avoid the risk of outbidding in awarding regional aid, the Commission created rules for co-ordination, including a ceiling for aid intensity.[28] Since that time, a number of documents further explained the way the Commission assessed regional aid in respect of the relevant Treaty

---

[28]   Council Resolution of 20 October 1971, OJ 1971 C-111.

Articles 87(3)(a) and 87(3)(c).[29] Regional aid is awarded to develop the less-favoured regions by supporting investment and job creation. Such aid should not interfere with the normal operation of market forces, that is, distortions of competition should be justified in the light of existing regional problems.[30]

The most recent Commission communication (1999a) with guidelines for assessing national regional aid (OJ 1998 C-74) stresses that such aid, in principle, should be exceptional. Therefore, the Commission states that the total extent of assisted regions in the Union must remain smaller than that of unassisted regions; this means that the total coverage of regional aid must be less than 50 per cent of the Community population.

The regions eligible under the derogation in paragraph (a) currently account for 22.7 per cent of the Community population, those under the derogation in paragraph (c) account for 24 per cent. Member States notify to the Commission the regions[31] that they want to be eligible for regional aid; the Commission approves the selection and also fixes, for each Member State, a ceiling on the coverage of such aid.

The eligible regions plus the aid intensity ceilings form a Member State's regional aid map. A draft map is notified to the Commission, who will adopt it for a fixed period. In the interests of consistency between the Community's competition policy decisions and decisions concerning regions eligible under the Structural Funds, the period of validity of the aid maps is in principle aligned on the timetable for Structural Funds assistance. Aid from the Structural Funds, as analysed in Chapter 10, has to follow the State aid rules in this respect.

In order to better control aid to investment in assisted regions, special attention is given to large-scale mobile investment projects. Investors in such projects often consider alternative sites in different Member States, thereby inviting governments to offer aid that may influence their location decisions. Member States have to take account of the allowable aid intensities, while the Commission has to make certain that the total amount of aid has no adverse effects on competition in the common market.

Under the guidelines for regional aid, Member States may support investments in the eligible regions; for example, investments in fixed capital relating to the setting-up of a new establishment, the extension of an existing establishment, or the starting-up of an activity involving a fundamental change in the product or production process of an existing establishment (through rationalisation, diversification or modernisation). To ensure that the productive investment aided is viable and sound, the recipient's own contribution to its financing ('counterpart') must be at least 25 per cent (see Box 9.2).

---

[29] Referred to as (a) regions and (c) regions.
[30] Case 730/79 *Philip Morris*.
[31] The individual regions proposed or the groups of contiguous regions must form compact zones, each of which must have a population of at least 100 000.

Box 9.2   Allowable aid intensity

> The intensity of the aid must take account of the nature and intensity of the regional problems that are being addressed. Therefore, a distinction must be made between the regions under paragraph (a) and those under paragraph (c) of Article 87(3). For the regions falling under paragraph (a), the intensity of regional aid must not exceed the rate of 50 per cent NGE (net grant equivalent), except in the outermost regions, where it may be as much as 65 per cent NGE.
>
> For the regions falling under paragraph (c), the ceiling is 20 per cent NGE, except in the low population density regions or in the outermost regions, where it may be as high as 30 per cent NGE.
>
> For SMEs these ceilings may be supplemented with 15 percentage points (paragraph (a) regions) or 10 percentage points (paragraph (c) regions).

After the setting up of a 'Multisectoral framework on regional aid for large investment projects' (OJ 1998 C-107), Member States are obliged to notify to projects that cost at least €50 million or when the aid amounts to at least €50 million.

In its assessment of the notification, the Commission uses a formula that combines criteria concerning competition, the capital-to-labour ratio, and the regional impact factor.

Environmental Aid (OJ 1994 C-72)

In every Member State governments are committed to improve the environment and the use of energy, through all sorts of activities. The Community as such contributes to these, as can be seen in Chapter 6.

These activities may involve State aid, when firms are encouraged to take into account environmental considerations in their investment decisions. The introduction of environmental taxes and charges can involve State aid because some firms may not be able to stand the extra financial burden immediately and require temporary relief. Such relief is operating aid.

In its assessment of the aid granted to such investments, the Commission makes allowances for the positive environmental goals. Aid for energy conservation will be treated like aid for environmental purposes, insofar as it aims at and achieves significant benefits for the environment and the aid is necessary, having regard to the cost savings obtained by the investor. Aid for renewable energy, the development of which is an especially high priority in the EU, is also subject to these guidelines, insofar as aid for investment is concerned. Operating aid for renewable energies will be judged on its merits. The Commission accepts aid to companies when such a support compensates for the production costs that are additional (compared with traditional costs). For example, when a company requests aid for a new, more environmentally-friendly installation, the Commission will only authorise aid to the extra costs of this installation by comparison with the costs of a standard installation. Also, the allowable aid will be differentiated according to the existing mandatory environmental standards (see Box 9.3).

Box 9.3   Allowable aid intensities

Aid to help firms adapt to new mandatory standards	15%
Aid that significantly increases the environmental performance of a firm than required by mandatory standard	30%
Aid to improve the environmental performance of a firm in an area where no mandatory standards exist	30%
Aid for information, advice, training	50%
These percentages may be increased with 15 percentage points when the enterprise is a SME, located in an assisted (a)-region and with 10 percentage points when located in an assisted (c)-region	

As in all cases of State aid, such aid must be strictly necessary to meet environmental objectives. Aid to investments in land, buildings, plant and equipment intended to reduce or eliminate pollution and nuisances or to adapt production methods in order to protect the environment, will be assessed in the light of the intended objectives.

The level of aid actually granted for exceeding standards must be in proportion to the improvement of the environment that is achieved and to the investment necessary for achieving the improvement.

Taxation

The Council (Ecofin) adopted a Resolution on a code of conduct for business taxation (OJ 1998 C-2). The code of conduct aims to improve transparency in the tax area through a system of information exchanges between Member States and of assessment of any tax measures that may be covered by it.

Tackling harmful tax competition is the objective of this exercise, and the State aid rules play a part. The Commission examines the compatibility of aid not in terms of the form which it may take, but in terms of its effect. The aid measure must give recipients an advantage which relieves them of charges that they normally have to pay out of their budgets. Such an advantage, that reduces the firm's tax burden, could be a reduction in the tax base (through special deductions or special or accelerated depreciation arrangements) or a reduction in the amount of tax.

When the tax authorities have the freedom to grant exemptions in a discretionary manner, the Commission readily assumes that there is State aid involved. However, the selective nature of a measure may be justified by 'the nature or general scheme of the system'[32].

In the application of the State aid rules, a loss of tax revenue is equivalent to consumption of State resources in the form of fiscal expenditure. State support may also be provided through the practices of the tax authorities. Just as in the case of subsidies granted, the fact that the aid strengthens the firm's position compared with that of other firms, which are competitors in intra-Community trade, is enough to conclude that intra-Community trade is affected.

Tax measures, which are equally accessible to all companies in a Member State, are in principle general measures. Examples of such measures which are allowed are the rate of taxation, depreciation rules, rules on loss carry-overs, provisions to prevent double taxation or tax avoidance. A tax measure whose main effect is to promote one or more sectors of activity constitutes aid. The Commission has taken the view that a measure which targets all of the sectors that are subject to international competition, constitutes aid[33].

Infringement Procedures

Infringement procedures start with the Commission formally asking from the Member State an official reaction concerning the possible infringement of the rules. If the Commission is not satisfied with the Member State's answer, it may require the Member State to alter or cancel the aid within a given period (normally two months). If the Member State fails to comply within the deadline, the Commission (or any other interested Member State) may refer the matter to the Court of Justice.

9.4 REGULATIONS

The Articles of the Treaty give exclusive competence to the Commission regarding the control on State aid. Member States, or the Council, have no decisive role to play, with the exception of Article 89:

> The Council may, acting by a qualified majority on a proposal from the Commission, make any appropriate regulations for the application of Articles 87 and 88 and may in particular determine the conditions in which Article 88,3 shall apply and the categories of aid exempted from this procedure.

Earlier attempts to legislate under this Article failed, because the Council was unable to agree[34] and/or the Commission feared for its exclusive

---

[32] Case 173/73 Italy vs Commission.
[33] Case Maribel bis/ter, OJ 1997 L-95.
[34] Article 89 has been used to exempt the major categories of aid to inland transport: Council Regulations 1191/69, 1192/69, 1107/79.

competence. It took until 1996 before the Commission again made proposals: on the exemption of certain categories of aid, and on procedures; this time, the Council accepted both.

Exemptions[35]

This Regulation enables the Commission to exempt from the notification requirements certain categories of aid (aid for small and medium-sized enterprises, research and development, environmental protection, employment and training, and regional aid). The implication is that these aids have a limited effect on competition. With this exemption, the Commission expects to lighten its caseload, so that it can give more attention to major cases. But this does not mean that control on State aid is neglected: Member States are obliged to keep records of all aid that is exempted for a period of ten years; the Commission can request all the information necessary to exercise its control.

Each category exempted from notification has to be specified in Commission Regulations, which also can attach further conditions for the compatibility of the aid exempted. Before adopting any such regulation the Commission has to consult the Advisory Committee on State Aid[36].

Three Commission Regulations have been proposed so far: small and medium-sized enterprises, training aid, and *de minimis* 'aid'.

SMEs

Aid for investment to small and medium-sized enterprises is exempted from the obligation to notify, when the intensity of that aid does not exceed 15 per cent (small enterprises) or 7.5 per cent (medium-sized enterprises). In areas which qualify for regional aid (see above), these percentages may be increased with 10 percentage points in (a) regions, and with 15 percentage points in (c) regions; there is an absolute ceiling on the total amount of aid received of 30 per cent and 65 per cent, respectively.

These percentages only regard the obligation to notify. Added as an extra condition is the obligation that the aided investment is maintained in the region for at least five years. The enterprise itself has to contribute at least 25 per cent of the financing needed.

SMEs have been defined in the Commission's policies as enterprises which have fewer than 250 employees and have either an annual turnover not exceeding €40 million, or an annual balance-sheet total not exceeding €27 million; as well as be independent, that is, 25 per cent or more of the capital or voting rights is not owned by others.

---

[35]   Council Regulation (EC)994/98 on the application of Articles 92 and 93 (now: 87 and 88) of the Treaty to certain categories of horizontal state aid, OJ 1998 L-142.

[36]   Established by Council Regulation (EC)994/98.

Excluded from the exemption is any aid that exceeds €50 million, or aid that finances a project that costs at least €50 million. Aid to export activities of an enterprise is also excluded.

Training

General training provides transferable skills and qualifications, and as such improves the competitiveness of European industry. The risk of distorting competition is small and, therefore, aid to such training is considered to be compatible with the common market. There is no need to notify such aid when the aid intensity is less than 50 per cent (for large enterprises) or 70 per cent (for SMEs).

Aid to specific training mainly benefits the enterprise involved and involves a greater risk for distortion of competition. The aid intensity of such aid may not exceed 25 per cent (for large enterprises) or 35 per cent (for SMEs).

In areas that qualify for regional aid, these percentages may be increased with 10 percentage points in (a) regions and 5 percentage points in (c) regions.

Whenever the amount of aid for training exceeds €1 million, the exemption to notify is not applicable.

De minimis

According to the Commission's experience, aid not exceeding a ceiling of €100 000 over a period of three years does not affect trade between Member States and does not distort competition. Therefore, it does not fall under Article 87(1) of the Treaty; in other words, it is not regarded as State aid and does not need to be notified.

Aid to the agriculture sector, as well as to the transport sector, is excluded from the exemption.

Whenever a Member State grants *de minimis* support to an enterprise, it has to inform that enterprise accordingly; in response, the enterprise has to confirm in writing that the support given does not raise the total amount of *de minimis* aid above €100 000 for a period of three years.

Procedures[37]

This Regulation (see Figure 9.1) codifies existing practice and case law, reaffirming the rule that aid must be notified in advance to the Commission and that Member States must not implement any aid that has not been

---

[37] Council Regulation (EC)659/1999, laying down detailed rules for the application of Article 93 (now: 88) of the Treaty, OJ 1999 L-83; see the flowchart annexed to this Chapter.

authorised by the Commission. Any aid that does not conform to this rule, will be unlawful aid.

Without giving a definition of aid, the Regulation not only codifies but also introduces new rules: concerning a limitation period (ten years), the rights of interested parties, recovery injunction, and on-site monitoring.

An 'interested party' is defined as: 'any Member State and any person, undertaking or association of undertakings whose interests might be affected by the granting of aid, in particular the beneficiary of the aid, competing undertakings and trade associations'. Any of these may submit comments and, when they do, shall be sent a copy of the Commission's decision on that case.

The Commission may require a Member State to recover any unlawful aid until a decision has been taken on the compatibility of the aid with the common market. Such a provisional recovery[38] can only be applied if the aid character is clear; if there is an urgency to act; and if there is a serious risk of substantial and irreparable damage to a competitor.

When the Commission takes a negative decision in cases of unlawful aid, the Member State shall be ordered to take all necessary measures to recover the aid from the beneficiary. With a view to past experiences[39], the Regulation states, that 'recovery shall be effected without delay and in accordance with the procedures under the national law of the Member State concerned, provided that they allow the immediate and effective execution of the Commission's decision'. In case national procedures do not make provision for a speedy action, the Member State concerned 'shall take all necessary steps which are available in their respective legal systems, including provisional measures.'

In order to achieve more transparency in State aid control, the Regulation demands the publication in the Official Journal of: a summary notice of the Commission's decision in an aid case (a copy of that decision may be obtained in the authentic language version); the decision to initiate the formal investigation procedure in the authentic language version (the Official Journal in other languages will publish a meaningful summary in that language); the decision to close the formal investigation procedure; short notices of decisions, such as the withdrawal of a notification by a Member State. On the Internet the Commission will publish the decision that a measure is not State aid and its decision not to raise objections to a notified aid (that is, approval).

In case of doubts about the compatibility of the notified aid with the common market, the Commission must initiate the formal investigation procedure of Article 88(2)of the Treaty.

---

[38] Applicable only to unlawful aid implemented after the entry into force of this Regulation, i.e. from 16 April 1999 onwards.

[39] There are cases, where recovery of aid is frustrated by national escape procedures, that can take as long as ten years or more.

Figure 9.1 Flowchart: procedure

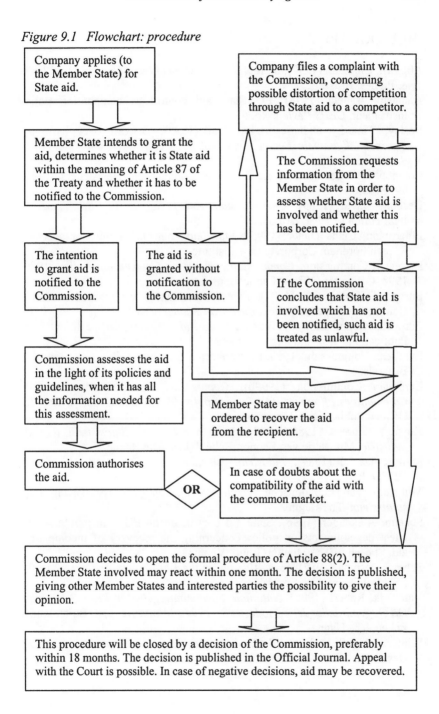

BIBLIOGRAPHY

Ahlborn, Christian (1997), *State Aid – Everything Under Control?* Linklaters & Paines, Brussels.

Atanasiu, Isabela (1998), EU State aid control as competition policy instrument, *CEPS Review* No. 6.

Besley, Timothy and Seabright, Paul (1999), Discord over harmony, *European Economic Perspectives* No. 21. Centre for Economic Policy Research.

Competition Directorate of the European Commission: Newsletters, 1994–99, Brussels.

Deacon, David (1989), *Current State Aid Policy in the EEC and the Implication of 1992,* Brussels.

Ehlermann, Claus Dieter (1995), State aid control – failure or success? Speech Fordham Corporate Law Institute.

European Commission, *Commission Reports on Competition Policy*, 1980-1998, Office for Official Publications, Luxembourg.

European Commission (1991), Fair competition in the internal market – Community State aid policy, *European Economy* No. 48.

European Commission, *Surveys on State Aid*, 1990-98, Office for Official Publications, Luxembourg.

European Commission (1999a), *Vademecum Community Rules on State Aid*, Brussels.

European Commission (1999b), *Competition Law in the European Communities, Volume IIA, Rules applicable to State Aid*, Office for Official Publications, Luxembourg.

Kuyper, Laurens (1986, 1989), *Industriebeleid en Staatssteun aan de industrie*, Ministerie van Economische Zaken, The Hague.

Malkin, Daniel (1989), *Industrial Subsidies and Structural Adjustment*, OECD, Paris.

Ministerie van Economische Zaken (1997), *Europese regelgeving over staatssteun,* The Hague.

Schaub, Alexander (1996), State aid control in the EU – in particular the latest developments on policy concerning the recovery of incompatible aid, Speech to The Mentor Group, Vienna.

Schina, Despina (1987), *State Aids under the EEC Treaty Articles 92 to 94*, ESC Publishing Ltd, Oxford.

Van Dijk, Robert (1995), *Nationale Steunmaatregelen en het EG-Verdrag, O&O gedurende de periode 1985-1994*, Ministerie van Buitenlandse Zaken, The Hague.

Winter, J.A. (1981), *Nationale Steunmaatregelen en het Gemeenschapsrecht*, Deventer.

UNICE (1996), *Reform of State Aid,* Brussels.

10. Structural Funds – Sources of Finance for Business in most EU Regions

Michael Darmer

The Structural Funds and the Cohesion Fund are the means by which the Community assists regions whose development is lagging behind or areas facing structural difficulties or to prevent and combat unemployment.[1] In that respect the Structural Funds and the Cohesion Fund are closely linked to the Regional Policy[2] of the European Union.

Even though the Structural Funds always have been an integrated part of the Treaty, it is only in the last 10–15 years that these funds, in financial terms, have reached a level which have put them on top as the number one EU source of finance for industry. For the period 2000–06, the Structural Funds including the Cohesion Fund have a budget of €213 billion. Even though not all the Structural Funds are equally important to industry, a large majority of the available financial means will be very attractive to business and industry, making the Structural Funds the number one EU source of finance for business and industry.

The increase in the financial means available is to a large extent due to the previous enlargements of the Union, which have increased regional disparities and added peripheral regions to the central location of the original six Member States. Section 1 gives the historical background for the regional policy of the EU and analyses the development in the financial means available for Structural Funds and regional policy.

Section 2 analyses the development of regional disparities within the EU, indicating that the regional policy of the EU has narrowed regional disparities. However, it is also indicated that in the most successful of the regions lagging behind, the reasons for their success is a mix of measures taken at regional, national and EU level. This section also makes clear that despite 10–15 years of massive financial support from the EU, large regional disparities still exist.

---

[1] The criteria for defining regions as lagging behind and areas as facing difficulties and so on are explained below.
[2] In EU terminology is the notion Cohesion Policy used instead of Regional Policy.

Section 3 outlines the objectives and means of the Union's regional policy. The section focuses on those Funds that are of particular importance to business and industry. These Funds also happen to be the ones that are the biggest in financial terms.

Section 4 focuses on the eligible regions. In terms of number of regions and geographical area coverage, the majority of regions of the EU is covered. Even more so when the regions and areas are included that are phasing out from the earlier period of the Funds.

Before we conclude in Section 6, Section 5 illustrates, through real life cases, how business and industry may benefit from the Structural Funds.

10.1   HISTORICAL BACKGROUND – THE AIM

Regional policy has been an integrated part of EU policy from the very beginning, although in the beginning it was rather small in financial terms. One of the reasons for the limited amount was that the original six Member States (France, Germany, Italy, the Netherlands, Belgium and Luxembourg) were rather homogenous, with southern Italy as the only exception. The European Social Fund (ESF) focused its activity on the south of Italy and the European Agricultural Guidance and Guarantee Fund, Guidance Section (EAGGF) was mainly distributing to the relatively wealthier agricultural areas in the north of the Community.

With enlargement, regional disparities increased and so did the importance of regional policy. The first enlargement took place in 1973 when Ireland, the UK and Denmark joined the EU. While Denmark was on equal footing with the others in terms of per capita income, the UK brought in some regions like the north of England and Northern Ireland which increased regional disparities. Ireland was significantly poorer than the rest of the EU with a per capita income that was only just half that of the original six Member States.

With the 1973 oil shock regional disparities increased even further since that shock had a different impact on different regions. Governments were put under pressure to react: in 1975, the European Regional Development Fund (ERDF) was established.

The second enlargement in 1981 (Greece) and the third in 1986 (Spain and Portugal) further increased regional disparities and established regional policy at the top of the European agenda. The reunification of Germany in 1990 added 17 million inhabitants whose average income at the time was only 35 per cent of the enlarged EU-12 average.

The latest enlargement with Sweden, Finland and Austria took place in 1995, and this enlargement had also regional policy implication. As a direct consequence a new objective[3] was added to the existing ones. The aim of the new objective was to assist sparsely populated areas in the north of Sweden and Finland.

The 1986 revision of the Treaty (The Single European Act) re-launched among other things the Internal Market. In that respect there was a fear that the creation of a strong internal market would mainly benefit the centre of the EU at the expense of the periphery, which at the same time were the poorest regions – Greece, Southern Italy, Spain, Portugal and Ireland. In order to balance the benefit of the Internal Market and assist the regions in the periphery of the EU, the Title of *'Economic and Social Cohesion'* was inserted in the Treaty, and in 1987 it was decided to double the amount allocated to the Structural Funds for the period 1989–93. In 1993, the amount was increased even further for the period 1994–99 (see Figure 10.1).

Figure 10.1   Structural Funds and the Cohesion Fund, million € 1970–2006

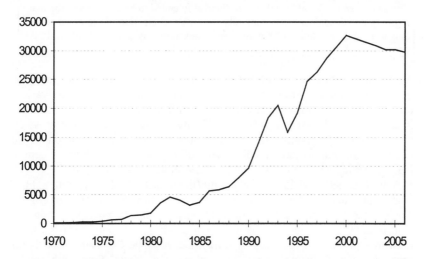

Note: 1970–98; outturn in payments. 1999; budget. 2000–2006; budget, fixed 1999 prices.
Source: European Commission (1999g)

In 1999, the EU budget, including the budget for the Structural Funds, for 2000–06 was decided. Because of budgetary restraints (due to the forthcoming enlargement with East and Central European Countries) the amount set aside for regional policy within EU-15 was reduced (see later).

---

[3]   Former Objective 6, now integrated in Objective 1. See below for an explanation of the different objectives.

The Treaty

As mentioned above, the Title on Economic and Social Cohesion (Articles 158–162) was inserted in the Treaty in 1986 (see Box 10.1).

Box 10.1   Articles from the Treaty related to economic and social cohesion

> **Article 158**
> In order to promote its overall harmonious development, the Community shall develop and pursue its actions leading to the strengthening of its economic and social cohesion.
> In particular, the Community shall aim at reducing disparities between the level of development of the various regions and the backwardness of the least-favoured regions, including rural areas.
>
> **Article 160**
> The European Regional Development Fund is intended to help to redress the main regional imbalances in the Community through participation in the development and structural adjustment of regions whose development is lagging behind in the conversion of declining industrial regions.

According to Article 158 of the Treaty the Community shall in particular 'aim at reducing disparities between the level of development of the various regions'. The main instrument to accomplish this is the Regional Fund which in accordance with Article 160 of the Treaty 'is intended to help redress the main regional imbalances in the Community through participation in the development and structural adjustment of regions whose development is lagging behind and in the conversion of declining industrial region'.

With the 1991 revision of the Treaty (the Maastricht Treaty), a new Fund was established – The Cohesion Fund. According to Article 161 of the Treaty the Council shall 'set up a Cohesion Fund to provide a financial contribution to projects in the fields of environment and trans-European networks in the area of transport infrastructure'. The Cohesion Fund is not regarded as a Structural Fund, but rather as a special fund with related objectives.

The financial instrument related to the fishing industry, the Financial Instrument for Fisheries Guidance (FIFG), operated previously outside the scope of the Structural Funds, but has now become an integrated part of the Structural Funds. The Structural Funds then consist of the European Regional Development Fund (ERDF), the European Social Fund (ESF), The European Agricultural Guidance and Guarantee Fund, Guidance Section (EAGGF) and the Financial Instrument for Fisheries Guidance (FIFG). These funds are usually referred to by their abbreviations or simply as the Regional Fund, the Social Fund, the Agricultural Fund and the Fishery Fund.

10.2 DISPARITIES AND CONVERGENCE

The two fundamental criteria in relation to EU regional policy are per capita income and unemployment. There are other criteria (see next section), but they are all linked to these two basic criteria.

Figure 10.2 shows the variation in per capita income within Member States and between Member States. Per capita income is measured in gross domestic product (GDP) at purchasing power parities (PPS). A per capita income of 100 is equal to Community average. Member States are organised in order of their average per capita income.

Figure 10.2 Regional variation in per capita GDP (PPS) and between Member States, 1996

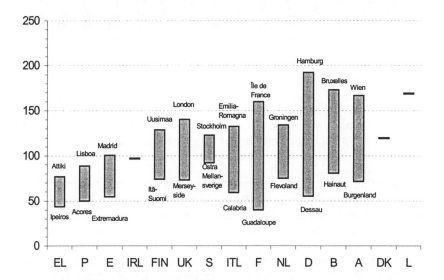

Source: European Commission (1999a)

Figure 10.2 shows that the largest regional variation within a Member State is found in Germany and France followed by Belgium and Austria. In Germany, the richest region, Hamburg, is almost four times as rich as the poorest, Dessau. Figure 10.2 shows no regional variation for Ireland, Denmark and Luxembourg, which is due to the fact that each of these countries statistically are regarded as one region when it comes to per capita income.

While it is very difficult to change per capita income in the short and even in the medium–long term, there is more fluctuation in the unemployment rate – the other main criteria. The development in Denmark and Ireland illustrates this. In 1994, the Danish and the Irish unemployment rate was 10.7 and 15.2 per cent respectively. In 1997, their unemployment rates were reduced to 5.7 and 10.1 per cent respectively. The 1997 figures are shown in Figure 10.3.

Figure 10.3   The average unemployment rate in percentages, 1997

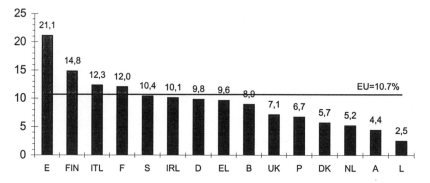

Source: European Commission (1999a)

Figure 10.3 shows that Spain has a tremendous unemployment problem. The Spanish unemployment rate is twice as high as the Community average and it is more than 6 percentage points higher than the second highest. To this must be added that Spain is one of the poorest countries in the Community as Figure 10.2 showed.

While Spain is in a league of is own, there are three other Member States with unemployment rates above Community average, that is, Finland, Italy and France. Five Member States have an unemployment rate just below average: Sweden, Ireland, Germany, Greece and Belgium. The UK, Portugal, Denmark, the Netherlands and Austria are all well below Community average. As with Spain, Luxembourg is in league of its own, although it is at the other end of the scale. With an unemployment rate of 2.5 per cent, less than one quarter of the Community average, Luxembourg can be regarded as having full employment.[4]

As shown in Figure 10.1 the financial means available for regional policy were increased substantially from the second half of the 1980s onward. It is therefore interesting to see whether any change can be recorded in regional wealth by now. Table 10.1 shows the changes in per capita income in the so-

---

[4]   An unemployment rate of 2.5 is normally regarded as 'frictional unemployment' that is unavoidable unemployment stemming from a short period of unemployment in connection with changing jobs, entering the job market for the first time and so on.

called Cohesion countries, that is the four countries, Greece, Spain, Ireland and Portugal receiving support from the Cohesion Fund.[5]

Table 10.1   Annual average growth in percentage of GDP in the Cohesion countries, 1986–99

	EL	E	IRL	P	EU-4	EU-11	EU-15
1986-1991	2.2	4.3	5.3	5.1	4.1	2.8	3.0
1991-1996	1.0	1.3	7.1	1.8	1.7	1.5	1.5
1996-1999	3.8	3.6	9.2	3.8	4.1	2.6	2.8

Note: Growth rate 1986–96 excluding the German new Länder. 1997–99: Projections.
Source: European Commission (1999a)

Table 10.1 shows that the four Cohesion countries, throughout the period 1986–99, have had a higher annual growth rate than the rest of EU. This was especially true in the second half of the 1980s while it is less obvious for the first half of the 1990s. In the beginning of the 1990s, Greece and Spain have had a lower annual growth rate than the non-Cohesion countries while Ireland and Portugal have had a higher growth rate than the non-Cohesion countries. In particular, take note of the remarkable growth rate of Ireland. It is remarkable not only compared to the non-Cohesion countries but to all Member States. In the period 1991–96 the annual growth rate of Ireland has been almost five times as high as the Community average. All together Table 10.1 shows that the countries benefiting the most from the Structural Funds are the ones which have had the highest growth rate leading to a narrowing of the income disparities in the EU.

While Table 10.1 shows that income disparities on average have narrowed for the Cohesion countries versus the rest of EU, it does not show whether this also is true for the poorest regions. Table 10.2 gives an indication thereof.

Table 10.2 shows that both the poorest and the richest regions have become wealthier. The poorest regions, and in particular the 10 most poor regions, have converged toward the Community average indicating that it is not only the more well-off regions in the poorest countries which have benefited from the regional policy.

---

[5]   Member states whose Gross National Product (GNP) is below 90 per cent of the Community average.

Table 10.2   GDP per capita (PPS) in the poorest and richest regions in the EU, 1986–96

	1986	1996
10 poorest regions	41	50
25 poorest regions	52	59
10 richest regions	153	158
25 richest regions	138	143

Note: Community average = 100.
Source: European Commission (1999a)

All together these statistics indicate that the regional policy of the EU has made a difference since income disparities have narrowed in the same period as the amount available for regional policy has been increased significantly. In particular Ireland but also Portugal have shown remarkable results. For Ireland, the per capita income has increased from 60.8 per cent of Community average in 1986 to 96.5 per cent in 1996. For Portugal, the per capita income has increased from 55.1 per cent of Community average in 1986 to 70.5 per cent in 1996. (See Table 10.6 for a comprehensive list of main regional indicators for all regions in the EU).

Also Spain and Greece have experienced a real convergence although not with the same speed as Portugal and Ireland. For Spain, the per capita income has increased from 69.8 per cent of Community average in 1986 to 78.7 per cent in 1996. For Greece, the per capita income has increased from 59.2 per cent in 1986 to 67.5 per cent in 1996.

Even though economic progress correlates with the time in which the Structural Funds contributions have been increased substantially there might be other factors of importance. Factors which are just as important or even more important than the Structural Fund's contribution. This seems to be the case in relation to the Irish 'miracle' (see Box 10.2).

Box 10.2   The Irish 'miracle'

In the mid-1980s, Ireland experienced a deep recession independent of the normal business cycle. From the mid-1980s onward, Ireland took radical measures to reverse the situation, and the economy started recovering. In the first half of the 1990s, where the full effect of the reforms could be expected, Ireland experienced an extraordinary high growth rate and increase in employment. Between 1993 and 1996 Ireland had an annual average growth of GDP at 8.8 per cent - four times as high as the rest of EU – and 139 000 net jobs were created. The increased growth rate was due to increased investment rather than increased consumption.

Ireland undertook a number of reforms including fiscal consolidation and labour market reforms. Combined with a low level of corporate tax in place since the 1960s these led to a major expansion of foreign investment, in particular in research and development.

In relation to fiscal consolidation, Ireland has reduced the budget deficit as a percentage of GDP from 10.6 in 1986 to 0.9 in 1996. This improvement has not been achieved by increased taxes. In the same period, 1986–96, Ireland has reduced its tax burden as a percentage of GDP with 2.2 per cent, compared to an average 1.8 per cent increase in the rest of the EU. As a result, government total expenditure as a percentage of GDP in Ireland has reached the lowest level in the EU.

On the labour market, Ireland has had a slower growth in employee compensation than the EU average and a low level of social security tax was introduced. Furthermore, wage moderation has been achieved through three-year national agreements between the government, employers and trade unions on pay policies. This has led to that the growth in unit labour costs in Ireland was the slowest among EU Member States in 1986-1996.

The Irish 'miracle' shows that there is not a single measure but rather a series of national measures that together with the Structural Funds contribution helped explain the strong performance in terms of GDP and employment growth.

Source: Commission (1998)

10.3   OBJECTIVES AND MEANS

In order to fulfil the obligation of Article 158 of the Treaty to 'aim at reducing disparities between the level of development of the various regions' the Community has for the period 2000–06 set up three Objectives and four Structural Funds to pursue the aim. The Objectives and the Structural Funds interact as described in Box 10.3.

Box 10.3   Objectives and means of EU regional policy

The Objectives

Objective 1:   Regions whose development is lagging behind, defined as regions whose per capita GDP, for an average of the last three years, is less than 75 per cent of the Community average.

Objective 2:   Areas facing structural difficulties, in particular areas undergoing socio-economic change in the industrial and service sectors, declining rural areas, urban areas in difficulty and depressed areas dependent on fisheries.

Objective 3:   Education, training and employment outside objective 1 regions.

Community Initiatives: Cross border, transnational and interregional co-operation (Interreg), regeneration of cities and of urban neighbourhoods (Urban), rural development (Leader), combating all forms of discrimination and inequalities in connection with the labour market (Equal).

The means

Objective 1:   Regional Fund, Social Fund, Agricultural Fund, Fishery Fund
Objective 2:   Regional Fund, Social Fund
Objective 3:   Social Fund

Interreg: Regional Fund
Urban: Regional Fund
Leader: Agricultural Fund
Equal: Social Fund

Related means – Cohesion Fund
Member States whose Gross National Product (GNP) is below 90 per cent of the Community average and who follow an economic convergence programme are eligible for assistance. For the moment, four Member States are eligible, that is Spain, Greece, Portugal, Ireland. The Cohesion Fund finances projects in the field of environment and transport infrastructure.

Source: Council (1999a, 1999b)

The Objectives

Objectives 1 and 2 are of a regional nature, limited to those regions that are eligible. Objective 3, however, is horizontal in nature, that is not limited to any specific region, but applicable throughout the Community outside Objective 1 regions.

Objective 1 covers regions whose GDP per capita is less than 75 per cent of the Community average. The only exceptions to this threshold are the sparsely populated regions in the north of Sweden and of Finland (the former Objective 6) agreed upon when Sweden and Finland joined the EU.

Areas covered by Objective 2 are areas undergoing socioeconomic change in the industrial and service sector, declining rural areas, urban areas in difficulties and depressed areas depending on fisheries. The industrial and service areas are determined by the rate of unemployment and the share of industrial employment. The rural areas are determined by the population density or the share of agricultural employment and the unemployment rate. Urban areas can be determined according to a number of criteria, for example, the rate of long-term unemployment, the level of poverty or the crime rate. The areas dependent on fisheries are determined by the number of jobs in the fisheries industry. The criteria for determining Objective 2 areas are very broad. Just think of the number of inhabitants in urban areas suffering from long term unemployment, poverty or crime. All larger cities will most likely have certain areas fulfilling one of these criteria. In order to maintain the total geographical concentration at 40 per cent of the total EU population, the population of the areas covered by Objective 2 may not exceed 18 per cent of the total population of the Community. The Commission has decided on a population ceiling for each Member State according to objective criteria.

The horizontal Objective 3 shall provide financial assistance outside the regions covered by Objective 1. It provides a policy frame of reference for all measures to promote human resources in a national territory without prejudice to the specific features of each region. Objective 3 supports the adaptation and modernisation of policies and systems of education, training and employment.

Of the four Community initiatives, Interreg is the most important in political, financial and industrial terms. Half of all the financial means available for the Community initiative are allocated to Interreg. The aim of Interreg is, after the removal of the physical barriers in the internal market, to assist overcoming the non-physical barriers, particular in cross-border areas.[6]

The means

The two most important instruments, both in terms of financial means and of importance to industry, are the Regional Fund and the Social Fund. Together they account for more than 80 per cent of the financial means available for the Structural Funds (see Figure 10.4). The Agricultural Fund and the

---

[6]   The reason for having both an Objective 2 covering urban areas and an Urban Initiative is that many urban problems are located in cities and areas located outside the Objective 2 areas. The aim of Equal is transnational co-operation to promote new means of combating all forms of discrimination. Leader will be structured around three strands, that is development strategies, co-operations between rural territories and networking between the actors.

Fishery Fund are only of limited interest to business. The main measures of the Agricultural Fund are 'accompanying measures', for example early retirement, and 'measures to modernise and diversity agricultural holding', for example farm investment and setting up of young farmers. The main objective of the Fishery Fund is to contribute to achieving a sustainable balance between fishery resources and their exploitation.

Figure 10.4   Financial allocation between the Structural Funds, 1999

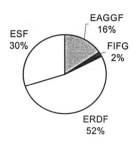

Source: European Commission (1999g)

The Regional Fund

The task of the Regional Fund is to promote economic and social cohesion by correcting the main regional imbalances and participating in the development and conversion of regions. To accomplish this, the Regional Fund shall contribute towards the financing of the following three activities:

1. Productive investments, that is direct investment in enterprises which creates and/or safeguard sustainable jobs.
2. Investment in infrastructure, which, in regions covered by Objective 1, helps to increase the economic potential or which, in regions and areas covered by Objectives 1 and 2, Interreg or Urban, concern the diversification of economic sites.
3. The development of endogenous potential by measures which encourage and support among other things activities of small and medium-sized enterprises. Under this heading it is possible to finance among other things services for enterprises, transfer of technology, improvement of access by enterprises to finance and loans.

The Social Fund

The task of the Social Fund is among other things to support measures to prevent and combat unemployment and to develop human resources. The financial support of the Social Fund shall mainly take the form of assistance to persons and be devoted to develop human resources. The financial support may include the following activities:

1. Education, vocational training and apprenticeships.
2. Employment aid and aids for self-employment.
3. In the area of research and technology development the Social Fund can support post-graduate training and the training of managers and technicians in for instance enterprises.

The Cohesion Fund

Four Member States fulfilled the eligibility criteria in 1999,[7] that is Spain, Greece, Ireland and Portugal. In the present period, 2000–06, the Cohesion Fund has a budget of €18 billion. The Council has decided to allocate the budget to these countries as follows: 61–63.5 per cent for Spain, 16–18 per cent for Portugal and Greece respectively and 2–6 per cent for Ireland.

The Cohesion Fund co-finances two types of projects: environmental projects and transport infrastructure projects. Environmental projects are projects which help achieve the objectives of the Community's environmental policy. In accordance with the environmental Directives in force, the Cohesion Fund gives priority to the supply of drinking water, wastewater treatment and solid waste disposal. Eligible transport infrastructure projects are projects that establish or develop transport infrastructure within the Trans-European Transport Network (TEN) or projects providing access to the TEN. For an analysis of the effects of TEN on business and industry see Chapter 5.

The Cohesion Fund is interesting for business and industry for at least two reasons. First, for those industrial sectors involved in providing transport infrastructure and environmental sites, the financial amount available is of interest. The Cohesion Fund Regulation allows financing up to 85 per cent of a project, which means that the total cost of all projects that the Cohesion Fund co-finances amount to at least €21 billion. However, these rates will be reduced for revenue-generating projects. Second, companies that use the finalised projects, in particular the transport infrastructure, will benefit from faster, more safe and cheaper infrastructures which improve their own competitiveness.

---

[7] In 1999, the eligible Member States were determined for the period 2000–06 with a mid-term review before end 2003 at which the Member States must fulfil the eligibility criteria in order to stay eligible in the second half of the period.

10.4   THE ELIGIBLE REGIONS

Due to the criteria for selecting the eligible regions mentioned above, the Commission took decisions on the objective 1 regions immediately. For the objective 2 regions, it determined the total population coverage for each Member State, within which each Member State should propose eligible regions. Table 10.3 shows the population coverage for each Member State.

Table 10.3   Population coverage in Objectives 1 and 2 (1000 inhabitants), 2000–06

	Objective 1	Objective 2	Objectives 1 and 2	Total population	Pct.
B		1.269	1.269	10.157	12.5
DK		538	538	5.262	10.2
D	14.153	10.296	24.449	81.896	29.9
GR	10.476		10.476	10.476	100.0
E	23.219	8.809	32.028	39.669	80.7
FR	1.644	18.768	20.412	58.372	35.0
IRL	965		965	3.634	26.6
ITL	19.302	7.402	26.704	58.450	45.7
L		118	118	416	28.4
NL		2.333	2.333	15.523	15.0
AU	275	1.995	2.270	8.059	28.2
P	6.616		6.616	9.927	66.6
SF	1.076	1.582	2.658	5.125	51.9
SV	452	1.223	1.675	8.841	18.9
UK	5.079	13.836	18.915	58.782	32.2
Total	83.257	68.169	151.426	374.589	40.4

Source: European Commission (1999b)

Table 10.3 shows that 40.4 per cent of total EU population lives in regions eligible under Objectives 1 or 2 for the period 2000–06. In the previous period 1994–99 this population coverage was 51 per cent. The reduced coverage is part of an overall political aim of concentrating the financial resources available on fewer regions. Those regions that were not re-appointed for the new period will benefit from a phasing-out arrangement, which means that these regions, for a period up to the end of 2005, can continue to receive support from the Regional Fund. However, the support in the phasing-out period will be reduced gradually.

Table 10.3 also shows that four Member States do not have any Objective 1 regions, that is Belgium, Denmark, Luxembourg and the Netherlands. Furthermore, two Member States, that is Ireland and Portugal have no Objective 2 regions. Greece is covered 100 per cent by Objective 1.

While it should come as no surprise that Member States that are less wealthy like Greece, Spain and Portugal have a high population coverage, it may be more surprising to realise that for instance in the richest country in the EU, Luxembourg, more than a quarter of the population is covered. But also other Member States in which per capita income is well above Community average, like Austria, Germany and France, have a fairly high coverage. In the case of Germany this is partly due to the reunification with the former East German Länder, which all qualify as Objective 1 regions. However, Table 10.4 shows that more than 10 million people in the western part of Germany live in regions covered by Objective 2.[8]

Table 10.4   Structural Funds allocation between Member States according to objectives, 2000–06, million €, fixed 1999 prices

	Obj. 1[1]	Obj. 2	Obj. 3	Com. Initiatives	Total[2]	PCT.
B	625	433	737	209	2.011	1.0
DK	-	183	365	80	668	0.3
D	19.958	3.510	4.581	1.608	29.679	15.4
GR	20.961	-	-	862	21.823	11.3
E	38.096	2.651	2.140	1.958	44.886	23.3
FR	3.805	6.050	4.540	1.046	15.487	8.0
IRL	3.088	-	-	166	3.254	1.7
ITL	22.122	2.522	3.744	1.172	29.580	15.3
L	-	40	38	13	91	0.0
NL	123	795	1.686	651	3.261	1.7
AU	261	680	528	358	1.828	0.9
P	19.029	-	-	671	19.700	10.2
SF	913	489	403	254	2.065	1.1
SV	722	406	720	278	2.138	1.1
UK	6.251	4.695	4.568	961	16.500	8.6
TOTAL	135.954	22.454	24.050	10.442[3]	193.125[3]	100.0

Notes:
1) Including phasing out.
2) Including the Structural Funds' contribution to the fishery sector outside Objective 1, allocated among Member States.
3) Including funds not yet distributed among Member States.

Source: European Commission (1999c), (1999d), (1999e) and (1999f)

At the European Council in Berlin in March 1999, the overall EU-budget for the period 2000–06 was decided upon, including the allocation of €195 billion to the Structural Funds. Of these the Commission has so far decided

---

[8]   Since all the former East Germany Länder are Objective 1 regions, the Objective 2 regions must be located in the western part of Germany.

to allocate €193 billion, as shown in Table 10.4. The allocation between Member States was decided by the Commission according to more or less objective criteria such as, for example, objective, population coverage, regional and national prosperity, unemployment rate and so on.

Table 10.4 shows that Spain receives most from the Structural Funds. Almost one quarter of the total amount available is allocated to Spain. This is not so surprising taking into account the findings of Figures 10.2 and 10.3. These show that Spain is one of the less wealthy countries in the EU with a per capita income of 79 per cent of Community average, and has a unique high unemployment of 21 per cent. Add to this that, in terms of population, Spain is a large country with 40 million inhabitants. Once again, it may be surprising to learn that Germany and Italy – both countries with a per capita income well above the Community average – each receive 15 per cent of the total amount available for the Structural Funds. This is mainly due to the large number of people living in Objective 1 regions in these countries. Almost half of the Member States receive less than 2 per cent, that is Belgium, Denmark, Ireland, Netherlands, Luxembourg, Austria, Finland and Sweden; showing at least some concentration on those regions and countries with the biggest needs, although the countries mentioned above also are the smallest in the EU. However, the concentration aspect is also clear from the fact that more than 70 per cent of the funds allocated so far have been allocated to Objective 1 regions.[9] Together Objectives 1 and 2 receive 82 per cent of the Structural Funds allocation. The geographical location of the regions covered by Objectives 1 and 2 is shown in Figure 10.5.

---

[9]   It should be taken into account, that not all funds are yet allocated and that Objective 1 regions also may benefit from the Community Initiatives.

Figure 10.5 Eligible regions under EU regional policy, 2000-06

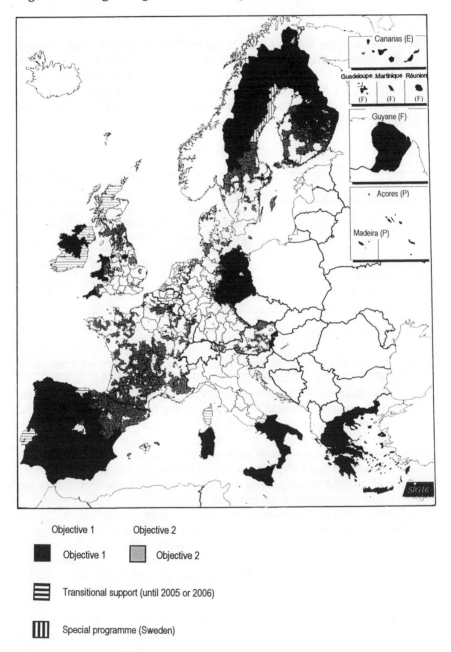

Objective 1   Objective 2

■ Objective 1   ▨ Objective 2

☰ Transitional support (until 2005 or 2006)

⦀ Special programme (Sweden)

Note: There are no Objective 2 regions in Italy. They have not been approved yet.
Source: European Commission, DG Regional Policy

10.5   STRUCTURAL FUNDS – IMPORTANT FINANCIAL INSTRUMENT FOR BUSINESS AND INDUSTRY

While the previous section looked at the amount available for each objective in each Member State, where the eligible regions are located and what type of activities are to be supported, we now turn to what the Structural Funds actually can do for a company located in an eligible region. The rate of contribution from the Structural Funds depends on the type of activity and where the activity is carried out as shown in Table 10.5.

Table 10.5   Maximum rates of contribution by objective and type of activity

	Objective 1			Objective 2
	Outermost regions and outlying Greek islands	Cohesion countries	Others	All
General activities	85	80	75	50
Infrastructure	50	50	40	25
Investments in firms	35	35	35	15
Non-direct investments in SMEs	45	45	45	25

Source: Council (1999a*)*

First, the rate of contribution depends on whether the activity is carried out in a region covered by Objective 1 or in an area covered by Objective 2. In the first case, it is sometimes also necessary to distinguish between where the Objective 1 region is located, depending on the type of activity. In general the rate of contribution is significantly higher in Objective 1 than in Objective 2. In some cases, as for example for 'general activities', a bonus in the form of higher contribution rates may be given within Objective 1 if the region is located in a Cohesion country or is an outermost region or outlying Greek island. The notion general activities covers all kinds of activities that do not generate substantial net revenues.

Secondly, the rate of contribution depends on the type of activity, that is whether the activity generates revenue, like for instance in some types of investment in infrastructure and investment in firms. If the activity generates revenue, the rates of contribution are in general lowered. How much depends on the location of the activity, that is the rate of contribution can be higher for an infrastructure project in an Objective 1 region if the Objective 1 region is located in a Cohesion country.

Thirdly, the rate of contribution depends on the type of intervention. If the intervention takes the form of direct investment in a firm, the rates of contribution are lowered, depending on the location. If, however, the intervention is directed to SMEs and takes the form of finance other than direct assistance[10] a bonus in terms of higher contribution rates may be granted.

In the following we will look at some concrete cases of Structural Funds assistance of importance to industry. All of the cases are from the previous period, 1994–99, since at present there are no experiences from the new period. However, all of the cases are also possible in the new period.

Objective 1, Direct Investment in a Manufacturing Company

This case illustrates how the Regional Fund can contribute towards the financing of 'productive investment to create and safeguard sustainable jobs' (European Parliament and Council, 1999a). The area, Sachsen in Germany, is one of the New Länder located in the former East Germany. With an average GDP of 63 per cent of Community average in 1994–96 (see Table 10.6), Sachsen is well below the eligibility threshold for objective 1. Furthermore, the unemployment rate was 17.2 per cent in 1997.

It is part of the development programme for Sachsen to give priority to productive investment with the aim of creating new jobs. The maximum rate of contribution for these types of investments was at the time (1994–99) 50 per cent for SMEs and 30 per cent for others.

One of the former State-owned monopoly companies producing chemical consumer products suffering a hard time after the reunification in 1989. After privatisation, new products were added to the list of products and the company started to expand into new markets – primarily in East and Central Europe. The investment necessary to undertake this expansion was co-financed by the Regional Fund. There have been several rounds of investments in order to modernise the company. In 1994 investments made it possible for the company to introduce new and more modern products. In 1996 a new machine was introduced which made it possible for the company to handle different kinds and sizes of bottles and to introduce more consumer-friendly caps on the bottles.

All together more than €26 million was invested in the company to which the Regional Fund contributed €8 million. The rate of contribution was approximately 31 per cent. Today there are 77 employees of which 30 are women and 4 are apprentices. In this respect the Structural Funds have contributed to integrate disadvantaged groups and individuals into the labour market.

In the new period, 2000–06, 17 per cent of the German population (14 million people) is living in regions covered by Objective 1. In the new period Germany will receive approximately €20 billion. If, for instance, the rate of contribution in general is at the same level as in the example mentioned

---

[10]   Finance other than direct assistance includes among other things repayable assistance, interest rate subsidy, guarantee and venture capital funding.

above, it means that the Structural Funds will co-finance projects to a volume of €65 billion.

Objective 2, NOVI, a Technology Science Park

This case illustrates how the Regional Fund can assist in the 'development of endogenous potential' (European Parliament and Council, 1999a). The area, Northern Jutland in Denmark, is an Objective 2 area. The focus of the project is technology transfer in particular for small and medium-sized enterprises and entrepreneurs. The Regional Fund contributed to the establishment of technology science park NOVI. The total cost of the project was €4.9 million to which the Regional Fund contributed €694 500.

The recent economic history of Northern Jutland indicates an area depending on large labour-intensive sectors such as shipbuilding, agriculture and fishery with a high unemployment rate. The aim of the Objective 2 programme for Northern Jutland is to improve conditions for growth of business through a strategy called 'Globalisation'. The globalisation strategy aims at strengthening the company's ability to compete internationally by supporting innovation and conversion capacity, by increasing competence and by increasing the educational and infra-structural frameworks. To put it in other words, the Objective 2 programme shall assist the area in transformation from an area depending on heavy industry to one relying on knowledge-based industry, trade and services.

NOVI fits well into this strategy, offering access to capital and technological, administrative and commercial assistance. NOVI provides shelter for entrepreneurs and provides numerous services especially of technical nature but also facilities like auditorium, meeting facilities and cantina. These types of facilities are free of charge, since the entrepreneurs only rent the space they occupy themselves.

NOVI is not only for entrepreneurs. Any high-technology based firm can establish themselves in NOVI. One of the first to make use of this opportunity was the Korean electronic enterprise Maxon – one of the leading producers of wireless telecommunication equipment.

NOVI has close connections with Aalborg University which is partly a technological university. NOVI plays a key role in the dissemination of research results to enterprises in the region, and assists the companies in making their needs for research known to the University.

NOVI is also venture capital. NOVI can provide small-scale venture capital, which makes it easier for entrepreneurs and small companies to get additional funding from external investors.

Today, there are 34 companies located at NOVI including world-leading companies like LM Ericsson and Nokia. In 1999, Nokia located a new department for the development of advanced applications and Wireless Application Protocol (WAP). The department will employ 30 people, developing software that will make it possible to make use of the Internet via mobile phones. NOKIA has decided to place this department in NOVI because of the close link between the Centre for Personal Communication at Aalborg University and NOVI.

In the new period, 2000–06, 10 per cent of the Danish population is living in areas covered by Objective 2. Denmark receives €183 million under Objective 2.

Co-ordinated Use of the Regional Fund and the Social Fund in North East of England

Throughout the 1980s and 1990s, the North East of England experienced major economic restructuring. Shipbuilding, steel, engineering and coal mining accounted for nearly a quarter of all employment in 1975. The decline of these industries has had a strong depressing effect on the regional economy due to the strength of the deeply rooted local linkages associated with traditional industries. Low levels of self-employment, a low proportion of small firms in the economy and a relatively low rate of firm formation point to the underlying difficulties of the region's economy. Some of the urban areas suffer from male unemployment with figures as high as 36.4.

To address this situation, the Objective 2 programme for the region has as one of its aims to seek to attract investment from outside the region. Three Regional Funds projects were approved to develop on-site and off-site infrastructure on a 2.47 hectare site at Wynyard Hall, Stockton in Cleveland. This infrastructure consisted of industrial units and a Research and Development Training Centre. A combined total of €2.3[11] million was approved for the projects against a total cost for the investment of €25.9 million. Approximately half of the development accommodated a major international electrical goods manufacturer with the remaining sites going to supply chain and other companies wishing to locate close to this company.

Output included by the investment included among other thing 1420 direct permanent jobs created, 400 direct temporary jobs created, 40 SMEs assisted. The Training Centre further provided 599 training places through which 866 trainees were trained and 69 firms assisted by the training with an additional 306 unemployed people receiving training.

The Social Fund under Objective 2 sought to assist the specific training needs of strategic businesses and inward investors. The Social Fund also supported a wage-subsidy programme to assist unemployed people into jobs on the site. Furthermore, a training programme for unemployed people to provide the necessary vocational skills to make them more employable and able to take advantage of emerging employment opportunities on the site. In addition to this, small programmes were funded through the Social Fund under Objective 3 to provide training for CNC operators in preparation for the skills needed at the site and a guidance and counselling programme to

---

[11] The exchange rate used was 0.6123.

make local residents more aware of the upcoming opportunities for employment.

For the period 2000–06, the UK receives €4695 million which covers both Regional Fund and Social Fund assistance under Objective 2. For the Social Fund under Objective 3, the UK receives €4568 million.

Interreg, IT-Bridge, Cross-Border Contact and Business Development

This case illustrates how the Regional Fund can assist in 'cross-border co-operation' within the Community Initiative Interreg. The IT-Bridge is a Swedish–Danish co-operation in the Öresund region between Denmark and Sweden. The project started in 1997. The enterprises (in majority SMEs) in seven municipalities in southern Sweden and nine municipalities in western Denmark get in the framework of the project new opportunities to enlarge their markets and to come into contact with similar enterprises concerning trade and size. The aim of the project is to promote business development and business connections and to create a network for business contacts across the border.

By using the possibilities within electronic infrastructure in the 'virtual society', the project has developed an Internet-based transnational corporate database. In October 1999 the database contained 13 267 Swedish as well as 13 700 Danish companies. Linked to the development of the database as a tool for creating contacts and knowledge across the border, the project's partners have also arranged several contact conferences and partner twinning meetings. These meetings have led to many co-operations and business agreements between Danish and Swedish enterprises.

The total cost of the project was approximately €220 000 (1 872 000 SEK) to which the Regional Fund has contributed 50 per cent. After the end of the project in the beginning of 2000, the project partners continued the development and co-operation with their own as well as national funding.

For the period 2000–06, €4875 million has been allocated to Interreg. Of this, Sweden will receive €154 million and Denmark €34 million.

Cohesion Fund, the M40 Madrid Ring Road

This case illustrates the importance of Cohesion Fund projects to business. It is a road transport project, the M40 Madrid ring road. The M40 ring road is 35 kilometres long and the Cohesion Fund has contributed with €282.8 million.

The importance of investment in road infrastructure in Spain reflects the need to complete and upgrade the extensive main-road system in response to the rapid growth of traffic. The M40 ring road meets the objectives of the Trans-European Road Network Guidelines.

The direct benefit of the project was to reduce through traffic in residential areas, reduce the quantities of exhaust fumes emitted in the centre, cut travel times and improve road safety. But due to the fact that Madrid is at the centre of a radial road transport system, the benefit of the project was expected to reach further than just the Madrid area. The M40 ring road has made communications between the regions smoother by improving links between the various main roads which begin and end in the capital.

The benefit for industry depends on the type of industry. There are the 'upstream industries', which benefit directly from creating the physical infrastructure, and there are the 'downstream industries' which are all the industries benefiting from a faster, more reliable and more safe transport system – all factors leading to lower costs and increased competitiveness in the region. For further discussion on the benefit for upstream and downstream industries of transport infrastructures and other trans-European networks, see Chapter 5.

A recent study carried out for the Commission (1999j) has tried to simulate the effect of the M40 ring road. The effect of the M40 ring road on the employment in the Madrid region, depending on the assumptions, varies from 21 000 to 56 000 more employed. When the model allows for interregional spillovers the employment effect in the Madrid region is lower. However, this last model indicates considerable spillover effects into the rest of the economy, with aggregated effects on output and employment some three times greater than the effect on Madrid alone.

In the new period, 2000–06, Spain can expect to receive approximately €11 billion from the Cohesion Fund.

How do Businesses Get Access to these Funds

The administration of the Structural Funds is organised in a 'partnership' between the Commission, the Member State and the regional or local level. The general regulation covering this field is decided by the Council by unanimous voting based on a proposal from the Commission. The overall amount available for the structural policy was determined by the European Council when deciding on the overall budget for the European Union for the years 2000–06. Hereafter, the Commission decided the eligible regions and areas in each Member State based on a proposal from and after dialogue with the Member States. The Commission also decides on the allocation of funds for Objectives 1, 2 and 3 and the Community Initiative for each Member State.

When the Commission has decided on the eligible regions and areas and the allocation of funds, the Member State draws up a development programme, on the basis of the funds available, for the region or area covered. The programme describes how to develop the region or area covered in the period 2000–06. The programme must be drawn up in partnership with local and regional authorities and economic and social partners. The Commission approves each programme. When the programme has been adopted by the Commission, the monitoring of the programme will be done by a Monitoring Committee in which the Commission, the Member State, regional and local authorities, social and economic partners and other relevant partners are present.

It is clear from this structure that the concept of the partnership has a significant influence in drawing up and monitoring of the programmes. It is also clear, however, that who these partners are will vary from region to region and programme to programme. In some Member States the programming and involvement of partners are carried out at local and regional level with only a supervisory function at national level. In other Member States the programming is done at national level with a hearing procedure at local and regional level. These differences reflect the differences in legal and administrative tradition between Member States. The participation of economic and social partners at local and regional level usually includes local and regional business organisations and forums.

The day-to-day administration, including decisions on individual projects, of the Structural Funds also depend on the legal and administrative tradition in each Member States. Therefore, the administrative set-up will vary from region to region. There are, however, some common characteristics which business and industry may observe in order to get access to the Structural Fund. In most Member States, the overall responsibility for the administration of the funds follows the following logic. The responsibility for the national administration of the Fishery Fund and the Agricultural Fund lie with the Ministry of Fishery (where such exist) and the Ministry of Agriculture. The responsibility of the national administration for the Social Fund lies with the Ministry of Labour. The responsibility for the national administration of the Regional Fund usually lies with the Ministry of Trade and Industry. As a starting point, a business may get the initial information about the national administrative set-up from the relevant national authorities.

However, in most Member States the day-to-day administration is delegated by the Member State to a Managing Authority that can be a public or private authority or body at national, regional or local level. Most Member States have delegated the administration to a Managing Authority at regional or local level. Who that may be varies considerably from region to region. However, the regional or local federation of business and industry or local Chamber of Commerce most likely participates in the partnership and will know who is the Managing Authority. Otherwise, one can ask the local Euro Info Centre. There are 227 Euro Info Centre in the EU-15, Norway and Iceland covering all regions of Europe. The Euro Info Centre have information on EU legislation and programmes of relevance for business and they answer some 400 000 questions a year. The concept of Euro Info Centres is further explained in Chapter 12.

Once identified, the Managing Authority has all the necessary information concerning how to apply for assistance, the conditions, the rate of contribution and so on. In this sense it is important to remember that any individual project has to fit in with the particular development programme objectives of the region.

10.6 OUTLOOK AND CONCLUSION

The chapter has shown that the Structural Funds and the Cohesion Fund are important sources of finance in most EU regions. For business and industry the Regional Fund is the most interesting because of the possibilities for, for example, grants for productive investment and infrastructure and the amounts available. But also the Social Fund and the Cohesion Fund are of interest for business and industry.

The present regulations, adopted in 1999, fix the financial resources available and the eligible regions and areas until the end of 2006. We are therefore not likely to see any major changes within that period, not even if a new enlargement of the Union should take place before the end of 2006. The EU budget is constructed in such a way that any enlargement will be financed outside the Structural Funds.

For the applicant countries there has been established a special structural policy instrument, called ISPA, which shall provide assistance to the preparation for accession to the EU. ISPA is very similar to the Cohesion Fund in its administration and approach to financing individual projects in the transport and environment sectors.

After accession, any new Member State will in principle participate fully in regional/structural policy. All of the regions in the applicant countries fulfil the criteria for becoming Objective 1 regions. But the financial figures referred to in this chapter are restricted to the present EU-15. See Chapter 14 for an explanation.

Table 10.6 Main regional indicators

Region	Economy					Labour market 1997		Population 1996	
	GDP/head (PPS) avg. 1994-96	Employment (% of total), 1997			Eur. Patent applications per million inh., avg. 1994-96	Unemployment rate (%)	Employment rate (% of poupulation aged 15-64	1000 inhabitants	Population density inh./km²
		Agriculture	Industry	Services					
EUR 15	100.0	5.0	29.4	65.3	90.7	10.7	60.9	373243	117.0
EUR 12	99.8	4.9	29.5	65.2	87.0	10.8	60.5	351218	148.9
BELGIUM	112.5	2.7	27.5	69.8	90.1	8.9	57.3	10157	332.8
Brussel	172.3	0.2	16.0	83.8	97.9	13.5	53.0	949	5882.0
Vlaanderen	115.8	2.9	30.6	66.5	107.8	6.3	60.1	5890	435.9
Antwerpen	137.6	1.7	30.0	68.3	166.5	7.2	58.5	1633	569.7
Limburg	110.4	3.0	37.8	59.2	41.8	8.3	55.4	778	321.0
Oost Vlaanderen	104.8	2.8	32.7	64.4	68.1	6.5	61.4	1353	435.8
Vlaams Brabant	96.8	2.3	21.3	76.4	159.3	4.5	63.5	1002	475.7
West Vlaandren	118.0	5.1	33.1	61.8	70.2	5.1	61.0	1123	358.4
Wallonie	89.4	2.9	24.5	72.6	55.4	12.5	53.3	3318	197.0
Brabant Wallon	89.0	1.7	18.5	79.8	203.7	7.9	58.7	340	312.0
Hainaut	81.3	2.7	26.9	70.5	22.5	15.4	49.8	1285	339.3
Liege	99.4	2.5	26.6	70.8	59.7	12.2	53.3	1014	262.6
Luxembourg	97.3	5.6	22.5	72.0	38.3	6.8	58.7	242	54.5
Namur	86.2	3.6	19.7	76.7	37.7	11.4	56.4	437	119.1
DENMARK	116.5	3.7	26.1	69.7	119.8	5.7	76.1	5263	122.1
GERMANY	109.8	2.9	34.7	62.4	169.1	9.8	64.2	81915	229.6
Baden-Württembrg	125.8	2.8	41.2	56.0	303.4	6.2	68.0	10347	289.4
Stuttgart	137.1	2.9	43.8	53.3	349.3	6.1	68.3	3872	366.8
Karlsruhe	127.1	1.3	38.5	60.2	278.1	6.6	65.9	2651	383.1
Freiburg	110.9	3.7	38.3	58.0	292.9	6.2	69.2	2093	223.7
Tübingen	116.2	3.7	42.9	53.4	252.0	5.7	69.2	1731	194.1
Bayern	125.9	3.7	36.4	59.9	245.5	5.9	69.6	12019	170.3
Oberbayern	158.4	3.0	31.5	65.4	362.0	4.8	71.4	3985	227.3
Niederbayern	98.6	6.8	40.2	53.0	102.6	5.5	70.2	1148	111.1
Oberpfalz	101.0	5.5	37.2	57.3	157.0	6.5	69.2	1057	109.1
Oberfranken	108.6	3.6	41.8	54.7	135.4	7.4	68.2	1112	153.8
Mittelfranken	124.8	2.7	37.7	59.6	277.8	7.1	68.3	1671	230.6

Table 10.6 continued

Region	Economy					Labour market 1997		Population 1996	
	GDP/head (PPS) avg. 1994-96	Employment (% of total), 1997			Eur. Patent applications per million inh., avg. 1994-96	Unemployment rate (%)	Employment rate (% of poupulation aged 15-64	1000 inhabitants	Population density inh./km²
		Agriculture	Industry	Services					
Unterfranken	105.9	2.4	39.5	58.1	205.0	6.4	67.3	1320	154.7
Schwaben	112.0	4.3	38.4	57.3	195.5	5.8	69.1	1726	172.7
Berlin	104.7	0.6	23.6	75.9	107.1	13.4	62.1	3465	3897.3
Brandenburg	66.2	5.3	34.0	60.7	22.0	17.2	62.8	2548	86.4
Bremen	152.0	0.9	32.1	67.0	58.6	12.3	59.7	679	1679.3
Hamburg	193.9	1.4	22.2	76.4	148.1	8.8	63.9	1708	2261.3
Hessen	149.4	1.7	32.1	66.3	264.4	7.4	64.8	6019	285.0
Darmstadt	172.8	0.9	30.5	68.6	354.3	6.7	65.5	3690	495.6
Giessen	106.3	2.5	35.1	62.4	166.5	7.8	63.7	1058	196.6
Kassel	116.9	3.4	34.3	62.3	83.8	9.0	63.7	1271	153.3
Mecklenburg-Vorp.	60.8	6.5	30.7	62.8	10.0	18.8	61.3	1820	78.6
Niedersachsen	104.2	4.5	32.5	62.9	94.1	9.4	63.4	7798	164.7
Braunschweig	108.1	3.6	36.1	60.4	93.9	11.4	61.0	1679	207.3
Hannover	118.8	3.8	30.9	65.3	130.4	9.1	63.0	2143	236.8
Lüneburg	85.2	5.0	31.7	63.2	98.3	8.0	66.9	1609	105.6
Weser-Ems	100.9	5.6	32.1	62.3	58.2	9.2	63.2	2367	158.2
N.Rhein-Westfalen	111.9	2.0	35.9	62.2	175.1	9.0	61.2	17920	526.0
Düsseldorf	121.4	1.6	35.0	63.4	218.4	9.6	60.4	5291	1000.4
Köln	115.9	1.1	30.6	68.3	231.7	8.3	61.5	4202	570.6
Münster	96.9	4.1	36.4	59.5	115.3	8.6	60.6	2580	373.8
Detmold	108.0	3.1	42.5	54.4	111.7	8.3	65.2	2020	309.9
Arnsberg	106.4	1.5	39.1	59.5	126.3	9.7	60.1	3827	478.5
Rheinland-Pfalz	97.3	2.8	35.8	61.3	226.5	7.2	63.8	3989	201.0
Koblenz	91.9	1.7	36.3	62.0	120.0	6.8	64.0	1495	184.7
Trier	87.5	4.7	32.5	62.7	79.1	6.3	65.6	507	102.9
Rheinhessen-Pfalz	103.8	3.2	36.3	60.5	343.7	7.7	63.3	1988	291.0
Saarland	107.1	1.0	30.3	68.7	92.1	10.1	57.8	1084	421.8
Sachsen	63.0	2.9	36.8	60.3	35.9	17.2	62.7	4556	247.5
Sachsen-Anhalt	60.9	4.4	34.0	61.6	20.1	20.6	59.6	2731	133.6
Dessau	55.2	4.3	36.0	59.7	18.9	21.5	58.8	572	133.6

Table 10.6 continued

Region	Economy					Labour market 1997		Population 1996	
	GDP/head (PPS) avg. 1994-96	Employment (% of total), 1997			Eur. Patent applications per million inh., avg. 1994-96	Unemployment rate (%)	Employment rate (% of poupulation aged 15-64	1000 inhabitants	Population density inh./km²
		Agriculture	Industry	Services					
Halle	68.4	4.5	34.3	61.2	25.2	19.9	60.5	906	204.7
Magdeburg	58.0	4.4	32.9	62.7	16.8	20.7	59.3	1253	106.8
Schleswig-Holst.	104.7	2.9	27.0	70.2	78.6	7.6	66.5	2734	173.8
Thüringen	60.4	3.9	35.9	60.2	32.4	17.6	63.0	2497	154.4
GREECE	66.4	19.8	22.5	57.7	3.7	9.6	56.7	10476	79.6
Voreia Ellada	63.7	27.5	23.1	49.4		9.1	57.7	3381	59.9
Anatoliki Makedon	59.9	40.0	17.9	42.1		8.3	62.2	561	39.6
Kentriki Makedonia	66.4	19.5	25.6	54.8		9.2	56.0	1777	94.5
Dytiki Makedonia	60.6	23.4	32.8	43.6		13.8	53.6	302	31.9
Thessalia	61.5	38.6	17.4	44.0		7.5	60.6	742	52.8
Kentriki Ellada	57.7	37.1	19.6	43.3		8.8	60.6	2635	48.9
Ipeiros	43.4	30.3	20.1	49.6		10.5	55.7	368	40.0
Ionia Nisia	61.1	26.7	15.8	57.6		6.2	68.5	199	86.4
Dytiki Ellada	56.9	41.5	17.6	40.9		7.9	59.9	733	64.6
Sterea Ellada	65.3	31.8	27.5	40.8		12.0	55.6	663	42.6
Peloponnisos	57.9	43.4	16.9	39.7		7.5	66.2	671	43.3
Attiki	75.0	1.0	25.3	73.7		11.6	52.4	3449	905.5
Nisia Aigaiou, Kriti	68.5	28.5	15.5	56.0		4.7	64.6	1011	57.9
Voreip Aigaio	50.3	24.2	19.6	56.1		7.1	52.5	184	48.0
Notio Aigaio	74.6	10.2	20.0	69.9		4.3	61.7	268	50.7
Kriti	71.6	37.8	12.5	49.8		4.3	70.1	559	67.1
SPAIN	78.5	8.3	29.9	61.8	12.0	21.1	48.3	39270	77.8
Noroeste	66.8	18.4	28.5	53.1	3.9	19.9	47.7	4322	95.4
Galicia	62.3	22.2	27.6	50.2	2.9	19.2	49.9	2724	92.5
Princ. Asturias	73.3	11.1	30.2	58.7	6.6	21.2	43.2	1071	101.4
Cantabria	76.7	11.3	30.1	58.6	3.6	21.1	45.9	527	99.4
Noreste	91.8	6.1	36.7	57.2	14.6	16.0	52.0	4037	57.4
Pais Vasco	92.5	2.7	36.9	60.4	14.9	18.8	49.7	2069	285.0
Com. Foral Navarra	97.4	8.9	40.0	51.0	27.8	10.0	56.1	527	50.5
La Rioja	89.0	9.2	39.0	51.9	6.7	11.8	54.0	261	51.7

Table 10.6 continued

| Region | Economy | | | | | Labour market 1997 | | Population 1996 | |
| | GDP/head (PPS) avg. 1994-96 | Agriculture | Industry | Services | Eur. Patent applications per million inh., avg. 1994-96 | Unemployment rate (%) | Employment rate (% of poupulation aged 15-64) | 1000 inhabitants | Population density inh./km^2 |
		Employment (% of total), 1997							
Aragon	88.7	10.1	34.2	55.8	10.3	14.4	54.0	1180	24.8
Com. Madrid	99.6	1.2	26.5	72.3	21.8	18.4	49.4	5016	627.4
Centro (E)	67.8	13.8	29.2	57.0	3.2	21.6	46.6	5279	24.6
Castlla y Leon	74.6	14.0	28.4	57.6	4.2	19.9	47.7	2510	26.6
Castilla-La Mancha	65.6	12.1	33.2	54.7	3.1	19.1	47.8	1694	21.4
Extremadura	55.0	16.3	24.5	59.3	1.6	29.5	41.8	1075	25.8
Este	89.4	4.2	35.8	60.0	21.6	18.5	53.3	10708	177.7
Cataluna	98.1	3.2	38.4	58.4	28.7	17.4	55.3	6066	190.0
Com. Valencia	74.4	6.4	33.8	59.8	13.7	21.4	49.4	3913	167.9
Islas Baleares	98.0	2.3	24.4	73.3	5.1	12.2	58.5	730	145.5
Sur	59.0	12.1	22.3	65.6	3.3	30.0	40.8	8346	84.6
Andalucia	57.4	12.4	21.7	65.9	3.2	32.0	39.5	7128	81.7
Region de Murcia	68.0	12.1	26.9	61.0	3.8	18.3	48.6	1084	95.8
Ceuta y Melilla	71.4	0.3	6.9	92.6		26.4	42.2	133	4296.8
Canarias	74.8	8.4	17.8	73.8	5.2	20.9	47.6	1563	215.9
LUXEMBOURG	170.3	2.4	23.3	74.2	86.4	2.5	60.3	416	160.6
FRANCE	105.6	4.6	26.6	68.7	94.6	12.0	59.7	58375	107.3
Ile deFrance	163.1	0.4	20.3	79.3	204.5	10.7	63.4	11044	919.4
Bassin Parisien	94.1	6.1	31.0	62.8	64.0	12.6	60.2	10483	72.0
Champgne-Ardenne	94.9	7.6	27.2	65.1	42.2	13.3	58.2	1352	52.8
Picardie	86.0	5.3	33.5	61.1	62.3	14.2	58.3	1866	96.2
Haute Normandie	107.8	3.3	33.5	63.2	63.5	13.6	60.3	1783	144.8
Centre	93.5	6.5	30.8	62.7	79.9	10.9	61.9	2438	62.3
Basse Normandie	90.4	7.3	29.6	63.1	47.0	13.2	59.3	1419	80.7
Bourgogne	91.5	7.6	30.0	62.4	75.9	11.0	61.8	1625	51.5
Nord-Pas-de-calais	86.9	2.9	31.4	65.6	33.5	16.6	49.5	4004	322.6
Est	96.6	3.5	34.3	62.2	82.0	9.6	60.6	5136	106.9
Lorraine	89.9	2.8	31.1	66.1	53.0	11.3	57.9	2311	98.2
Alsace	107.5	2.6	35.9	61.4	122.1	7.8	63.7	1708	206.3
Franche-Comté	93.8	5.9	37.4	56.6	81.4	9.1	61.1	1117	68.9

Table 10.6 continued

Region	Economy					Labour market 1997		Population 1996	
	GDP/head (PPS) avg. 1994-96	Employment (% of total), 1997			Eur. Patent applications per million inh., avg. 1994-96	Unemployment rate (%)	Employment rate (% of poupulation aged 15-64	1000 inhabitants	Population density inh./km²
		Agriculture	Industry	Services					
Ouest	88.5	8.1	28.4	63.4	44.4	10.7	61.5	7660	90.0
Pays de la Loire	92.2	6.3	32.6	61.1	39.7	11.0	62.1	3167	98.7
Bretagne	86.8	8.7	25.1	66.1	47.4	9.9	61.0	2868	105.4
Poitou-Charentes	84.4	10.9	26.2	62.9	48.1	11.4	61.2	1625	63.0
Sud-ouest	89.6	8.4	23.2	68.4	50.8	11.4	60.0	6126	59.1
Aquitaine	92.9	8.0	21.7	70.2	40.7	11.9	58.3	2895	70.1
Midi-Pyrénées	87.9	8.4	24.5	67.1	68.4	11.2	61.7	2513	55.4
Limousin	82.4	9.8	25.3	64.9	30.6	9.2	61.4	718	42.4
Centre-est	98.9	4.6	29.9	65.4	142.1	10.6	61.9	6940	99.6
Rhone-Alpes	102.2	3.5	30.5	65.9	162.8	10.5	62.5	5625	128.7
Auvergne	84.7	9.8	27.2	62.9	54.0	11.0	59.2	1315	50.5
Méditerrannée	88.8	4.4	19.6	76.0	55.5	16.9	53.2	6981	103.5
Languedoc-Roussill	80.2	7.8	19.4	72.8	41.3	17.8	52.0	2254	82.4
Provence-Alps-Azr	93.6	2.7	19.8	77.5	65.4	16.5	54.5	4465	142.2
Corse	82.8	6.6	14.5	78.9	8.7	15.2	38.9	261	30.1
Dép. D'Outre-mer	46.5							1644	18.4
Guadeloupe	40.1							425	249.4
Martinique	54.0							390	345.7
Guyane	48.0							160	1.9
Réunion	45.7							670	265.7
IRELAND	94.8	10.9	28.5	60.4	33.3	10.1	57.7	3626	51.6
ITALY	102.1	6.5	31.7	61.8	46.3	12.3	51.3	57461	190.7
Nord ovest	117.3	4.6	34.8	60.7	70.0	9.0	55.9	6064	177.9
Piemonte	116.4	4.6	39.6	55.8	80.4	9.7	57.1	4294	169.1
Valle d'Aosta	130.4	6.6	22.7	70.9	27.0	4.1	61.9	119	36.5
Liguria	118.7	4.4	21.6	74.0	46.2	10.2	52.2	1651	304.7
Lombardia	131.5	2.7	40.7	56.6	102.0	6.2	58.3	8959	375.3
Nord est	123.3	5.8	37.9	56.3	62.7	5.0	59.6	6558	164.7
Trentino-Alto Adge	126.6	9.7	27.2	63.0	40.4	3.8	62.3	919	67.5
Veneto	122.3	5.2	41.1	53.7	62.7	4.8	59.7	4453	242.5

Table 10.6 continued

Region	Economy					Labour market 1997		Population 1996	
	GDP/head (PPS) avg. 1994-96	Employment (% of total), 1997			Eur. Patent applications per million inh., avg. 1994-96	Unemployment rate (%)	Employment rate (% of poupulation aged 15-64	1000 inhabitants	Population density inh./km²
		Agriculture	Industry	Services					
Emilia-Romagna	130.9	6.3	34.6	59.1	99.6	6.7	63.2	3938	178.0
Centro	106.9	5.0	35.0	60.0	34.0	8.1	56.6	5802	141.0
Toscana	109.8	3.9	34.3	61.8	37.0	8.5	56.4	3525	153.3
Umbria	98.0	6.2	31.3	62.5	21.1	8.2	55.0	830	98.1
Marche	104.9	6.8	38.7	54.5	34.0	7.1	58.0	1448	149.3
Lazio	113.3	4.6	19.9	75.6	29.1	13.3	50.1	5217	302.8
Abruzzo-Molise	87.0	10.2	31.4	58.4	23.8	10.6	51.8	1604	105.3
Abruzzo	89.5	8.9	32.5	58.7	29.1	8.8	52.3	1274	118.0
Molise	77.4	15.5	27.1	57.5	3.5	17.2	49.6	331	74.5
Campania	66.3	10.3	22.4	67.3	5.9	26.1	38.8	5785	425.5
Sud	67.2	12.2	23.6	64.1	3.6	20.5	40.4	6770	152.4
Puglia	71.2	11.6	25.2	63.2	4.5	18.3	41.3	4088	211.2
Basilicata	68.1	13.7	30.8	55.4	6.3	20.6	42.1	608	60.8
Calabria	59.1	13.1	18.0	69.0	1.3	24.9	38.2	2074	137.5
Sicilia	66.3	12.0	20.1	67.9	9.8	24.0	38.1	5101	198.4
Sardegna	74.0	12.5	22.8	64.7	7.2	20.5	43.1	1663	69.0
NETHERLANDS	105.8	3.5	21.6	69.1	120.6	5.2	68.0	15531	374.0
Noord Nederland	102.1	4.9	24.1	64.6	66.6	6.8	63.4	1631	143.2
Groningen	129.6	4.1	24.4	64.1	68.4	8.3	61.2	558	188.1
Friesland	87.5	5.1	24.4	65.5	63.2	6.4	63.4	614	106.9
Drenthe	88.0	5.8	23.3	64.1	68.9	5.6	66.2	459	171.2
Oost-Nederland	92.6	4.2	24.2	66.0	105.0	4.8	67.9	3214	292.9
Overijssel	93.1	3.3	26.7	63.9	102.2	5.1	67.5	1056	308.8
Gelderland	94.5	4.4	23.6	66.5	113.4	4.6	68.0	1881	365.7
Flevoland	76.6	6.3	18.4	70.1	56.6	5.1	69.0	277	114.9
West-Nederland	114.0	2.8	17.2	74.1	96.9	5.1	69.1	7253	611.0
Utrecht	118.7	1.8	15.9	75.6	99.9	4.1	72.2	1075	749.5
Noord-Holland	119.0	2.4	16.9	74.6	81.6	5.3	69.9	2472	608.9
Zuid-Holland	109.9	3.0	17.1	74.3	111.7	5.3	67.7	3339	968.9
Zeeland	103.5	6.5	25.4	62.7	56.8	4.6	67.1	368	125.5

Table 10.6 continued

| Region | Economy | | | | | Labour market 1997 | | Population 1996 | |
| | GDP/head (PPS) avg. 1994-96 | Employment (% of total), 1997 | | | Eur. Patent applications per million inh., avg. 1994-96 | Unemployment rate (%) | Employment rate (% of poupulation aged 15-64 | 1000 inhabitants | Population density inh./km² |
		Agriculture	Industry	Services					
Zuid-Nederland	102.7	3.7	27.2	63.3	210.4	4.8	67.6	3432	470.7
Noord-Brabant	105.4	3.9	26.9	63.6	259.3	4.6	68.3	2297	452.1
Limburg	97.2	3.3	28.0	62.8	112.0	5.4	66.2	1135	513.7
PORTUGAL	70.1	13.3	31.0	55.7	1.7	6.7	67.4	9927	108.0
Continente	71.0	13.2	31.3	55.4		6.7	67.8	9428	106.2
Norte	62.1	11.6	39.9	48.5		6.9	66.7	3538	166.3
Centro	59.8	31.9	29.7	38.5		3.4	81.4	1711	72.3
Lisboa,Vale Tejo	88.5	3.8	25.2	71.0		7.9	63.5	3312	277.6
Alentejo	58.0	14.2	24.5	61.2		10.4	62.5	522	19.4
Algarve	70.2	11.8	19.6	68.6		8.2	64.7	346	69.3
Acores	49.9	16.0	21.2	62.9		5.4	58.5	242	103.9
Madeira	53.8	12.5	27.6	59.8		5.4	63.3	258	330.9
FINLAND	94.8	7.7	27.3	64.6	165.5	14.8	62.2	5125	15.2
Manner-Suomi	94.7	7.7	27.4	64.6	174.3	14.9	62.2	5099	15.1
Uusimaa	123.9	1.4	21.4	76.7	307.1	11.4	67.8	1335	128.3
Etela-Suomi	90.0	7.6	34.1	57.9	164.2	15.1	62.5	1797	30.9
Ita-Suomi	74.0	12.5	23.5	63.8	55.1	18.7	54.7	703	8.3
Vali-Suomi	81.7	16.4	29.5	54.0	73.0	14.9	61.0	706	15.1
Pohjois-Suomi	83.0	9.6	23.8	66.4	171.9	18.6	57.3	559	4.1
Ahvenanmaa/aland	119.5	20.7	15.5	63.8		4.6	75.8	25	16.2
AUSTRIA	111.3	6.9	29.6	63.5	96.9	4.4	67.8	8059	96.1
Ostösterreich	126.0	6.0	26.8	67.2	86.6	4.6	68.4	3395	144.1
Burgenland	71.3	8.2	34.6	57.3	19.7	3.8	66.2	275	69.4
Niederösterreich	94.8	11.5	30.3	58.2	84.2	3.4	69.6	1524	79.5
Wien	165.1	0.4	22.2	77.4	100.4	5.9	67.7	1595	3844.3
Südösterreich	89.2	9.4	31.2	59.4	82.4	5.1	65.0	1770	68.3
Karnten	89.7	8.0	28.8	63.2	71.9	5.8	63.4	563	59.0
Steiermark	89.0	10.0	32.3	57.6	87.2	4.8	65.7	1207	73.7
Westösterreich	107.5	6.5	32.1	61.4	115.7	3.8	68.9	2894	84.2
Oberösterreich	100.9	8.2	35.4	56.4	114.4	3.0	69.8	1381	115.3

Table 10.6 continued

| Region | Economy | | | | | Labour market 1997 | | Population 1996 | |
| | GDP/head (PPS) avg. 1994-96 | Agriculture | Industry | Services | Eur. Patent applications per million inh., avg. 1994-96 | Unemployment rate (%) | Employment rate (% of poupulation aged 15-64 | 1000 inhabitants | Population density inh./km² |
		Employment (% of total), 1997							
Salzburg	121.4	5.6	25.4	69.0	81.9	3.9	69.5	509	71.2
Tirol	108.1	5.5	26.0	68.5	95.9	5.4	66.6	660	52.2
Vorarlberg	111.9	3.0	40.0	57.0	209.1	4.1	68.9	344	132.3
SWEDEN	100.3	3.1	25.8	70.9	191.4	10.4	67.7	8841	21.5
Stockholm	122.1	0.6	16.4	82.9	311.6	7.9	68.1	1735	267.3
Östra Mellansverige	91.0	3.8	28.6	67.4	165.2	10.2	67.6	1500	39.0
Smaland med Öarna	97.4	5.7	34.0	60.3	98.9	8.6	71.2	793	24.2
Sydsverige	92.5	4.0	25.9	70.2	197.1	11.9	66.0	1265	90.6
Vastsverige	96.8	3.1	28.0	68.8	183.4	10.4	68.8	1770	59.2
Norra Mellansverge	96.1	3.7	30.4	65.6	154.4	12.3	65.0	860	13.4
Mellerstra Norrland	99.4	5.1	26.0	68.9	20.2	13.0	69.0	393	5.5
Övre Norrland	97.5	2.4	23.5	73.8	148.5	13.3	64.6	525	3.4
UK	98.0	1.9	26.8	71.1	75.3	7.1	70.7	58801	243.2
North	86.2	1.7	31.3	66.7		9.3	65.1	3091	200.5
Cleveland, Durham	81.6	1.0	32.8	65.9		9.6	65.6	1166	385.3
Cumbria	101.5	6.3	31.5	61.9		6.9	70.3	491	71.9
Northumberl. Tyne	84.6	0.5	30.1	69.2		9.9	62.9	1435	257.8
Yorkshire	88.3	1.5	30.0	68.4		7.9	68.2	5036	326.8
Humberside	92.7	1.9	34.4	63.4		8.7	65.8	887	252.8
North Yorkshire	99.3	4.5	24.1	71.5		4.8	75.8	735	88.4
South Yorkshire	73.7	0.4	32.0	67.5		10.0	61.5	1305	836.9
West Yorkshire	91.8	0.7	29.3	69.7		7.4	70.7	2109	1037.0
East Midlands	93.7	1.8	33.5	64.6		6.0	73.4	4141	265.0
Derbysh, Nott.shire	88.7	1.1	34.4	64.3		7.1	71.1	1994	416.3
Leicestersh, Northa	102.1	1.3	34.9	63.7		4.8	76.3	1532	311.5
Lincolnshire	89.2	5.6	26.5	67.7		5.7	73.2	616	104.0
East Anglia	98.3	3.5	27.7	68.4		5.5	73.6	2142	170.4
South east	114.7	1.1	21.1	77.7		6.6	73.3	18120	665.6
Bedfors, Hertfordsh	99.7	0.9	24.9	73.8		4.1	77.2	1565	544.2
Berks,Buckh,Osfrd	120.2	1.9	24.1	73.9		3.2	80.0	2066	359.8

Table 10.6 continued

Region	Economy					Labour market 1997		Population 1996	
	GDP/head (PPS) avg. 1994-96	Employment (% of total), 1997			Eur. Patent applications per million inh., avg. 1994-96	Unemployment rate (%)	Employment rate (% of poupulation aged 15-64)	1000 inhabitants	Population density inh./km²
		Agriculture	Industry	Services					
Surrey	99.3	1.6	20.6	77.6		4.1	77.3	2519	461.4
Essex	84.8	1.5	27.0	71.4		5.7	72.7	1586	431.6
Greater London	138.4	0.3	15.7	83.7		9.7	69.0	7074	4483.1
Hampshire, Wight	97.2	1.6	25.9	72.4		4.7	74.7	1753	421.5
Kent	90.2	1.8	25.5	72.7		6.3	72.5	1557	417.0
South West	93.3	3.2	25.4	71.2		5.7	76.0	4842	203.2
Avon,Glouc, Wiltsh	105.9	1.9	26.3	71.6		5.0	78.5	2134	286.1
Cornwall, Devon	79.9	5.0	24.1	70.7		7.3	72.2	1543	150.3
Dorset, Somerset	88.0	3.5	25.3	70.9		5.1	76.4	1165	190.8
West Midlands	91.7	1.9	34.3	63.7		7.0	70.6	5317	408.8
Herefr,Worc, Warw	96.1	2.8	29.8	67.2		4.6	78.1	1197	202.8
Shropsh,Staffordshr	84.7	3.1	35.0	61.8		4.9	72.4	1477	238.1
West Midl County	93.7	0.5	36.3	62.9		9.4	66.0	2642	2939.3
North West	88.4	0,8	29.0	70.1		7.7	67.6	6401	871.8
Cheshire	110.6	1.2	30.0	68.7		5.4	71.1	980	420.4
Gr. Manchester	89.8	0.4	29.1	70.4		7.4	67.2	2576	2002.7
Lancashire	86.4	1.7	31.0	67.1		5.7	71.6	1425	464.1
Merseyside	72.5	0.1	25.3	74.2		12.1	61.7	1420	2168.6
Wales	82.0	3.4	28.7	67.6		7.5	66.3	2921	140.7
Clwyd,Dyfed,	79.4	7.4	26.7	65.5		7.2	68.0	1134	66.2
Gwent, Mid Gla	83.7	0.8	30.0	68.9		7.8	65.2	1787	492.2
Scotland	96.8	2.7	26.8	70.4		8.0	68.0	5128	66.5
Fife-Lothian-Taysd	100.9	2.7	25.7	71.4		7.3	70.4	1891	105.9
Dumfries, trathclyd	89.5	1.3	26.9	71.8		9.3	63.4	2425	121.9
Highlands, islands	79.7	5.6	26.3	68.1		8.4	73.9	280	9.2
Grampian	124.8	6.1	30.3	63.1		4.8	77.1	531	61.0
Northern Ireland	80.2	5.2	27.0	66.8		10.3	64.2	1663	123.4

Source: European Commission (1999a)

BIBLIOGRAPHY

Council (1999a), *Council regulation No. 1260/1999 of 21 June 1999 laying down general provisions on the Structural Funds,* OJ L 161 of 26.06.1999.

Council (1999b), *Council regulation No. 1264/1999 of 21 June 1999 amending Regulation (EC), No. 1164/94 establishing a Cohesion Fund,* OJ L 161 of 26.06.1999.

European Commission (1996), *First Report on Economic and Social Cohesion 1996. Preliminary Edition,* EUR-OP, Luxembourg, CM-97-96-928-EN-C.

European Commission (1997), *Regional Success Stories. Profiles of 36 Projects in Europe,* EUR-OP, Luxembourg, CX-94-96-372-EN-C.

European Commission (1998), *Benchmarking the EU against Ireland and New Zealand,* Benchmarking papers, No. 1, 1998.

European Commission (1999a), *Sixth Periodic Report on the Social and Economic Situation and Development of the Regions of the European Union,* EUR-OP, Luxembourg, CX-21-99-472-EN-C.

European Commission (1999b), *Kommissionens beslutning af 01.07.1999 of fastsættelse af befolkningslofter for de enkelte medlemsstater under strukturfondsmål 2 for perioden 2000–2006,* K(1998) 1771 endelig udgave.

European Commission (1999c), *Kommissionens beslutning af 01.07.1999 om fastsættelse af vejledende fordeling på de enkelte medlemsstater af forpligtelsesbevillinger under strukturfondsmål 1 for perioden 2000 til 2006,* K(1999) 1769 endelig udgave.

European Commission (1999d), *Kommissionens beslutning af 01.07.1999 om fastsættelse af vejledende fordeling på de enkelte medlemsstater af forpligtelsesbevillinger under strukturfondsmål 2 for perioden 2000 til 2006,* K(1999) 1772 endelig udgave.

European Commission (1999e), *Kommissionens beslutning af 01.07.1999 om fastsættelse af vejledende fordeling på de enkelte medlemsstater af forpligtelsesbevillinger under strukturfondsmål 3 for perioden 2000 til 2006,* K(1999) 1774 endelig udgave.

European Commission (1999f), *Kommissionens beslutning af 01.07.1999 om fastsættelse af vejledende fordeling pr. medlemsstat af forpligtelsesbevillinger for det Finansielle Instrument til Udvikling af Fiskeriet i områder uden for strukturfondsmål 1 for perioden 2000–2006,* K(1999) 1760 endelig udgave.

European Commission (1999g), *The Community Budget: The facts in figures 1999,* EUR-OP, Luxembourg, C6-23-99-281-EN-C

European Commission (1999h), *Annual Report of the Cohesion Fund, 1998,* COM(1999) 483 final, Brussels, 15.10.1999.

European Commission (1999i), *The Cohesion Fund in pictures,* EUR-OP, Luxembourg, CX-11-97-035-EN-C.

European Communication (1999j), *The Socio-Economic Impact of Projects Financed by the Cohesion Fund – A modelling approach. Volume 1:*

Introduction and summary – Literature review – Vector auto-regression models, EUR-OP, Luxembourg, CX-46-97-001-EN-C.

European Commission (1999k), *10th Annual Report of the Structural Funds, 1998,* COM(1999) 467 final, Brussels, 15.10.99.

European Council (1999), *Presidency conclusions – Berlin, 24–25 March 1999,* SN 100/1/99 REV 1.

European Parliament and the Council (1999a), *Regulation No. 1261/1999 of the European Parliament and of the Council of 21 June 1999 on the European Regional Development Fund,* OJ L 161 of 26.06.1999

European Parliament and the Council (1999b), *Regulation No. 1262/1999 of the European Parliament and of the Council of 21 June 1999 on the European Social Fund,* OJ L 161 of 26.06.1999

Reiner, Martin (1998), *Regional Policy in the EU. Economic Foundations and Reality.* Centre for European Policy Studies, Brussels.

Udenrigsministeriet (1997), *Strukturfondenes funktion og fremtid. Rapport til regeringen,* Embedsmandsudvalget om strukturfondenes funktion og fremtid, juli 1997

11. EU Research for Industrial Competitiveness

Robert-Jan H.M. Smits

After agriculture and regional development, research and technological development (RTD) is the third largest expenditure item in the EU budget. But while the first two policies account for more than 75 per cent of total EU spending, the percentage of the Community budget allocated to RTD does not exceed 4 per cent. Still, this accounts in absolute figures today for about €3.5 billion per year.

All RTD activities of the EU are grouped under Framework Programmes, which are 5-year action plans covering EU RTD actions in all different fields and disciplines, from environment to energy and information technologies to biomedicine. The concept of the Framework Programme was introduced in 1984 and so far four Framework Programmes have been completed. The current Framework Programme V runs from 1998 to 2002.

Framework Programme V is very different from its predecessors. It is characterised by concentration and selectivity and it focuses on a limited number of socio-economic issues ('key actions'). To address these issues, it intends to mobilise Europe's best brains via calls for proposals, whereby interested researchers from both large and small enterprises, universities and research centres are invited to put forward their proposals for the relevant areas. Only the very best are selected.

About half of the Community funds for research and technological development go to industry. This makes the Framework Programme one of the largest public instruments for industry in Europe. Each year some €1.7 billion is allocated to both large and small enterprises.

Section 1 of this chapter deals with the legal basis of the EU RTD actions as well as their objectives and the decision-making process. Section 2 describes the EU Framework Programme in a broader context. In Section 3, the implementation of the EU RTD Programmes is discussed. Section 4 presents both quantitative and qualitative results of the Framework Programme. The current Framework Programme V is presented in Section 5. Section 6 focuses on the special measures for SMEs. Finally, in Section 7, some concluding remarks are made. The special annex to this chapter provides sources for further information and assistance.

11.1 LEGAL BASIS

For a long period of time, the legal basis of the Community RTD activities was rather narrow: the general Article 308 of the Treaty. However, with the Single European Act and later the Amsterdam Treaty on the European Union, a sound legal frame was given to the Community research policy.

Chapter XVIII of the Amsterdam Treaty deals with research and technological development. The most important articles of this chapter define:

The Objectives (Article 163)

The research policy of the EU aims at:

* Reinforcing the scientific and technological base of European industry.
* Strengthening the competitiveness of European industry.
* Promoting research activities in support of the other policies of the EU (for example, in the fields of environment and consumer protection).

The Means (Articles 164 and 166)

Article 166 stipulates that the research policy of the EU is implemented through multi-annual Framework Programmes that cover all RTD actions of the Community. Article 164 defines four types of activity that the Community may undertake:

* Implementation of RTD programmes.
* Promotion of international co-operation.
* Dissemination and exploitation of research results.
* Encouragement of the training and mobility of researchers.

However, all four types of activity are implemented by means of specific RTD Programmes (and not just the first activity).

The Treaty clearly defines in Article 166 that the four types of activities mentioned above are complementary to those carried out by the Member States. In other words, it has to be avoided that the EU RTD Programmes duplicate the research efforts undertaken by the Member States (the famous subsidiarity principle). [1]

---

[1] According to the subsidiarity principle, intervention should take place at the level that is most appropriate and ensure an added value. At EU level, only those issues which require a European approach should be addressed.

The Link with the Member States (Article 165)

Article 165 stipulates that the Community and the Member States shall co-ordinate their activities in the field of research. According to the same article, the Commission may undertake any initiative to promote such co-ordination. An important instrument enhancing such co-ordination is COST (European Co-operation in the field of Scientific and Technical research), a legal mechanism of an intergovernmental nature, outside the Framework Programme under which mainly public research institutes co-ordinate their research efforts voluntarily without receiving EU funding (only the travel and meeting costs are reimbursed). This co-ordination is, however, done on an ad-hoc 'project-basis' and not on a 'programme basis'.

Decision-Making Process

The mechanisms for approving a Framework Programme are rather complex. The Maastricht Treaty provided for an adoption of the Framework Programme through a co-decision procedure involving the European Parliament and Council (unanimity vote). After this, each specific RTD Programme has to be adopted by qualified majority by the Council after consultation of the European Parliament.

The cumbersome procedure of co-decision provides for two readings by Council and Parliament. In case of disagreement, a conciliation procedure will start. Due to this procedure it took 20 months before Framework Programmes IV and V were decided, which led to criticism, in particular from the side of industry. With the entry into force of the Amsterdam Treaty (on 1 May 1999), a major change was introduced in the decision-making process. In future, Council will accept the Framework Programme by qualified majority (and no longer unanimity).

In the decision-making process, an important role is played by CREST (Scientific and Technical Research Committee), which is a consultative body to both Council and the Commission and is composed of senior officials from the Member States. CREST is the body that normally re-works the Commission proposals for a Framework Programme and the specific RTD programmes to allow an adoption by Council.

The research activities of the EU in the nuclear field find their legal basis in Articles 4 to 11 of the Euratom Treaty. They are decided upon by the Council (unanimity vote). Under this procedure, the consultation of the European Parliament is not obligatory, although in recent years an informal consultation has been carried out.

Rules for Participation and Dissemination (Article 167)

Article 167 of the Treaty refers to the 'Rules for Participation of undertakings, research centres and universities and for the dissemination of research results' for which the Commission normally has to make a special proposal for each Framework Programme. The decision by Council on the Commission proposal for the Rules under Framework Programme V was taken on 22 December 1998. The rules define conditions for participation and financing, selection criteria, ownership of knowledge and so on. Under the new rules, greater attention is put on the exploitation of the results from Community research. For example, proposers have to submit as part of their proposal a 'dissemination and exploitation plan', which, once the proposal has been selected, should be transformed into a more detailed 'Technological Implementation Plan'.

11.2   THE FRAMEWORK PROGRAMME IN A BROADER CONCEPT

Not only does the Framework Programme represent 4 per cent of the total EU budget, but it also represents only 4 per cent of *total* public spending on research in Europe as a whole. This means that the overall majority of public RTD support Programmes are still run in and by the Member States.

Therefore the impact of the Framework Programme has its limits, but were it to concentrate on real European issues (that is, transnational problems such as global change) this impact could be substantial.

Framework Programmes I to IV were to some extent shopping lists of national research priorities, which meant that their strategic leverage was limited. Amongst the reasons for this was the decision-making process. Since each Member State could veto a decision, difficult compromises had to be sought which often led to a watering down of the priority setting process.

The impact of the Framework Programme also varies by country and by sector. As an example, for the smaller Member States, such as Greece, Ireland and Portugal, the Framework Programme largely influences and affects the national research activities. For the larger Member States, such as France and Germany, this is much less the case. Besides this, the Framework Programme's impact in some industrial sectors, such as IT and aeronautics, is much larger than in others (for example, car manufacturing).

Compared to the United States and Japan, public spending on research in Europe lies behind both as far as quantity and quality is concerned. The EU spends only 1.9 per cent of its GDP on research, whilst for the United States and Japan these figures are 2.7 per cent and 2.9 per cent respectively.[2]

As far as the qualitative aspect is concerned, one needs only to look at the nationality of recent Nobel prize winners and the number of patents filed in Europe compared to the other continents to assess Europe's position with regard to its main competitors. Also, other indicators can be used to assess

---

[2]   EU S & T Indicators Report, p. 25.

Europe's position as far as science and technology are concerned (Table 11.1). In general, it can be said that, although Europe's fundamental research base is solid, its contribution to new industrial innovations is lagging behind.

Table 11.1   Indicators of RTD intensity

	USA	Japan	EU
Business expenditure on RTD per capita (1997)	€456	€369	€175
Value added from 'High-Tech' companies as a percentage of total manufacturing (1997)	16.4	14.7	10
Higher education expenditure on RTD per capita (1997)	€98	€86	€65
Applications for patents by domestic residents per 10 000 population (1996)	4	7	2.6
Number of computers per 1000 population (1997)	450	228	215
Researchers working in business per 10 000 of the labour force (1996)	59	58	23

Source: UNICE study

One of the most striking features of the European research landscape is that there is too much duplication and overlap between the national research programmes of the Member States. This is particularly the case in the area of fundamental research. A way forward could be better co-ordination of the public research efforts in Europe. The first attempt by the European Commission to arrive at some kind of co-ordination was not very successful. Its Communication 'Co-ordination through Co-operation' (1995) was too prudent and never received a concrete follow-up.[3]

It is clear that in the co-ordination debate there are many national interests and obstacles that have to be overcome. The vested interests of the research community in universities and large institutes (for example, Max Planck Gesellschaft in Germany, CNRS in France) are very well protected. Besides this, the large Member States dislike the thought that their national RTD programmes will be co-ordinated by Brussels.

Co-ordination of research efforts in Europe should not affect only the research policies and programmes of the Member States. There are other European programmes on science and technology that are often of an inter-

---

[3]   Although the Commission Communication was presented to, and discussed by many committees, a concrete action plan as follow-up never emerged.

governmental nature. EUREKA, ESA, COST, EMBL, EMBO and CERN[4] are examples of this. Also, for these programmes there is a need for better division of labour with the Framework Programme.

To re-launch the debate on this issue, Mr Busquin, the Commissioner for Research, presented in January 2000 a Communication to Council and Parliament entitled 'Towards a European Area'. This document is considered as the first official Commission paper on the road to Framework Programme VI (2002–06). But instead of focusing narrowly on the mechanism of the Framework Programme, the Commission Communication addresses the overall European landscape for science and technology. Only after a political debate has taken place on this document will the Commission present a formal proposal for Framework Programme VI in 2001.

11.3 IMPLEMENTATION OF EU RTD PROGRAMMES

As said before, it takes on average 20 months from the presentation of a formal Commission proposal for a Framework Programme to its actual adoption by Council and Parliament (including the adoption of the specific RTD Programmes). And even then the actual implementation cannot start before Committees composed of representatives from the EU Member States have given a positive opinion on the 'work programmes' which are the detailed technical annexes of the specific RTD Programmes (and include the topics of the calls for proposals as well as the related 'roadmaps'). This may take an additional 4 months, which brings the total duration of the decision making process to 24 months. In the fast-changing world of science and technology, where developments occur at an increasing speed, these delays are believed to be too long. For this reason it was decided in Framework Programme V to update the work programmes of the research programmes at regular intervals in order to meet new emerging challenges and needs of industry and society as a whole.

Based on the work programmes, the Commission organises, at regular intervals 'calls for proposals' in which interested parties are invited to put forward proposals for the areas covered by the calls. The minimum duration of each call is three months, however, for specific target groups (for example, SMEs) and special types of activities (for example, studies) there are open calls for proposals, meaning that proposals may be submitted during the whole duration of the programme.

Proposals have to meet certain criteria such as having at least two partners from different Member States, being innovative, indicating the European

---

[4]   EUREKA (European Research Co-ordination Action), ESA (European Space Agency), COST (European Co-operation in the field of Scientific and Technical Research), EMBL (European Molecular Biology Laboratory), EMBO (European Molecular Biology Organisation), CERN (European Organisation for Nuclear Research).

added value, contributing to EU policies, containing plans on how the project will be managed and its results will be exploited.

Following the submission deadline of a call, the Commission services carry out an eligibility check, which means that for each submitted proposal it is verified whether the appropriate application forms were used, if the original signatures are present and whether the basic number of partners from different countries are available. After this, all eligible proposals are examined by panels of independent experts ('evaluators') from outside the Commission. At least three experts grade each proposal on the basis of clearly defined and published criteria upon which they also rank them in order of priority (highest grades on top; lowest grades on the bottom).

Although the Commission is not obliged to follow this priority ranking when deciding which proposals are considered for funding, it does so in most of the cases. Successful applicants, whose proposals have received the highest grades and best ranking, are invited for contract negotiations with the Commission. Unsuccessful proposals are rejected.

It should be noted that the contract negotiations between the Commission and successful applicants might take some time (in several cases up to 4–6 months). The main reasons for this are the following:

- Additional forms (Contract Preparation Forms) have to be completed.
- Applicants have to modify their proposal on basis of the findings of the evaluators (sent to them in the form of evaluation summary reports).
- Specific requests from the Commission concerning certain proposed costs (for example, labour, travel, co-ordination, overheads).
- Applicants need to arrange between themselves how they will divide the results that may arise from the research project. This arrangement is normally laid down in a 'Consortium Agreement' in which the Commission does not interfere as long as it is not in violation with the terms of the standard contract used by the Commission.

Box 11.1   Timetable for evaluation of project proposals

Date	Activity
⊗	Launch of a call for proposals
⊗ + 3 months	Deadline of the call for proposals
⊗ + 4 months	Start of proposal evaluation
⊗ + 5 months	End of proposal evaluation
⊗ + 6 months	Start of contract negotiations
⊗ + 8 months	Commission selection decision on first projects
⊗ + 9 months	First contracts signed
⊗ + 10 months	Start of first RTD projects
(EC advance payment: 40 per cent)	

Once the contract negotiations are completed and the contracts have been signed by both parties – the Commission and the applicants – the research work may start. Since the Commission as 'college' takes all decisions concerning rejected and selected proposals, additional delays of four weeks may occur (Box 11.1).

Selected proposals never receive more than 50 per cent Community funding of the total eligible costs.[5] The remaining 50 per cent have to be born by the participants themselves. Universities may request a 100 per cent funding of additional costs, that is, the extra costs for carrying out the project (for example, additional staff, special equipment).

Besides the instrument of the call for proposals, parts of the specific RTD programmes are implemented by the eight institutes of the Joint Research Centre (Box 11.2), which are the Community's own research laboratories, located in several of the Member States. This, however, concerns less than 10 per cent of the EU research budget as a whole, and it is very likely that this percentage will be reduced in future Framework Programmes.

The Joint Research Centre (JRC) is an inheritance of the past, the old 'Euratom Days' when Commission officials from the different Member States jointly carried out research projects in the nuclear field. Although over the years the eight JRC institutes have changed their mission and today deal with more 'modern' topics such as materials research and the environment, the fundamental question of the real mission and core business of these institutes is still under discussion.

Box 11.2   Joint research institutes

Institute	Location
• Institute for Advanced Materials	NL – Petten
	I – Ispra
• Institute for Reference Materials and Measurements	B – Geel
• Institute for Transuranium Elements	D – Karslruhe
• Institute for Prospective Technological Studies	E – Sevilla
• Environment Institute	I – Ispra
• Institute for Systems, Informatics and Safety	I – Ispra
• Institute for Space Applications	I – Ispra
• Institute for Health and Consumer Protection	I – Ispra

The current Commission policy, as regards the JRC, is aimed at concentrating the activities of the eight institutes on supporting EC policy. Drastic decisions (for example, the closing of certain institutes) will be

---

5   For RTD projects, these eligible costs consist of: personnel costs, durable equipment, consumables, travel and subsistence, computing, subcontracting, protection of knowledge and facilitation of knowledge exploitation and other specific costs.

difficult since the Member States that host these sites will oppose this for political reasons.

11.4 RESULTS

From a quantitative point of view, the research programmes of the EU are impressive. In 1997 the European Commission received more than 24 000 proposals which resulted in 7000 contracts involving about 30 000 participants. By the end of 1997 more than 11 000 RTD projects were running, including those that were selected in 1995 and 1996. In 1998 6200 new projects were started with over 28 000 participants (European Commission, 1999c, p. 6).

About 40 per cent of the participants in the Framework Programme are companies, of which more than half can be characterised as SMEs. The other 60 per cent are universities and research centres. The most important industrial sectors involved are Information and Communication Technologies (ICT), chemicals and automotive.

From a qualitative point of view, the Community Research Programmes are more difficult to evaluate. There are of course success stories, individual projects that led to breakthroughs, but the overall strategic impact of the Framework Programme is difficult to assess. Did it contribute to enhancing the competitiveness of European industry? Did it make certain European sectors more competitive as regards their American and Japanese competitors?

The answer to these questions is difficult to give. Each year, the European Commission carries out monitoring exercises whereby independent experts are requested to write reports on the progress made by the individual specific research programmes. In addition to this, there are the 'Five-year Assessment Reports', which assess the impact of the Framework Programme and the specific RTD Programmes as a whole (Box 11.3). Although the overall tone of these reports is positive, they do not – or perhaps cannot – go further than making general statements, about how these instruments could be developed further. As the Commission puts it itself in one of its publications: 'Although it is accepted that the impact of RTD activities on competitiveness and employment is neither direct nor immediate, the fact that they are crucial for the long term remains uncontested' (European Commission, 1999c, p.11).

Box 11.3   Impact assessment of 123 completed RTD projects funded by the Industrial Technologies Programme

• 123 completed RTD projects which involved 836 partners.
• 836 partners came from SMEs (33 per cent), large industry (16 per cent), contract research organisations (11 per cent) and non-profit (that is, public and university) research centres (30 per cent).
• 75 per cent of the projects have reached their original objectives.
• 40 per cent of the industrial partners and contract research organisations have created or safeguarded jobs.
• 49 per cent of the industrial partners have obtained 'environmental' benefits (energy saving, material savings)
• 56 per cent of the partners have obtained additional turnover.
• 43 per cent of the partners have achieved cost savings.
• Each € invested by the European Commission generated €12 of economic activity.

Source: IMT, impact study, pp. 13–14

What is perhaps more interesting is to hear what individual participants, industry in particular, have to say about the Framework Programme. In 1995, David Fishlock, a former journalist of the *Financial Times*, was asked by IRDAC, the Industrial Research and Development Advisory Committee of the European Commission, to interview[6] eight senior industrialists to obtain their views on Framework Programme IV. As advantages of the Framework, the industrialists saw 'bringing Europe's industry and universities close together' and 'facilitating vertical integration of suppliers, manufacturers and users'. They also mentioned 'the networking, the making of new technical contacts outside their own nations, the benchmarking and training of staff'. The interviewees were less concerned about the amounts of money coming from Brussels. For them the financial advantage was less important than the other ones. However, the industrialists also expressed some criticism on the Framework programme and the specific research programmes. They were of the opinion that these programmes were still too much oriented towards academia and lacked a sharp industrial focus. They also criticised the lack of concentration and selectivity. On the exploitation of the results of the Community Research Programmes, they called for 'a more rapid transfer of research results into development and the marketplace, perhaps through demonstration projects, pull through projects and venture capital schemes'.

The views of the eight industrialists were echoed by a panel of wise men[7] that assessed Framework Programme IV in 1997. In their report, these wise

---

[6]   The results of this was the booklet 'Lets Talk Research'.
[7]   Chaired by former Commissioner Etienne Davignon

men mentioned that, although the quality of the individual research projects was high, there was a lack of strategic orientation and concentration:

> the Framework Programme is not fulfilling its promise. It lacks focus and is underachieving. This is not the fault of individuals, but of a structure that inhibits the formulation of real strategy and makes effective implementation difficult. As it is currently conceived and managed, the programme is not flexible enough to respond to new challenges and opportunities. Nor is it clearly related to the goals and objectives of the European Union. For too long it was intended to be an aggregate of national and sectoral desires and ambitions. It must be more than that in the future (European Commission, 1997c, p. 10).

11.5 FRAMEWORK PROGRAMME V

On basis of the findings of the Davignon Panel, the European Commission began in 1997 with the preparation of Framework Programme V.

This process comprised a broad consultation of industry, universities, research centres and other stakeholders. One of the first organisations that presented coherent advice on Framework Programme V was IRDAC (the Industrial Research and Development Advisory Committee of the Commission), which made a plea for:

* Concentration and selectivity around four main themes.
* A challenge-led approach, 'whereby specific targets are set which enhance both national wealth creation and the quality of life simultaneously'.
* Greater emphasis on SMEs.
* Training and mobility of researchers.
* Less complex and less time-consuming procedures (IRDAC, 1996).

The Commission proposal for Framework Programme V was issued in April 1997 and very much resembled the IRDAC opinion. It consisted of six specific programmes and 16 key actions. The proposed budget was €16.3 billion. However, the lengthy discussions with Council and Parliament led to an increase of specific programmes to 7 and of key actions to 23. The proposed budget was reduced to €14.96 billion.

At their meeting of 22 December 1998, the Council reached an agreement on the Commission proposal for Framework Programme V. This action plan runs from 1999–2002 with a total budget of €14.96 billion, which is 3 per cent higher in real terms than that for Framework Programme IV. The areas with the biggest increase in budget are Quality of Life (32 per cent increase) and Human Potential (29 per cent increase).

Framework Programme V consists of 7 specific RTD Programmes: 4 thematic and 3 horizontal ones (Box 11.4). To a large extent, the role of the horizontal programmes is to support the thematic ones.

Box 11.4   Framework Programme V, 1998–2002

Programme	Budget (million €)	%
Thematic Programmes:		
1. Quality of life and management of living resources	2 413	16
2. User-friendly information society	3 600	24
3. Competitive and sustainable growth	2 705	18
4. Energy, environment and sustainable development	2 125	14
Horizontal Programmes:		
5. Confirming the international role of Community research	475	3
6. Promotion of innovation and encouragement of SME participation	363	2
7. Improving human potential and the socio-economic knowledge base	1 280	9
Joint Research Centre	1 020	7
Nuclear Fission and Nuclear Fusion	979	7
	14 960	100

Compared with previous Framework Programmes, Framework Programme V constitutes a break with the past. This is largely due to the following new features:

Concentration and Selectivity
Framework Programme V consists of only 7 specific RTD Programmes while its predecessor comprised 22. It is more than just the continuation of previous programmes. As the former member of the European Commission responsible for research put it: 'Research focused on performance for its own sake has given way to research concentrating on current socio-economic problems. Also, the available resources have been concentrated on carefully targeted priorities, thereby avoiding spreading finances thinly which has too often limited the impact of the Union's efforts' (European Commission, 1998–99, No. 21, p. 3).

Key Actions

Framework Programme V embraces a 'problem solving' approach by means of the key actions. Some 23 strategic problems and topics have been defined which Community research should address in an interdisciplinary way. These topics range from 'ageing' to 'sustainable management of water' and are mainly implemented via the four thematic programmes (Box 11.5).

These key actions are the real innovations of the Fifth Framework Programme, because they 'concentrate the resources of all the disciplines and technologies concerned on a series of well-defined themes' (European Commission, 1998–99, No. 15, p. 3).

The key actions are a step away from the traditional fundamental research oriented projects that were funded under previous Framework Programmes and which served mainly to generate new know-how. Some 70 per cent of Framework Programme V's budget is allocated to the key actions.

Research Infrastructure

Under Framework Programme V, special attention is given to the optimal use of existing research infrastructure and to the development of new research infrastructure through transnational co-operation. In this context, researchers are provided with access to unique infrastructure in other European countries.

Small and Medium-Sized Enterprises (SMEs)

Largely due to the pressure of the European Parliament, special attention is given to the involvement of SMEs, to which an average of 10 per cent of the budget of each thematic programme has to be allocated. In addition, special instruments are provided for to encourage the participation of SMEs in the Framework Programme (see below).

Innovation

Emphasis is put on the exploitation of the research results generated by the thematic programmes. In this regard, special actions are undertaken in the field of venture capital and protection of Intellectual Property Rights (IPR).[8] While in previous Framework Programmes, dissemination of research results was the key obligation for the participants, under Framework Programme V dissemination is only obligatory when the research results are not exploited.

In addition, contractors in the EU RTD programmes are required to present and update at regular intervals 'Technology Implementation Plans' (TIPS) in which they have to indicate how they intend to exploit the research results.

Many of the Community activities in the field of SMEs and innovation are co-ordinated and supported by the horizontal programme 'Promotion of Innovation and the Encouragement of SME Participation'. Not only does this programme manage the IPR Helpdesk; it also updates the innovation trend-

---

[8] For example, through the creation of an intellectual property rights helpdesk.

chart which is an overview of the innovation related actions of the Member States.

Box 11.5   Framework Programme V – 23 key actions (million €)

Quality of life and management of living resources		Budget
Key Action 1:	Food, nutrition and health	290
Key Action 2:	Control of Infectious diseases	300
Key Action 3:	The 'cell factory'	400
Key Action 4:	Environment and health	160
Key Action 5:	Sustainable agriculture, fisheries and forestry and internal development of rural areas including mountain areas	520
Key Action 6:	The ageing population and disabilities	190
User-friendly information society		
Key action 1:	Systems and services for the citizen	646
Key Action 2:	New methods of work and electronic commerce	547
Key Action 3:	Multimedia content and tools	564
Key Action 4:	Essential technologies and infrastructures	1363
Competitive and sustainable growth		
Key Action 1:Innovative products, processes and organisation		731
Key Action 2:	Sustainable mobility and intermodality	371
Key Action 3:	Land transport and marine technologies	320
Key Action 4:	New perspectives for aeronautics	700
Environment and sustainable development		
Key Action 1:	Sustainable management and quality of water	254
Key Action 2:	Global change, climate and biodiversity	301
Key Action 3:	Sustainable marine ecosystems	170
Key Action 4:	The city of tomorrow and cultural heritage	170
Energy		
Key Action 1:	Cleaner energy systems, including renewables	479
Key Action 2:	Economic and efficient energy for a competitive Europe	547
Nuclear Energy		
Key Action 1:	Controlled thermonuclear fusion	788
Key Action 2:	Nuclear fission	142
Improving human research potential and the socio-economic knowledge base		
Key Action: Improvement of the socio-economic knowledge base		165

Participation of Candidate Countries

Traditionally the Framework Programme is the test-bed for future Member States of the EU. Long before Austria, Sweden and Finland joined the EU, these countries were already actively involved in the Community research programmes. And also under Framework Programme V, all 11 candidate countries participate as if they were already members of the EU (in return for a contribution to the Community Research budget based on their gross national product). This will allow these future Member States to get familiar with the Brussels way of working. Besides the 11 candidate countries, 5 other countries are fully associated to the Framework Programme and participate as full members. These are Iceland, Norway, Liechtenstein, Israel and soon Switzerland (Box 11.6).

Box 11.6   Framework Programme V – participation of non-EU States

European Economic Area: Liechtenstein, Iceland, Norway
Applicant Countries: Bulgaria, Cyprus, Czech Republic, Estonia, Hungary, Latvia, Lithuania, Poland, Romania, Slovak Republic, and Slovenia
Other Countries: Israel, Switzerland

However, Framework Programme V does not only constitute a break with the past as far as the content is concerned, but also as regards the implementation of the research programmes. In this context, a number of Commission initiatives[9] have been taken aimed at creating more transparency, efficiency and rapidity:

A Common Evaluation Manual[10]

This manual informs potential participants in the Framework Programme on how their proposal will be dealt with. But it also harmonises the rules between the different RTD Programmes[11] which was really necessary given the discrepancies in approach in previous Framework Programmes. The manual sets out five blocks of criteria that are common for all specific research programmes (Box 11.7). In addition it describes the different steps, after the submission of proposals. These range from the 'administrative

---

[9]   These initiatives were discussed at an informal Ministerial Colloquium which was held in London on the 28 April 1998.

[10]   Manual of Proposal Evaluation Procedures, 24 March 1999.

[11]   Evaluation Manual, p. 2. It should be noted that nationality of applicants is not amongst the evaluation criteria. In other words, proposals are selected on basis of their quality and relevance.

check on eligibility' to 'proposal evaluation and selection' and 'contract negotiations with successful applicants'.

Box 11.7   Evaluation criteria – five blocks

• Scientific and technological quality and innovation. • Community added value and contribution to EU policies. • Contribution to Community social objectives. • Economic development and scientific and technological prospects • Resources, partnership and management.

Source: Manual of Proposal Evaluation, 24 March 1999, *pp 13–14.*

Over-Subscription

In 1998, the last year of Framework Programme IV, the average selection rate of proposals was 37 per cent, compared to 30 per cent in 1997 and 26 per cent in 1996 (European Commission, 1999c, p. 8).

Since many applicants complained about the low selection rate and related chance of success, the Commission introduced measures to address this over-subscription problem. Amongst these is a better definition of research topics. In this regard, the introduction of the 'key action' concept has proved to be a success. Framework Programme V will encourage larger and more focused proposals. This move towards larger projects could already be seen in 1998 when compared to the previous year, the newly started projects were 20 per cent bigger with an average Community contribution of €660 000 and an average six partners per project (ibid.).

National Contact Points

The participation of organisations, in particular SMEs, in the Framework Programme stands or falls according to the quality of information and assistance available to them at national level. Although in the context of Framework Programme V, the provision of information and assistance is seen as a responsibility of the Member States, the Commission has a clear role as far as the training and co-ordination at European level is concerned.[12]

Consultative Structures

Consulting the stakeholders (for example, universities, industry, research centres) is of great importance for the formulation and implementation of Community RTD Programmes. In the past, such meetings mainly took place

---

[12]   *Guidelines for Setting up Networks*, p. 3.

in the context of IRDAC and ESTA.[13] Under Framework Programme V, both bodies have been abolished and replaced by a new organisation, which is called: the Forum for European Research.

Besides the strategic advice given by the Forum, 17 special External Advisory Groups have been created to advise on the key actions. These groups consist of around 25 persons each nominated in a personal capacity from industry, university, research centres and end-user communities.

The European Group on Ethics in Sciences and New Technologies is providing advice on ethical issues (European Commission, 1999c, p. 2).

Simplification of Procedures

Framework Programme V should have brought a simplification of rules and procedures, but this did not really occur in the first year of its implementation. The information packages and application forms of the specific programmes are more voluminous and complex than ever before. However, the Commission has promised to review the situation and propose simplifications in the course of 2000–01. This will include the introduction of new internal Commission procedures which allow to provide applicants with a rapid feedback on the results of the evaluation of their proposals.

Electronic Proposal Submission

Traditionally proposals for Community RTD programmes could only be submitted in paper form. Under Framework Programme V, submission in electronic form is offered via the software tool 'Pro-Tool' (which stands for 'Proposal Preparation Form'). Although the first use of Pro Tool in 1999 during the first calls for proposals was far from being successful due to problems of a technical nature it is expected that the instrument will become fully operational in the course of 2000–01.

11.6 SPECIAL MEASURES FOR SMEs

In recent years, SMEs have become an important target group of the Framework Programme. The reason for this is their contribution to economic growth and job creation. SMEs need to innovate constantly, and access to new technologies is therefore essential for their competitiveness in the internal market.

To enhance the participation of SMEs in the Framework Programme, special instruments have been developed. These consist of:

---

[13] European Science and Technology Assembly, the academic consultative body.

Exploratory Awards

Exploratory awards are financial grants of up to €22 500 (75 per cent of total costs up to €30 000) allowing two SMEs from two different Member States or one Member State and an Associated State to prepare a proposal for a European research project. The grant may be used by the SMEs to carry out themselves, or to ask a consultant to carry out on their behalf, a number of activities: searches for partners, novelty verification, market analysis, feasibility checks, project planning and writing of research proposals.

Co-operative Research (CRAFT)

CRAFT is a scheme allowing at least three SMEs from two different Member States or one Member State and an Associated State to sub-contract the research necessary to solve their common problem to a third party (who is called the 'RTD performer'). The SMEs involved normally have little or no in-house research capability and therefore cannot solve their problems themselves. Many of the SMEs involved in CRAFT projects are working in so-called traditional sectors such as textiles, clothing, metalworking, construction, leather, and so on.

The maximum duration of co-operative research projects is two years. The total costs may not exceed €2 million, of which the European Commission will pay 50 per cent. All the intellectual property rights resulting from the projects belong to the SMEs (who are obliged to exploit the research results). The RTD Performer is paid 100 per cent for his work.

During Framework Programme IV, some 2700 SMEs received an Exploratory Award and more than 4200 were selected for a CRAFT project. Besides the Exploratory Awards and the Co-operative Research scheme, over 7600 SMEs were involved in the regular RTD Programmes of Framework Programme IV. These SMEs have their own in-house research facility and can for this reason be classified as 'research-intensive' SMEs.

In 1997, at the request of the European Commission, an independent study was undertaken to assess the experience of 4000 SMEs with the Framework Programme, and in particular with the SME-specific instruments (that is, Exploratory Awards, CRAFT). The main findings of the study were the following:

- two-thirds of the participating SMEs have less than 50 workers;
- 64 per cent of SME participants are newcomers;
- 63 per cent of SME participants have never been involved in a regional, national or other European research programme;
- half of the participating SMEs did not know their project partners beforehand;

- 96 per cent of all SMEs are satisfied with their participation in the Framework Programme and intend to participate again.

In Framework Programme V (1999–2002), the SME-specific instruments – Exploratory Awards, Co-operative research – have been strengthened. In addition, a number of additional initiatives have been developed to enhance SME involvement in the EU research programmes further. These initiatives consist of:

The Creation of a Single Entry Point

Since SMEs tend to think in terms of problems and opportunities instead of 'programmes', the European Commission is offering to the SMEs a single gateway to the Framework Programme.

SMEs can send all their queries to this point concerning the EU research activities and the SME-specific instruments in particular. The single entry point also carries out pre-screening of proposals and ensures a rapid feedback to SMEs on their submitted proposals (not exceeding 13 weeks).

In the context of the single entry point, a special SME Helpline is run which provides SMEs with feedback on their oral and written questions within a maximum of 24 hours.

A Network of SME National Contact Points (NCPs)

This network consists of organisations (mostly governmental agencies) which are nominated by and located in the Member States and Associated States with the task of informing and assisting SMEs on the Framework Programme. Although the members of the network are funded by their national authorities, the European Commission may support special events of a transnational dimension (for example, brokerage events, workshops) as well as transnational co-ordination meetings between members of the SME NCP network. The tools which the SME NCPs use (for example, information brochures, application forms, 'success stories') are normally prepared by the European Commission.

Economic and Technological Intelligence

This action allows existing information networks, services and intermediaries to make proposals for providing SMEs with information and assistance on technological trends that may result in participation in the Framework Programme. These proposals may include training actions and technological audits.

The EU contribution for such proposals may go up to 100 per cent of their total costs. Examples of networks that may introduce proposals are: the SME

National Contact Point Network and the different networks of European industrial federations.

Although the involvement of SMEs in the Framework Programme is a well-established political priority, it should be clearly understood that for the vast majority of SMEs, there is no reason or need whatsoever to participate in Community research programmes. The average greengrocer, butcher or baker at the corner of the street is not the target group. This means that for some 85 per cent of all SMEs in Europe, the Framework Programme is not of interest as far as direct involvement is concerned. However, this still leaves some 15 per cent of industrial and service-related SMEs in Europe, which is in absolute terms a very large community. For these SMEs, which have high or medium research intensity, the Framework Programme is an excellent mechanism to innovate and internationalise at the same time. And it is not difficult to calculate that although the figure of 14 500 SMEs involved in Framework Programme IV is impressive, it represents only a fraction of the target group of potential participants.

To allow SMEs themselves to determine if they are potential participants in the Framework Programme, the European Commission has prepared five questions (Box 11.8):

Box 11.8   Five questions: should you take part in a Framework Programme?

• Are you exporting or searching for new business opportunities?   • Are you facing competition in your home market?   • Are you interested in developing or acquiring new technologies?   • Are you willing to invest in RTD?   • Are you willing to work with other companies?   If your answer to all these questions is 'yes', then you are a potential participant in EU RTD Programmes.

Source: European Commission

11.7 CONCLUDING REMARKS

Although it is logical that after Framework Programme V there will be a Framework Programme VI, a number of issues will have to be addressed before the new Framework Programme begins in 2003. Amongst these issues are the following:

Co-ordination of Research in Europe

It is time that new initiatives are taken with regard to the division of labour in Europe as far as public support of research is concerned. There is currently an enormous overlap and duplication in publicly-funded fundamental research programmes in the Member States. The Commission may, on basis of the Treaty, propose measures to tackle this problem and it should do so.

At the same time, a better division of labour has to be reached with the other main European programmes in the field of research: EUREKA, ESA and the activities of the ESF. The Commission's Communication 'Towards a European research Area' is therefore a step in the right direction, since it will encourage the debate on the co-ordination topic and has a broader dimension than the instrument of the Framework Programme as such.

More Concentration and Selectivity within the Framework Programme

Although the introduction of the 'key action' concept (the problem-solving approach) in Framework Programme V was a major step forward, the majority of the key actions still have objectives that are too vague. Therefore, under Framework Programme VI, the number of key actions could be reduced and better deliverables defined. This will also contribute to solving the existing problem of 'over-subscription'. However, at the same time a 'free space' has to be created in which innovative SMEs can submit their proposals in a 'bottom-up' way. A good model for such an SME-friendly action could be SBIR (Small Business Innovation and Research) in the United States.

Simplification of Rules and Procedures

Although Framework Programme V brought a big leap forward as far as content is concerned, the requested and promised simplification of rules and procedures did not really occur at its start. In Framework Programme VI, this effort must be made.

Information packages and application forms have to be made more user-friendly and certainly less voluminous. Also, the Commission's internal procedures for evaluating and selecting project proposals have to be streamlined. A delicate balance will have to be found between budgetary and legal rigour and a user-friendly approach.

APPENDIX: INFORMATION AND ASSISTANCE

Information and assistance on the Framework Programme and the specific
RTD Programmes can be obtained from the National Contact Points (NCPs)
in the Member States and Associated States. In addition, the Commission
itself provides information and assistance (for instance pre-screening of
proposals). These services are made available via Internet (Box 11.9).

Box 11.9   Information on the EU RTD projects

The Commission's general EUROPA site:	http://europa.eu.int
The CORDIS site:	http://www.cordis.lu
Directorate-General for Research site:	http://europa.eu.int/comm/dgs/ research/index-fr.html
The Joint Research Centre (JRC) site:	http://www.jrc.org
The EUROSTAT site:	http://europa.eu.int/comm.eurostat

Potential participants may also collect information from those organisations
that have already participated in Community Research activities. This will
allow them to obtain a good overview of the advantages and disadvantages
of participation in the programmes. (Box 11.10). The CORDIS database
gives examples of completed Community RTD projects (Box 11.11).

Box 11.10   Costs/benefits of participation in the Framework Programme

Benefits
- Sharing costs of research
- Sharing risks of research
- Establishing contacts in other countries; exploring new markets (internationalisation)
- Access to new know-how
- Prestige
- EU funding
- Training of staff
- Benchmarking of own competence

Costs
- Financial investment (half a man-year to prepare a proposal)
- Investment in time
- No guarantee of success (30 per cent get accepted)
- Sharing knowledge with other parties
- Paperwork
- Time lags (6 months to prepare a proposal; 9 months before the start of RTD work)

Box 11.11   Examples of EU RTD projects

• *Soundproofing AIRCRAFT CABINS:*
In the BRAIN project (Basic Research in Aircraft Interior Noise) seven industries and ten research centres and universities have developed new mathematical models, which can be used to predict the level of noise inside an aircraft cabin. These models will play an important role in the design of future aircraft since passenger comfort is a growing factor of importance in the design stage. The participation industries were: Aérospatiale, Alenia, CASA, Daimler-Benz, DASA Airbus, Fokker and Saab.

• *A cleaner process for leather tanning:*
Three European companies located in France, Italy and Germany have developed a new technique for pre-processing hides. This technique eliminates pollution and allows the production of high quality leather at lower manufacturing costs. In this way, Europe's tanneries can meet the strict EU regulations on environmental protection since part of their waste problem has been solved by a new pre-processing technique.

• *Recycling Toxic Chips:*
In a CRAFT project, a German university and six European SMEs developed automated machines to recycle used toxic chips. These machines identify and recover valuable parts and components while at the same time separating and discarding toxic waste.

BIBLIOGRAPHY

André, M. (1995), Thinking and debating about science and technology at the European level, *Science and Public Policy*, vol. 22, no. 3, pp. 205–7.

Callon, M., Laredo, P. and Rabeharisoa, V. (1990), *The management and evaluation of technological programmes and the dynamics of techno-economic networks: the case of Agence Française de la Maîtrise de l'Energie (AFME)*, Centre de Sociologie de l'Innovation, Ecole des Mines, Paris.

Cawson, A. and Holmes, P. (1995), Technology policy and competition issues in the transition to advanced television services in Europe, *Journal of European Public Policy*, vol. 2, no. 4, pp. 650–71.

European Commission (1995), *A Brief History of European Union Research Policy*, Office for Official Publications, Luxembourg.

European Commission (1996a), *Inventing Tomorrow*, Office for Official Publications, Luxembourg.

European Commission (1996b), *RTD Strategies of the Top 500 European Industrial Companies and their Participation in the Framework Programme and Eureka*, Office for Official Publications, Luxembourg.

European Commission (1997a), *Joint Research Centre*, Office for Official Publications, Luxembourg

European Commission (1997b), *The Threat of Natural Disasters*, Office for Official Publications, Luxembourg.

European Commission (1997c), *Five-year Assessment of the European Community RTD Framework Programmes*, Office for Official Publications, Luxembourg.

European Commission (1998a), *Better Health for All*, Office for Official Publications, Luxembourg.

European Commission (1998b), *Water: A Vital Resource Under Threat*, Office for Official Publications, Luxembourg.

European Commission (1998c), *Industrial Technologies: Impact Predicted, Impact Delivered*, Office for Official Publications, Luxembourg.

European Commission (1998–99), *RTD Info, Magazine for European Research*, Office for Official Publications, Luxembourg.

European Commission (1999a), *The Fifth Framework Programme*, Office for Official Publications, Luxembourg.

European Commission (1999b), *Second European Report on S & T Indicators, Key figures*, Office for Official Publications, Luxembourg.

European Commission (1999c), *Annual Report 1999*, Office for Official Publications, Luxembourg.

European Commission (1999d), *Innovation in Europe: Research and Results*, Office for Official Publications, Luxembourg.

Freeman, C. and Soete, L. (1997), *The Economics of Innovation*, Pinter, London.

Galimberti, I. (1993), *Large Chemical Firms in Biotechnology: Case Studies of Learning in a Radically New Technology*, DPhil Thesis, SPRU, University of Sussex.

Gibbons, M., Limoges, C., Nowotny, H., Schwartzman, S., Scott, P. and Trow, M. (eds) (1994), *The New Production of Knowledge: The Dynamics of Science and Research in Contemporary Society*, Sage, London.

Grieco, J.M. (1995), The Maastricht Treaty, economic and monetary union and the neo-realist research programme, *Review of International Studies*, no. 21, pp. 21–40.

Guzzetti, L. (1995), *A Brief History of European Union Research Policy*, Brussels, European Commission, DG Research.

IRDAC (1996), *Towards Framework Programme V*, Luxembourg.

IRDAC (1995), *Let's Talk Research*, Luxembourg.

Larédo, P. (1995), *The Impact in France of the European Community Programmes for RTD*, Presses de l'Ecole des Mines, Paris.

UNICE (1999), *Fostering Entrepreneurship in Europe*, Brussels.

12. Small and Medium-Sized Enterprises Create Growth and Jobs

Michael Darmer

Small and medium-sized enterprises (SMEs) have had considerable political attention for many years now. It is perhaps not obvious why this particular group of enterprises should receive special attention, what their problems are and how they should be addressed. This chapter provides some of the answers to these fundamental questions and gives an overview of the Community's actions in this field.

Section 1 analyses the rationale behind the political attention devoted to SMEs and the economic contribution of SMEs. In Section 2 we look into the specific problems of SMEs and in Section 3 we discuss the role and competence of Member States versus the EU in this particular policy field. We give an overview of the main EU initiatives towards SMEs in Section 4 and look at some of the new initiatives in Section 5.

12.1 POLITICAL AND ECONOMIC IMPORTANCE OF SMEs

Since the mid-1980s, Member States and the Commission have given political priority to small and medium-sized enterprises. During the same period, Member States have expressed serious concern about the economic performance of the European Union. The political priority given to SMEs should be seen in relation to the growth potential of SMEs and in particular their ability to create new jobs.

During the past decade economic growth has declined and the number of unemployed has increased dramatically. In 1965, the rate of unemployment was 2.3 per cent in the EU. It increased from 8.3 per cent in 1991 to 11.2 per cent in 1993. By way of comparison, the rate of unemployment in the US and Japan in 1994 was 6.1 and 3.1 per cent respectively. In order to face this challenge, the Commission, in 1993, presented a White Paper on Growth, Competitiveness and Employment. In the White Paper, the Commission recommended the setting of a target to create 15 million jobs by the year 2000 to be able to halve the actual level of unemployment.

The aim of halving the actual level of unemployment is by no means easy. The level of unemployment can be influenced by a number of different factors, which are beyond political control. The task can be illustrated by the following facts. The working-age population was expected to increase annually by 0.3 per cent. But the increase in participation in the work force was expected to be more than twice this, 0.7 per cent, mainly due to the increased participation of women. This meant that a 0.5 per cent increase in employment annually was needed just to prevent the unemployment rate from increasing. In order to reduce the rate of unemployment by 50 per cent between 1995 and 2000, a constant annual rise in employment of 2 per cent was required.

This should be compared with the fact that between 1974 and 1985 the annual average growth in employment was negative (European Commission, 1998e). Between 1986 and 1995 it was positive but less than 0.5 per cent. In 1996 and 1997 it was positive too, though the annual growth in employment was slightly higher (approximately 0.5 per cent).

In order to fulfil this job-creating aim, much attention has been given to the job-creating capacity of SMEs. But the job-creating potential of SMEs is not unchallenged. Some argue that SMEs are the greatest potential job creators, whilst others question the sustainability of the jobs created due to the relative low survival rate of new firms.[1] During the period from 1988 to 1995 enterprises with less than 100 employees are believed to have been responsible for almost all net job creations (European Commission, 1996b). On the other hand, only half of the newly created enterprises are still active after five years. However, in general, SMEs are expected to create jobs faster than large firms and to be more consistent job creators than large firms because they are less affected by macroeconomic factors.

So the increased political importance of SMEs is mainly due to the economic and, in particular, the employment crises in the Union. SMEs are expected to play a significant role in creating new jobs. Since the beginning of the 1990s, SME-related issues have been on the agenda of almost every European Council, which illustrates the political importance attached to SMEs.

This may explain *why* there has been a significant and increasing interest for SMEs. But it does not explain the economic contribution of SMEs in relation to, for instance, employment. This will be the subject for the next sub-section.

---

[1]   For a discussion of the job creating potential of SMEs, see European Commission (1995a).

Economic Importance of SMEs

In statistical terms, SMEs are defined as enterprises with less than 250 employees.[2] Small companies dominate the enterprise structure of the Union. There are approximately 18 million (non-agriculture) enterprises in the EU-15; of these, 99 per cent have less than 50 employees, and the number of SMEs account for 99.8 per cent of all enterprises (see Figure 12.1).

Figure 12.1 Number of enterprises, employment and turnover according to size, 1995

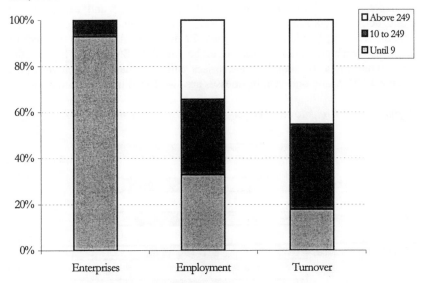

Source: European Commission (1998h)

What Figure 12.1 does not show is that half of all the enterprises are one-man businesses where the entrepreneur and his family members are the only staff. Another 41 per cent of the enterprises have less than 10 employees (micro enterprises). Together, 91 per cent of the enterprises have none or less than 10 employees. So, the business structure in the EU is dominated not only by SMEs but in particular by micro enterprises with less than 10 employees.

All together, there are 150 million people employed in the EU. More than two thirds (112 million) of these are employed in the private non-agricultural sector referred to in Figure 12.1 and they generate a total turnover of €17 109 billion. SMEs provide two-thirds of the jobs and generate more than half of the turnover. The micro enterprises with less than 10 employees provide one-

---

[2]   The official European definition of SMEs is explained later in this chapter.

third of the jobs and 18 per cent of the turnover. So even though there are only 1.2 million enterprises with between 10 and 250 employees, these enterprises provide one-third of the jobs and 37 per cent of the turnover. Large companies with 250 employees or more provide the last third of employment and turnover. There are only 36 000 large enterprises in the EU. This means that a very small number of enterprises account for a very high proportion of the employment.

The economic importance of micro enterprises can partly be explained by the industrial structure in the EU. In general SMEs dominate sectors where economies of scale are not significant or where capital intensity is low, for example, sectors like trade, HoReCa (hotel, restaurant and catering) and construction. Retail trade and HoReCa account for 38 per cent of all enterprises and provide 30 million jobs (27 per cent). Around 80 per cent of the employment in these sectors is to be found in SMEs and half of the employment is to be found in enterprises with less than 10 employees (see Figure 12.2). Many one-man businesses are also found in these sectors.

Figure 12.2   Breakdown of employment into size and sectors, 1995

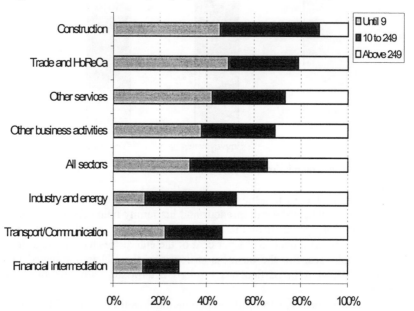

Source: European Commission (1998h)

Also the construction sector has a relatively high share of SMEs. Around 60 per cent of all enterprises in the construction sector are SMEs and around 90 per cent of the employed in the sector is employed in SMEs. Contrary to the trade and HoReCa sectors, the construction sector has a relatively high share of small and medium-sized enterprises with between 10 and 250 employees.

Large enterprises play a more significant role in capital-intensive sectors like energy and manufacturing. The latter is dominated by a few but very large firms, such as car assembly units and steel plants. The energy sector is dominated by former national public monopolies.

The industrial structure cannot only be explained by the distribution between sectors. Also differences in enterprise culture between the 15 Member States of the EU play a significant role. In the southern part of the EU, there is a greater tradition of small family-owned enterprises in retail trade activities and craft sectors than in the northern part of the Union. These differences in enterprise culture help explaining why there are more than 80 enterprises per 1000 inhabitants in southern countries like Greece while there are less than 67 enterprises per 1000 inhabitants in, for example, the Netherlands.

The differences in enterprise culture can also be seen in the average enterprise size in the different Member States. Member States can be divided into three groups according to the average size of their enterprises. One group with the southern countries Greece, Italy, Portugal and Spain has on average less than five employees per enterprise. At the other end of the scale, enterprises in countries like Ireland, Luxembourg, the Netherlands and Austria have on average more than double as many employees. Most of the rest of EU-15 have on average between six and seven employees (see Figure 12.3).

Figure 12.3   Average turnover and employment in the EU

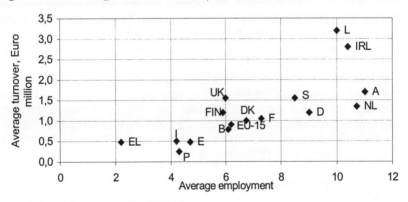

Source: European Commission (1998h)

The economic importance of SMEs is considerable and due to their growth potential and employment creation they have received (and still do) much political attention. SMEs dominate almost all sectors but particularly in sectors like trade, HoReCa and construction as well as in countries with a tradition for small family-owned enterprises.

Having analysed the political and economic importance of SMEs, the next questions immediately pop up. What are the specific problems of SMEs and how are they addressed? These questions will be analysed in the next sections.

12.2　BARRIERS TO ECONOMIC GROWTH AND JOB CREATION FOR SMEs

In a report to the Madrid European Council (European Commission, 1995b), the Commission identifies five major markets and policy imperfections or failures. The failures are seen as inhibiting economic growth and job creation in SMEs. Many of the barriers are of a general nature in the sense that they affect all enterprises, large and small, but they are regarded as much more damaging to SMEs. The five failures are excessive administrative burdens, barriers to transfers of technology, barriers to the labour and human resource market, insufficient capital markets and barriers in the product and service market.

Excessive Administrative Burdens

Administrative burdens are unavoidable in the modern and complex society of today. The problem is that they affect enterprises differently depending on their size. Administrative burdens have a relatively much higher impact on SMEs than on large enterprises. The reasons are that SMEs neither have the human resources to cope with the burdens nor the financial resources to pay for outside help. As a result, the administrative burdens are expected to be more than 20 times higher in smaller enterprises than in larger ones (European Commission, 1995b).

Administrative costs are caused by many things like, for example, registering, licensing or the tax system. An example of the last is the fiscal burden to successful transfer of business from one generation to the next. The Commission estimates that at least 30 000 enterprises and 300 000 jobs are lost each year due to unsuccessful transfer of business in the EU (European Commission, 1995b; see also 1998f).

Barriers to Transfers of Technology

Europe does not create as many new technology-based firms as its main competitors like the US. This is a problem because new technology-based firms can open new areas of economic growth and job creation. There are in particular two barriers in this field. The first is to transfer the results of successful research into marketable innovations. The second is the lack of risk capital for these kinds of investments. One of the most effective ways to transfer technology is to create new technology-based firms. But early-stage venture capital in this field is highly risky and Europe has not been able to develop the same kind of financial markets for risk capital as, for example, the US.

Technology-intensive SMEs need constant access to innovation and research results in order to stay competitive and develop themselves. But it is more difficult for SMEs to stay updated because of their size and because the access to this knowledge is complicated and difficult to obtain.

Furthermore, the use of information technology is expected to be of particular importance to SMEs, since it can help overcome the disadvantage of being an SME, for example, in relation to administrative burdens. But SMEs make less use of the information technology than non-SMEs.

Barriers in the Labour and Human Resource Market

Non-wage labour costs as tax on labour and social security contributions reduce the incentive to employ more people. Therefore reducing the non-wage labour costs is thought of as one way of encouraging companies to recruit more people in general, and in particular in SMEs, since non-wage costs hit SMEs harder than larger enterprises.

SMEs also undertake less training than larger enterprises due to several reasons. One is that the training available does not meet the needs of SMEs in terms of content and form. SMEs need multidisciplinary training focusing on their particular problems and have difficulties in attending traditional away-from-the-job training.

Furthermore, new entrepreneurs need vocational and management training. Only half of the newly started enterprises are still active after five years. This rate can perhaps be improved with more training in this field.

Insufficient Capital Market

SMEs have special problems in obtaining capital. Because of their size they have fewer financing options than lager enterprises, and the ones they have are more difficult and more expensive to obtain.

SMEs have difficulties in obtaining equity capital for two reasons. First, most Member States discriminate in favour of debt financing and against equity financing. For example, an entrepreneur who invests a given sum from his business earnings in his company is being taxed, whereas if he borrows the same amount from a bank, he will be able to deduct interest from his tax bill. This can become a problem since debt repayment must continue even in times of recession, whereas dividends can be temporarily suspended. Secondly, there is not a well-functioning market for equity for SMEs in most Member States. After the American model, the EU has assisted in creating a secondary market for equity financing for smaller companies at the European level called EASDAQ. However, the number of enterprises that have actually financed themselves through EASDAQ is still much smaller than the number of American enterprises financing themselves on the American equivalent.

SMEs also have difficulties in obtaining debt financing in the form of loans. Due to higher administrative costs (many small loans) and higher risks (only half of the newly started enterprises are still active after five years), SMEs typically pay a significantly higher interest rate than larger enterprises. This additional financial burden has a negative impact on the growth and job potential of SMEs.

Barriers in the Product and Service Market

While State aid distorts competition between enterprises, the distorting effect on SMEs becomes even higher since a large part of total State aid is given to non-SMEs. Only 7 per cent of the total volume of State aid to the manufacturing sector is given with the purpose of supporting SMEs (European Commission, 1999a). State aid to the manufacturing sector amounts to €37 680 million per year (annual average 1995–97). SMEs may, however, benefit from other, more general, support schemes as support for research and development or aid spent on regional objectives.

The creation of the Internal Market is of particular importance for SMEs since they do not have the resources to overcome the difficulties in exporting to another Member State with different standards, requirements and so on. The fact that the Internal Market is still not a single market for many products and services is a particular obstacle for SMEs. Persistence of technical barriers to trade, lack of acceptance of the mutual recognition principle, the slow pace of the European standardisation and certification procedures and the costly and burdensome requirements for participating in public procurement prevent SMEs in particular from enjoying the full benefits of the Internal Market.

There are other barriers and policy imperfections than the ones mentioned above, but these are the ones which according to the Commission should be addressed at Community level. However, many of the barriers SMEs face, including the ones mentioned above, are also being dealt with at national level, as we will see in the next section.

12.3   THE ROLE OF MEMBER STATES VERSUS THE EU IN SME POLICY

Some of the problems that SMEs have to face may be of local or regional nature calling for a local or regional initiative. However, many of them are indeed of a more general nature and therefore also need to be approached more generally. Usually the problems fall within national competence like, for instance, taxation on labour or they are related to national cultural practices like for example administrative practices. It is therefore not surprising that all Member States have an active SME policy of their own (see Table 12.1).

Table 12.1   Implemented and planned national actions by fields and countries, 1996–97

	Business environment	Financial environment		Internationalisation and information		Labour, training and innovation	
	Administrative burdens	Late payment	Finance	Internationalisation	Information	Labour	Innovation
AT	X		X	X		X	X
B	X		X	X		X	
D	X		X	X	X		X
DK	X		X	X	X	X	X
FI	X		X	X	X	X	X
N							
F	X	X	X	X	X	X	X
GR			X	X	X	X	X
IR	X	X	X	X	X	X	X
L							
I	X	X	X	X	X	X	X
L	X		X	X		X	X
NL	X		X	X	X		X
P	X		X	X	X	X	X
E	X		X	X	X	X	X
S	X			X	X	X	X
UK	X	X			X	X	X

Source: European Network for SME Research (1997)

Except in relation to late payment almost every Member State has planned or is already active in the areas where significant barriers or market failures have been identified. For instance, only Greece has not implemented or planned any actions in order to reduce 'administrative burdens', and only Sweden and the UK have not taken any actions in relation to 'finance'. In relation to 'internationalisation', the UK is the only Member State that has not taken any actions, and in relation to 'information' only Austria, Belgium and Luxembourg have not taken any actions. In relation to the 'labour market' the Netherlands and Germany have not taken any actions and in relation to 'innovation', Belgium is the only Member State without any implemented or planned actions. It is worth noticing that three Member States have implemented or planned actions in all areas. These are France, Ireland and

Italy. It should be taken into consideration that these observations are some years old. Furthermore, a missing mark for a Member State is not the same as to say that the Member State in question is not doing enough in that area. In some cases it can be interpreted as the Member State in question does not feel it has a problem in that area, or that the problem is of minor importance compared to the other problem areas for SMEs in that specific Member State.

Simplification of *administrative burdens* includes modification or abolishing of existing business-related administrative burdens such as registering, licensing and mergers of outlets of authorities into 'One-stop Shops'. In most Member States improvement of the business environment also includes reforms of the tax system.

Improvement in the *financial environment* focuses mainly upon improving SMEs' access to risk and venture capital. Private capital is channelled into SMEs by means of guarantees. Furthermore, in most Member States start-ups are offered new credit lines, loan guarantees and related allowances. For example, in Finland €60 million is earmarked for subsidised loans aimed at start-ups in the manufacturing and service sectors.[3]

In relation to *information*, the general tendency in most Member States is to centralise information sources into One-stop Shops either physically or via the Internet.

Labour market initiatives include more flexible labour market regulations, tax rebates on recruitment of personal, reduced social security contributions by employers. For example, in regions in France hampered by high unemployment, SMEs with less than 50 employees can benefit from social security contributions and income/corporate tax exemptions.

Many Member States try to improve SMEs' *innovative competitiveness* by stimulating SMEs to co-operate with research centres and universities. For example, the Danish Ministry of Business and Industry supports the establishment of 5–10 regional innovation centres in Denmark. Their task is to provide entrepreneurs with special training and access to research, development and capital, as well as to initiate a range of innovative projects.

These examples show that almost all Member States have a very active SME policy of their own. The activities of the Member States leave little room for the Community to conduct a SME policy at Community level which is different from and adds value to what Member States already do. The Subsidiarity Principle highlights the problems with a Community policy in this field. According to this Principle, any action should only be carried out at Community level 'if and insofar the objective of the proposed action cannot be sufficiently achieved by the Member State and can therefore, by scale or effects of the proposed action, be better achieved by the Community'.[4] Add to this that most SMEs are very locally oriented by nature

---

[3]   The examples in this section stem from European Network for SME Research (1997).
[4]   Article 5 of the Treaty.

and therefore difficult to address directly for both Member States and even more so for the Community.

Furthermore, SMEs are by no means a homogeneous group. There are start-ups, micro enterprises, small enterprises and medium-sized enterprises and their problems vary very much depending on their size. For starts-ups the lack of capital and managerial training are major problems. For very small enterprises with less than 10 employees, administrative burdens are usually the biggest problem. They have to apply the administrative rules, but they neither have the human resources to cope with the burdens nor the financial resources to pay for outside help. For a small enterprise with between 10 and 50 employees it can be difficult to maintain its innovative competitiveness, and for medium-sized enterprises with between 50 and 250 employees it can be difficult to expand into new foreign markets within the EU or into third countries.

So one may ask: does it make any sense to have an SME policy, which by definition should be different from a general industrial policy but on the other hand addresses 99.8 per cent of all enterprises? If yes, does it then make sense to conduct an SME policy oriented at all SMEs. Should it rather not conduct a start-up policy, a policy for very small enterprises and so on since the problems seem to differ depending on the enterprises' stage of evolution. And finally, does it make sense to have a Community policy in this field since most SMEs by nature are very locally oriented and in view of the fact that all Member States are very active in this field? Some of the answers will be given in the following sections where we analyse what the Community actually does in relation to SME policy.

12.2 MAIN SME INITIATIVES IN THE EU

The beginning of the SME policy at Community level dates back to 1983 which was the 'European Year of Small and Medium-Sized Enterprises and Craft Industry'. The initiative was originally proposed by the European Parliament. In 1986, the European Commission set up an SME Task Force and an SME action programme was adopted (European Commission, 1986). In 1989 the Council adopted the first multiannual programme (Council, 1989). A budget of €110 million, later raised to €135 million, was allocated to the programme for the period 1990–93. In 1993 this programme was followed by the second multiannual programme for which €112 million was allocated for the period 1993–96 (Council, 1993).

With the Treaty of the European Union agreed in Maastricht in December 1991, industrial policy as such entered into the Treaty for the first time. The article in the Treaty about industrial policy (Article 157) highlights among other things SMEs and co-operation between companies to which should be paid special attention. See also Chapter 1 for an analysis of Article 157 of the Treaty. In December 1993 the Commission's White Paper on Growth,

Competitiveness and Employment recommended the setting of a target to create 15 million jobs and in that context proposed a complementary strategy to help enterprises and particularly SMEs to fully develop and exploit their growth and job potential (see above). As a response to the White Paper and in view of the obligation of Article 157 of the Treaty to 'encouraging an environment favourable to initiative and to the development of undertakings throughout the Community, particularly small and medium-sized undertakings' and to 'encouraging an environment favourable to co-operation between undertakings' the Commission adopted the first integrated programme (European Commission, 1994). The aim of the integrated programme was to assemble the various initiatives into a global framework, with a view to ensuring their coherence and giving them a high profile.

In December 1995, the Commission presented a report to the Madrid European Council. The report identified major markets and policy imperfections or failures and advocated a more focused approach to enterprise policy as mentioned above. The Madrid European Council called on the Commission to put these aims into practice as speedily as possible in the framework of the next Integrated Programme for SMEs (European Commission, 1995b). In response, the Commission in July 1996 adopted a Communication which updated the first Integrated Programme. This 1996 Integrated Programme (European Commission, 1996b) is still in action.

In December 1996 the Council adopted the Third Multiannual Programme (Council, 1996). The programme runs from 1997 to 2000 with a financial reference amount of €127 million. The programme fits within the Integrated Programme framework, providing the legal and budgetary basis for the Community's specific SME policy actions of today.

This means that while the Commission's report to the Madrid European Council sets out the problem areas to be addressed, the Integrated Programme and the Third Multiannual Programme respond to the request of the Madrid European Council. The Integrated Programme and the Third Multiannual Programme form the Community's SME policy of today.

The Integrated Programme for SMEs

As we have seen, all Member States have an active SME policy. The Community has, too, taken a number of initiatives which are of particular importance to SMEs. Following the line of the first Integrated Programme, the aim of the 1996 Integrated Programme is to co-ordinate and ensure coherence and visibility of all efforts being made in favour of SMEs and the craft sector. This should be done in close partnership between all parties concerned with the development of SMEs at Community, national and regional level.

It follows from Article 157 of the Treaty that 'The Member States shall consult each other in liaison with the Commission and, where necessary, shall co-ordinate their action. The Commission may take useful initiative to promote such co-ordination'. The Integrated Programme is the most direct response. The overall aim of the Integrated Programme is to achieve greater consistency, effectiveness and transparency of the individual actions taken. While the report to the Madrid European Council pointed at the areas to be addressed, the Integrated Programme sets the priorities for the efforts to be made. The five priorities are:

1. Simplify and improve the administrative and regulatory business environment.
2. Improve the financial and fiscal environment for SMEs.
3. Help SMEs to Europeanise and internationalise their strategies in particular through better information and co-operation services.
4. Enhance SME competitiveness and improve their access to research, innovation, information technologies and training.
5. Promote entrepreneurship and support special target group.

Within these priorities the Integrated Programme distinguishes between three types of measures:

A. Concerted actions.
B. Actions under other Community policies.
C. The third Multiannual Programme for SMEs.

All three measures should be used in each of the five priorities, thereby facilitating greater co-ordination of Member States' and the Community's actions affecting SMEs.

A. Concerted actions

The concerted actions intend to increase the efficiency of Member States' actions by exchange of best practices between Member States. One form these concerted actions may take is to hold a forum. If the Commission finds that special attention is needed in one of the priorities mentioned in the Integrated Programme, it organises a forum, as for example the Helsinki SME Forum which was held in September 1999 (see Box 12.1).

The participants of these SME fora are usually not enterprises. The main target group is those dealing with SMEs at national and regional level. This includes national and regional civil servants, industrial organisations, technological institutes, One-stop Shops, consultants and so on.

The many different fora all relate to the phases of business development that is, the start-up phase, growth phase, transfer phase and so on and the content of each forum builds on the findings of previous fora.

Box 12.1   The Helsinki SME Forum, a concerted action

> The Helsinki SME Forum on '*Rapid Growth and Competitiveness through Technology*', 16–17 September 1999.
>
> The theme of the Forum was the use and impact of information technology and other new technologies on SMEs and their competitiveness, and the role of public and private support services in this. It attracted some 400 participants: SME policy makers, representative organisations and business people from the EU Member State.
>
> The Forum had the following workshops: Workshop A on '*administrative services for SMEs in the information technology era*'. Here the Forum aimed at providing the Member States with new and innovative good practices on how administrative services may be improved by the use of IT and technology. In Workshop B on '*support services for users of new technology*', the Forum aimed at providing new ideas of how support services can assist SMEs to use new technology to improve competitiveness and growth. In Workshop C on '*how can support services boost the rapid-growth suppliers of IT and technology*', the Forum discussed how these companies and the networks of high-technology SMEs may be helped by support services.

Source: Finnish Ministry of Trade and Industry (1999)

B. Actions under other Community policies

The co-ordination of the actions under other Community policies is the responsibility of the Commission. The objective is to ensure better co-ordination of the various contributions that the Community makes in favour of SMEs through its different policies and programmes. The idea is to ensure better recognition of the SME dimension throughout Community policies and programmes with the view to facilitate increased participation of SMEs in Community supported actions and more effective consultations with SME organisations.[5] Some of the policy areas where SMEs have a privileged status include State aid policy, regional policy and research and development policy.

State aid policy   In general, Article 87(1) of the Treaty bans State aid that distorts competition. As such, State aid may threaten the functioning of the internal market. In principle, Article 87(1) regards State aid as incompatible with the common market. However, the principle of incompatibility does not amount to a full-scale prohibition. Articles 87(2) and 87(3) of the Treaty specify a number of cases in which State aid could be considered acceptable. These acceptable circumstances fall within three categories, that is, regional aid, horizontal rules and sectoral rules. One of the horizontal rules is the rule for aid to SMEs. For further details see Chapter 9.

---

[5]   For a comprehensive list of EU activities in favour of SMEs see European Commission (1998i).

State aid to SMEs is allowed because of the job-creation effect of SMEs, the market imperfections suffered by SMEs and the assumption that aid to SMEs distorts less than aid to larger companies.

In European policy areas, such as State aid, an SME is defined as an enterprise which satisfies all of the following three criteria. First, the number of employed must be less than 250. Second, either the annual turnover has not exceeded €40 million or the balance sheet has not exceeded €27 million. Third, the SME must be independent, that is, not owned as to 25 per cent or more of the capital or the voting rights by one enterprise, or jointly by several enterprises (European Commission, 1996d).

SMEs also have a privileged status in most other State aid rules. For instance, the State aid rules for research and development and those for environmental protection allow the aid to be increased up to 10 per cent for SMEs compared to non-SMEs. The same 10 per cent 'bonus' is given in training aid, while the 'bonus' within regional aid varies from 10 to 15 per cent depending on the status of the region.

Regional policy In 1999, the Council agreed to a reform of regional policy for the period 2000–06. According to the new rules (Council, 1999a), the rate of contribution from the Structural Funds for investments in firms cannot, as a general rule, exceed 35 per cent of the total eligible costs in Objective 1 regions (regions which are economically lagging behind). In Objective 2 regions (regions with structural difficulties), the rate of contribution for investments in firms cannot exceed 25 per cent of the total eligible costs. However, in case of investments in SMEs, these percentages can be increased with up to 10 percentage points if finance takes another form than direct assistance, that is interest-rate subsidies, guaranties, equity holdings, venture capital holdings or other forms of finance. See Chapter 10 for an analysis of the Structural Funds including an outline of the different rates of contribution.

SMEs also have a privileged status in the European Regional Development Fund (European Parliament and Council, 1999). The European Regional Development Fund can co-finance three types of investments, that is productive investment, investment in infrastructure and assistance to the development of the region's endogenous potential in particular for the benefit of SMEs. The latter type of investment covers, for instance, assistance towards services for enterprises, financing of technology transfer and improvement of access by enterprises to finance and loan.

Research and development policy Within the Framework Programme there are several instruments in favour of SMEs. For instance, an average of 10 per cent of each thematic programme is reserved for the involvement of SMEs.

Furthermore, special financial instruments like the Exploratory Award and the CRAFT scheme have been developed to promote the participation of SMEs in the Framework Programme. The Exploratory Award is a financial grant of up to €22 500 allowing two SMEs from two different Member States or from a Member State and an Associated State to prepare a proposal for a European Research project. The CRAFT scheme allows at least three SMEs from at least two different Member States or from a Member State and an Associated State to sub-contract to a third party the research necessary to solve their common problem.

See Chapter 11 for an outline of other non-financial instruments connected to the Framework Programme which facilitate the participation of SMEs in the programme.

C. The Multiannual Programme for SMEs

The Third Multiannual Programme for SMEs is an essential part of the Integrated Programme. It provides the legal and budgetary basis for the Community's specific actions in favour of SMEs, which are not covered by other Community policies. The programme covers the period 1997–2000 with a budget of €127 million. It follows the five priorities set out in the Integrated Programme adding a sixth which is *'Improve SME policy instruments'* (Council, 1996). The programme contains specific measures within all six priority areas.

The Council decision on the programme sets clear limitations to what the Community actually can do with this programme, since the decision makes it clear that any measure in the programme must be complementary and not be part of other Community policies or be better carried out at Member State level.

Euro Info Centre The Multiannual Programme covers altogether 23 types of measures divided between the six priority areas. A mid-term external evaluation report[6] shows that, half-way through the programme, 57 per cent of the amount is spent on the aims of helping SMEs to *'Europeanise and internationalise their strategies'*. Within this priority we also find the financially largest measure in the programme, where 38 per cent of the total amount is spent on developing Community information services. One of the aims of the measure is to develop the Euro-Info-Centre network as a 'first-stop-shop' directing requests to the most appropriate Community service provider. In general, the evaluators give the Euro-Info-Centre a positive evaluation, but recommend the 'first-stop-shop' concept to be clarified and to allow the Euro-Info-Centre to be better integrated in the national SME support structure. The Euro-Info-Centre concept is illustrated in Box 12.2.

---

[6] Summarised in European Commission (1999b).

Box 12.2   Euro-Info-Centres

The Euro-Info-Centres are joint ventures which link local organisations and the European Commission on a contractual basis with the common goal of serving SMEs. Locally, Euro-Info-Centres are accommodated by a host structure. The hosts include Chambers of Commerce, development agencies, banks and Chambers of Trade. Alltogether there are 227 Euro-Info-Centres in EU-15, Norway and Iceland.

The Euro-Info-Centres are close to the businesses in their respective regions the special regional and national circumstances. They perform the role of interface between the measures taken at Community level and in particular SMEs. The status as 'first stop shop for European information' should make it simple and efficient to get information about what is going on in the Community.

The Euro-Info-Centres have information concerning EU legislation and programmes of relevance for business. This includes information related to, for example, the EU research and development programmes, public contracts, standardisation, the Euro, the information society and the environment.

The Euro-Info-Centres answer some 400 000 questions a year.

As an example, The Euro Info Centre North West (in the UK) can illustrate the kind of services provided by Euro Info Centres:

Euro Info Centre North West works in partnership with other organisations to help smaller firms in the region to become more competitive and more internationalised. Euro Info Centre North West is part of a network of Euro Info Points around the North West of England which companies can contact for information about Europe, locally. Euro Info Centre North West provides fee-based services to help smaller firms to do business in the European Single Market. As a first-stop-shop for European information, the Euro Info Centre North West helps companies through the maze of EC legislation and programmes, carries out desk research to track down key market information, uses their Europe-wide network to identify potential business partners and monitor public sector contracts across Europe. Euro Info Centre North West works closely together with the Business Links and other Business Support Organisation in the North West. Together with these partners, initiatives for local firms, such as international business to business meetings are organised. To keep local firms informed of contract opportunities, the Euro Info Centre North West also works together with the Regional Supply Office.

Source: European Commission, *Euro Info Centre Network: Europe close to SMEs*

Europartenariat Another important measure related to the aims of helping SMEs to Europeanise and internationalise their strategies is the Europartenariat. The aim of the Europartenariat is to promote direct contact between SMEs by organising two contact events a year where SMEs can meet. According to the evaluators of the Third Multiannual Programme, 12 per cent of the total amount in 1997 and 1998 has been spent on Europartenariat (and the Interprise programme[7]). The evaluators gave

---

[7]   The amount spent on Europartenariat and the Interprise programme cannot be separated. The Interprise programme is the same concept as Europartenariat, but smaller, sector-oriented events. The Interprise programme also takes place more frequently than the Europartenariat.

Europartenariat a positive evaluation. Of the companies researched by the evaluators, 44 per cent claim that a form of useful co-operation has started as a result of participating in a Europartenariat.

The Europartenariat is a joint regional and SME measure. It can only take place in a region which is eligible as an Objective 1 or 2 region according to the regional policy. For an explanation of the differences between Objectives 1 and 2, see Chapter 10. The host region sets up the event with SMEs from the host regions and then invites SMEs from all over EU and from third countries to participate (see box 12.3).

Box 12.3   Europartenariat Denmark 2000

The region Aalborg – North Jutland proposed 450 regional companies from which the Commission selected 350 companies to be host companies. The host companies were presented in a catalogue which was distributed in 65 000 copies in 5 languages to 80 countries. National Counsellors, appointed by the Commission in all 80 countries, promoted the event. Europartenariat Denmark 2000 calculated more than 1700 visiting companies to the event.

From the catalogue presenting the host companies, the visiting companies in advance indicated which companies they would like to meet, and meetings were arranged in advance to ensure that both host and visiting companies were matched as often at possible in order to optimise the outcome of the event. It was also possible to arrange meetings during the event by booking meetings in a large database.

During the two days of the event the host company had between 20 to 30 meetings with new, possible, international partners for co-operation who themselves were looking for partners for co-operation. The visiting companies got a chance to meet host companies from the region but they had also the opportunity to meet other visiting companies which often can be just as, or even more, beneficial as meetings with the host companies.

The benefit of participating in a Europartenariat can be illustrated by the experiences of a Danish printing company 'H & M Etikettrykkeri A/S' from Vojens, Denmark which was able to increase the number of employed from 10 to 25 after participating in a Europartenariat, where it received a large order and was able to establish its own business network easily and effectively with a limited financial investment/fee.

JEV   The Multiannual Programme can also play a useful role for testing innovative measures. This is, for example, the case within the priority area of improving the financial environment for enterprises where the Multiannual Programme has co-financed the Joint European Venture (JEV) initiative. In November 1997 the Commission decided to set aside €5 million of the Multiannual Programme to the new JEV initiative (European Commission, 1997).

The aim of the JEV initiative is to support and encourage the development of transnational joint ventures between SMEs in the Community in order to create viable and stable jobs. The argument for creating this new initiative was the fact that transnational joint ventures were rather rare. The reason for this was seen as reluctance on the parts of banks to support such projects because of the high risk factor stemming from, among other things, the limited knowledge of the partner from another Member State. JEV should then stimulate the interest of financial institutions and make them more receptive to these kinds of projects.

Box 12.4 The JEV programme

The JEV initiative finances up to a maximum of €100 000 per project, to cover part of the costs involved in setting up a joint venture in the European Union between at least two European SMEs. In the initial phase, each project can receive a repayable advance of a maximum €50 000 which represents up to 50 per cent of the cost for conceiving and setting up the joint venture. In a second phase, once the joint venture is operational, the project can receive the rest of the contribution, up to 10 per cent of the total investment. The initiative is channelled to the SMEs through a network of financial intermediaries.

One year after the adoption of the JEV programme in May 1998, the Commission regarded it as a success story and published it as such on its home page. It was regarded as a success for three reasons. First 86 financial intermediaries had joined the JEV network. The financial intermediaries assisted the SMEs in their projects and informed them about the opportunities offered by the JEV programme. Second, in order to further inform SMEs about JEV, a promotion facility was put in place, under which Euro-Info-Centre, Chambers of Commerce, SME-organisations and so on could organise seminars on JEV. Third, one year after the adoption, 100 SMEs had submitted proposals for the setting up of 50 joint ventures. Half of the proposals had then already been accepted.

A concrete example of joint venture, which has received support by the JEV programme, was an Italian company that sat up a joint venture with a British company in the virtual reality computer system sector. The purpose of the joint venture was the production of virtual reality driving simulators for scooters. The Italian company worked in the software service business, whereas the British company was leading in the supply of PC-based virtual reality software.

Source: Council (1998)

The evaluators found that the JEV initiative was welcomed by almost all of those involved, but that the initiative was still unknown to a large number of SMEs. The criticism was not new for the Commission, and in May 1998 the Council decided to allocate another €100 million to a JEV programme for the period 1998–2000 (Council, 1998) and in early 1999 the Commission launched a promotion facility to help SME organisations organise JEV events bringing together SMEs. The JEV programme was financed outside the Multiannual Programme.

The evaluation report also highlighted some of the problems of an SME policy at Community level. Part of the overall conclusion was that there were too many small pilot projects and actions which were inadequately feeding into genuine policy development. There were also 'too many publications-type actions which do not directly relate to policy development or to tangible benefits for SMEs, or which are inadequately disseminated to have major effect' (European Commission, 1999b).

The Commission has presented a new Multiannual Programme in the spring of 2000 (European Commission, 2000) to leave enough time for the proposal to be negotiated with Member States in the Council before the Third Multiannual Programme runs out by the end of the year 2000. The legal base is Article 157 of the Treaty which requires unanimity.

12.5   NEW SME INITIATIVES IN THE EU

Since the publication of the 1996 Integrated Programme and the adoption of the Third Multiannual Programme, the Commission has taken a number of initiatives of which the two most promising in relation to SMEs should be mentioned here. These are the Commission's proposal for a directive combating late payment in commercial transactions (European Commission, 1998a; Council, 1999b) and the BEST Task Force.

Late Payment

Late payment in commercial transactions is a problem especially for SMEs since late payment leads to cash-flow difficulties, undermines profitability and damages competitiveness. In the worst case, it results in insolvency and job losses. SMEs are more vulnerable, rely more frequently on a limited number of suppliers and are weaker *vis-à-vis* the large firms they usually supply, especially when cash-flow needs have to be met with short-term bank loans or overdrafts with relatively high interest charges. Furthermore, lack of efficient implementing procedures are particular harmful to SMEs which are often unable to pursue their claims through lengthy legal proceedings because the cost of these proceedings exceeds the value of their claims.

According to the Commission, 33 per cent of businesses in Europe regards late payment as a serious problem or a problem threatening the survival of their business. With 17 million unemployed and only half of the newly started enterprises still active after five years, the Commission felt that it had to take action. In 1995 the Commission issued a recommendation to Member States to tackle the problem of late payments (European Commission, 1995c). Only a limited number of actions were taken in a few Member State and therefore the Commission in 1998 brought forward a proposal for a European Parliament and Council Directive to combat late payment. After the conciliation procedure, the European Parliament and the Council agreed on a common position in the spring of 2000

As a result of the Directive, SMEs will, as a general rule, benefit from a statutory right to interest 30 days after the date of the invoice. The interest should be sufficiently high to compensate the creditor for the loss incurred through late payment. The level is composed of the European Central Bank's rate for refinancing operations plus 6 per cent. Interest will automatically be payable 30 calendar days after the receipt of the invoice unless otherwise specified in the contract. No reminder will be necessary. For certain categories of contract, Member States will be able to fix a period of 60 instead of 30 calendar days after which interest will become due. However, if they choose to do so, they will have to prevent the parties from exceeding this delay. In order to improve the creditor's ability to pursue the debtor throughout the EU and to collect the claims with speed and efficiency, the Member States are obliged to ensure that the creditor will be able to obtain an enforceable title within a period not exceeding 90 calendar days.

BEST

The BEST Task Force was established by the Commission at a request from the European Council meeting in Amsterdam in June 1997 (European Commission, 1997). The Task Force consisted of entrepreneurs, civil servants and academic experts. Its task was to draw up a report with concrete proposals for improving the quality of legislation and for removing unnecessary burdens.

However, the Task Force found it necessary to take a wider perspective of the problems of companies than just the issue of administrative burdens. Furthermore, the Task Force did not regard it as its task to produce new research, since all the relevant facts were already well-known. Instead it felt it should go through all relevant areas, identifying which to be given priority and to recommend for further actions within these areas.

The BEST Task Force finalised its report in 1998 (European Commission, 1998b, 1998c). It contained 19 recommendations within five areas to the Commission as well as the Member States. The five areas were better public administration, education and training, employment and working conditions, finance, and finally research and innovation. The Commission responded to the recommendation of the BEST Task Force (European Commission, 1998d) by setting up an action plan which provides for measures to be taken at appropriate levels in the Community, nationally and regionally. The Council (1999c) endorsed a modified action plan, and the coming years will show how many of the Task Force's recommendations will be carried out in the ongoing strive to improve the business environment for SMEs

12.6 CONCLUSION

The chapter shows that the political attention to SME is due to the SME's job-creating effect in an EU with severe and constant unemployment problems, and that the contribution of the SMEs to European economy is substantial. Certain barriers and problems, though general in nature but with particularly damaging effects to SMEs, have been identified.

The chapter also shows that all Member State have an active SME policy of their own which due to the Subsidiarity Principle leaves only little room for Community actions in this field. The question whether it makes sense to have a separate SME policy, since SMEs count for 99.8 per cent of all enterprises, is raised and discussed.

The 1996 Integrated Programme and the Third Multiannual Programme form the Community's SME policy of today. The Integrated Programme provides an overall framework for all actions taken in favour of SMEs and sets out the priorities for the efforts to be made. The Multiannual Programme provides a legal and budgetary basis for the Community's specific actions which are not covered by other Community policies such as State aid policy, regional policy and research policy.

Both the Integrated Programme and the Third Multiannual Programme can be expected to change within a few years. The Integrated Programme needs to be updated with the latest developments, including integrating the result of the Late Payment Directive. The Third Multiannual Programme expires by the end of the year 2000. The Commission has brought forward a proposal for a new Multiannual Programme in the spring of 2000 to be negotiated throughout 2000 in order to come into force on 1 January 2001.

BIBLIOGRAPHY

Council (1989), *Council decision of 28 July 1989 on the improvement of the business environment and the promotion of the development of enterprises, and in particular small and medium-sized enterprises, in the Community,* OJ L 239 of 16.08.1989.

Council (1993), *Council decision of 14 June 1993 on a Multiannual Programme of Community measures to intensify the priority areas and to ensure the continuity and consolidation of policy for enterprises, in particular small and medium-sized enterprises, in the Community,* OJ L 161 of 02.07.1993.

Council (1996), *Council decision of 9 December 1996 on a Third Multiannual Programme for Small and Medium-Sized Enterprises (SMEs) in the European Union (1997–2000),* OJ L 6 of 10.01.1997.

Council (1998), *Council decision of 19 May 1998 on measures of financial assistance for innovative and job-creating small and medium-sized enterprises (SMEs) – the growth and employment initiative,* OJ L 155 of 29.05.1998.

Council (1999a), *Council Regulation No. 1260/1999 of 21 June 1999 laying down general provisions on the Structural Funds,* OJ L 161 of 26.06.1999.

Council (1999b), *Common position adopted by the Council on 29 July with a view to the adoption of the Directive of the European Parliament and the*

Council on combating late payment in commercial transactions, Council document 8790/1/99 REV 1.

Council (1999c), *Council Conclusions on Promoting Entrepreneurship and Competitiveness (BEST),* Council document No. 7422/99.

European Commission (1986), *SME Action Programme,* COM(86) 445 final. OJ C 287 of 14.11.86.

European Commission (1993), *Growth, Competitiveness and Employment. The Challenges and Ways forward into the 21st Century, White Paper,* COM(93) 700 final, Brussels 5 December 1993.

European Commission (1994), *Integrated Programme in favour of SMEs and the Craft Sector,* COM(94) 207 of 3 June 1994.

European Commission (1995a), *Panorama of EU Industry 95–96,* Office for Official Publications of the European Communities, 1995.

European Commission (1995b), *Small and Medium-Sized Enterprises. A Dynamic Source of Employment, Growth and Competitiveness in the European Union,* Report presented by the European Commission for the Madrid European Council, CSE(95) 2087.

European Commission (1995c), *Commission's Recommendation of 12 May 1995 on payment periods in commercial transactions,* OJ L 127 of 10.06.1995.

European Commission (1996a), *Enterprises in Europe, Fourth report,* EUR-OP Luxembourg, CA-94-99-162-EN-C.

European Commission (1996b), *Integrated Programme for Small and Medium-Sized Enterprises (SMEs) and the Craft Sector, The Multiannual programme, Concerted Actions and other Community Actions in support of SMEs,* COM(96) 329 final of 10.07.1996.

European Commission (1996c), *Maximising European SMEs' full Potential for Employment, Growth and Competitiveness, Proposal for a Council Decision on a Third Multiannual Programme for Small and Medium-sized Enterprises (SMEs) in the European Union (1997–2000),* COM(96) 98 final of 20.03.1996.

European Commission (1996d), *Definition of Small and Medium-sized Enterprises,* COM(96) 261 final.

European Commission (1997a), *Commission Decision of 5 November 1997 approving for SMEs in the Community a support mechanism for the creation of transnational joint ventures,* OJ L 310 of 13.11.1997.

European Commission (1997b), *The Euro Info Centre Network: Europe close to SMEs,* European Commission, Directorate-General XXIII.

European Commission (1998a), *Proposal for a European Parliament and Council Directive combating late payment in commercial transactions,* COM(1998) 126 final, Brussels 25.03.1998.

European Commission (1998b), *Report of the Business Environment Simplification Task Force, BEST, Volume 1,* EUR-OP, Luxembourg CT-79-98-001-EN-C.

European Commission (1998c), *Report of the Business Environment Simplification Task Force, BEST, Volume 2*, EUR-OP, Luxembourg CT-79-98-002-EN-C.

European Commission (1998d), *Promoting Entrepreneurship and Competitiveness. The Commissions Response to the BEST Task Force Report and its Recommendations*, COM(98) 550, Brussels, 30.09.1998.

European Commission (1998e), *The Competitiveness of European Industry–1998 Report*, EUR-OP, Luxembourg CO-17-98-556-EN-C.

European Commission (1998f), *The Transfer of Small and Medium-Sized Enterprises*, OJ C 93 of 28.03.1998.

European Commission (1998h), *Enterprises in Europe, Fifth Report, SME project, Eurostat*, EUR-OP, Luxembourg, CA-12-98 174-EN- C

European Commission (1998i), *Activities in favour of SMEs and the Craft Sector*, EUR-OP, Luxembourg, CT-08-97-795-EN-C

European Commission (1999), *On Concerted Action with the Member States in the field of enterprise policy*, COM(99) 569 final, Brussels 09.11.99

European Commission (1999a), *Seventh Survey on State aid in the European Union in the Manufacturing and Certain Other Sectors*, COM(1999) 148 final, Brussels 30.03.1999.

European Commission (1999b), *Report on the Evaluation of the 3rd Multiannual Programme for SMEs in the European Union (1997–2000)*, COM(1999) 319 final, Brussels 29.09.1999.

European Commission (1999c), *Commission Regulation of the Application of Articles 87 and 88 of the EC Treaty to State Aid to Small and Medium-Sized Enterprises*, Draft.

European Commission (1999d), *On Concerted Action with the Member States in the Field of Enterprise Policy*, COM(1999) 569 final, Brussels 09.11.99.

European Commission (2000), *Challenges for Enterprise Policy in a Knowledge-Driven Economy: Proposal for a Council Directive on a Multiannual Programme for Enterprise and Entrepreneurship (2001–2006)*, COM(2000) 256 final, Brussels 26.04.2000.

European Council (1995a), *Presidency Conclusions – Cannes, 26–27 June 1995*, SN 211/95 part A.

European Council (1995b), *Presidency Conclusions – Madrid, 15–16 December 1995*, SN 400/95.

European Council (1997), *Presidency Conclusions – Amsterdam, 16–17 June 1997*, SN150/97.

European Parliament and Council (1999), *European Parliament and Council Regulation No. 1261/1999 of 21 June 1999 on the European Regional Development Fund*, OJ L 161 of 26.06.1999.

European Parliament and Council (2000), *Directive of the European Parliament and the Council on Combating Late Payment in Commercial Transactions*, PE-CONS 3620/00+COR1(en).

European Network for SME Research, ENSR, (1997), *The European Observatory for SMEs. Fifth Annual Report, 1997,* EIM Small Business Research and Consultancy, Zoetermeer, the Netherlands.

Finnish Ministry of Trade and Industry (1999), Rapid Growth and Competitiveness through Technology, SME FORUM during the Finnish Presidency, Helsinki, 16–17 September 1999, Press release, 18 May 1999.

13. European Policy and Specific Sectors

Oscar Schouw

European policy towards business determines the framework conditions under which business operates. In the previous chapters several policy fields have been analysed. Trade policy, environmental policy, enterprise policy, research policy, and so on, all affect business to a certain degree and follow in principle a generic approach towards industry. In addition to and within those policies, sector-oriented measures may be taken, to influence developments within a sector or because of the specific characteristics of a sector, for instance, measures relating to products in the pharmaceutical market need to be seen in the wider context of public health.[1]

The main purpose of this chapter is to show how those policies affect economic sectors in practice. To address this issue, this chapter focuses on three sectors: the shipbuilding industry, the steel industry and the Information and Communication Technology (ICT) industry. Many sectors could have been chosen, but this chapter is limited to those three for various reasons.

The shipbuilding industry has always been a politically sensitive sector[2] within Europe. It is the only industrial sector mentioned in the Treaty of Rome (Article 87(3)(c) referring to an obligation to gradually reduce State aid to shipbuilding subject to certain conditions. The policy towards the shipbuilding industry is interesting because it shows the involvement of the Community through its State aid and trade policy.

The policy towards the steel industry is interesting, because the relevant Treaty that regulates this sector will expire in July 2002, implying major consequences for the rules of the game the steel industry is subjected to. The special regime, which applied since 1951, will thus come to an end. After 2002 the steel industry will be in principle subject to the normal EU regulations.

---

[1] Commission communication on the single market in pharmaceuticals, COM(98) 588 final, 25.11.1998.

[2] Other examples of sensitive sectors are the textile industry, the coal, automobiles and synthetic fibres industry. It concerns sectors with chronic structural problems, which usually operate in mature markets characterised by overcapacity and stagnating or falling demand. They are called sensitive sectors because there may be strong political pressure at a national level to protect the sector for strategic, industrial or employment reasons.

Special attention is given to the ICT industry, because of its huge importance for the future competitiveness of European industry. The information industry is a very rapidly growing sector, especially in terms of growth of employment and value added. Under the flag of the information society the Commission has taken a number of initiatives to create a favourable business climate for ICT industry.

13.1 SHIPBUILDING

The Market

The market for shipbuilding is highly competitive. It is characterised by overcapacity, depressed prices and aggressive policies by non-Community yards. The difficult market conditions for the shipbuilding industry have already existed for a long time. Since 1976, demand and supply have been structurally in imbalance. In the beginning, excess capacity resulted from a fall in demand.[3] At a later stage, the market imbalance continued because new capacity was added to the market, especially by Asian countries through the years.[4] The structural imbalance between supply and demand always results in fierce competition, because every yard tries to fill up its construction capacity; in order to obtain orders it might reduce its prices. In particular, South Korea developed itself as market leader during the latter part of the 1990s following a low price policy to fill up its increased production capacity.

According to the OECD, an improvement in market conditions is not to be expected in the first years of the third millennium: 'the world shipbuilding industry is still in crisis with prices plummeting and future demand likely to remain weak for years'.[5] OECD expects further that overcapacity in the industry will be increasing during the first years of the third millennium, 'thanks to a combination of increased productivity, the coming on line of new facilities and the conversion of naval shipyards to commercial production, while at the same time, the growing participation in shipbuilding by emerging countries such as China is adding to the market imbalance'. The European Commission shares these expectations.[6]

---

[3] After the oil crisis of 1973 a decline in the order intake of the world's shipbuilding industry began. However, the effect on output became clear in 1976. Between 1976 and 1979 vessel completion around the world fell by some 37 per cent. In the EU this decline was some 42 per cent.

[4] For instance, shipbuilding capacity grew 170 per cent in Korea, from 1.7 million cgt in 1988 to 4.6 million cgt in 1997. Also China increased its capacity, in particular in the 1990s.

[5] Press release of 2 June 1999 of the OECD Council Working Party on Shipbuilding.

[6] Report from the Commission to the Council on The Situation in World Shipbuilding, COM(1999) 474 final.

In this highly competitive market, European shipbuilding industry has been confronted with a considerable loss of market share. European yards have to compete on the one hand with low-wage countries like China, and on the other with South Korea and Japan; countries that might be more efficient in their shipbuilding production. It should be noted that the loss of market share of the European industry did not start in the mid 1970s, but much earlier. In 1960 the EU produced around 50 per cent of the world shipbuilding's output; by 1970 this had fallen to 27.8 per cent and by 1994 its market share had fallen to 20.5 per cent of world production. Measured in new orders the market share has fallen further to below 20 per cent in the first half of 1999. However, it remains to be seen whether this is a continuation of the structural trend or whether this last figure represents an exceptional year. South Korea increased its market share from under 5 per cent in 1980 up to around 30 per cent in 1998. Japan and South Korea together produce nowadays nearly 60 per cent of the world output measured in cgt[7] as shown in Figure 13.1. World new building capacity amounted up to around 20 million cgt in 1998.

Figure 13.1   World market shares by country/region (new orders, based on cgt), first half of 1999

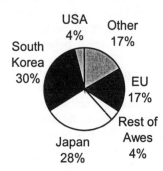

Source: European Commission (1999)

In this context, it is hardly a surprise that the European shipbuilding industry has been intensively restructuring since the mid 1970s. The market situation, the fierce competition at global level and the loss of market share to the Asian countries forced them to rationalise and restructure in order to restore competitiveness.

---

[7]   Cgt: compensated gross tonnes, a measurement combining ship size and ship type-specific building effort.

Restructuring

The restructuring process resulted in a workforce reduction within the EU shipbuilding industry by 70 per cent between 1976 and 1997. Production capacity within the EU has been reduced by 60 per cent. These figures show the dramatic adjustment process of the sector. In some countries like Belgium shipbuilding of seagoing vessels completely disappeared (Simon, 1999). But, European industry is still not able to take advantage of economies of scale, because it is too fragmented. The five largest shipbuilders within the EU represent about 36 per cent in cgt terms in 1996, while the top five shipbuilders in South Korea represent 99 per cent of South Korean capacity. Furthermore, productivity in Europe is lower in many segments of the market compared to Japan and South Korea. It is an indication that the grade of efficiency is still lagging behind. European industry still has a relatively strong position in the higher added value segment of shipbuilding (like building cruiseships). There are, however, indications that Asian countries are penetrating those market segments.

The Community Approach

The adjustment process of the European shipbuilding industry raised intensive discussions in the Council about the content of its shipbuilding policy. It should be considered that, because of the nature of ships, it is difficult to rely on trade measures to protect industry against distortive competition. Trade measures can be to the disadvantage of shipping companies. Tariff measures (custom duties, anti-dumping measures) and quantitative measures can result in higher prices of ships. That could be a reason for European shipping companies not to 'flag in' their new ships, but to carry a flag from a non-EU country. Therefore, traditional trade measures are not suitable for this sector to defend it against outside (unfair) competition.

In this context, the Council adopted in 1969 for the first time a so-called Shipbuilding Directive allowing production aid[8] to protect the sector against the fierce international competition on the basis of social and regional considerations. Since then, State aid policy has been a major pillar within the Community's approach towards shipbuilding: 'it takes account of the industry's structural problems and should therefore not be regarded simply as a legal framework for limiting the granting of aids but as an essential element

---

[8]   The First Shipbuilding Directive provided that aid should be no more than 10 per cent of the price contractually fixed before the beginning of the works, for the purchase of new vessels or for the 'work of transformation'. Ten per cent was chosen because this was estimated to be the level of harm suffered by the EC shipyards as a result of the distortion of competition in the world market. The terminology 'operational aid' is being used in the remainder of this chapter for these price subsidies.

of an industrial approach'.[9] Six other Directives followed: they established the framework under which the Member States could grant subsidies to the shipbuilding and ship-repair industry. The Seventh Shipbuilding Directive (90/684/EC, OJ L-380) emphasises the main reason behind this approach by stating:

> a competitive shipbuilding industry is of vital interest to the Community and contributes to its economic and social development by providing a substantial market for a range of industries, including those using advanced technology; whereas it also contributes to the maintenance of employment in a number of regions, including some which are already suffering a high rate of unemployment.[10]

The Community, therefore, relied on its State aid approach. Table 13.1 shows the support to the EU shipbuilding industry in the last decades. The aid covered 20 per cent of the sector's value added in the period 1995–97. In comparison, aid to the total manufacturing sector within the EU amounted to 2.8 per cent of the sector's value added in this period.

Table 13.1   Aid to the shipbuilding sector as a percentage of added value

Period	86–88 *	88–90	90–92	92–94	94–96	95–97 **
%	33.8	33.3	24	25	25	20

Note: * Third survey, ** Seventh survey
Source: Sixth survey on State aid in the European Union in the manufacturing and certain other sectors, COM(98) 417, p. 14.

The aid amounts involved are quite considerable. Table 13.1 shows that the shipbuilding industry has been heavily supported within the community for some decades. The average annual level of total aid to shipbuilding in the period 1993 to 1995 amounted to €1720 million. This annual level decreased to €1445 million in the period 1995–97, of which €753 million[11] in the form of restructuring aid, which was concentrated in a few countries. The new German Länder received aid for restructuring to about €890 million between 1994 and 1996. In 1997 the Council allowed restructuring aid in Germany (€371 million), Spain (€812 million) and Greece (€175 million).[12] This aid was allowed under strict conditions such as capacity reduction and the

---

[9]   Comments by the Commission, as cited in Power (1992).
[10] Council Directive of 21 December 1990 on aid to shipbuilding, 90/684/EEC, OJ L-380
[11] Seventh survey on state aid in the European Union in the manufacturing industry, March 1999.
[12] Council Regulation (EC) No. 1013/97 of 2 June 1997 on aid to certain shipyards under restructuring, OJ L-148, 6.6.1997.

availability of a viable business plan.[13] Those conditions are meant to contribute to the restructuring process of the sector. Capacity reduction diminishes the excess capacity within the sector. It is an example of how aid for restructuring works out in practise, of which the general regime is explained in Chapter 9. Box 13.1 provides some examples of approved aid and shows that the Commission acts when the conditions under which the aid has been implemented are not respected.

Box 13.1   Aid and restructuring

The Commission monitors closely whether permitted restructuring aid meets its conditions, for instance the conditions to implement the restructuring plan. The Commission may demand reimbursement of the aid granted when a company does not respect those conditions. Bremer Vulkan Group misused €400 million of approved aid. It had received the aid under the condition that it would be used exclusively for the restructuring of its two East German shipyards. But the aid was used for other purposes. In 1998, the Commission decided consequently that the German government should recover this misused aid.[14]

Another example of reimbursement of aid relates to Spanish shipyards. In 1999 the Commission decided that Spain's publicly owned merchant shipyards should repay €110 million. The Commission was of the opinion that Spain had flouted an agreement over restructuring aid for the yards reached in 1997, when the Commission had approved a restructuring aid package. This included €349 million in special tax credits to be used between 1995 and 1999 to compensate the yards for not being able to take advantage of tax credits under a general programme. The yards were, however, integrated into a state-owned holding company which was able to benefit from the tax credits.

An example of a successful restructuring process is the restructuring of Lloyd Werft Bremerhaven GmbH, a medium-sized shipyard which is specialised in ship repair and conversions. The yard was severely affected by the collapse of its mother company, Bremer Vulkan. LWB went into a debt composition procedure in April 1996. It was separated from Bremer Vulkan and started negotiations with new investors. The liquidity situation became very tight in 1997 for various reasons (unclear future ownership, the debt composition procedure). A state guarantee was asked by the commercial banks of 80 per cent on a short-term credit line for working capital up to €6.13 million. Restructuring aid is not allowed for this sector under the shipbuilding directive in force at that time.

The Commission approved the guarantee in 1997, because the aid intensity was still below the allowed level of operational aid. The guarantee made it possible to continue the regular operations of the company and to implement the restructuring plan. It gave time to find new investors. After new investors were found and the debt composition procedure was ended, the company regained viability and became profit making.

---

[13] Capacity reduction around 240 000 compensated gross registered tonnes (cgrt) in yards involved, plus non-reopening to shipbuilding of the public yard at Astano (135 000 cgrt capacity) and some additional capacity reductions in Spain.

[14] European Commission: 28th Report on Competition Policy, 1998.

According to the Treaty, aid to shipbuilding will be diminished gradually. However, only the sixth (1987) and the seventh Directive managed to implement such degressivity – lowering ceilings to 9 per cent of contract value for ships with a contract value exceeding €10 million and 4.5 per cent of contract value, both for ships with a contract value of less than €10 million and for conversions.[15] Table 13.1 shows as well that, given the yardstick of aid as percentage of value added, the aid seems to decrease gradually since the end of the 1980s. However, the amounts spent are still quite considerable.

A New Shipbuilding Policy

In line with general European policies, the Community is trying to implement market-oriented policies towards the shipbuilding industry. Its actual policy (European Commission, 1997a) aims at improving industry's competitiveness and allowing it to face the challenge of global competition without any further sector-specific aid. The Commission's starting point is that industry's future lies primarily in the hands of industry itself. It is the responsibility of management to carry out the actions to improve the competitive position of their yards. The role of the Community is to establish and assure a framework which helps industry to improve competitiveness. In this context, the Community directs its efforts towards ensuring a global level playing field, promotion of research and development, support of industrial co-operation and stimulation of demand for European yards. Redesigning State aid policy is an important element of this new approach. Hereto, the Council adopted a regulation establishing new rules on aid to shipbuilding.[16] This regulation came into force on 1 January 1999 and will apply until December 2003.

The key issue of the new aid policy is the abolishment of operational aid after 31 December 2000. Only aid to promote and encourage competitiveness of the industry may be allowed, because, in the long term, non-specific aid, such as aid for R&D, training aid and so on, may benefit the sector more. Such aid encourages modernisation and innovation and structural improvements within the sector. Box 13.2 shows the essential elements of the new aid policy.

---

[15] The Third Directive did not mention any subsidy ceiling: by 1977 Italy, France and the UK were offering price subsidies of 20–30 per cent end of cost. The Fourth Directive (1978) set aid ceilings at 30 per cent.

[16] Council Regulation (EC) 1540/98, OJ L 202 18.7.98.

Box 13.2   New aid policy of the Commission towards shipbuilding

• No more operating aid after 31 December 2000.
• Aid for innovation will be permitted during a transitional period of 5 years.
• Home and export credits in conformity with OECD 'Rules on Export Credits for Ships' will still be allowed.
• Contract related aid granted in the form of development assistance to developing countries continues to be permitted.
• Stricter conditions in relation to closure aid.

Under the Regulation aid to shipbuilding will basically be subject to the general Community regime. R&D aid, environmental aid, rescue and restructuring aid have to comply with the relevant frameworks that have been discussed in detail in Chapter 9. Regional aid may also be allowed, provided that the aided project is to improve the productivity of existing installations. The Commission acknowledged 'that such aid can make a valuable contribution towards overcoming structural handicaps in disadvantaged regions' (1997a). A transitional aid regime applies for aid to innovation.[17] Aid to innovation may be compatible with the common market up to an aid intensity of 10 per cent provided that it relates to the industrial application of innovative products and processes that are genuinely and substantially new.[18]

To facilitate the further structural adjustment of the sector, it is allowed to grant aid to close production facilities. In order to get approval of such aid, the accessory capacity reductions should be genuine and irreversible.[19] In cases of restructuring aid, the one-time/last-time principle will be applied strictly.

Research Policy

Shipbuilding industry may benefit from the research policy of the Commission. The Fifth Framework Programme, of which the general objectives have been explained in Chapter 11, includes the key action 'Land transport and marine technologies,' targeting promotion of research in the field of advanced technologies that are necessary for the development of advanced ships which are safe and efficient and respect the environment. Other activities will promote research concerning the use of the sea and inland waterways and the transport of good and passengers. The research will relate to vessels, intermodal equipment and new technologies for cargo handling. Furthermore, technologies for the rational and sustainable

---

[17] Under the 1996 - R&D framework on State aid costs for innovation are not eligible for State aid.

[18] That is, are not currently used commercially by other operators in the sector within the European Union, and which carry a risk of technological or industrial failure.

[19] The closed facilities must remain closed for a period of five years and may not re-open for a further period of five years without the Commission's prior approval.

management of the sea are being promoted relating amongst others to offshore and subsea technologies in the field of sustainable exploitation of the sea as a source of energy and mineral resources.

As one of the results of the work within the R&D framework, all major European ship-equipment manufacturers accepted the development platform for an integrated ship control standard. This will contribute to bring together the fragmented European industry.[20]

The Community is also involved in Maris (Maritime Information Society), a project adopted by the G-7 countries and co-chaired by the EU and Canada. The project[21] aims to provide an open framework under which subprojects demonstrate the potential benefits of information technologies and telematic applications for a broad range of marine activities. One of the projects (MARVEL) aims to provide for a user-oriented project for intelligent manufacturing of ships interlinking shipyards and their suppliers in a common global network.

Trade Policy

Shipbuilding business is global by its very nature. As explained before, unfair trade practises are difficult to neutralise by traditional trade measures, such as custom duties, because ships might not be imported at all by shipping companies. Therefore, there are no direct instruments to combat injurious pricing. The only instrument at hand is the WTO Agreement on Subsidies and Countervailing Measures, which establishes a presumption of serious prejudice when it is demonstrated that subsidies of 5 per cent ad valorem or subsidies to cover operating losses and direct forgiveness of debt exist. This mechanism has, however, not been applied to the shipbuilding sector so far.

It is clear that the world shipbuilding industry would benefit from fair trade conditions in the long run. It could lead to a restoration of market balance, because necessary structural adjustment processes, in which uncompetitive excess capacity has to be closed down, would not be influenced by State interventions to keep yards in business. The Community has been pushing for fair trading conditions for many years, as explained in Chapter 7. Initiatives to regulate competition conditions in shipbuilding have, so far, not been successful. An interesting initiative to reach normal competitive conditions in shipbuilding was the OECD Agreement Respecting Normal Competitive Conditions in the Commercial shipbuilding and Repair Industry, concluded on 21 December 1994. This was initiated by the United States and agreed upon after a long period of negotiations, but it never entered into force, because the same country did not ratify it.

---

[20] Research and Technological Development activities of the European Union, 1999 annual report, COM(1999) 284 final/2.

[21] Maris is one of the eleven pilot projects in the Global Information society.

The value of this OECD Agreement is that it could establish a level playing field for the main shipbuilding countries and set fair trading conditions.[22] In principle all measures of support specifically provided, directly or indirectly, to commercial shipbuilding are prohibited under the agreement. However, for certain categories of aid such as support to encourage R&D, exceptions have been made. The OECD Agreement contains an injurious pricing instrument designated to counter price dumping. The developments in the shipbuilding market since 1994, however, make it unlikely that the OECD Agreement will come into force.

Near Future

The expectations are that in the coming years the market will remain weak and that prices will stay under pressure. Production and price policies of South Korean yards will continue to influence the market, forcing the European shipbuilding industry to continue its restructuring processes and to specialise in those fields in which it is competitive. This restructuring process could be painful if the market conditions deteriorate further.

Given the policy of the Community to end operational aid after 31 December 2000, the European shipbuilding industry will be more vulnerable to trade-distorting practises of non-Community countries. Member States may put pressure to change Community policies if the situation in the European shipbuilding industry becomes worse. There seem to be two scenarios. In the first one the Community will stick to its present policy which will likely accelerate restructuring processes in shipbuilding. Only yards that are viable without operating aid will stay in business. In this scenario, the only way to act against trade-distorting practices seems to be to find a way to use WTO procedures. This requires evidence that shipyards benefit from subsidies within the definition of the Agreement on Subsidies and Countervailing Measures. In this respect, it should be noted that the Commission already monitors the shipbuilding market very closely (1999a). It reported on its investigations concerning the costs of shipbuilding of Korean yards. WTO procedures, with its panels, take time; something European industry may not have.

In the other scenario, the Community would, given the importance of the shipbuilding industry for the EU, reconsider its aid policy. The restructuring process could slow down as a consequence, which would not be in the long-term interest of European shipbuilding industry.

---

[22] As soon as the OECD agreement would have been ratified by all countries, it shall replace the new EU regulation for the new aid on shipbuilding.

13.2 STEEL INDUSTRY

Traditionally, the steel industry has been a sensitive sector, because of its strategic value due to economical, military, employment or regional motives. The process of economic integration within Europe started with this strategic sector, as well as the coal industry: the Treaty of Paris (on 18 April 1951) establishing the European Coal and Steel Community (ECSC). It provided the steel sector with an institutional framework on the basis of which special measures could be taken. Thus the steel industry became a 'special case' within European policy.

The steel industry is a capital-intensive industry subject to the cyclical phases of the international iron and steel market. Investments are normally taken during periods of economic growth. Capacity added to the market is there to stay for many years. Therefore, a fall in demand results easily in overcapacity. The supply side is rather inflexible.

Since the 1970s the steel industry has been hit by two periods of deep crisis. The first crisis appeared after the oil shock of 1973. A fall in demand of steel resulted in overcapacity in 1975. European steel producers lost nearly $3000 million in the year 1977.[23] The overcapacity lasted up to the mid-1980s. The second steel crisis took place during the beginning of the 1990s. Once more industry was faced with the problems of depressed prices resulting in losses due to overcapacity. The Asian financial crisis of 1998 also hit the market, but not as severe as the former crises. European policy responded differently to the crises. It evolved from an interventionist policy at the end of the 1970s to a more market-oriented approach at the end of the 1980s and the beginning of the 1990s.

During the first crisis, in accordance with the ECSC Treaty, the Commission declared the state of 'crise manifeste'[24] and by doing so empowered itself to take fargoing measures, starting with the introduction of voluntary production quotas, which were replaced by compulsory production quotas at a later stage. Furthermore, a minimum price system for steel imports was introduced. The purpose of these measures was to establish an equilibrium between supply and demand within the EU at reasonable prices. At the same time, Member States supported the steel industry intensively. As can be seen from Table 13.2, the aid intensities related to gross value added were in some countries extremely high compared to the rest of the manufacturing industry (excluding shipbuilding) with a percentage of 5.5 in the given period.

---

[23] Industrial policies in the European Community, Victoria Curzon Price, 1981.
[24] Article 58 ECSC Treaty.

Table 13.2 Aid to steel as a percentage of gross value added in steel, average 1981–85

IRL	I	F	UK	B	DK	LUX	D	NL
107.2	71.4	58.3	57.6	40.4	18.0	14.6	8.6	4.3

Source: First survey on State aids in the European Community. The figures should be regarded as 'best estimates' and are given as indicators only.

At the beginning of the 1980s, the Commission regulated the total EU steelmarket. It decided on the production amount through its compulsory production quota and it influenced the price of steel through its minimum price system. The measures aimed at providing industry with time to restructure and restore competitiveness. Looking back with hindsight, it is doubtful of this interventionist policy was successful. The upswing of the market in 1984 was the most important element in why the crises ended. If a market-oriented policy had been followed from the beginning, it may be assumed that the structural adjustment processes would have taken place at a faster pace. The minimum price systems did not stimulate efficient producers to become more efficient. It hampered, therefore, the development of industry and may have slowed down the speed of the restructuring process. The production quotas hindered, for instance, the development of efficient electric arc furnace technology (mini-mills) in the Community (Meiklejohn, 1999). Politically, however, there was wide agreement that Europe should protect its steel industry against distortive outside competition at that time.

When in the mid-1980s the steel market recovered, all these measures came to an end. A new, more market-oriented, policy wind started to blow through Europe. When the second crisis hit at the beginning of the 1990s, industrial policy had evolved in the direction of more market-oriented policies. This has been explained in more detail in Chapter 2. The current steel aid code at that time restricted aid basically to research and development, environmental protection, closures and regional aid to certain specified regions.

Nevertheless, there was strong political pressure to support the steel industry in the EU. Steel companies in financial difficulties in Germany, Italy, Spain and Portugal asked for aid to survive the crisis. They were prepared to reduce capacity by five million tonnes. The Commission used as a yardstick that for every €1 billion of State aid at least 750 000 tonnes of capacity needed to be reduced. The Council decided unanimously to allow aid up to €6974 million[25] for restructuring or privatisation of loss making companies for six companies from four Member States Box 13.3) in December 1993, under strict conditions relating to capacity reduction and closures of production facilities: totalling up to 5.5 million tonnes annually.

---

[25] Amounts contain restructuring aid, as well as regional investment aid.

The implementation of the aid and the capacity reduction measures would be strictly monitored. Furthermore, industry ministers agreed that this would be the last round allowing massive state aid. The Council and the Commission emphasised that no further aid would be approved for these companies, unless it would be in line with the steel Aid Code.

Box 13.3   Council decision of December 1993

COMPANIES	AID AMOUNT	REMARKS
ILVA, Italy	€2573 million	Closing of some of the production facilities
Sächsische Edelstahlwerke Freistal, former East Germany	€177 million	Capacity reduction
Sidenor , Spain	€515 million	Capacity reduction
Eko Stahl, former East Germany	€586 million	Closing production facilities
CSI, Spain	€2817 million	Closing of some of the production facilities
Siderurgia Nacional, Portugal	€306 million	Capacity reduction

Source: European Commission: 23rd Report on competition policy, 1993

The decision of the Council saved the future of these companies at the costs of the taxpayer. Basically as a result of this decision, the annual average of aid to the steel industry amounted to €1700 million in the period 1993–95 and amounted to €1130 million in the period 1995–97.[26]

Policies Towards the Steel Sector

Although the steel market recovered after 1994, the steel industry is still confronted with problems. The concentration grade is still very low, whereas the demand side becomes increasingly concentrated. The economic scale of steel companies in Europe is smaller compared to its competitors in Japan and the US. The steel industry can improve its economics of scale through mergers, joint ventures, take-overs and co-operation. In Europe this will imply crossborder co-operation. The single market within the EU will ease the concentration process, which will transform former national champions into European companies. The merger between British Steel and the Dutch

---

[26] European Commission, Seventh Survey on State aid in the European Union in the manufacturing and certain other sectors. The figures do not include aid granted under the objectives of supporting R&D and environmental protection.

Hoogovens group in the second half of 1999 is an indication that the concentration process in the steel industry will continue and will contribute to the continuous restructuring process of industry to maintain competitiveness.

For the future the environmental issue, as well as the enlargement process adding new production capacity to the EU market, will be on the agenda. After the expiry of the ECSC Treaty in 2002, the steel industry will become subject in principle to the normal EU regulations. Accordingly, the situation of the steel industry being a special case will come to an end, except as far as State aid rules are concerned.

State Aid Rules

State aid is not allowed under the ECSC Treaty: Article 4 prohibits State aid in normal circumstances. However, Article 95 may lead to derogation from this principle. The Council may, unanimously, adopt measures aiding the iron and steel industry in times of unforeseen difficulties. On this basis the Council adopted the Steel Aid Code, giving the criteria for approving State aid. One of the differences between the 1980s and 1993 was that the steel aid code did not allow aid for restructuring, although it allowed aid for closures. Therefore, in 1993 the unanimous consent of the Council was necessary to take the State aid decisions concerned, individually on the basis of Article 95 of the ECSC Treaty.

The aid policy became more strict after 1993. In 1996 the Commission adopted 19 partially negative or negative decisions. The fifth steel Aid Code expired in 1996 and a sixth Code was adopted which limits further the conditions under which State aid is permitted (Council Decision 2496/96/ECSC). Only aid for research, the promotion of the environment or the (partial) closure of companies will be authorised. This Code will apply during 1997–2002.

Under the State aid rules, Member States have the possibility to act as a private market investor[27]. This principle stimulates Member States to find market conform solutions for business problems. It implies for business that a State acting as market private investor is not longer prepared to pay the bill, but expects an upward potential of its investment in line with the underlying risk.

The question is what will happen after the expiry of the ECSC Treaty in 2002. There are two options. The first is to apply the normal State aid regime

---

[27]   In 1997 the Commission decided that an injection of capital of €76.6 million was outside the scope of Article 1 of the Steel Aid Code. The shareholders in Stahlwerke Bremen, namely Sidmar, a private company, and Hanseatische Industriebeteiligungen (Hibeg), a regional investment company controlled by the City of Bremen, infused capital proportionate to their shareholding of respectively 67.7 per cent and 32.3 per cent. The Commission considered Hibeg's capital injection as normal behaviour of a private investor which did not contain State aid. Source: 27th Report on Competition Policy 1997.

of the Community for this sector after 2002. In this option the industry would no longer be subject to special sector rules. When the normal State aid regime would be applied, the strict control would be relaxed in some perspectives. Restructuring and training aid, for example, are not allowed under the sixth Steel Aid Code, but can be allowed under the Community State aid regime.

The second option is to continue with a special State aid framework for the steel industry and to maintain more strict rules compared to the rules of the normal community regime. The Commission announced that a new 'Steel Aid Code' in the form of Commission guidelines is being prepared and seems, therefore, to have chosen to prolong the present strict aid policy: 'These rules, to be applied for a sufficient period, should be based on the approach adopted in the existing aid code' (European Commission, 1999b).

Research Policy

As for other industries, technological innovation is a key factor for industry to improve competitiveness. The Community tries to shape a favourable R&D climate. Research has always been financed out of the ECSC reserves. These reserves were originally financed through levies paid by industry. The Commission estimated the amount of these reserves up to €1.3 billion at the end of 2002. The expiration of the ECSC Treaty will change the system of financing. Steel research will be phased in to the Fifth Framework Programme. In addition, research may be financed from the ECSC money that remains after 2002: that is, the proceeds of the fund, that are approximately €40 million yearly, will be available for R&D in the coal and steel industry and related sectors.

Through promoting R&D the Community tries to encourage co-operation between industry and customers. Such co-operative research can result in improved product requirements and standards. According to the Commission projects focussing on innovative and durable building materials and steel packaging have a favourable impact on co-operation between steel producers, manufacturers, clients, researchers and designers. Research in the fields of optimising energy consumption, reducing polluting emissions and more efficient use of raw materials is promoted as well.

Trade Policy

For the steel industry, with its relatively homogeneous products and large number of suppliers, free and fair competition constitutes an essential element in securing the future. During the Uruguay Round most OECD countries committed themselves to completely abolishing their tariffs on steel imports by the year 2004. The Community's tariffs were around 3.2 per cent in 1998 and will fall to around 2.2 per cent in 2000 before disappearing completely in 2004. The process of liberalisation of international steel trade will, therefore, continue. As a consequence, an increase in international competition may be expected.

The Community aims for an open common market and further liberalisation of international trade. An equivalent access to other markets is a pre-condition for fair trade. In this context the EU has launched a Market Access Strategy. Although markets throughout the world are increasingly open for foreign competition, exporters may still be faced with trade barriers: anti-dumping measures, technical barriers to trade, minimum import prices, and so on, which can cause material injury to the Community's industries and put employment at risk. The Commission may, therefore, act to ensure that its industries are not disadvantaged by these practises. It might restore fair competition where needed. It initiated 175 anti-dumping and anti-subsidy investigations on imports during the period from 1994 to 1998 of which 24 were in the field of iron and steel. In the majority of cases where the Commission considered measures necessary, they took the form of duties.[28]

Nevertheless, the Commission considers 'the best chance of creating a level playing field on subsidies at the global level would be to make full use of the provisions of the WTO Agreement on Subsidies and Countervailing Measures'(European Commission, 1999b). This agreement binds Members to a subsidy discipline prohibiting export subsidies and importation substitution subsidies.[29] The agreement applies, however, to all economic sectors except the steel sector.

Enlargement

After the unification of Germany in 1989 and the new political developments in Eastern Europe, a number of Central and Eastern countries became candidate Member for the EU. The 'Europe Agreements' concluded with the associated Central and Eastern European countries provide for trade without any restrictions and with zero duty in respect of steel exports to the EU. The EU followed an asymmetric approach: the EU market was opened up more rapidly by bringing import tariffs faster down than the market of the candidate countries. The associated countries are progressively dismantling tariffs.

The Europe Agreements contain a protocol on ECSC products, which includes provisions on public aid for restructuring. In this context the Commission sets conditions (sound national restructuring programmes and viability plans for individual companies). The Commission strictly monitors these conditions, especially in view of the delay in the privatisation and restructuring process in most of the CEEC countries.

---

[28] The Community's anti-dumping and anti-subsidy activities, Seventeenth annual report from the Commission to the European parliament, 1998.

[29] Subsidies for R&D, environmental and regional aid do have a 'green light' status.

The enlargement of the EU with new Members from Central and Eastern Europe will bring new steel companies and steel capacity into the common market. Opportunities for the EU industry are open access to potential growth markets and possibilities for industrial specialisation, based on comparative advantages that the CEEC offers: such as relatively low labour costs and a relatively good level of technical qualification of the workforce. Outdated production facilities and a slow implementation of modern production techniques are, however, weak points.

Environmental Policy

The steel industry affects environment through emissions to the atmosphere, landfilling of solid materials (byproducts) and water discharge. Emissions to the atmosphere can be, amongst others, NO_x, the greenhouse gas CO_2, or the acid rain contributor, SO_2. In particular the latter two result from the energy-intensive steelmaking process. Energy accounts for up to 20 per cent of costs within the steel industry.[30]

The Community tries to improve the environment through its environmental policy. Part of this policy is promoting the development of environmentally friendly technologies, which contribute to the reduction of contaminating emissions. New techniques, such as the development of continuous casting to replace primary rolling mills, has reduced the amount of energy required to produce a tonne of steel. The energy consumed per tonne of steel fell from approximately 17.2 GJs in 1986 to approximately 15.8 GJs in 1996 in the EU. This resulted in a corresponding reduction of CO_2. The challenge of the future is to bring down the energy consumed per tonne of steel further by improving and implementing environmentally friendly technology. Box 13.4 presents an example of support to new environmental friendly technology by the Commission.

Box 13.4   Demonstration project aiming to reduce energy consumption

The European Commission supported the building of a demonstration plant for the continuous direct casting of thin strip (2–8 mm) stainless steel of the Italian steel company Voest Alpine. With thin-strip casting all the energy-intensive and very expensive hot rolling becomes unnecessary. According to the European Commission, the successful demonstration of this technology will be a major breakthrough in steel making. The support of the Commission amounted up to €4.5 million.

In Chapter 6, the IPPC (Integrated Pollution Prevention and Control) Directive has been explained. The steel industry will be subject to the

---

[30] In 1996 the EU consumed 50 million tonnes of coal and coke, 3.6 million tonnes of fuel oil, 75000 million kWhs of electricity and 800 000 GJs of gas (including steel industry own generated blast furnace gas and coke oven gas).

provisions of this Directive. It ensures that industry operations will move in the direction of *best available techniques*. Applying such techniques will contribute to the reduction of carbon dioxide emissions. Identifying the *best available techniques* is a difficult task. The Commission makes efforts in this field, for instance within the co-ordinated steel–environment programme the Commission aimed at determining the *best available techniques* at various stages of the production process.[31]

An interesting programme in the field of new technology concerns CARNOT: a multiannual programme promoting the use of clean and efficient technologies in industrial plants using solid fuels. The aim is to limit emissions, including carbon dioxide emissions, from such use and to encourage the uptake of advanced clean solid fuel technologies in order to achieve improved Best Available Technologies at affordable costs.

Steel is the world's most recycled material and the steel industry produces an environmental friendly product in this respect. Measures to increase the percentage of steel which is recycled will contribute to energy conservation, materials conservation and waste minimisation.

Within the Kyoto Protocol CO_2 reduction targets have been agreed. Given the energy intensive character of steel industry, it may be expected that the CO_2 issue will stay on the agenda of the steel industry the coming years. The introduction of a CO_2 tax is still under discussion within the Union. Such a tax could have a big impact on the steel industry. The steel industry will have to pay attention to the Kyoto instruments such as joint implementation projects and tradeable CO_2 reduction units, which Member States may introduce.

13.3 INFORMATION AND COMMUNICATION TECHNOLOGY (ICT) INDUSTRY

The information revolution is rapidly changing the world. Modern information and communication technology enables companies in principle to communicate, process and store information unconstrained by distance, time and volume. New network technologies and software produce a significant expansion of communication capacity.

Although the impact on business and society of the new ICT technology is already tremendous, its effects will be felt even more in the future, as the penetration of ICT technology increases and the potential of the new technologies are better utilised. ICT affects business in all its aspects. It changes organisation and production methods, it leads to innovative products and services and it shapes new markets and market structures. The modern

---

[31] Co-ordinated study 'steel–environment', technical steel research, C. Roederer and L. Gourtsoyannis, European Commission, 1996.

IC technology is, for instance, challenging the traditional distribution channels: in the US an increasing number of cars are sold directly or indirectly through the Internet.

The worldwide ICT market has enjoyed a period of high growth since the 1980s.[32] During the period 1997–99 the ICT industry was the fastest growing sector of the EU economy with a growth rate 5 per cent higher in comparison to the GDP growth rate. The ICT market had an estimated volume of around €1225 billion in 1997. Figure 13.2 shows the worldwide ICT markets by products.

Figure 13.2   Worldwide ICT markets by product, 1997

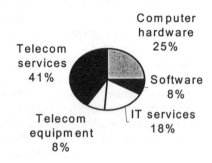

Source: European Commission (1998c)

During this period market growth was driven mainly by software and services although hardware segments such as semiconductors, microprocessors and 'network superservers' also performed strongly. The telecommunications revolution, the strong development of the Internet and the growth of electronic commerce were some of the prime movers.

Digital technology and the liberalisation of the telecommunications market have contributed to the telecommunications revolution, with new telecommunications services and new products entering a liberalising market. In particular, mobile telecommunications have become a booming business. The number of mobile phone subscribers grew by 52 per cent in 1997 worldwide. The growth in West Europe was even faster, at 57 per cent. The number of jobs related to mobile telephony grew from around 50 000 in 1993 to over 200 000 in 1998 in the EU (European Commission, 1998b). The new

---

[32]   The OECD estimated that the average compound growth rate was 10 per cent for the industry as a whole over the period 1985–95, European Commission, 1998a.

communication technologies and the deregulation of the communication market resulted in a big reduction of communication costs.

A second reason for the impressive growth rates is the use of the Internet. Internet use within the EU is growing exponentially. It is estimated that about 150 million people were connected to the Internet at the end of 1999. In the year 2000 this figure could approach 200 million, in particular because the possibilities of connecting to the Internet will increase. Connection will be possible via television combined with set-top boxes or via mobile devices. Through the Internet a global electronic market place has been created. E-commerce or electronic business is rapidly developing. The EU market already exceeded €6.5 billion in 1998 (European Commission, 1998b). The OECD estimated that the world market would reach $1 trillion by 2005, mainly in business-to-business trading.

A third reason is the rapid technological development in the field of hardware. Available computer power is doubling every 18 months and transmission capacity every 12 months. In many segments the US has gained leadership, for instance in the market for software packages, due to a very dynamic ICT industry, as is shown in Box 13.5.

Box 13.5   IT industry in the US: a dynamic industry

In Silicon Valley alone eleven new companies are formed every week and one is floated on the stock exchange every five days. Every year 300 venture capital companies invest US$1 to 3 billion in start-ups in the US. Compaq, Cisco, Sun, Oracle and Apple did not exist 20 years ago.

Source: European Commission, 1998c.

Growth rates within the EU are consistently lower than those of the US. Europe's share of worldwide IT markets declined from 35 per cent in 1990 to 27.5 per cent in 1997. Also IT expenditure as a percentage of GDP is lower in the EU (around 5 per cent in 1997) compared to the US (around 7 per cent in 1997).

Key Importance for the European Economy

The Commission (1997b) emphasises that the ICT industry is a critical component of the European economy, not only because of its present size (Table 13.3 shows some data relating to the ICT industry as a percentage of the manufacturing industry) but in particular because it accounts for a growing part of the industrial activities; it is a key to the future competitiveness of all industrial processes, products and services and it will be vital for the information society in the twenty-first century.

Table 13.3 ICT industries as a percentage of manufacturing industry, 1995

Turnover	8.3
Employment	6.5
Production	7.8
Total gross value added	9.1

Source: European Commission (1997b)

In the first place, the fast-growing ICT industry provides for new jobs. More than 300 000 jobs were created between 1995 and 1997. If the EU can assure its share in the expected future growth of the ICT sector, it will contribute to lowering Europe's high unemployment rates.

Secondly, information and communication technology is of great strategic importance for the competitiveness of European industry. The success of firms seems to depend more and more upon their capacity to generate, process and market knowledge-based information. In this context, business processes and corporate value chains are re-engineered. The information and communication technology makes it possible, directly or through a network of linkages between economic agents, to organise production and distribution on a global scale. This is true for the production factors of labour, capital raw materials, management and for ICT itself as well. The new ICT technology reconfigures corporate boundaries.

Therefore, industry should have access to the latest ICT to be able to keep the products, services and production methods up to date. Failure to keep up with the fast developments in this field will result in a loss of welfare within Europe.

Thirdly, excessive dependency on key technologies should be avoided. The ICT equipment industry, for example, supplies a large number of other industries. IC products are responsible for 20 per cent of the added value in the consumer electronics industry. For more advanced products, like personal computers, this value can be as high as 50 per cent. Technological developments within the equipment industry are, therefore, indirectly of major importance for a large part of the European industry.

Fourthly, the EU should benefit from growing markets. Concerning future innovation ICT industry should be positioned at the forefront to profit as much as it can from new markets.

Given the importance of the ICT industry for the future of the European economy, the Community, under the flag of the information society, is undertaking a large number of activities to encourage the development of the ICT industry.

Improving Framework Conditions

A clear and predictable framework is important for markets to develop. This is especially true for the ICT market. The new communications technology has raised a number of legal questions. Trying to take away uncertainties about those issues, the Community has a whole series of directives dealing with copyright, privacy, security and authentication, electronic signature, commercial communications, electronic contacting, liability and consumer protection. The aim of all these directives is to implement a clear and predictable environment for the digital economy in Europe. The legislative package tries to bring closer a single market for electronic commerce in Europe.

Internal Market Policy

European ICT standardisation policy is in principle market driven. Industry itself proposes standards and tries through international consortia to achieve market acceptance. The European Commission supports the creation of flexible and open workshops to enable European companies to participate in the International ICT standardisation process. The main objective is to provide European industry with an effective platform for identifying user requirements and implementing them in a flexible manner.

One of the success stories within the EU concerns mobile telephony: the GSM standard (Global System for Mobile Communications). It is a demonstration of how a common Europe-wide initiative can contribute to the development of the European economy in terms of job creation and growth. Europe's GSM standard has become *de facto* the world standard used by over 300 operators in 130 countries. In 1999 there were around 120 million mobile subscribers. Within the next five years many expect the penetration rate of GSM to go up further.

Box 13.6 The GSM standard and the success of Nokia

The European Conference of Postal and Telecommunications Administrations (CEPT) decided to develop a common standard for digital mobile telephony at the end of the 1980s. This standard is known as GSM.

Nokia, headquartered in Finland, has been one of the main developers of the GSM technology. The first GSM call was made in Finland with a Nokia phone on a Nokia-equipped network in 1991. Eight years later Nokia ranks as one of the world's leading suppliers of GSM networks. It has supplied GSM technology to 87 operators in 39 countries. Nokia has become one of the European companies at the forefront of ICT. Its success within the field of GSM has contributed considerably to the growth of the company. In 1998 net sales totalled €13.3 billion and the company employed more than 53 000 people.

It is still uncertain whether the third generation mobile telephony will allow the EU to build further on this success. Universal Mobile Telecommunications System (UMTS) is foreseen as its successor. A world-wide standard will result in economic benefits against the background of the forecast that worldwide there will be over 600 million mobile phones with e-commerce capabilities by 2004.

Research Policy

Substantial R&D investments are required to maintain competitiveness in the fast-changing ICT business environment. To promote R&D in the field of ICT the fifth R&D programme framework, which has been explained in Chapter 11, includes a programme 'User-friendly Information Society'. The budget for this programme amounts to up to €3600 million. Box 13.7 shows the key actions which categorise the research fields.

Box 13.7   Key actions of 'User-friendly Information Society'

The R&D programme will focus on the following four key actions:
<ul><li>Systems and services for the citizen.</li><li>New methods of work and electronic commerce.</li><li>Multimedia content and tools.</li><li>Essential technologies and infrastructures.</li></ul>

Source: Fifth Framework Programme

Furthermore, research projects of a more generic nature can be supported under this programme, aimed at emerging technologies such as nano-scale, photonic, bio-electronic technologies, ultra high performance computers and super-intelligent networks. In particular, support is provided to implement Europe-wide advanced high-speed computer and communications systems.

There are other international frameworks that promote research and development under the condition of international co-operation. In this context EUREKA has to be mentioned. EUREKA was created in 1985 to reinforce European industry through stimulating cross-border R&D-activities. EUREKA follows a bottom up approach, that is, the R&D projects are proposed by industry. When projects receive the 'EUREKA status', national governments might support the project.

One of the larger initiatives of EUREKA is MEDEA[33] (Box 13.8). Key European Silicon IC manufacturers and Electronic Systems industries will carry out the programme. The following countries are actively participating in MEDEA: France, Germany, Italy, Belgium, the Netherlands and the UK.

---

[33]   MEDEA was formally adopted as 'EUREKA project 1535' by Ministers on 29 June 1996.

Box 13.8 Medea

MEDEA is an acronym for MicroElectronics Development for European Applications. The programme is targeting collaborative work in two broad basic domains, which are strongly interdependent:

- The IC Technologies domain (silicon technology platforms and manufacturing) covered by the IC manufacturers themselves, supported by their key equipment suppliers.
- The 'system-on-a-chip' domain, incorporating skills and collaborative contributions from both the IC manufacturers and the electronic system houses, to form the basis for new systems products.

The co-operation in MEDEA is organised around six industrial core competencies: multimedia technologies, communication technologies, automobile and traffic applications, design techniques and libraries, CMOS-based technology platforms and manufacturing technologies.

Research in the field of manufacturing technologies addresses amongst others the issue of the evolution to 300 mm manufacturing. The conventional wafer size is 200 mm. The enlargement of the wafer size to 300 mm will lead to a new generation of machines and equipment to produce ICs. The larger the wafer the more ICs can be produced per wafer.

At the time of the start the programme costs were estimated to be about €2000 million. The time frame for MEDEA is 4 years (1997–2000).

Under this Eureka programme, France granted State aid up to €14.95 million for R&D concerning pilot production lines for integrated circuits on 300 millimetre wafers. Companies receiving aid, which were involved in the project, were SGS-Thomson, Air Liquide, Gressi, Incam and Recif.

The Netherlands provided assistance for research in the field of manufacturing technology in the form of loans and grants up to €88 million to stimulate international co-operation with a large number of companies. The main recipients were ASML, ASMI, and Philips semiconductors.

13.4 CONCLUSION

This chapter demonstrated how Community policies affect business. It focussed on three sectors: the shipbuilding industry, the steel industry and the ICT industry. It showed that many measures were and are taken within the Community affecting those sectors directly. Trade policy, R&D policy, environmental policy, sector-specific measures, and so on, together, the measures taken within those fields can be called the industrial approach of the Community.

Basically, the Community's approach is to create a favourable business climate and to stimulate adjustment processes in industry which improve competitiveness. Its approach towards the ICT sector is a clear example in this respect, where under the flag of the information society the Commission took many initiatives to improve the framework conditions. The example of the steel industry shows the shift the Community made from an interventionist policy controlling prices and production at the beginning of the 1980s to a more market-oriented policy since the mid 1980s. The shipbuilding sector, although operational aid was allowed for many years, is still not competitive. By ending authorisation to grant operational aid by 2000, the Commission emphasises that aid should be used to speed up structural adjustment processes within the sector. Shipbuilding may in the long term benefit more from investments in innovation, R&D, environment, and so on, than from operational aid.

ICT will change business tremendously in the coming years: it is becoming more and more an integral part of production processes and products. The digital economy is driving competitiveness. Business has to keep up with the developments in this field in order to benefit from the huge opportunities the new ICT technology provides. The Community's approach of an open common market in combination with the globalisation process will result in more competition between businesses. In the long run this approach will strengthen competitiveness. All industrial sectors will undergo profound structural changes due to the globalisation process and the information and telecommunications revolution. Industry will have to improve continuously its effectiveness and efficiency to compete successfully in this rapidly changing world.

BIBLIOGRAPHY

Curzon Price, Victoria (1981), *Industrial Policies in the European Community,* Trade Policy Research Centre, London.

Dudly, G. and Richardson, R. (1997), *Competing Policy Frames in EU Policy Making: the Rise of Free Market Ideas in EU Steel Policy 1985–96.*

European Commission, *Reports on Competition Policy 1991, 1992, 1993, 1994, 1995, 1996, 1997, 1998,* Office for Official Publications, Luxembourg

European Commission (1987), *Second Communication from the Commission on Shipbuilding – Industrial, Social and Regional Aspects*, Office for Official Publications, Luxembourg.

European Commission, *Surveys on State Aid in the European Union in the Manufacturing and Certain other Sectors,* Reports 1990–99, Office for Official Publications, Luxembourg.

European Commission (1995), *Proposal for a Council Regulation on Aid to Shipbuilding*, COM(95) 410, Brussels.

European Commission (1996), *Shaping Europe's Maritime Future,*

European Commission (1997a), *Towards a New Shipbuilding Policy*, Office for Official Publications, Luxembourg.

European Commission (1997b), *The Competitiveness of the European Information and Communication Technologies Industries,* COM(97) 152, Office for Official Publications, Luxembourg.

European Commission (1998a), *ICT Investment in the Intangible Economy*, Office for Official Publications, Luxembourg.

European Commission (1998b), *Job Opportunities in the Information Society,* Office of Official Publications, Luxembourg.

European Commission (1998c), *The Competitiveness of European Industry,* 1998 Report prepared by IFO, NEI, Prometeia Calcolo Srl, WiFo, Brussels.

European Commission (1998c), *The Competitiveness of European Enterprises in the Face of Globalisation: how it can be encouraged*, COM(1998) 718, Office for Official Publications, Luxembourg.

European Commission (1999a), *The Situation in World Shipbuilding*, COM(99) 474 final, Office for Official Publications, Luxembourg.

European Commission (1999b), *The State of the Competitiveness of the Steel Industry in the EU,* COM (99) 453, Office for Official Publications, Luxembourg.

European Commission (1999c), *Industrial Change in the Knowledge Economy: the Role of ICTs in Growth and Competitiveness*, Staff Working Paper, SEC(1999) 1713, Brussels

Meiklejohn, R. (1999), State Aid and the Single Market, *European Economy, Reporst and Studies*, No. 3, European Commission Directorate-General for Economic and Financial Affairs, Brussels.

High-level Group on the Information Society (1994), *Europe and the Global Information Society,* Recommendations to the European Council of June.

Ministry of Economic Affairs of the Netherlands (1997), *Enabling the Information Society*, a study presented to the informal Council of Industry Ministers.

Power, Vincent (1992), *EC Shipping Law*, Lloyd's of London Press Ltd.

Simon, S. (1999), Recent Developments in State Aid Policy, *European Economy, Reports and studies*, No. 3, European Commission Directorate-General for Economic and Financial Affairs, Brussels.

PART FOUR

The Future

14. EU Industrial Policy in an Enlarged and Changing European Union

Michael Darmer

It is difficult to predict – especially the future. However, there are certain trends and there are decisions taken in the past which mark the road for future development. The purpose of this chapter is to analyse the trends and study the roads in order to give an idea of the direction in which the European Union is heading. It is clear that in a chapter about the future where tomorrow's events may change the preconditions for the analyses, the opinion expressed can only be the personal opinion of the writer. Readers are – as always – entitled to disagree and have their own opinion. Indeed, it is also the purpose of the chapter to stimulate discussions!

The chapter is divided into four sections. Section 1 draws on the findings of the previous chapters trying to see them in perspective and give some indication of possible future developments. Section 2 focuses on the ongoing Intergovernmental Conference. The Intergovernmental Conference is intended to finish by the end of 2000. Therefore this section focuses in particular on the problems, which was the reason for calling on an Intergovernmental Conference. In this way, it should hopefully be possible to compare the outcome with the initial problems. The third section deals with enlargement, that is the state of the enlargement process, the state of the candidate countries and how enlargement might affect EU industrial policy and the other policies of importance to industry. Finally, Section 4 concludes.

14.1 THE EU INDUSTRIAL POLICY OF TOMORROW

The industrial related policies of the European Union are dynamic policies that have developed since the very beginning of the Union. It is part of an ongoing process which will continue into the future. The general tendencies for tomorrow's industrial policy will certainly take into account the new policy areas of importance to industry such as environment and increased globalisation.

Furthermore, the integration process will go on and continue to influence the basic conditions for doing business in the European Union. Of particular importance to industry are the completion of the internal market, the coming into force of the single currency and the development of genuine Trans-European Networks.

The cornerstones of the Union's industrial policy such as the regulatory bases of competition policy and the control of State aid, and financial instruments like the Structural Funds are under revision at this moment. The Structural Funds policy has recently been revised, but without fundamentally changing its present weaknesses. As such, a new reform is already called for. In relation to the research programmes, the Commission has already launched a political debate on the state of science and technology in Europe upon which new research programmes will be defined. Competition policy is in the beginning of a modernisation process and we can only guess to what extent the forthcoming reforms will be sufficient for maintaining and improving the execution of that policy in the new European Union.

New Industrial Policy Concept

A new industrial policy concept is probably about to emerge, simply because it is needed. Increasing globalisation and other new challenges from new policy areas of importance to business and industry, a new Commission (since the autumn of 1999) and a forthcoming new Treaty; all 'demand' a new concept.

Industrial policy – a dynamic concept

Just as any other policy, industrial policy is a dynamic policy which has developed over time from something not even recognised as industrial policy, over a more sectoral approach, towards the more horizontal approach of today's EU industrial policy. This development is clearly illustrated in Chapter 2. However, several factors indicate that a new development is underway.

First of all, as we saw in Chapter 1, Article 157, the fundamental article of the Treaty concerning industrial policy, requires unanimity. The intergovernmental conference (which started in February 2000) that should be finished by the end of the year 2000 will among other things consider in which articles unanimity should be changed to qualified majority. If Article 157 is changed to qualified majority, it will most likely change the industrial policy of the European Union. See later for an analysis of such a scenario.

Second, new areas of importance to industry emerge. Chapter 1 discusses which policy areas are of importance to industry and which are not. Consequently, we included new policy areas such as environmental policy and Trans-European Networks. At the same time, we excluded policy areas such as consumer policy, which have a growing impact (although still limited) on business and industry. As these new policy areas are developed further, the effect on companies will increase.

Third, increased global competition will put European companies under pressure. With the development of ICT, the Internet and e-commerce, this process has become extremely visible.

How will this affect the present competitiveness of EU industry as outlined in Chapter 2? European industry will no doubt benefit from the growth potential of increased integration, that is the completion of the Internal Market, the coming into force of the single currency and the further development of the Trans-European Networks. On the other hand, the EU has had a persistent unemployment problem for decades, which besides its personal consequences is also an unusual waste of resources, which points to structural problems. Such structural problems hamper the competitiveness of EU industry.

The Council will address this challenge in the year 2000 and in the years to come. In the year 2000, the Commission has produced a staff working paper which addresses this issue and has presented a proposal for a new Multiannual Programme to succeed the present Third Multiannual Programme for SMEs described in Chapter 12. The aim of this working paper is to outline the new industrial policy concept. It focuses on ICT, innovation and entrepreneurship. The new multiannual programme will form the legal and budgetary basis for this new industrial policy concept. Therefore the focus of the new multiannual programme is broader than the previous ones whose main focus was on SMEs.

A broader multiannual programme will also reflect the trend that the concept of SMEs needs to be more qualified. SMEs are too general a group and the problems of SMEs are not homogeneous. They depend to a large degree on the stage of evolution as highlighted in Chapter 12. Start-ups do not have the same problems as micro-enterprises which do not have the same problems as small enterprises which do not have the same problems as medium sized enterprises.

The SME concept will not disappear. It will probably survive in the sense that SMEs will continue to have a privileged status within other Community policies, such as, for example State aid, research and technological development and Structural Funds.

The new industrial policy concept will probably follow on the present horizontal approach, making it even harder to conduct sector policy.[1] There will no longer be room for traditional sector policy like in shipbuilding and steel. One can no longer protect 'old' sectors from increased global competition. There will, however, still be a need for regional policy in order to overcome regional problems resulting from diversification of economic activity – not to be confused as sector policy.

In shipbuilding, the regulation allowing operational aid runs out by the end of the year 2000 as mentioned in Chapter 13. At this stage, it is still

---

[1] At least in the short run. In the medium term this tendency might be affected by the Intergovernmental Conference and enlargement. See the next sections.

uncertain what, if any, the alternative should be. The traditional argument for continuation of operational aid is that the European shipbuilding sector is faced with unfair competition. However, in a truly global market State aid is not a very good instrument to counteract suspected unfair behaviour.

Also, the privileged status of the steel sector as a sector with its own legal regime will come to an end in 2002 after more than 50 years. The ECSC Treaty has in many ways been an important treaty that inspired the first Treaty of the European Union (the Treaty of Rome). For the first period after 2002, the steel industry will most likely have a stricter State aid regime compared to other sectors. One of the reasons for this is that the steel sector is still a sensitive sector as described in Chapter 13. The forthcoming enlargement of the Union will add to this sensitivity because enlargement will bring in social and regional problems from a sector under reconstruction in the new Member States. See also later for a further analysis of this situation.

New areas of importance for industry
New policy areas of importance to industry, such as the environmental policy, continue to develop. Some of the new policies of importance to the industry of tomorrow might very well include consumer policy and food safety.

Environmental policy has created new policy standards, with the development of a number of new principles and concepts, for example, sustainable development and the precautionary principle. Today's environmental policy affects business decisions like business location, research decisions, choice of inputs, product design and marketing decisions every day, as analysed in Chapter 6.

Environment is one of the relatively new policy areas, which sometimes clash with other policy areas like industrial or trade policy. As shown in Chapter 6, genetically modified organisms (GMOs) have on the one hand contributed to a fast growing biotechnology sector but on the other hand led to a number of problems connected with the precautionary principle and to trade-related problems.

Having said this, there are also positive industrial effects of environmental policy. A whole new environmental sector has emerged. The market size of the eco-industry in the EU, US and Japan was estimated at €124 billion in 1990 with an annual growth of approximately 5 per cent.

The clash between environmental policy and other policy areas led to the need for new policy instruments to be developed. It is simply not possible to regulate everything, especially if the regulation has to be changed again and again due to new developments in the regulated area. In that respect, regulation is too static an instrument. What is needed is a new set of incentive instruments, which give companies (and others) an incentive to behave environmentally correctly in the first place. Here economic instruments and environmental agreements seem to have some potential for further developments.

Globalisation

Globalisation may not be a new concept. It has been on the political agenda for many years now because of increased global economic integration. But so far it has not changed the way we do business significantly. The expansion of the Internet and e-commerce seems to give the concept of globalisation new impetus. The basic rules can no longer be applied and the way we do business is likely to be changed fundamentally. In this respect, trade policy will be of increased importance – not as a tool to protect local industries but as an instrument of securing open trade as explained in Chapter 7.

The developments of the trade policy and in particular of the WTO can be illustrated be the fact that when GATT started in 1947 it had only two dozen members while the WTO of today accounts for more than 130 members. And, as mentioned in Chapter 7, most of the non-members in the world are queuing for membership, including important participants in the world economy like China, Taiwan and Saudi Arabia. With the development of the WTO, the possibilities to use trade policy for protective industrial policy reasons has been limited and this general tendency is expected to continue despite the setback of the Third Ministerial Meeting of WTO in Seattle in 1999. Seattle was not a setback in the traditional sense, but in the sense that it was a missed opportunity to develop open trade even further especially in agriculture and services.

With increased globalisation, trade policy and the WTO seems to be of increased importance in the years to come. In that sense the idea behind the dispute settlement mechanism could be important. However, the dispute settlement mechanism needs to be more effective in order to be a real value added. The administrative set-up is complicated, burdensome, takes too long and is too easily blocked.

Further Integration

The integration process will go on and continue to release growth potential for the industry of the European Union. Of particular importance to business and industry are the completion of the Internal Market, the coming into force of the single currency and the further development of the Trans-European Networks.

Internal market

The basic principles of the internal market, the free movement of goods, persons, services and capital, have been fundamental elements since the first treaty of the European Union (the Treaty of Rome). However, it was not until 1985 that the development towards an internal market gained pace. For the last 15 years, the EU has accomplished much more than during the first 30 years. However, there still is a long way to go – especially in relation to standardisation, public procurement and financial services as explained in Chapter 3.

Most of the regulations needed for creating an internal market have already been adopted. However, many of these regulations require common standards to be developed and this has turned out to be a bottleneck for the completion of the internal market. Standardisation presently is slow and burdensome because of structural problems in the decision-making process. Business and industry must share this responsibility since they themselves take active part in formulating standards.

Another problem is related to public procurement. Public procurement does not have the effect of being a catalyst for competition as one would have expected taking into the account its size and importance. With an estimated market size of around €700 billion, public procurement accounts for more than 10 per cent of the Community's GDP.

While significant progress has been made in the free movement of goods and persons, there is still no internal market to speak of in financial services. That sector accounts for 6 per cent of the Union's GDP and offers essential financial products to both industry and individual consumers. The coming into force of the single currency may change this.

Single currency

Today 11 Member States participate in the single currency. But it will probably not be long before all the present EU Member States have joined. Greece has already applied for participation. Denmark will have a referendum in September 2000. All the polls unanimously predict a yes from the Danish people to join the single currency. The discussion in both the UK and Sweden is more focussed on when to join than if to join.

In 2002 we will have the euro coins and notes which will make it more than just a technical standard for most people. The benefits of a single currency in the form of price transparency, and the reduced cost of doing business due to the removal of the exchange rate risk within the EU, will be directly visible as shown in Chapter 4

Trans-European Networks

Efficient Trans-European Networks (TEN) are the backbone for a competitive European industry as demonstrated in Chapter 5. TEN both safeguard jobs and create new ones.

Traditionally TEN cover telecommunications networks, energy networks and transport networks. While the liberalisation of telecommunications has more or less been completed, this is not the case with energy networks and transport networks. The completion of the telecommunications network has led to both lower prices and new products and services for the benefit of European industry and consumers. The energy network is still suffering from too weak an interconnection among some Member States which might serve as a stumbling block for exploiting all the economic benefits from the recent liberalisation of the energy markets.

The transport network and especially the railway system still suffers from national and bureaucratic structures. As pointed out in Chapter 5, one could categorise railway services as an outdated technology for which should not cause too much concern if it were completely marginalised, were it not for environmental and social reasons. Therefore both Member States and the European Union are trying to revitalise railway services for both goods and passenger transport in the years to come. In relation to TEN the challenge is also to extend them to the Central and East European Countries.

Other Development Trends

There are other development trends than the ones covered by 'the new industrial policy concept' and 'further integration'. These other trends include competition policy, control of State aid, Structural Funds and the research programmes.

Competition policy
Modernisation of competition policy is underway as mentioned in Chapter 8. The Commission wants to leave it up to Member States to decide the majority of competition cases. Most Member States are in general positive while companies in general are worried. The companies are among other things, worried about whether the proposed decentralisation would lead to an unequal practice of competition law in different Member States.

The Commission presented its idea in the form of a White Paper, which has been sent out for reactions. The subsequent hearing of interested parties showed that a number of important issues have to be addressed and satisfactory solutions have to be found. At this stage we do not know the ultimate proposal of the Commission, as it cannot be expected before the end of year 2000. The negotiations are expected to take at least a year and implementation will also take time. Consequently, a fully operational system cannot be expected to be in place and functioning before the end of 2002 or beginning of 2003 in the best case scenario.

State aid
Despite several appeals over the years from the Commission, the overall volume of State aid has remained relatively high. In the future, the overall volume of State aid may go down, because the Commission and some of the Member States believe that this total volume is too high. On the other hand, this has been the situation for many years now without any significant change in the overall volume. It seems to follow the economic circle. During economic recessions State aid tends to go up while it tends to go down a little during periods of economic growth.

It is more likely that the issues receiving State aid will change in accordance with the industrial policy concept. Less aid will probably be given as rescue and restructuring aid, while aid to RTD, innovation, entrepreneurship and environmental matters will be more acceptable. In general, most Member States regard State aid as a valuable industrial policy instrument. However, there is a tendency toward a distinction between 'good' and 'bad' State aid in accordance with the development mentioned above. Rules on 'bad' State aid may be tighten up while rules on 'good' State aid might be loosened a little.

Structural Funds

Even with the new lower geographical coverage of the regional policy (see Chapter 10) the Structural Funds support too many regions and too many people. With the forthcoming enlargement of the EU, the geographical coverage needs to be concentrated further.

For the present period 2000–2006, there will be no changes, even if new Member States should join the Union. A special financial reserve would finance any new Member States' participation until the end of 2006. The overall financial volume for the Structural Funds will probably not increase but it is not likely to decrease either, taking into account the regional problems and challenges of an enlarged EU. However, when the next budget has to be negotiated, the new Member States will be present around the table and make sure that their problems are not forgotten. See later for a possible scenario for the period 2007 onward.

Research and development

Improved conditions for research and innovation will most likely be part of the new industrial policy concept to be presented by the Commission. The present concept should be improved to ensure a greater strategic impact (for example, by having greater concentration) and placing it into a broader political context (for example, by creating more links with other EU policies). If these issues are dealt with successfully, EU research and development programmes might be an appropriate answer to the challenges outlined in a new industrial policy concept.

The Fifth Framework Programme for Research and Technical Development runs until the end of 2002. The Commission has launched a political debate on the state of science and technology in Europe, upon which a proposal for the Sixth Framework Programme will be presented.

14.2 THE INTERGOVERNMENTAL CONFERENCE 2000

One of the purposes of the Intergovernmental Conference (IGC) which led to the present (Amsterdam) Treaty was to prepare the European Union for enlargement. Some progress was made, for example the ceiling of the total number of members of the European Parliament was fixed at 700 regardless of the number of Member States in the Union. However, the Amsterdam Treaty postponed a number of important institutional points, for example the size of the Commission and the weighting of votes in the Council. According to a Protocol to the Amsterdam Treaty, these issues should be dealt with in two steps. First, the size of the Commission. On the date of the first enlargement, the Commission should consist of one and only one national from each Member State.[2] The reason for this first step was that in this way it would be possible to take in up to five new Member States and make sure that they had a Commissioner each without increasing the total number of Commissioners. Second, when the number of Member States was about to exceed 20 an IGC should carry out a general revision of the Treaty with the aim of reforming the composition and the functioning of the European Institutions.

The Amsterdam Treaty came into force 1 May 1999. One month later, the European Council, meeting in Cologne, 3–4 June 1999, called for a new ICG to be finalised by the end of 2000 (European Council, 1996). The aim of the conference would be to resolve the institutional issues left open in Amsterdam that needed to be settled before enlargement. The European Council meeting in Cologne decided that the ICG should cover the following topics:

- size and composition of the Commission;
- weighting of votes in the Council (re-weighting, introduction of a dual majority and threshold for qualified-majority decision-making);
- Possible extension of qualified-majority voting in the Council.

Other necessary amendments to the Treaties arising as regards to European institutions in connection with the above issues and in the implementing the Treaty of Amsterdam could also be discussed.

At least one thing should be noted in relation to the decision taken by that European Council and that is the very precise and limited scope of the IGC. This limited scope did not please the Commission and in particular its new President Romano Prodi. The Commission wanted a far-reaching reform of

---

[2]   Today (2000) the Commission consists of at least one national from each Member State. The larger Member States (UK, France, Germany, Spain and Italy) have two Commissioners.

the composition of the Union's Institutions and the decision-making process (see, for example, European Commission, 1999a).

There are objective as well as political reasons behind the opinion of the Commission. Among the more objective reasons is the fact that the enlargement process foreseen when the Amsterdam Treaty (and protocol) was signed in 1997 was a two-step process. The first step was a relatively fast enlargement with the five applicant countries most advanced (Hungary, Poland, Estonia, the Czech Republic and Slovenia). The second step was a much later enlargement with the rest of the applicant countries. However, since the Amsterdam Treaty was signed the enlargement process had been speeded up considerably and the distinction between the first and second enlargement has been blurred (see later). Therefore the first enlargement may bring the number of Member States above 20 and the timespan between the first and the second enlargement may be considerably shorter than initially projected.

The present (2000) institutional structure is basically unchanged since it was formed to serve a Community of six Member States. In the present Union of 15 Member States, this institutional structure shows signs of weaknesses and lack of efficiency. The problems broadly recognised include sluggish decision making, lengthy debates, lack of co-ordination between too many different Councils, numerous operational and legislative problems sent for decision to the Heads of Government (see, for example, von Weiszäcker et al., 1999). Decision-making and management problems are expected to increase exponentially with the increased number of Member States since interest will be different, discussion slower, decisions more difficult and management more complex.

The Commission

Today the Commission takes decisions collectively with one vote per Commissioner. All Member States appoint at least one Commissioner each. The Commission consists of 20 Commissioners. In theory, the Commissioners should only work for the interest of the European Union and not represent the Member State who has appointed them; they are not allowed to receive instructions from any Member State. It is the general feeling that this is also, in general, the case in practice. However, for understandable reasons most Member States do not accept the perspective of a Commission in which their country would not be represented. The Finnish Presidency at the European Council in Helsinki, 10 and 11 December 1999, did prepare a report, based on consultations of the Member States, stating that 'the overwhelming view is that there should be one national from each Member State in the Commission'[3].

Another point in relation to the functioning of the Commission concerns the power of the President and the collective responsibility of the Commission. The Santer Commission resigned collectively in mainly because of criticism of one Commissioner. President Prodi dealt with that in an informal manner requesting in advance the agreement of a Commissioner to resign if he so requires. On this issue, the Finnish Presidency reported to the European Council in Helsinki that 'the general view was that the IGC should consider whether this *de facto* form of accountability of individual Commissioners to the President of the Commission needs to be reflected somehow in the Treaty'.

Qualified Majority Voting

In an enlarged Union, divergences of national interests will inevitably increase together with the risk of blockage whenever unanimity is required. Hence, an increased use of qualified majority voting would facilitate the decision-making process. The experience of the Community shows that qualified majority voting creates a dynamic decision-making process and paves the way for compromises. The change from unanimity to qualified majority voting was the most significant instrumental factor in helping push through the single market programme.

The consultations undertaken by the Finnish Presidency show that most Member States regard an increased use of qualified majority voting as the key to efficient decision making. However, even in an enlarged Union, most Member States are of the opinion that a number of issues should remain subject to unanimity. The IGC will decide which articles in the Treaty should be changed from unanimity to qualified majority decision making. An extended use of qualified majority voting is likely to be seconded by a parallel extension of the co-decision procedure with the European Parliament.

Two of the articles up for discussion to change from unanimity to qualified majority are of particular importance to industry, that is, Article 161 concerning Structural Funds and Article 157 concerning industrial policy. While the use of qualified majority voting in Article 161 is expected to be of less importance,[4] the change in the decision-making process in Article 157

---

[3] In comparison with the alternative view; a Commission consisting of a limited and fixed number of members, which would result in a Commission with fewer members than Member States (Presidency of the European Union , 1999).

[4] The latest (1999) negotiation of the general Structural Fund regulation which has article 161 of the Treaty as its legal base showed that some Member States used the unanimity requirement to obtain special arrangement which would not have been accepted with qualified majority voting. For instance, regions covered by the former Objective 6 are in the new period covered by Objective 1 even though they do not fulfil the strict Objective 1

may change the industrial policy of the Union more substantially as the scenario in Box 14.1 shows.

Box 14.1   Possible scenario of a change in the voting requirement in Article 157, industrial policy

---

As shown in Chapter 1, Article 157 about industrial policy requires that 'the Council, acting unanimously on a proposal from the Commission, ...,may decide on specific measures ...'. The industrial policy of the European Union has to a large extent been liberal. As mentioned in Chapter 1, the liberal attitude has not been due to consensus among the 15 Member States, but rather a consequence of the fact that a small group of Member States has taken a liberal attitude. The majority of Member States has been in favour of a more interventionist attitude. This was also the case in relation to a proposal from the Commission for a tourism programme called Philoxenia (Council, 1998). After lengthy negotiations, 13 Member States could agree to the compromise text while 2 Member States were against. The proposal could not be adopted since the legal base required unanimity.[5]

If the decision-making mechanism of Article 157 is changed from unanimity to qualified majority voting and co-decision with the European Parliament, it is likely to change EU industrial policy due to the following three reasons. First of all, the majority of the present Member States is in favour of a more interventionist industrial policy. The most liberal countries like the UK, the Netherlands, Denmark and Sweden do not by themselves have enough votes to block more interventionist proposals. Second, even if the more liberal countries at present could gather enough votes to form a blocking minority, this situation would most likely change with enlargement. Because of their historical heritage of strong State intervention, it can be expected that the new Member States will sign up with the more interventionist countries. Third, in the past, the European Parliament has been very supportive of sector programmes like Philoxenia. With qualified majority voting and co-decision with the European Parliament one can expect more support for these types of programmes.

So what is the most likely form of proposals to be adopted if Article 157 is changed to qualified majority and co-decision? Due to the traditional way the Commission is organised, the Commission has always been good at producing Communications analysing the competitive situation of specific sectors. Usually these kinds of Communications end up with recommendations to the industry itself, to Member States and to the Community. In these cases they are not very far from a situation where the Commission proposes sector-oriented programmes. The total number of programmes and the financial amount allocated to such programmes is restricted by the overall budget for the budget line 'Internal Policies'.[6]

---

criteria. A qualified majority was against the inclusion of the former regions covered by Objective 6 in Objective 1. See Chapter 10 for a study of the different objectives.

[5]   The legal base of the Philoxenia tourism programme was article 308 (former 235) which, like Article 157, requires unanimity.

[6]   The budget line 'Internal Policies' is the budget line in the overall budget under which industrial policy (and for instance EU research programmes) is financed.

Weighting of Votes in the Council

The voting allocation of the Council originally reflected the population size and balance between small, medium and large Member States. The threshold for attaining a qualified majority has remained largely unchanged at 71 per cent. In the Community of 6 Member States, 12 out of 17 votes, equal to 71 per cent, was needed to attain a qualified majority. Today 62 out of 87 votes, also equal to 71 per cent, are needed. However, in going from 6 to 15 Member States the minimum population required for a qualified majority has fallen from 67 per cent to 58 per cent. As qualified majority voting today requires 62 out of 87 votes, a blocking minority of 26 votes can prevent a Council decision requiring qualified majority from being adopted. The minimum population required for a blocking minority is 12 per cent.

Most of the applicant countries are smaller countries, which will add to the problem analysed. With the present way of allocating votes, a proposal following qualified majority voting in an enlarged Union of 27 Member States could be blocked by a group of Member States representing only 10 per cent of the population and adopted by a group of Member States representing only 50 per cent of the population.

In order to address this problem, two alternative solutions have been discussed. One is re-weighting of the votes. A second is introducing a so-called dual majority system, that is, an agreed majority voting of both votes and population. In the report to the European Council the Finnish Presidency found broad support for the option of re-weighting of votes.

Other Subjects in Relation to the IGC

In the roundup to the IGC, other topics than the three mentioned in the conclusions of the European Council in Cologne have been discussed, that is, increased use of flexibility and reorganisation of the Treaty text. These topics and others might be discussed at a later stage of the IGC even though they are not on the agenda from the beginning.

Flexibility
Enlargement will undoubtedly increase diversity. With increased diversity and a large group of old and new Member States, some will wish to go further or faster than others. They will wish to pursue forms of closer co-operation between themselves. At present, the absence of such flexibility has forced Member States to co-operate outside the Union, as has been the case with the Schengen[7] agreement and Euro-11.[8]

---

[7]   The Schengen agreement is a co-operation between some EU and non-EU countries to create a territory without internal borders.

[8]   Euro 11 is a co-operation between the 11 Member States that have signed up for the single currency.

The idea of flexibility is not invented so that the present 15 Member States can continue integration while leaving the new Member States with the struggle of adapting to the present Community regulations and policies. Therefore a flexibility possibility inserted in the Treaty is likely to be accompanied by insurance that any flexibility initiative will be open to all Member States that fulfil the necessary conditions.

The Amsterdam Treaty introduced the concept of flexibility, but the conditions and criteria for applying this flexibility make it unworkable in practice. Therefore it is likely that requirements for such a co-operation initiative would be qualified majority or super-qualified majority, that is without the possibility of veto by any single Member State, but with an obligation to respect the interests of non-participants.

The concept of flexibility is likely to be discussed at the IGC. It could very well be included in the forthcoming Treaty, one way or the other.

Reorganisation of the Treaty

In their report, von Weizsäcker et al. (1999) point to the fact that for the past 10 or 15 years, the Union has lived through a permanent process of treaty modifications – either preparing, negotiating or ratifying treaty changes. Constant treaty revisions are a source of political difficulties in several Member States, for example in Denmark.[9] Constant treaty revisions contribute to the feeling of legal insecurity. These problems will increase in an enlarged Union, when each Treaty change has to go through up to 27 Member States' parliamentary system with the foreseeable delays, frustrations and risks of complete paralysis.

In order to overcome these problems von Weizsäcker et al. suggest the Treaty text to be divided in two separate parts, that is a basic treaty and a separate text along the following lines:

> The basic treaty would only include the aims, principle and general policy orientations, citizen's rights and the institutional framework. These clauses, as is the case now, could only be modified unanimously, through an IGC, with ratification by each Member State. Presumably such modification would be infrequent.

> A separate text (or texts) would include the other clauses of the present treaties, including those which concern specific policies. These could be modified by a decision of the Council (acting on the basis of a new superqualified majority or on unanimity, depending on the subjects) and the assent of the European parliament (eventually with a special majority).

Amendment of the basic articles of the Treaty should then be done more or less as treaty changes of today,that is, through an IGC followed by a

---

[9]   In Denmark, any change of the Treaty has to be ratified by a super-qualified majority of 5/6 of the Danish Parliament and in most cases also by a referendum.

ratification process, but much less frequent. Amendment of the rest of Treaty should not require an ICG and ratification process and could therefore be done much easier.

The idea of von Weizsäcker et al. has, for the moment, been rejected by most Member States. However, the idea is now out in the open to be discussed and it might be on the agenda in the future since it does point at some real and unsolved problems, that is, ongoing treaty modifications and the lengthy and burdensome ratification process.

14.3 ENLARGEMENT

The main reason for having the IGC is to prepare the European Union for enlargement. Without the forthcoming enlargement there was no urgent need for institutional reforms. However, as analysed above, the present institutional weaknesses would probably paralyse the decision-making system and create management problems in an enlarged Union. So institutional reforms are needed in order for the Union to prepare itself for enlargement. But institutional reforms are in themselves not enough. A budgetary reform was also needed. So when deciding the overall budget for the period 2000–06, the Berlin European Council (1999c) carried out a budgetary reform in order to prepare for enlargement. In the overall budget for the period 2000–06, a special heading is preserved for pre-accession aid and another for enlargement, as shown in Table 14.1.

Table 14.1 Financial framework— EU-21, million €, fixed 1999 prices

	2000	2001	2002	2003	2004	2005	2006
Pre-accession instrument	3 120	3 120	3 120	3 120	3 120	3 120	3 120
PHARE	1 560	1 560	1 560	1 560	1 560	1 560	1 560
Agricultural	520	520	520	520	520	520	520
Structural (ISPA)	1 040	1 040	1 040	1 040	1 040	1 040	1 040
Enlargement			6 450	9 030	11 610	14 200	16 780
Agriculture			1 600	2 030	2 450	2 930	3 400
Structural			3 750	5 830	7 920	10 000	12 080
Internal policy			730	760	790	820	850
Administration			370	410	450	450	450

Source: European Council (1999c)

The financial allocation to the pre-accession instruments is independent of any future enlargement. As more Member States join the Union the same financial allocation will be available for the remaining applicant countries. The financial allocation for enlargement includes additional own resources from the accession of six new Member States as from 2002. If fewer than six applicant countries join the Union before the end of 2006, the financial allocation for enlargement will be smaller due to the fact that the budget foresees that the new Member State will contribute to the budget through additional own resources. If the applicant countries enter into the Union later than 2002, the unused funds from previous years could not automatically be accumulated. That would require a new decision.

It seems fair to conclude that with the budget reform decided in Berlin and a successful conclusion of the IGC, the European Union will structurally be ready for enlargement.

The Road to Enlargement

The road to enlargement is paved by a number of important decisions taken by the Heads of Government and State in the European Council. The Copenhagen European Council decided on the criteria for membership. The Luxembourg European Council decided on the method, and the Helsinki European Council on the timeframe.

In 1993, the Copenhagen European Council agreed upon the membership criteria, since then referred to as the Copenhagen Criteria. These Criteria can be divided into three categories as shown in Box 14.2.

Box 14.2 The Copenhagen Criteria of membership of the European Union

---

Political criteria
Membership requires that the candidate country has achieved stability of institutions guaranteeing democracy, the rule of low, human rights, and the respect for and protection of minorities

Economic criteria
The existence of a functioning market economy and the capacity to cope with competitive pressure and market forces within the Union.

Other criteria
The ability to take on the obligation of membership, including adherence to aims of political economic and monetary union.

Source: European Council (1993)

In December 1997, the European Council of Luxembourg decided to launch the enlargement process by taking the decision to launch an accession process on 30 March 1998 comprising the ten Central and East European countries and Cyprus. The European Council pointed out that these countries were destined to join the European Union on the basis of the same criteria and that they were participating in the accession process on an equal footing. Furthermore this European Council also decided to begin negotiations (in the spring of 1998) with 6 of the 11 applicant countries, that is, Cyprus, Hungary, Poland, Estonia, the Czech Republic and Slovenia. It was underlined that the decision to enter into negotiations did not imply that they would be successfully concluded at the same time for every applicant. Conclusion of the negotiations and subsequent accession depends on the extent to which each country complies with the Copenhagen Criteria and the Union's ability to assimilate new Member States.

Malta, which had 'frozen' its application for membership in 1996, reactivated it in October 1998. During 1999, Turkey was accepted as an applicant country bringing the total number of applicant countries up to 13.

In December 1999, The Helsinki European Council decided to start negotiations in the beginning of 2000 with six more applicant countries, that is, Romania, Slovakia, Latvia, Lithuania, Bulgaria and Malta. So, at present accession negotiations are taking place with 12 applicant countries, leaving Turkey as the only applicant countries for which accession negotiations have not yet started. The reason for this is that the Helsinki European Council underlined that: 'compliance with the political criteria laid down at the Copenhagen European Council is a prerequisite for the opening of accession negotiation and that compliance with all the Copenhagen criteria is the basis for accession to the Union'. At present Turkey does not fulfil the political criteria. The Commission has expressed its concern about shortcomings in terms of respect for human rights and the rights of minorities and about the constitutional role that the Turkish army plays in political life through the National Security Council (European Commission, 1999).

Besides deciding to open accession negotiations with the rest of the Central and East European countries and Malta, the Helsinki European Council also decided when the first enlargement could take place. The IGC must end by December 2000 and after ratification by the Member States 'the Union should be in a position to welcome new Member States from by the end of 2002'.

So when will the first enlargement take place and with which of the applicant countries? The above quotation from the Helsinki European Council could and has been interpreted in a number of ways. However, it seems likely that the first enlargement will take place 1 January 2004 with from 8 to 10 countries. Which countries depend on the progress made. As the Helsinki European Council points out; 'each candidate State will be judged on its own merits'.

The Candidate Countries

As stated above, all of the candidate countries except Turkey fulfil the Copenhagen Criteria. On the economic criteria, there are big differences between candidate countries.

Economic criteria

The economic performance of the candidate countries has been affected by the recent crises in Asia, Russian and the Balkans. Some of the candidate countries have been more affected than others. Economic indicators together with other main statistical indicators are shown in Table 14.2 Economic growth has varied significantly from negative growth in the Czech Republic and Romania of –2.3 and –7.3 respectively to a positive growth of 5.1 in Hungary and Lithuania.

Table 14.2 Main statistical indicators (1998) of the Candidate Countries

	Area	Popula-tion	Density	GDP in Purshasing Power Standards			GDP change	Agriculture	
	1000 Km^2	Million inhab.	Inhab. / Km^2	Billn €	€/ inhab.	€/ inhab. % EU-avge	%	% gross added value	% employ-ment
Bulgaria	111	8.3	75	38.2	4 600	23	3.4	21.1	25.7
Cyprus	9	0.7	78	10.4*	14 787*	77*	5.0	4.6	9.6
Czech Republic	79	10.3	130	125.7	12 200	60	–2.3	4.5	5.5
Estonia	45	1.4	32	10.2	7 300	36	4.0	6.2	9.4*
Hungary	93	10.1	109	99.0	9 800	49	5.1	5.9*	7.5
Latvia	65	2.4	37	13.2	5 500	27	3.6	4.7	18.8
Lithuania	65	3.7	57	22.9	6 200	31	5.1	10.1	21.0
Malta	0.3	0.4	1333	n.d.	n.d.	n.d.	4.1	2.8	1.8
Poland	313	38.7	124	301.8	7 800	39	5.0	4.8	19.1
Romania	238	22.5	94	123.7	5 500	27	–7.3	17.6	40.0
Slovakia	49	5.4	110	50.2	9 300	46	4.4	4.6	8.2
Slovenia	20	2.0	100	27.4	13 700	68	3.9	3.9	11.5
Turkey	775	63.4	82	404.7	6 383	32	2.8	16.1	42.3

* 1997
Source: European Commission (1999b)

The economic prosperity of the candidate countries is also very different. The economic performance of the most well-off countries, in terms of GDP per capita, like Cyprus, Slovenia and the Czech Republic, is equal to the economic performance of existing regions and Member States of the Union. On the other hand, the less well-off candidate countries like Bulgaria and Romania only have a GDP per capita equal to around one quarter of the Community average.

In order to make long-term investments, companies as well as foreign investors need a stable, predictable and supportive regulatory framework, enforced by an efficient public administration. The European Round Table of industrialists has underlined that the candidate countries need to continue targeted reforms of the existing regulatory environment and clarification of property rights. Furthermore, a legal framework which will facilitate investments in transport and environment infrastructure should be completed and the candidate countries should accelerate the pace of acquis adoption and implementation, primarily for single market issues.

In accordance with the Copenhagen economic criteria, the Commission regards Poland, Hungary, Cyprus, Estonia, Slovenia, the Czech Republic, Latvia and Malta as 'functioning market economies'. With respect to 'the capacity to cope with competitive pressure and market forces within the Union', the Commission finds that Cyprus and Malta have this capacity, while Poland, Hungary, Estonia, Slovenia and the Czech Republic have improved their ability to cope with competitive pressure and market forces within the Union in the medium term. Taken together only Cyprus and Malta fulfil both economic criteria.

Some Consequences for EU Industrial Policies

Before the applicant countries can access the Union, they also have to apply the rules of the Union ('aquis Communitaire') including the ones related to the industrial policy of the Union and the other policies of importance to industry. In these areas most of the applicant countries have to make progress.

A solid legal base of *internal market* legislation is in place in most candidate countries. However, further effort is needed in all countries to align and effectively implement the EC approach to standards and certification.

EMU is an integrated part of the Community acquis. However, a clear distinction should be made between participation in EMU and adoption of the euro as a singly currency. New Member States are not expected to adopt the single currency immediately upon accession, even though they will be taking part in the EMU.

None of the candidate countries are very advanced in the transposition of *environmental* laws. Without additional legislative and implementation effort, all countries will face serious difficulties to achieve significant progress with the environment acquis in the near future.

In *State aid*, no country has a fully functioning system of State aid control. A concerted effort is needed in all candidate countries to make the control and monitoring systems operational.

In order for the applicant countries to familiarise themselves with the Union's policy and working method, some of the *Community programmes*, for example education, training and research programmes have been opened for the applicant countries.

In relation to regional policy and the *Structural Funds*, all of the applicant countries do have access to the structural pre-accession instrument ISPA. ISPA is very similar to the Cohesion Fund in its administration and in the sense that it supports transport and environment projects. When some of the applicant countries actually enter into the Union, they will also be eligible to financial support from the Structural Funds. Until the end of 2006, the funding will be taken from the reserve set aside for structural purposes under the heading 'Enlargement' as shown in Table 14.1, which outlines a possible scenario for a future Structural Funds reform.

Box 14.3   A possible scenario for a future reform of the Structural Funds

In relation to the Structural Funds, the big question is how the objectives will be defined from 2007 onward. A possible scenario is that the overall financial envelope will remain in the same relative magnitude today as mentioned in Chapter 10. Consequently, there will be a need for further geographical concentration in order to ensure that the funds available are concentrated on the regions with the greatest need. The present Objective 1 criteria, that is, regions with GDP per capita below 75 per cent of Community average, will probably be maintained.[10] Enlargement will add many new regions with GDP well below the 75 per cent threshold. As a consequence, the Community average will be lowered. This means that EU regions with an average GDP today close to the threshold, most likely will be above the threshold and therefore no longer eligible as Objective 1 regions from 2007. In order to maintain the financial resources needed, it is likely that the present relative part to Objective 1 (about 2/3) will be increased. Consequently, the relative part of the other objective will be reduced. With reduced resources to objectives other than Objective 1, it is questionable whether the present Objective 2 could be maintained. Regions covered by Objective 2 are after all located in the better off countries.

It seems more likely that the present Community Initiative, Interreg, in the future could be a new Objective 2. In a Community without physical barriers, it is the aim of Interreg to assist in overcoming non-physical barriers. Non-physical barriers as differences in languages, cultural and administrative heritage still prevent cross-border co-operation taking place. Interreg contributes to cross-border and inter-regional co-operation and as such to further integration in disintegrated areas.

Objective 3 will most likely be maintained. Persistent unemployment is a clear indication of structural problems in the labour market. These structural problems are not easy to deal with and continued Community assistance can be expected.

In all, it is likely that Objective 1 will continue, covering all of the regions in the new Member States and a significantly smaller number of existing Objective 1 regions in EU-15. There will be a new Objective 2 following on the tradition of the existing Community Initiative, Interreg. The present Objective 3 will continue in one form or another. A relatively higher ratio of the Structural Funds will most likely be given to Objective 1, perhaps as high as 80 per cent. Except for the limited number of regions covered by objective 1, the regions of the present EU-15 will benefit from the new Objectives 2 and 3, which only should cover areas and regions outside Objective 1.

---

[10]   Except that the former Objective 6 regions will probably not be eligible as Objective 1 regions after 2006.

From 2007 onward the new Member States will participate on an equal footing with the present Member States. As Table 14.2 shows, all East and Central European Countries are presently below the 75 per cent criteria for being eligible under Objective 1.[11] As the only applicant country, Cyprus is above the 75 per cent threshold while there are no GDP statistics available for Malta. Box 14.3 outlines a possible scenario for a future Structural Funds reform.

As we have seen above, two of the largest challenges for the applicant countries are 'to cope with competitive pressure and market forces within the Union' and to apply the rules of the Union (aquis Communautaire). In a number of sensitive sectors, such as the steel sector, this will inevitably lead to significant job losses and regional and social problems. For the steel sector, the necessary restructuring process will be particularly painful, as the steel plants in the East and Central European countries tend to be concentrated in industrial regions where they are the principal economic activity.

The aim of the restructuring programmes for the steel sector is therefore to establish a viable and competitive steel industry in Central and Eastern Europe. The bulk of funds required for the restructuring of these countries' steel industry has been estimated at the level of $10 billion between 1994 and 2002 (see European Commission, 1998). At present is the competitive advantage of the EU steelworks partly offset by the availability of a skilled and relatively cheap workforce. However, in the future, cost increases can be expected due to the increased labour costs. Furthermore the customs tariffs for imports of steel from the EU should be phased out by 2001 to 2002 (under the Europe Agreements), which will increase the competitive pressure on the CEEC. So restructuring the steel industry is proving difficult due to the social and regional consequences. According to the Commission, the restructuring of the steel industry is not advancing at a sufficient pace in Poland and is also proving difficult in Romania, Slovakia, the Czech Republic and Bulgaria. 'Governments need to take on this challenge, as it will affect greatly their future capacity to compete successfully in the Union' (European Commission, 1999b). The situation in the steel industry in Central and Eastern Europe is analysed in Box 14.4.

The EU steel industry has been through a restructuring process in the 1980s and 1990s like the one the Central and East European countries face now. In 1998, the EU steel industry represented 20 per cent of worldwide production of crude steel, and in 1996 the EU had an export surplus of 11 million tonnes. To achieve this level of competitiveness, the EU steel industry underwent profound restructuring since 1980. Production capacities were reduced by 60 million tonnes and the workforce employed in the sector has been reduced from 900 000 to 280 000 in 1998. That significant reduction in employment in the last 15–20 years has been

---

[11]   See Chapter 10 for a study of the different objectives related to the Structural Funds.

accompanied by significant levels of public aid, estimated at €45 billion. Aid has been granted mainly by Member States (see also Chapter 13), but also by the Community through its social and regional interventions.

Box 14.4   The steel sector in the Central and East European countries

---

The market
The steel industry of the Central and East European countries (CEEC) accounts for approximately 4 per cent of worldwide production of steel. The area is a net exporter of steel products. Export surplus in steel products amounted to 10 million tons in 1996, of which 4 million tons originated in trade with the EU. This reflects the increase of exports from these countries to the EU since the collapse of their previous market including the former Soviet Union

Demands
Since 1990, demand for steel in the CEEC has fallen sharply. Between 1990 and 1992 consumption of crude steel in the applicant countries fell from 32 to 16 million tonnes and from 25 to 13 million tonnes for rolled products. In response to the collapse in consumption in these countries and their previous export markets, the CEEC turned to the European Union. Consequently, the share of exports to the EU rose from 21 per cent in 1990 to 40 per cent in 1995. This increase was mainly created by selling low value-added products at unprofitable prices.

Production
Under central planning the steel industry was an important part of the industrial fabric of the economies of the CEEC. Between 1986 and 1992, the per capita steel production per year fell from 565 kg to 312 kg. As way of comparison, the per capita steel production per year in the Union was 330 kg.

Productivity
Between 1990 and 1995, productivity increased the production of crude steel per person per year from 76 to 98 tonnes. As way of comparison, the production in EU-12 increased from 355 to 496 tonnes. So productivity growth has been slower in CEEC than in the EU. In the CEEC productivity increased 29 per cent while it increased 40 per cent in the EU.

Social and regional dimension
In CEEC, the steel industry represents 3 per cent of employment and 8 per cent of industrial production. However, in some regions the steel and coal industry combined makes up for around 37 to 46 per cent of industrial employment. The largest steel mills are concentrated in an industrial zone of around 5 to 6 million inhabitants located in the border area of Poland, the Czech Republic and Slovakia. This region represents 40 per cent of total employment in the steel industry of the CEEC. Between 1990 and 1995, employment has been reduced from around 580 000 to 350 000 employees. Based on the working hypothesis that productivity in the CEEC reaches, by 2002, the productivity level of the EU in 1995, a further reduction of 276 000 jobs (estimated) would take place between 1995 and 2002.

Source: European Commission (1998)

14.2 CONCLUSION

The EU is in the beginning of probably the most important transformation in its history – the enlargement process. The challenge of bringing 12(13) new Member States requires institutional reforms, a budgetary reform and political reforms. There is no doubt that in the medium term, reforms and changes in the industrial policy of the European Union and the other policies of importance to industry are required.

In the short term, a new industrial policy concept is under development which most likely will continue the general horizontal industrial approach of today. Focus will probably be on such issues as innovation, information and communication technology (ICT), market access, globalisation and entrepreneurship. The Commission has recently presented a staff working paper and a proposal for a Multiannual Programme which back up this new industrial policy concept.

In the medium-long term, when the first enlargement has taken place, the industrial policy of the Union may very well be changed toward a sector approach. This could be the case if Article 157 of the Treaty concerning industrial policy was changed from unanimity to qualified majority voting and if the new Member States, as expected, join the more interventionist Member States of the Union today. Together they will most likely have the qualified majority to undertake such a change. Changes may also be foreseen in other areas such as, for example, regional policy and competition policy.

It is for sure an exiting and changing period of the history of the European Union. One can – sometimes with great pleasure – speculate about the future, as we have done in this chapter, but in the end , luckily, nobody knows it.

BIBLIOGRAPHY

Council (1998), *Proposal for a Council Decision on a First Multiannual Programme to Assist European Tourism (1997–2000) (PHILOXENIA)*, Council document 13834/98, 4 December 1998.

European Commission (1998), *A Global Approach to Promote Regional and Social Conversion and to Facilitate Industrial Restructuring in the Central and Eastern European Countries: The Case of Steel*, COM(1998) 220 final, Brussels, 07.04.1998.

European Commission (1999a), *Adapting the institution to make a succes of enlargement*, Contribution by the European Commission to preparations for the Intergovernmental Conference on institutional issues, 10 November 1999.

European Commission (1999b), *Composite paper, Reports on progress towards accession by each of the candidate countries*. European Commission, IP/99/751, 13 October 1999.

European Commission (2000), *Dialogue on Europe: The Challenges of Institutional Reform,* Memorandum to the Commission from the President, Mr. Barnier, and Mrs. Reding, in association with Mr. Verheugen, 14 February 2000.

European Commission (2000b), *Challenges for Enterprise Policy in a Knowledge-Driven Economy: Proposal for a Council Directive on a Multiannual Programme for Enterprise and Entrepreneurship (2001–2006),* COM(2000) 256 final, Brussels 26.04.2000.

European Commission (2000c), *Staff Working paper, Towards Enterprise Europe; The Work Programme for Enterprise Policy 2000–2005, SEC(2000) 771, Brussels, 08.05.2000.*

European Council (1999a), *Presidency Conclusions. Helsinki European council, 10 and 11 December 1999.* SN 300/1/99 REV 1.

European Council (1999b), *Presidency Conclusion. Cologne European Council, 3 and 4 June 1999.* SN 150/99 REV 1.

European Council (1999c), *Presidency Conclusion. Berlin European Council, 24-25 March 1999.* SN 100/1/99 REV 1.

European Council (1993), *Presidency Conclusion. Copenhagen European Council, 21-22 June 1993.SN 180/93.*

Presidency of the European Union (1999), *Efficient Institutions after Enlargement. Options for the Intergovernmental Conference, Presidency Report.* 13636/99, 7 December 1999.

von Weizsäcker, Richard; Dehaene, Jean-Luc and Simon, David (1999), *The Institutional implications of Enlargement. Report to the European Commission.* Brussels, 18 October 1999

Index